JESUS' DEFEAT OF DEATH

Persuading Mark's early readers

Peter Bolt explores the impact of Mark's Gospel on its early readers in the first-century Graeco-Roman world. His book focuses upon the thirteen characters in Mark who come to Jesus for healing or exorcism and, using analytical tools of narrative and reader-response criticism, explores their crucial role in the communication of the Gospel. Bolt suggests that early readers of Mark would be persuaded that Jesus' dealings with the suppliants show him casting back the shadow of death and that this in itself is preparatory for Jesus' final defeat of death in resurrection. Enlisting a variety of ancient literary and non-literary sources in an attempt to illuminate this first-century world, this book gives special attention to illness, magic and the Roman imperial system. This is a new approach to Mark which attempts to break the impasse between narrative and historical studies and will appeal to scholars and students alike.

PETER G. BOLT is Head of New Testament at Moore Theological College, Sydney. He has edited (with M.D. Thompson) and contributed to *The Gospel to the Nations: Perspectives on Paul's Mission* (2000).

SOCIETY FOR NEW TESTAMENT STUDIES

MONOGRAPH SERIES

General Editor: Richard Bauckham

125

JESUS' DEFEAT OF DEATH

Jesus' Defeat of Death

Persuading Mark's early readers

PETER G. BOLT

Moore Theological College, Sydney

CAMBRIDGE
UNIVERSITY PRESS

PUBLISHED BY THE PRESS SYNDICATE OF THE UNIVERSITY OF CAMBRIDGE
The Pitt Building, Trumpington Street, Cambridge, United Kingdom

CAMBRIDGE UNIVERSITY PRESS
The Edinburgh Building, Cambridge, CB2 2RU, UK
40 West 20th Street, New York, NY 10011–4211, USA
477 Williamstown Road, Port Melbourne, VIC 3207, Australia
Ruiz de Alarcón 13, 28014 Madrid, Spain
Dock House, The Waterfront, Cape Town 8001, South Africa

http://www.cambridge.org

First published 2003

Printed in the United Kingdom at the University Press, Cambridge

Typeface Times 10/12 pt.   *System* LATEX 2$_\varepsilon$ [TB]

A catalogue record for this book is available from the British Library

Library of Congress Cataloguing in Publication data
Bolt, Peter, 1958–
Jesus' defeat of death : persuading Mark's early readers / Peter G. Bolt.
    p.   cm. – (Society for New Testament Studies monograph series ; 125)
Includes bibliographical references and index.
ISBN 0 521 83036 2
1. Death – Biblical teaching.   2. Bible. N.T. Mark – Reader-response criticism.   3. Bible.
N.T. Mark – Criticism, Narrative.   4. Jesus Christ – Miracles.   5. Exorcism in the Bible.
6. Healing in the Bible.   I. Title.   II. Monograph series (Society for New Testament
Studies) ; 125.
BS2585.6.D45B65   2003
226.3′06 – dc21   2003043930

ISBN 0 521 83036 2 hardback

To my wife, Barbara, who, for better and for worse, shares my life under the shadow of death, my fellow heir in our Lord's gracious gift of life; and to our four daughters, Grace, Jana, Sara and Alice, who are kissed each night with the thought that tomorrow they might rise again.

CONTENTS

PREFACE

This book attempts to understand the potential impact of Mark's Gospel upon its early Graeco-Roman readers.

It focuses upon the role of the healing/exorcism accounts in this communicative process. These scenes forge a link with Mark's flesh-and-blood readers by:

(1)   strongly aligning the 'implied readers' with the suppliants in the scenes;

(2)   enabling the 'flesh-and-blood' readers to recognise their own world in the circumstances of the suppliants and to 'become' the implied readers;

(3)   thus drawing the flesh-and-blood readers into the story-world which seeks to move them by its message about Jesus and the coming kingdom.

To appreciate the impact of these stories on early readers, the book attempts to recover relevant aspects of the pre-understanding which Graeco-Roman readers could be expected to bring to their reading of Mark. This requires a special focus on ancient perceptions of sickness and death, as well as due attention to magic, which could be either cause or cure of the afflictions.

When read from this reconstructed perspective, the healing/exorcism scenes show Jesus dealing with death.

These scenes are read within Mark's wider framework of the expectation of the kingdom of God, to be inaugurated by the resurrection of the dead.

Portrayed as a king who brings life to those under the shadow of death, Jesus would be seen as an alternative to the deified rulers familiar to the Roman world. He had no apotheosis which removed him from death, but he truly died. His emptied tomb therefore speaks of a genuine resurrection which inaugurated the kingdom of God, and which provides genuine hope for those who continue to live under the shadow of death.

Mark's Gospel had the potential to make an impact upon the early readers' sense of mortality. Jesus had defeated death.

I trust that this small offering towards a greater understanding of Mark's message might help others better appreciate the wonder of this 'gospel about Jesus Christ, the Son of God'.

ACKNOWLEDGEMENTS

This book is a revision of my PhD thesis, which was accepted by King's College, London in 1997. I would like to express my gratitude to many who assisted me in various ways during the writing of my thesis: my supervisor, Prof. Graham N. Stanton; Dr Peter Jensen, former Principal of Moore Theological College, Sydney, and his Council; Dr Bruce Winter, Warden of Tyndale House Centre for Biblical Research, Cambridge, and his Council; the Trustees of Rev. and Mrs F.W.A. Roberts Scholarship and the Joan Augusta McKenzie Travelling Scholarship; the British Pro-Vice Chancellors' Committee for an Overseas Research Scholarship; the Australian College of Theology, for their Faculty Research Scholarship; the Cambridge University Bethune Baker Fund; and Deutscher Akademischer Austauschdienst (DAAD); and last, but by no means least, the various friends and family members whose support has often been beyond their better interests.

I am also grateful for feedback on parts of my argument, during both the writing of the thesis and the preparation of this book. My thanks go to the participants in the King's College London New Testament Postgraduate Seminar and in the Tyndale House Study Groups (New Testament and Theology); Prof. David Jordan; Prof. Roy Kotansky; John Hoskin; Darryl Palmer; Bruce Winter; and Prof. Edwin Judge. Comments made by my two examiners, Dr Richard Burridge and Prof. Morna Hooker, the Cambridge University Press reader, and the editor of the Monograph Series, Prof. Richard Bauckham, have also been greatly appreciated. Special thanks must also go to my good friend David Thurston and to Melody Machin for undertaking the gruelling task of compiling the initial indexes for this book.

NOTE ON THE RENDERING OF
PAPYROLOGICAL/INSCRIPTIONAL TEXTS

I have rendered texts as they appear in the edited versions. It should
be noted that the magical texts often have unusual spelling and the ac-
centuation is not always supplied by the editors. The following guide
to the standard sigla, taken from P.W. Pestman, M. David and B.A. van
Groningen, *The New Papyrological Primer* (Leiden: E.J. Brill, 1990),
should be noted, although the practice of some editors varies.

[ ]	lacuna
< >	omission in the original
( )	resolution of a symbol or abbreviation
[ca. 3]	approximately 3 letters are missing
ca. 3	traces of approximately 3 letters survive
. (subscript dot)	uncertain letter. (This needs to be distinguished from the subscript dot used in transliterations, which does not indicate uncertainty.)
|	edge of text
[?]	where, in irregularly spaced material (such as in lead tablets), it is impossible to know whether to assume a lost letter. This sign is introduced by D.R. Jordan, 'Southwest Corner Agora', 213.
σ, ς, c	I have retained the type of sigma used by the editors of the various pieces.

If the symbol | is not used in translations, the beginning of lines is of-
ten indicated by capitalisation. I have also followed this fairly standard
practice when citing poetic literary texts.

ABBREVIATIONS

Abbreviations, in both text and bibliography, generally conform to the practice of the *Journal of Biblical Literature*, and to either the *Oxford Classical Dictionary* or H.G. Liddell, R. Scott, H.S. Jones, *Greek-English Lexicon* (Oxford: Oxford University Press, ^{9}1940). The following abbreviations are used in quotations of primary sources. I have referred to text numbers in collections of primary sources in **bold**, and page numbers in normal type. [TLG] following a work indicates that the source was accessed solely through the TLG computer database. I have also occasionally used a preceding ? to indicate that a translation or interpretation is either debated or possible.

ACBM	C. Bonner, 'Amulets Chiefly in the British Museum', *Hesperia* 20 (1951), 301–45.
AG	W.R. Paton, *The Greek Anthology*: vol. II (LCL; London and Cambridge, Mass.: W. Heinemann and Harvard University Press, 1917, repr. 1970); vol. V (LCL; Cambridge, Mass. and London: Harvard University Press and W. Heinemann, 1918, repr. 1979).
AMB	J. Naveh and S. Shaked, *Amulets and Magic Bowls. Aramaic Incantations of Late Antiquity* (Jerusalem: Magnes, 1985).
ANET	J.B. Pritchard, *Ancient Near Eastern Texts Relating to the Old Testament* (Princeton: Princeton University Press, ^{3}1969).
AnonLond	H. Diels (ed.), *Anonymi Londinensis ex Aristotelis Iatricis Menoniis et aliis medicis eclogae* (Supplementum Aristotelicum iii pars i; Berlin: Reimer, 1893) [TLG].

AthAg | D.R. Jordan, 'Defixiones from a Well Near the Southwest Corner of the Athenian Agora,' *Hesperia* 54 (1985), 205–55.

AthAg**IL72** | D.R. Jordan, 'A Curse Tablet from a Well in the Athenian Agora,' *ZPE* 19 (1975), 245–8.

Braund | D.C. Braund, *Augustus to Nero. A Sourcebook on Roman History 31 BC–AD 68* (London: Croom Helm, 1985).

Carlini | A. Carlini et al. (eds), *Papiri letterari greci* (Pisa: Giardini editori e stampatori, 1978).

Carthage | D.R. Jordan, 'New Defixiones from Carthage,' in J.H. Humphrey (ed.), *The Circus and a Byzantine Cemetery at Carthage* (Ann Arbor: University of Michigan Press, 1988), 117–34.

Cartlidge | D.R. Cartlidge and D.L. Dungan (eds), *Documents for the Study of the Gospels* (Minneapolis: Fortress, ^{2}1994 (1980)).

CIL | T. Mommsen et al., *Corpus Inscriptionum Latinarum* (Berlin: Reimer, 1862–1963).

CLE | F. Bücheler, *Carmina Latina Epigraphica* (Leipzig: Teubner, 1897, repr. 1921).

Diels-Kranz | H. Diels and W. Kranz, *Die Fragmente der Vorsokratiker* (Zurich and Berlin: Weidmann, ^{6}1964).

DT | *Defixionum Tabellae* (Paris: A. Fontemoing, 1904).

DTA | R. Wünsch, *Defixionum Tabellae Atticae* (IG III^3; Berlin: Reimer, 1897). Reprinted in A.N. Oikonomides, *Inscriptiones Atticae: supplementum inscriptionum Atticarum* I (Chicago: Ares, 1976).

EJ | V. Ehrenberg and A.H.M. Jones, *Documents Illustrating the Reigns of Augustus and Tiberius* (Oxford: Clarendon Press, 1949).

Epig.Gr. | G. Kaibel, *Epigrammata Graeca ex lapidibus conlecta* (Berlin: Reimer, 1878).

E-W | R.H. Eisenman and M. Wise, *The Dead Sea Scrolls Uncovered* (Shaftesbury, Dorset: Element, 1992).

Farber | W. Farber, '*MANNAM LUŠPUR ANA ENKIDU*: Some New Thoughts about an Old Motif,' *JNES* 49 (1990), 299–321.

FGr H | F. Jacoby, *Die Fragmente der griechischen Historiker* (Berlin: Weidmann, 1923–58).

Fox	W.S. Fox, 'An Infernal Postal Service', *Art and Archeology* 1 (1914), 205–7.
Gager	J. Gager (ed.), *Curse Tablets and Binding Spells from the Ancient World* (Oxford: Oxford University Press, 1992).
GM	F. García Martínez, *The Dead Sea Scrolls Translated* (Leiden: E.J. Brill, 1994).
GMPT	H.D. Betz, *The Greek Magical Papyri in Translation Including the Demotic Spells* (Chicago: University of Chicago Press, ²1986).
Grant	F.C. Grant (ed.), *Ancient Roman Religion* (New York: Liberal Arts Press, 1957).
IG	A. Kirchhoff et al., *Inscriptiones Graecae* I–XV (Berlin: Reimer, 1923→).
IKyme	H. Engelmann, *Die Inschriften von Kyme* (Bonn: Habelt, 1976).
ILS	H. Dessau, *Inscriptiones Latinae Selectae* (Zurich: Wiedemann, 1974 (1892–1916)).
Isbell	C.D. Isbell, *Corpus of the Aramaic Incantation Bowls* (SBLDS 17; Missoula: Scholars Press, 1975).
Kock	T. Kock, *Comicorum Atticorum Fragmenta* II *Novae Comoediae Fragmenta pars I* (Leipzig: Teubner, 1884).
Kotansky	R. Kotansky, *Greek Magical Amulets. The Inscribed Gold, Silver, Copper, and Bronze Lamellae* (Opladen: Westdeutscher Verlag, 1994).
L&R.I	N. Lewis and M. Reinhold, *Roman Civilization*. I: *The Republic* (New York: Columbia University Press, 1951).
L&R.II	N. Lewis and M. Reinhold, *Roman Civilization. Sourcebook* II: *The Empire* (New York: Harper, 1966).
Lattimore	R. Lattimore, *Themes in Greek and Latin Epitaphs* (Urbana, Ill.: University of Illinois Press, 1942).
LKA	E. Ebeling, *Literarische Keilschrifttexte aus Assur* (Berlin, 1953).
LSCG	F. Sokolowski, *Lois sacrées des cités grecques* (Paris: De Boccard, 1969).
LSJ	H.G. Liddell, R. Scott and H.S. Jones, *Greek-English Lexicon* (Oxford: Oxford University Press, ⁹1940).
LSSupp	F. Sokolowski, *Lois sacrées des cités grecques, Supplément* (Paris: De Boccard, 1962).

McCullough   W.S. McCullough, *Jewish and Mandaean Incantation Bowls in the Royal Ontario Museum* (Toronto: University of Toronto Press, 1967).

MES   C. Bonner, 'A Miscellany of Engraved Stones,' *Hesperia* 23 (1954), 138–57.

MGP   D.R. Jordan, 'Magica Graeca Parvula,' *ZPE* 100 (1994), 321–35.

Migne *PG*   J.-P. Migne, *Patrologiae cursus completus, Series Graeca* (Paris: J.P. Migne, 1857–87).

Migne *PL*   J.-P. Migne, *Patrologiae cursus completus, Series Latina* (Rome: Typis Vaticanis, 1906–8, repr. 1968).

Montgomery   J.A. Montgomery, *Aramaic Incantation Texts from Nippur* (Philadelphia: University of Pennsylvania Museum, 1913).

NewDocs   *New Documents Illustrating Early Christianity* (7 vols; G.H.R. Horsley, vols. I–V, S.R. Llewelyn, vols. VI–VII, eds; Sydney: Macquarie University AHDR Centre, 1981–94).

OGIS   W. Dittenberger (ed.), *Orientis Graeci Inscriptiones Selectae* (Leipzig: Hirzel, 1903–5).

Page   D.L. Page, *Select Papyri* III *Literary Papyri, Poetry* (LCL; London and Cambridge, Mass.: Heinemann and Harvard University Press, 1941, repr. 1970).

PDM   Demotic spells in H.D. Betz, *The Greek Magical Papyri in Translation Including the Demotic Spells* (Chicago: University of Chicago Press, ²1986).

Peek, *GG*   W. Peek, *Griechische Grabgedichte* (Berlin: Akademie-Verlag, 1960).

Peek, *GV*   W. Peek, *Griechische Vers-Inschriften* I (Berlin: Akademie-Verlag, 1955).

P.Giss   O. Eger, E. Kornemann and P.M. Meyer, *Griechische Papyri im Museum des oberhessischen Geschichtsvereins zu Giessen* (Leipzig and Berlin: Teubner, 1910–12).

PGM   K. Preisendanz and A. Henrichs (eds), *Papyri Graecae Magicae: Die griechischen Zauberpapyri* (2 vols; Stuttgart: Teubner, 1973–74).

P. Tebt.   B.P. Grenfell and A.S. Hunt, *The Tebtunis Papyri vol. II* (London: Egypt Exploration Society, 1907, repr. 1970).

Ramsay   W. Ramsay, *Cities and Bishoprics of Phrygia* Vol. I,
                 Part II: *West and West-Central Phrygia* (Oxford:
                 Clarendon Press, 1897).
RG   *Res Gestae divi Augusti.* Text: EJ**1**; Translation:
                 Sherk**26**, Braund**1**, L&R. II.**2**.
SB   *Sammelbuch griechischer Urkunden aus Ägypten*
                 (successively published by F. Preisigke, F. Bilabel,
                 E. Kiessling, H.-A. Rupprecht; 1915→).
Scurlock   J.A. Scurlock, *Magical Means of Dealing With
                 Ghosts in Ancient Mesopotamia* (unpublished PhD
                 dissertation; University of Chicago, 1988).
SEG   J.J. Hondius et al. (eds), *Supplementum Epigraphicum
                 Graecum* (Leyden: Sijthoff, 1923).
SGD   D.R. Jordan, 'A Survey of Greek Defixiones Not
                 Included in the Special Corpora,' *GRBS* 26 (1985b),
                 151–97.
Sherk   R.K. Sherk, *The Roman Empire: Augustus to Hadrian*
                 (Cambridge: Cambridge University Press, 1988).
SMA   C. Bonner, *Studies in Magical Amulets Chiefly
                 Graeco-Egyptian* (Ann Arbor and London: University
                 of Michigan Press and Oxford University Press,
                 1950).
Small.   E. M. Smallwood, *Documents Illustrating the
                 Principates of Gaius, Claudius and Nero* (Cambridge:
                 Cambridge University Press, 1967).
SuppMag   R. Daniel and F. Maltomini, *Supplementum magicum*
                 (Papyrologica Coloniensia 16; Opladen:
                 Westdeutscher Verlag, 1990–2).
TGF   A. Nauck, *Tragicorum graecorum fragmenta*
                 (Hildesheim: Georg Olms, 1964 (^{2}1889)), Supp.
                 B.Snell (1964)
Thompson   R.C. Thompson, *The Devils and Evil Spirits of
                 Babylonia. Being Babylonian and Assyrian
                 Incantations against the Demons, Ghouls, Vampires,
                 Hobgoblins, Ghosts, and Kindred Evil Spirits, which
                 attack Mankind. I: Evil Spirits. II: "Fever Sickness"
                 and "Headache", etc.* (London: Luzac, 1903 and
                 1904).
                 Most of the tablets can be abbreviated without
                 confusion; however, it is necessary to distinguish the
                 following:

1.III	Volume 1, tablet III
am.III	Volume 2, tablet III, Ašakki maršûti series
ṭ.III	Volume 2, tablet III, Ṭïï series
X	Volume 1, tablet X
"X"	Volume 2, tablet "X"
am.IX	Volume 2, tablet IX, Ašakki maršûti series
ṭ.IX	Volume 2, tablet IX, Ṭïï series
ṭ.VIII	Volume 2, tablet VIII, Ṭïï series
lk.VIII	Volume 2, tablet VIII, Luḫ-ka series

TOTP   J.H. Charlesworth (ed.), *The Old Testament Pseudepigrapha* (2 vols; New York: Doubleday, 1983 and 1985).

1

INTRODUCTION

The project

General orientation to the topic

This project is an inquiry into the impact of Mark's Gospel on its early Graeco-Roman readers. It argues that the suppliants in the thirteen healing/exorcism scenes have an important role in engaging the implied readers, and, because they represent a sample of life from the real world, the suppliants enable flesh-and-blood Graeco-Roman readers to 'become' the implied readers, enter the story, and so feel its impact.

Each suppliant begins under the shadow of death, but their circumstances are changed as a result of their encounter with Jesus, who brings life where there once was death. Their stories are told as part of a larger narrative which presents Jesus, as Son of God, as an alternative leader for the world, who leads the way into the coming kingdom of God. Mark's early flesh-and-blood readers also lived under the shadow of death. When they entered the story through 'becoming' the suppliants, the larger narrative would have caused them to focus upon Jesus whose life, death and resurrection addressed their mortality and gave them the hope of their own future resurrection. In this way, Mark's message about Jesus' defeat of death had the potential to make a huge impact upon Graeco-Roman readers, and so to play a large role in the mission, and the remarkable growth,[1] of early Christianity.

---

[1] This remarkable growth is plainly a fact of history, even if it cannot be adequately described. Although the portrait of growth depicted in the NT cannot be taken as entirely informative, for there was no-one who had the means to gain accurate statistics, it is 'a fact of great importance' that the church took encouragement from its own 'consciousness of steady and irresistible growth'; Judge, 'Penetration', 6.

General orientation to the method

The Gospel's 'powerful drama and impact'[2] are often acknowledged, but its exact nature and the means by which it is achieved await further exploration.

In the last decades there have been many good studies engaging in literary analysis of Mark, paying attention to the role of plot, character, space, time, movement and the like.[3] Although literary study can be done ahistorically,[4] an examination of Mark's potential impact on its early readers must take into account the fact that the Gospel appears to be written as history, albeit in apocalyptic mode.[5]

Many literary studies deal well with Mark's 'narrative world', i.e., the world within the text, constructed by the text, but stop short of the problematic interface between 'text' and 'real world'. This is often due to a profound scepticism about whether this divide can or should be crossed. When such a crossing is attempted and questions of textual impact on real readers are actually broached, it is usually *(post-)modern* rather than ancient readers who are in view. But, since 'one of the principal means of bridging or at least diminishing the distance between later readers and the text is examination of the presumed effect of the story on its original audience',[6] this study seeks to assess Mark's 'narrative impact' on its *early* readers. As such, it is an exercise in 'literary reception', for it seeks to move beyond the literary study of Mark's *narrative world*, to understand Mark's reception in the *real world of first-century Graeco-Roman society*.[7]

In order to do this, this ancient reading experience (which for most in the first century would have been a 'hearing' experience)[8] is approached

---

[2] Dwyer, *Motif*, 201.

[3] For discussion of such methods, see, for example: Moore, *Literary Criticism*; Anderson and Moore, *Mark*; S.H. Smith, *Lion*.

[4] This is the complaint levelled at Fowler, *Loaves*, by Beavis, *Audience*, 10. It has been a self-conscious strategy amongst many literary interpreters to restrict themselves to the world in the text, rather than the world outside the text. This is an extremely important step, for it allows the narrative to be understood on its own terms. Nevertheless, understanding of the impact of the narrative on real people requires a further important step.

[5] See Collins, *Life?*   [6] Van Iersel, *Mark*, 24.

[7] My method is similar to that of Beavis, *Audience*, 11, who seeks to apply insights of reader-response criticism and Graeco-Roman rhetoric – complaining that this has rarely been done. In my case, I seek to combine reader-response criticism and social description of relevant aspects of the first-century Graeco-Roman world. This combination enables reflection on Mark's narrative rhetoric, i.e., the potential persuasive power of this narrative in that setting.

[8] This point is now commonly recognised and, in what follows, it should be assumed at every mention of the early 'reader'.

from two directions: first, 'outwards' from the text towards the textual construct known as the implied reader, and, secondly, 'inwards' from the real, flesh-and-blood readers towards the text. This twofold approach will now be explained in more detail.

Text to (implied) reader

The approach taken in this analysis is reader-oriented.[9] Although there is a variety of approaches with an interest in readers, the method adopted here is one which grants control of the reading experience to the text.[10] This means that, instead of simply providing what amounts to a set of subjective impressions, the analysis seeks to identify and explain textually embedded devices which are oriented towards producing an effect in the reader.

A text-controlled reader-response approach assumes that reading is a temporal experience,[11] in that the early parts of the narrative prepare the reader for the later parts through such devices as anticipation and retrospection, gaps, repetition and variation, in which a later scene echoes an earlier one, and the like. Adopting such a dynamic view of the reading process renders certain formalist approaches to Mark somewhat inadequate.[12]

---

[9] There are now three commentaries that provide a sustained focus upon the reader: Heil, *Gospel of Mark*; and van Iersel, *Reading Mark* and *Mark*. Heil's reader orientation consists in using each character in a particular scene to draw out exemplary lessons for the reader. Van Iersel's work is more sophisticated, paying attention to the interpretive value of the larger formal features of the text.

[10] Cf. Steiner's imagery, in which the critic is 'judge and master' of the text, the reader is its 'servant'; '"Critic"/"Reader"', 449. Text-controlled critics include Wayne Booth, and the early Stanley Fish, i.e., in *Self-Consuming*, and see also *Surprised*; see Fowler, 'Reader – Reader-Response?', 13, who says they both believe in 'the rhetorical power of the text'. Fowler positions himself with Booth's view of the implied reader being 'the reader implied *in* the text' (p. 15, cf. p. 13). Iser's phenomenology of reading, which speaks of an interaction between text and reader, is, in practice, a close relative. This is also evident in Fowler's method ('Reader – Mark', 53), for he grants to the text the role of 'direction', and to the reader the responsibility of making sense of the 'indirection' (ambiguity, irony, paradox, etc.). He later explored this method at length in *Let the Reader*. Van Iersel, *Mark*, 28 n. 21, dismisses the more subjective approaches, arguing that he has adopted an approach which is concerned with 'objective textual phenomena'.

[11] Cf. Iser, 'Reading Process'; 'Interaction'; Fowler, 'Reader – Reader-Response?', 18–21. This is acknowledged by van Iersel, *Mark*, 24–5, who therefore adopts the 'fiction of the first reading' in his commentary, although his work still shows an abiding influence of formalism.

[12] For example, the dynamic experience of reading can be somewhat lacking in analyses of Mark which rely upon 'concentric structures'; e.g., Standaert, *L'Évangile*; Stock, *Method*; Dewey, *Public Debate*, and even van Iersel, *Mark*.

This discussion adopts an analysis of the parties involved in a narrative transaction that is now fairly commonplace amongst reader-response critics. These 'narrative dynamics' can be diagrammed as in figure 1.[13] The inner box represents the text itself, with the real author and reader existing in the real world outside of the text and so not being easily accessible through simply reading the text. On the other hand, the *implied* author and reader are textual constructs, that is, their portraits are painted by the text itself. The implied reader, therefore, 'amounts to the textual elements that invite the actual reader to respond to the text in certain ways'.[14]

In regard to the movement from text to implied reader, this study assumes the distinction, still not widely utilised in Marcan studies, between the 'story' level of a narrative (i.e., what actually happens in the narrative) and the 'discourse' level (i.e., how the narrative connects with readers).[15] Literary studies of Mark have tended to deal with aspects of the 'story' level. However, given that the focus of this study is the interaction between text and reader, it is mainly concerned with the 'discourse' of Mark. It should be noted, however, that it is artificial to suggest that the two can be discussed in isolation from one another, especially since any study of the 'discourse' must also deal with the 'story', since the former also encompasses the latter.[16] The key analytical tools used here are drawn from Booth (dynamics of distance) and Genette/Bal/Rimmon-Kenan (focalisation), but frequent reference will also be made to Fowler's work, since it represents the only sustained treatment of Mark at the level of 'discourse'.[17]

[13] Chatman's diagram suffices for my purposes, although I have added 'characters' to it, for they can operate on either 'side' of the equation, speaking for the author or aligning themselves with the reader. It has been slightly modified by Danove and van Iersel. For discussion and diagrams, see van Iersel, *Mark*, 16–21. Fowler also discusses the place of the 'critic' and the 'critical reader'; 'Reader – Reader-Response?', 5–10; *Let the Reader*, 4–5, 263–4. The 'narrator/narratee' axis is not useful for Mark, for the transaction simply involves the implied author/reader; Fowler, 'Reader – Mark?', 40.

[14] Van Iersel, *Mark*, 17–18. That the 'implied reader' is a textual construct must be stressed, given the tendency for some to use the term loosely, in such a way as to bestow a real-world existence upon the implied reader.

[15] The distinction is drawn by Chatman, *Story*, 10, 19, who deals with Story in chs 2 and 3, and Discourse in chs 4 and 5. Fowler, *Let the Reader*, 256, complains that a failure to distinguish these two levels often troubles literary analyses of Mark. Van Iersel, *Mark*, 22, correctly stresses that the discourse level 'totally embraces the narrative level'.

[16] Van Iersel, *Mark*, 22.

[17] There are, of course, many 'literary' studies of Mark, but Fowler's almost unique contribution is his analysis of the 'discourse' level, i.e., the level at which the text communicates with the reader. In 1989 Beavis, *Audience*, 14, referred to his *Loaves* (1981) as 'the most important reader-response interpretation to date' (cf. p. 10), and *Let the Reader* (1991) focused even more sharply on the discourse level.

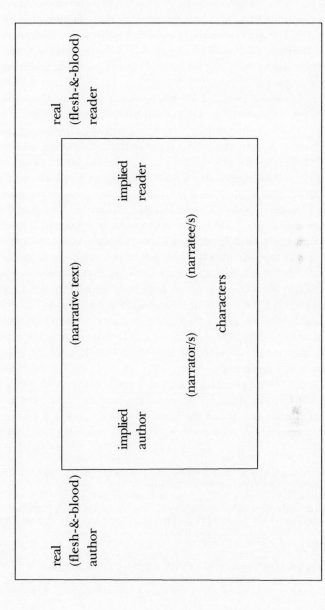

Figure 1 Chatman's narrative dynamics

A key question at the 'story' level of Mark's communicative dynamics is the role played by the various character groups with respect to the reader. It is usual to identify Mark's 'major' characters as Jesus, his disciples, and his opponents. The other characters are labelled as the 'minor' characters. Alongside the many studies discussing the role of the disciples in Mark's process of communication, the key role of these 'minor' characters has also been recognised.[18]

Since Williams has provided the fullest and most recent discussion of the 'minor' characters, he will be another conversation partner in this study. He divides the 'minor' characters into those appearing before Bartimaeus in the narrative and those appearing after him, arguing that the former play the role of 'suppliant', whereas the latter act as 'exemplars'[19] – Bartimaeus being a transitional figure with both roles. I suggest that a further subdivision is possible, however, for there is a group of 'minor' characters who change allegiance and so can be called the 'cross-over characters'.[20] These subdivisions enable a group of thirteen 'minor' characters to be isolated,[21] beginning with the man in Capernaum and ending with Bartimaeus, who, with greater precision, can be termed 'suppliants'[22] because they need healing or exorcism (for themselves or others) and they receive extraordinary help from Jesus (1.21–28; 1.29–31; 1.40–45; 2.1–12; 3.1–6; 5.1–20; 5.21–24a, 35–43; 5.24b–34; 7.24–30; 7.31–37; 8.22–26; 9.14–29; 10.46–52). These are the 'minor characters' of interest to this study, although, since I will be arguing that they play a 'major' role in Mark's communicative dynamics, I prefer the more descriptive label 'suppliants'.

The role of these suppliants in Mark's communication process has not yet been satisfactorily discussed. Considering them as 'foils for disciples'[23] has effectively eclipsed their own importance and perhaps even opened up the possibility of the disciples usurping Jesus' role as the story's

---

[18] Minor characters have received attention from Rhoads and Michie, *Mark*, 129–35, Malbon, 'Disciples', and, most recently, J.F. Williams, *Other Followers*.

[19] Williams, *Other Followers*, 167f., refining Malbon, 'Jewish Leaders', 159.

[20] The eager young man (10.17–23); the scribe (12.28–34), see S.H. Smith, 'Opponents', 177f.; the centurion (15.39); Joseph of Arimathea (15.42–47); and Judas. Although the category is my own, these characters have often been recognised as exceptions.

[21] The 'unknown exorcist' (9.38ff.) and the children (10.13–16) involve interactions between Jesus and his disciples, rather than properly being 'minor character' stories. A number of features distinguish them from the thirteen healing/exorcism scenes.

[22] The term, adopted from others, is not entirely satisfactory, since the actual 'supplication' can be made by the needy person, or by someone on behalf of another, or be absent altogether.

[23] Cf. Rhoads and Michie, *Mark*, 132–4.

protagonist.[24] Even Williams so subordinates these figures to the disciples that their role towards the reader is negligible. Although he admits that Mark also moves the readers to associate with characters other than the disciples,[25] he means those after and including Bartimaeus. His study therefore deems most important the 'minor' characters about whom the narrative says least and overlooks the importance of those about whom it says most.

In contrast to Williams, the present study argues that, when the analysis proceeds beyond the story level to the discourse level, it becomes clear that it is the suppliants in the healing and exorcism stories with whom the narrative most strongly associates the implied readers (see pp. 11–25 below). This, in turn, means that they play an extremely important part in the production of Mark's impact upon his real readers.

The (flesh-and-blood) readers to the text

This work seeks to understand Mark's persuasive impact on its early readers. The step of crossing from text to early audience to examine Mark's rhetoric has not often been taken: 'Mark has rarely been studied against the background of reader-response criticism and Graeco-Roman rhetoric, and [...] scholars have rarely undertaken to describe the Gospel's social setting.'[26] In order to understand Mark's persuasive power, it is necessary to move from the reader-oriented analysis of the text to an attempt to recover the 'cultural mind' of Mark's early readers through social description.

Understanding Mark has been likened to understanding a joke from another culture: 'You have to know what ideas and information are being assumed before you can "get" the meaning.'[27] Discussion of the healing and exorcism scenes, i.e., those involving the 'suppliants', has rarely delved into the ancient assumptions about the conditions represented in them, which limits the extent to which the interpreter 'gets' these scenes. Through an examination of relevant ancient literary and non-literary sources this study attempts to recover some of these assumptions as a step towards appreciating the impact the scenes would have made.

---

[24] Although it is true that, in Mark's web of relationships, these figures will have points of comparison and contrast to the disciples, their more important role will be to act in some way as 'foils' for the protagonist. In this web they take the part of 'the ficelle', who 'in innumerable ways [acts] as foil to the protagonist, creating [...] the perspectives of depth' (Harvey, 'Human Context', 242).

[25] J.F. Williams, *Other Followers*, 151.   [26] Beavis, *Audience*, 11.

[27] Rhoads, 'Social Criticism', 137.

The flesh-and-blood readers of interest to the study are not Mark's 'first', or 'original', readers, but its 'early' readers, i.e., those who potentially read/heard Mark once it was placed in the public domain. If all we can say about Mark's provenance is that 'the [G]ospel was composed somewhere in the Roman Empire',[28] it makes good sense to conceive of its early readers in correspondingly general terms, i.e., as those who lived in the Graeco-Roman world of the latter part of the first century.

Such generality allows Mark to be examined in terms of three broad features of first-century Graeco-Roman culture. These features are not chosen arbitrarily, but because they share vocabulary and/or concepts with Mark.

(1)   The expectation of the coming kingdom of God is the framework within which Mark's story is played out and its themes gain meaning. This intersects with the political framework of the Roman world, and, in particular, with the place of its rulers within it.

(2)   The healing/exorcism stories, which are the main interest of the study, inevitably touch upon various sicknesses. This project considers them as forms of 'illness', i.e., the social condition of being ill, rather than 'disease', i.e., the product of some pathological causality.[29] Such a focus avoids the 'etic' question of how a modern person might diagnose an ancient disease, in favour of the 'emic' question of how the ancient sufferer might have experienced it.[30]

(3)   Any interest in illness and *daimones*[31] in the ancient world automatically requires a corresponding interest in ancient magical practice. The various conditions experienced by Mark's sufferers overlap with those found in magical curses and spells. Jesus' treatment of these conditions has similarities to the practice of the magicians, albeit with important differences.

---

[28] Hooker, *Mark*, 8, who adds 'a conclusion that scarcely narrows the field at all!'. Cf. Fowler, *Loaves*, 183. This generality, however, is an asset, not a liability; cf. Bauckham, 'For Whom?'.

[29] Douglas, *Purity*, 29, labelled the fallacy that the only task called for is 'scientific explanation' of the disease 'medical materialism'; cf. Pilch, 'Leprosy', 108.

[30] For this sociological distinction see Pike, 'Etic', 152ff.

[31] Except in quotations from other authors, this study consistently uses the transliteration '*daimon*', instead of the more common English term 'demon'. Even though the English spelling finds the occasional counterpart in the sources (e.g. *P.Harris* 55 1.8–9 (2nd c. AD); *DT* 22–36 (3rd c. AD)), in popular parlance it tends to connote a metaphysical view of these beings which, I suggest, needs re-examination.

Flesh-and-blood readers come to a text with a 'repertoire' already in place, i.e., the conceptual resources which they bring to the reading of the narrative.[32] To put it more linguistically – and perhaps in a way that highlights the real-world context a little more – when a text is heard by an audience, its vocabulary and concepts have to engage with the 'mental register' that the audience already possesses. In order to make an impact, the language of the Gospel of Mark would have to engage in a meaningful way with its early readers' mental register. The particular features of Graeco-Roman life highlighted here are chosen because they share Mark's particular vocabulary and conceptualisation. They would be important – in fact, probably unavoidable – components of the mental register of the early readers seeking to make sense of Mark. Although local variation no doubt existed, each is a general feature of the Graeco-Roman world: it would be a rare place in the Roman world in which the effects of the Caesars, or illness and death, or magic, were not felt and experienced.

To understand the rhetoric of Mark, the persuasive strategy of the narrative itself *vis-à-vis* the reader needs to be understood, which is where reader-response criticism is useful. But real flesh-and-blood readers come to the text with an already-established 'repertoire' in their minds, by which they seek to understand Mark's narrative. The more we can understand the repertoire of a particular set of readers, the more we can understand the potential impact the narrative holds for them. If we wish to understand the potential impact of Mark on its early Graeco-Roman readers, then it is important to attempt to understand the repertoire of someone whose social setting was the first-century Graeco-Roman world.

In seeking to recover aspects of the early readers' mental register, the study attempts to assess the evidence of primary material not sufficiently utilised in previous Marcan studies. This has required the discussion of secondary material to be necessarily brief, although it will be obvious that decisions have been made about textual and exegetical issues discussed in the literature. This curtailment of lengthy discussion of secondary material is not meant to suggest that this discussion is irrelevant or inadequate, but simply represents a necessary compromise allowing the less familiar primary evidence to speak, at the expense of more familiar secondary material.

---

[32] Cf. van Iersel, *Mark*, 23–4, who speaks of the 'intended' reader, with whom the flesh-and-blood author shares much in common, such as language, literary conventions, shared presuppositions, world-view, fund of general knowledge, and a number of comparable experiences and ideas.

A focus on the Graeco-Roman readers does not imply that all of Mark's readers were Graeco-Roman, for, in fact, it is highly likely that there was a substantial Jewish component amongst Mark's readership. Neither does it imply that the Jewish material is not relevant to the concerns here. On the contrary, Mark is a Hellenistic document arising from a Jewish context, much the same as the LXX, the *Sentences* of Pseudo-Phocylides, and the writings of Philo and Josephus. The OT is essential for understanding the theological framework by which Mark evaluates Jesus. The Jewish thought world is important as a context from which the events of the story arose and against which they make sense. From time to time, in order to understand our text, reference will be made to this background, but much more could have been said. It should also be remembered that any Jewish readers would also be part of the Graeco-Roman world,[33] and by virtue of that position, despite their Jewish distinctives, they would share much of the same mental register as Gentile Graeco-Romans.

For the sake of a clear focus, the flesh-and-blood readers of interest here are those who inhabited the Graeco-Roman world of the first century. If Mark played a part in the movement towards the 'conversion of Rome',[34] then these were the people who read it. In order to understand how Mark's narrative rhetoric would have worked on them, we must attempt to expose relevant features of their cultural repertoire.

Jesus' defeat of death

This study argues that such text-to-reader and reader-to-text analysis leads to the conclusion that, in Mark, Jesus deals with death and its many invasions into human life. It will suggest that this message would have had a high potential impact on early readers, since their world provided ample occasion to feel the distress inflicted by human mortality, since, as depicted by Seneca (4 BC/AD 1–AD 65): 'Most men ebb and flow in wretchedness between the fear of death and the hardships of life; they are unwilling to live, and yet they do not know how to die' (*Ep.* 4.6).

A few studies have recognised in passing that Mark's presentation confronts the problem of human mortality, – either in parts,[35] or as a

[33] Cf. Cotter, 'Cosmology', 119, who complains that, in regard to cosmology and miracles, 'although we are now agreed that a common cultural influence was shared throughout the Mediterranean world, we have yet to take seriously the implications of Hellenization on the first-century Jewish understanding of the cosmos'.

[34] The phrase alludes to the title of the essay by Edwin Judge, *Conversion*.

[35] For example, 4.35–5.43 is clearly about Jesus' defeat of death in various forms. See McVann, 'Destroying Death', 125–9; Kotansky, 'Jesus'.

whole[36] – but there has been no full-scale exposition of this theme. These few studies have tended to adopt a moralistic framework (cf. pp. 11–25 below) which has inhibited the full appreciation of this theme for Mark's early readers.[37] Wegener probably comes closest to the conclusions reached here, although by vastly different means and to vastly different ends,[38] when he argues that the three major arenas of conflict in Mark all involve death, 'with the result that one might think that the overarching opponent is death itself'.[39] In arguing that Mark's narrative concerns Jesus' defeat of this opponent, this study also endorses Robert Smith's insistence that Jesus battles the 'dark powers' of human existence (demons, illness and death).[40]

Having sketched the general orientation of the project, three features require further introduction: the role of the suppliants in Mark's overall rhetorical strategy; the place of magic; and the place of the Caesars in first-century Graeco-Roman society.

The role of the suppliants

The suppliants, i.e., the so-called 'minor characters' involved in the healing and exorcism scenes, play a key role in the communication process between Mark's Gospel and its readers. Discussions of Mark's narrative dynamics, however, have tended to overlook their role in favour of that played by the disciples.[41]

[36] For Rhoads and Michie, *Mark*, Jesus' 'way' led inexorably to death, 64, 70f., 112; his end showed the awesome nature of death, 116; the disciples were to follow to their death, 91, but were hindered by their fear of death, 125–9, and Jesus had to prepare them for it, 92, 94f., yet their fear prevailed over their loyalty, 96, cf. 92, 95, 124. Later Rhoads, 'Losing Life', repeats much of this and shows that he regards 'death' largely as a metaphor, as does Olson, 'Between Text'. See also, Garland, ' "I am the Lord" ', 340; van Iersel's construction of Mark moving from desert to tomb, both places of death, van Iersel, *Mark*, 21; and Wegener, 'Reading Mark's Gospel', 468–9. Others recognize the anti-death theme, but blunt its impact by regarding it as a baptismal motif; cf., e.g., McVann, 'Destroying Death', 124, 129; Scroggs and Groff, 'Baptism', 542; Niedner, 'Gospel Dramaturgy', 459.
[37] Cf. Rhoads and Michie, *Mark*, 127–9, 139f.
[38] Wegener, *Cruciformed*, 3, 7, 80, 199, 209. His work explores responses to Mark expected from a fairly closely defined set of modern American readers, 'independent of how ancient auditors may have understood it' (p. 2).
[39] Ibid., 78; cf. Rhoads and Michie, *Mark*, 100, 96, following Wesley Kort (n. 31).
[40] R. Smith, 'Wounded Lion', 342, although the usual exemplary approach still protrudes (e.g. p. 343).
[41] Literary studies focusing on the disciples stretch from Tannehill, 'Disciples' and 'Narrative Christology', through Rhoads and Michie, *Mark*, to Shiner, *Disciples*, and Wegener, *Cruciformed*.

The role of the disciples: 'weak' identification

The relationship between reader and disciples is usually described as 'identification'. According to this conception, this supposedly 'natural'[42] process normally occurs with the protagonist, but, because Jesus is said to be too exalted and removed from them, the readers 'identify' with the disciples instead.[43]

This 'identification' can be labelled 'weak identification' (as opposed to the 'strong' identification described below), for it consists merely in the readers recognising a character as a role model.[44] This is reflected in the fact that, on this conception, the characters are often labelled 'exemplars', and that discussion centres upon their positive and negative traits of (moral) character.[45] It is 'weak' because it assumes a distance between the character and the reader which is crossed when the reader makes a rational choice to adopt a particular character as their exemplar.

Thus, Tannehill's influential presentation assumes 'identification' of the 'weak' type. The reader initially 'identifies' with the disciples in the opening call scenes (1.16–20; 3.13–19; 4.10–12; 6.7–13), because these scenes provide a strongly positive portrayal of them.[46] Later on, however, a shift occurs and the disciples are increasingly evaluated negatively (4.35–41; 6.45–52; 8.14–21),[47] until the passion narrative pictures them in strongly negative terms and the story ends with their failure.[48]

On closer examination, the 'strongly positive portrayal' of the disciples amounts, in total, to 'their immediate, unquestioning compliance'[49] with Jesus' call. Apart from this, the narrative contains no devices which close the distance between disciple and readers, who remain 'observers'.[50] The initial scene (1.16–20), for example, by erecting the expectation that the disciples will become 'fishers of men', certainly 'commissions'[51] them

---

[42] Cf. Tannehill, 'Disciples', 139; 'Narrative Christology', 70, 82f.; Wegener, *Cruciformed*, 7, 65, 69f.

[43] Wegener, *Cruciformed*, 212; cf. Harvey, 'Human Context', 243. Dewey, 'Point of View', argues for 'identification' with Jesus (for values) and the disciples (for situation). She mentions that Tolbert, in an unpublished paper, argues for identification *with Jesus* (p. 98).

[44] Cf. Tannehill, 'Disciples', 139–40.

[45] 'The narrator indicates which characters are approved and which scorned in the narrative world', Dewey, 'Point of View', 97.

[46] Tannehill, 'Disciples', 141, 144–5; 'Narrative Christology', 69–70; cf. J.F. Williams, *Other Followers*, 27–34; Wegener, *Cruciformed*, 74.

[47] Tannehill, 'Disciples', 145–51; 'Narrative Christology', 70.

[48] Tannehill, 'Narrative Christology', 82.

[49] Wegener, *Cruciformed*, 108; cf. Tannehill, 'Disciples', 144.

[50] As Wegener, *Cruciformed*, 109, himself admits.

[51] Tannehill, 'Narrative Christology', 62, 64f.

for their narrative role, but this commissioning is clearly a sub-set of Jesus' commissioning. These expectations are erected by a promise on his lips: '*I* will make you fishers of men.' The call to follow invites the readers to read further on into the story, watching Jesus to see whether and how he achieves this goal on the disciples' behalf. But, since they remain observers, this is not identification in any strong sense.

Despite its key role in previous discussions, this 'weak' concept of identification has major inadequacies.

(1) Its assumption of an autonomous and sovereign reader who must appropriate the story by means of 'choosing to identify' is an impoverished understanding of the act of reading. It is far too uni-directional and uni-dimensional and minimises the rhetorical power of the text itself. The more power granted a text to engage the reader, the more inadequate this view becomes.[52]

(2) It reflects a functional view of character,[53] in which the plot is all-important and the characters within a story, because subordinate to that plot, are of only typological interest.[54] This entails an interest in the (moral) character of characters, almost solely in terms of the 'traits' that can be distilled from their narrative presentation.[55]

(3) Although this focus on 'traits' was a feature of certain ancient approaches to character, it was not a feature of all,[56] and, in any case, it is doubtful whether this 'fits' with Mark's Gospel.[57] The assumption that

[52] This can be contrasted with Booth, *Company*, 141: 'A large part of our thought-stream is taken over, for at least the duration of the telling, by the story we are taking in.'

[53] Chatman, *Story*, 108–13; Rimmon-Kenan, *Narrative Fiction*, ch. 3; Culler, *Poetics*, 230.

[54] Tolbert, 'Character', 72–3. The view regarding character as subordinated to plot does injustice even to the ancient writers; see Pelling, 'Conclusion', 261.

[55] For example Rhoads and Michie, *Mark*, 130; J.F. Williams, *Other Followers*, 176, 177, 181, 183, 186f., 173, 202–5.

[56] Apart from Theophrastus, there were other writers on character, even if the fragmentary nature of their survival precludes their examination: Satyrus (*On Characters*, cited only once in Athenaeus 4.168c); Ariston of Keos (*On Relieving Arrogance*, in Philodemus, *On Vices* 10); Lycon (*On Drunkards*, in Rutilius Lupus 2.7 = Lycon fr. 26 Wehrli). Seneca, Plutarch and Posidonius (fr. 176 Kidd) also show a debt to character writing. Characterisation by type was already a feature of Aristophanes, and the 4th c. BC comics brought stock characters to the fore. It is interesting, however, that of the 'stock' traits dealt with, e.g., by Theophrastus, almost none are present in the Gospel of Mark. Characterisation by type was a feature of the orator, whose context militated against the wisdom of portraying people as 'individuals seen in the round'; see D.A. Russell, '*Êthos*' (citation from p. 198).

[57] Tolbert, 'Character', 72, refers to the typological nature of all character depiction in ancient writing, citing Theophrastus; cf. Malbon, 'Jewish Leaders', 278. But his approach cannot really be universalised. Gill, 'Character-Development', 469, complains about Theophrastus' 'relative triviality' and lack of clarity and shows that other ancient

Mark is operating within a moralistic framework and that his characters are therefore assembled for their exemplary role begs, amongst other things, questions of genre and purpose,[58] as well as of the societal level of Mark's audience. It also assumes that the flesh-and-blood readers of Mark would be interested in a story that helped them to make a rational, detached choice to follow some exemplary figure towards some moral goal.

(4) These assumptions encourage the tendency to overlook or disregard important rhetorical features of Mark's narrative. Greater attention to the dynamics of distance, i.e., how features of the text encourage the increase or decrease of the distance felt between the reader and the various parties in the text,[59] and the related notions of focalisation, i.e., the mediation of a perspective (not necessarily that of the narrator) in the text,[60] and the creation of sympathy, is essential if the concept of 'identification' is to be helpful. Furthermore, once these dynamics are taken into account, the 'weak' sense of identification becomes increasingly inadequate. While an exclusive interest in character 'traits' encourages a rationalistic/moralistic approach to the text, attention to the emotional features of the text,[61] for example, leads to a greater appreciation of the potential impact of the text upon real human beings. Despite the obvious value of attention to plot movements and character traits, if an approach ignores the dynamics of distance, focalisation and sympathy, it cannot be said to have dealt adequately with the narrative, for these things are crucial to the narrative engagement of the reader.

(5) The quest for character 'traits' also leads interpreters to overlook important features of the text. For example, it is an interesting feature of Mark's healing and exorcism scenes that, while traits of character are distilled only with effort,[62] the text itself always provides detail about

writers' interests were more complex (pp. 469f., 472f.). See also Pelling, 'Conclusion'. S.H. Smith, *Lion*, 93, admits that Mark shows little interest in character traits. It should also be noted that the focus on 'traits' probably assumes one particular approach to human psychology.

[58] Even *bioi*, to which Mark seems akin, pursued various purposes; cf. Burridge, *What Are the Gospels?*, 149–52.

[59] For the concept of 'distance', see Booth, *Fiction*, 155–8, 243–66, and the discussion to follow below. Dewey, 'Point of View', 99, mentions the importance of 'distance and perspective', but she apparently means distance between narrator and reader, rather than character and reader.

[60] Rimmon-Kenan, *Narrative Fiction*, ch. 6, drawing on Genette. Despite the 'visual' metaphor, it includes cognitive, emotive and ideological orientations (pp. 71, 79–82). Dewey, 'Point of View', uses the distinction, but underestimates its importance (p. 102).

[61] Cf. Booth, *Fiction*, 86.

[62] 'Faith' is sometimes so regarded, but is this really a 'trait'?

the characters' circumstances, sometimes at some length. Although the interest in (moral) character is entirely appropriate within a moralistic framework informed by a philosophical interest in the progress of the soul, this descriptive material suggests that Mark is more interested in the physical (including the social and emotional) state of his characters, than their moral progress.[63]

In fact, the focus upon the role of the disciples, with its associated interest in character traits, has meant that the role of Mark's healing/exorcism stories in the communicative process has been virtually overlooked,[64] despite these scenes being a major portion of Mark's early narrative (approximately 30 per cent of chapters 1–10) and an important vehicle for his portrayal of Jesus.

The trait approach has also led interpreters to be more attracted to the 'minor' characters in the text after Bartimaeus than those before him, since their brief treatment makes them amenable to being regarded as 'types'. The characters in the healing/exorcism scenes are described too richly to act as types. They have circumstances, needs, relationships, names, addresses, physical, social and economic problems; they are too much like real people! Mark is apparently not interested in a 'trait' or a 'character' that can be extracted, instead he appears to be interested in human beings.[65] As such, they are not so much 'exemplars' of what readers *ought to be*,[66] but, as representatives of the world of which the readers themselves are part, they are pictures of what readers *already know themselves to be*.[67] Mark's early flesh-and-blood readers would have seen them as more than simply 'characters' within a narrative-world, but as *intra-narrative reflections of themselves*. In other words, the role of these 'characters' towards the reader involves 'identification', understood in a strong sense.

---

[63] This is also true for the disciples. In contrast to other Graeco-Roman call stories, Mark's presentation of the call of the disciples ignores any moral changes and highlights the forsaking of property, family and profession; Shiner, *Disciples*, 196.

[64] Cf. Tannehill, 'Narrative Christology', 67; Wegener, *Cruciformed*, 76f. They are subordinated so strongly either to the disciples, cf. 'foils for the disciples', Rhoads and Michie, *Mark*, 132–4, or to the disciples and the minor characters after Bartimaeus (who are disciple-replacements), J.F. Williams, *Other Followers*, cf. Tannehill, 'Disciples', 152, that the importance of their narrative role is lost.

[65] Despite the link sometimes made between him and the 'trait' approach to characters, Aristotle's ethical-cum-empirical approach focused upon 'the human being' in the real world as a basic ethical norm; see Gill, 'Human Being'. It would be interesting to explore how this was linked to his views on literary/staged characters.

[66] Cf. Rhoads and Michie, *Mark*, 132.

[67] Cf. Rimmon-Kenan, *Narrative Fiction*, 33: although characters within a text 'are by no means human beings in the literal sense of the word, they are partly modelled on the reader's conception of people and in this they are person-like'.

Strong identification

It is more helpful to think of identification in the stronger sense that the readers somehow recognise themselves in a character and 'find [their] subjectivity in that representation'.[68] Rather than readers (arbitrarily?) choosing to adopt an ethical exemplar, the narrative is so constructed that it engages the readers and makes them see things as if they stood in another person's shoes.[69] If 'identification' is the feeling of *being* the character in some sense, then it is, in fact, only one end of a spectrum of possible distance relations between readers and characters.

Distance

Before Wayne Booth, discussion of 'distance' referred to aesthetic distance, namely, the awareness in a person that they are dealing with an aesthetic object and not real life.[70] Following Booth, 'distance' refers to 'the extent to which one is identified with or polarized from the action or, more pertinently, a particular point of view'.[71]

In order to understand 'distance relations' it is necessary to identify the textual dynamics involved in the reading process (see, again, figure 1). Once these parties are identified, it becomes clear that a number of different 'distance relations' are possible:[72]

> In any reading experience there is an implied dialogue among author, narrator, the other characters, and the reader. Each of the four can range, in relation to each of the others, from identification to complete opposition, on any axis of value, moral, intellectual, aesthetic and even physical.[73]

In what follows, I am especially interested in the distance relations between the flesh-and-blood readers and the thirteen characters identified as 'suppliants'. In order to communicate effectively, the (real) author must construct the text so as to make maximal impact upon the (real) readers, moving them from where they were when the text found them, to where

---

[68] Cohan and Shires, *Telling Stories*, 137.

[69] 'My consciousness behaves as though it were the consciousness of another' (Poulet), from Booth, *Company*, 139.

[70] Booth, 'Distance and Point of View', 97. The notion of aesthetic distance goes back to Bullough, ' "Psychical Distance" ', and is also the forefather of the 'critical distance' that is useful for analysing a text; cf. Fowler, 'Reader – Reader-Response?', 9–10.

[71] S.H. Smith, *Lion*, 173.

[72] These relations are also discussed by Fowler, 'Reader – Reader-Response?', 12–13, drawing upon Chatman, *Story*, 259–60.

[73] Booth, *Fiction*, 155.

the text wants them to be at the end of the reading experience. In rhetorical terms, they would then be thoroughly persuaded. The degree to which this successfully occurs is related to the degree to which the flesh-and-blood readers have 'become' the implied reader.[74] Booth put this desired result in terms of 'distance':

> From the author's viewpoint, a successful reading of his book will reduce to zero the distance between the essential norms of his implied author and the norms of the postulated reader.[75]

In order to reach this desired outcome for the whole work, it stands to reason that the various parts of the work will also have to manipulate the distance between the reader and the author's 'essential norms'. In what follows, I will argue that the suppliants play a key role in this reduction of distance. Mark's process of persuasion begins by engaging the readers with the suppliants.

Telling and showing

The control of distance is usually related closely to the formal distinction between 'telling' and 'showing' which goes back to Plato's distinction between 'simple narration' (διήγησις) and 'imitation' (μίμησις) (*Resp.* 3.392–4), and which became so important in twentieth-century fiction.[76] So, for example, Bal explains that distance 'has to do with the old distinction between showing and telling or the even older one between mimesis and diegesis'.[77] Or, at greater length, Smith comments:

> It has been widely established that control of distance (the extent to which one is identified with or polarized from the action or, more pertinently, a particular point of view) is regulated essentially by the relative proportions of 'telling' and 'showing' in a work. 'Telling' signifies the narrative mode [. . .], the narration of a story by a more or less intrusive third-person narrator; 'showing', on the other hand, represents the dramatic mode in

[74] 'The implied reader is the reader we must be willing to become, at least momentarily, in order to experience the narrative in the fullest measure'; Fowler, 'Reader – Reader-Response?', 12. Cf. Booth, *Fiction*, 138. The real reader who becomes the implied reader can be termed the 'ideal' reader, although this term is used variously; cf. Fowler's discussion, 'Reader – Reader-Response?', 15–18.

[75] Booth, 'Distance and Point of View', 99.

[76] For a convenient listing of 'some representative high spots in the history of aesthetics and criticism regarding this distinction', see Friedman, 'Point of View', 110 n. 3, along with his own discussion, pp. 109–117. For 'telling and showing', see Booth, *Fiction*, ch. 1.

[77] Bal, 'The Narrating', 234.

which the narrator appears to recede into the background, allowing the story to tell itself, as it were, by means of direct speech and superfluity of pictorial detail.[78]

Mark's Gospel contains both 'scenes' ('showing', *mimēsis*) and 'summaries' ('telling', *diēgēsis*). A large part of Mark's scenic material is devoted to the suppliants. Because their stories are given in scenes, the readers are 'shown' them, rather than being 'told' about them. The reader is made to feel like a first-hand observer of the action. Already this means that the distance between these characters and the readers is diminished. But, beyond this formal distinction, distance is also manipulated in other ways. It is at this point that the notion of focalisation becomes important.

Focalisation

The notion of 'focalisation' arose out of lengthy discussions concerning 'point of view' in narrative,[79] i.e., 'the position or perspective from which a story is told.'[80] Following this debate,[81] Genette offered a major revision of the traditional notion of 'point of view' by insisting upon the difference between narration and focalisation.[82] Mieke Bal further clarified the notion of focalisation.[83]

In many narratives, including Mark, it can be observed that 'often the object of the story's interest is not the same character from whose point of view the story is told'.[84] The basic distinction of importance here is, to use Genette's terms, that between external and internal focalisation, or, to use Bal's, that between the focaliser and the focalised. The distinction can be put simply through the use of prepositions: a scene can be focalised *on* a character, but focalised *through* another. In the analysis that follows, it will be seen that as the scenes involving suppliants open, they are focalised *through* the suppliants themselves. This is the start of the reduction of distance that ensures that the readers are aligned with these figures.

---

[78] S.H. Smith, *Lion*, 173.
[79] For a history of the discussion, see Friedman, 'Point of View', 109–17.
[80] Berlin, 'Point of View', 75.
[81] Chatman proposed perceptual, conceptual, and interest points of view; *Story*, 151–3. Berlin, 'Point of View', 75–7, offers some critique of his classifications. Uspensky, *A Poetics of Composition*, also differentiated a number of levels of point of view, see Berlin, 'Point of View', 85. Distinctions among kinds of points of view were made as early as Beach, see Friedman, 'Point of View', 112–13.
[82] Culler, *Poetics*, 'Introduction', 10.
[83] Bal, 'The Narrating'.   [84] Berlin, 'Point of View', 77.

There is more to the reduction of distance between reader and character than the use of showing rather than telling, or being focalised through a character. The narrative can reduce distance even further, even towards zero, through causing the reader to be sympathetically aligned with a character.

Sympathetic alignment

The close relationship between reader and character is usually expressed in terms of 'identification'. Despite its frequent use, this term seems to be rarely analysed and is not without problems.[85] As already argued, if rhetorical power is granted to the text, interest should fall upon what I have termed 'strong identification'. But, since the term 'identification' really implies a movement from reader to text, in order to maintain the text-controlled perspective it is better to speak of 'alignment', that is, the process by which a text aligns the implied reader with a particular character.

The creation of sympathy is a complex process,[86] using a variety of devices such as naming, positive characterisation, explanation (especially of perceived weaknesses or failings), emotion, and inside views. In ancient rhetorical declamation, characterisation by gender was also perceived to aid the promotion of sympathy. According to Hawley, the use of women in declamation was tied more to the construction of πάθος (feeling) than ἦθος (character). The same could be said of the use of children, and of description revealing relations between characters, which both appear to serve πάθος rather than ἦθος.[87]

[85] 'Identification' is, in fact, a modern notion which owes a heavy debt to romanticism. Tolbert, 'Character', 73; referring to Burns, *Character*, 6–15.

[86] 'What we call "involvement" or "sympathy" or "identification", is usually made up of many reactions to authors, narrators, observers, and other characters,' Booth, 'Distance and Point of View', 100.

[87] Dealing with Libanius (4th c. AD), Hawley, 'Female Characterization', 265–6, argues that these women were 'literary stereotypes' and the rhetors transmitted these stereotypes from the classical world to the world of the Empire, especially for use in the education of young men. If it is justified to extrapolate forwards from such 'literary stereotypes' from the classical world, and backwards from the rhetors' transmission of them to the later Empire, we can assume that these stereotypes may have also operated in the first century. Mark has four females (Simon's mother-in-law; Jairus' daughter; the bleeding woman; the Syrophoenician's daughter). Three of them are also relationally described, if not four (cf. 5.34). He also has three children (Jairus' daughter; the Syrophoenician's daughter (offstage); the boy at the base of the mountain) amongst the suppliants, and children also occupy an important place in the story on another occasion (10.13–16). None of these characters is really inspirational for ἦθος (being the lowly and despised of this world, rather than the wise and important), but they all generate πάθος. This also speaks against a moralistic understanding of them, for they were not those who would easily serve as role models.

Distance and the disciples

The more 'identification' is defined in terms of the readers' sense of *being* the character, the less satisfactory the notion becomes as the sole description of the role of the disciples in Mark. This role is complex and, since it changes as the narrative progresses, dynamic.[88] As the disciples are one of the three major character groups (with Jesus and his opponents) who appear practically from the start to the finish of the narrative, the reader has plenty of opportunity to evaluate them against the various narrative norms, and, as is common knowledge, they do not always perform well under such evaluation.

However, what needs to be recognised is that, wherever this evaluation occurs in the narrative, it actually excludes the disciples from being those with whom the reader identifies (in the strong sense). Strong identification with a character occurs most powerfully when the character is not evaluated at all – let alone negatively.[89] The presentation of their non-evaluated viewpoint creates the sympathy which leads to the feeling of 'identification'. Booth comments on a fictitious heroine:

> She must be accepted at her own estimate from the beginning, and that estimate must, for greatest effect, be as close as possible to the reader's estimate of his *own* importance. Whether we call this effect identification or not, it is certainly the closest that literature can come to making us *feel events as if they were happening to ourselves*.[90]

Strong identification in Mark

When the disciples are assessed against such criteria, it becomes clear that, in the early to mid stages of the narrative, they are not the characters who create the strongest sense of 'identification' in Mark's readers. Their sustained evaluation across the course of the narrative works *against* strong identification. The narrative only rarely uses textual devices which encourage the readers' sympathy, and so identification, with them. To be sure, when these devices do appear, they are present at key points in the

[88] This is acknowledged by Tannehill, 'Narrative Christology', 69ff., whose presentation vastly improves on, e.g., Weeden, *Mark*, but still needs to go further. These two represent the extremes of opinion on the disciples, see Dewey, 'Point of View', 98. 'Complex' is preferable to her 'ambiguous' (p. 97).

[89] See the discussion in Booth, *Fiction*, 274–7, commenting on Miranda, the heroine of Katherine Anne Porter's *Pale Horse, Pale Rider* (1936).

[90] Ibid., 276f., my italics.

story and their presence ensures that the disciples do have a role *vis-à-vis* the reader, but they are usually accompanied by evaluation.[91] Greater attention to these features would certainly strengthen the understanding of the disciples' reader-oriented role, enabling the discussion to move beyond the normal shallow 'exemplar' paradigm.[92] For instance, it is only in the passion narrative that sympathy-promoting devices begin strongly to appear and, at that point, even their 'failure' is sympathetically portrayed.[93] And so, as the implied readers are strongly aligned with the disciples, real readers find themselves 'identifying' with the disciples – *in the end*. But the way they are delivered up to the disciples in the final stages of the narrative is through previously being strongly aligned with the suppliants.

In the early to mid stages, the text encourages the greatest identification with the suppliants.[94] In terms of items which promote strong identification with a character,[95] Mark presents these characters statically, often revealing what they see, think, feel or know; and, despite the attempt by some to say otherwise, the norms erected by the story do not encourage a negative evaluation of them.[96] The reader sees their situation, and often even the main character in the story, through their eyes. Even though the narrator is not completely absent in these scenes, and his presence potentially threatens close identification by encouraging the readers to adopt an observer's stance, in fact it merely strengthens their sympathy with the character.[97] The various situations of these characters are often described rather fully,[98] decreasing the distance between them and the

[91] Dewey's list of devices supposedly encouraging closeness is demolished when the content is dealt with as well as the formal indicators, for they are almost always accompanied by negative evaluation; Dewey, 'Point of View', 101.

[92] Even within a moralistic framework, her more complex treatment leads Dewey, 'Point of View', 103, to move away from the emulation model, concluding that the suggested comparison between readers and disciples 'is not a question of the implied reader emulating the disciples' behavior; rather both the disciples and the implied reader are to live according to the behavior demanded by Jesus'.

[93] Cf. Boomershine, *Mark, the Storyteller*; 'Peter's Denial'.

[94] Cf. Wilder, *Rhetoric*, 65, who noted that we recognise ourselves in the minor characters.

[95] Booth, *Fiction*, 274–7.

[96] J.F. Williams, *Other Followers*, wrongly, as we shall see, attributes 'disobedience' to most of these characters, preventing him from acknowledging how important they are to the story.

[97] Often the readers are moved to the observer's role after the identification with the character is complete, in order that they might 'see' the interaction between Jesus and 'their' character.

[98] Admitted by Dewey, 'Point of View', 101, who misses the significance of this observation, despite being aware that 'showing [= a reducer of distance] is heightened by the sheer quantity of information, the inclusion of unnecessary concrete details and by direct speech' (p. 99).

reader and slowing the narrative tempo which enables them to come into even greater prominence. In short, these characters are the ones who are presented in such a way as to promote 'identification' in the strongest sense.

Mark's reading dynamics: a model

I have previously outlined a model which views Mark's reading dynamics in terms of six interlocking 'stories'.[99] The 'Main Story' about Jesus is set against the 'Big Story' of the kingdom of God,[100] promised in Israel's past, but expected in the future. The 'Counter Story', concerning Jesus' opponents; the 'Vacillating Story', of Jesus' disciples who oscillate between times of being for Jesus and times of sharing the hard-heartedness of his opponents; and the 'Episodic Stories', i.e., when other 'minor characters' interact with Jesus, all work together to make an impact upon the 'Readers' Story', in order to move them to adopt a positive stance towards Jesus and the kingdom of God.

Mark's narrative shows what Friedman calls 'multiple selective omniscience'.

> The tendency is almost wholly in the direction of scene, both inside the mind and externally with speech and action; and narrative summary, if it appears at all, is either supplied unobtrusively by the author by way of 'stage direction' or emerges through the thoughts and words of the characters themselves.[101]

The beauty of this kind of narrative is that it allows 'a composite of viewing angles', rather than limiting the reader to 'the fixed center'.[102] To earth this comment in my proposed model of Mark, this means that Jesus is at the centre, and the other stories provide the angles from which the reader is enabled to view him at the centre.[103]

This model assigns the disciples a very important role towards the reader which is both complex and dynamic. In brief, the disciples provide a source of continuity between scenes and across the narrative which the 'minor' characters cannot. The healing and exorcism scenes, however,

---

[99] Bolt, 'The Gospel', 43–9. A similar model could be distilled from Rhoads and Michie, *Mark*, chs 4 and 5. Cf. Tannehill, 'Narrative Christology', 63ff.

[100] Cf. Rhoads and Michie, *Mark*, 73–5.

[101] Friedman, 'Point of View', 127.   [102] Ibid., 128.

[103] Such a mode would be chosen 'if the author is concerned with the way in which personality and experience emerge as a mosaic from their impingement upon the sensibilities of several individuals', ibid., 134. In Mark, it is the 'personality and experience' of Jesus that emerge.

are 'not progressive but reiterative'.[104] But this study seeks to show that, far from being 'subordinate' to the material that forms 'a sequence leading toward the passion story, the narrative climax of the Gospel',[105] the two types of material work in a complementary fashion in order to achieve Mark's narrative impact. The sustained focus on the suppliants in this book should not be taken as an attempt to diminish the importance of the disciples in Mark. Just as studies focusing on the disciples do not claim that Mark is only about them,[106] so too this study acknowledges that there is more to Mark than the suppliants. The disciples and the suppliants, as well as Jesus, his opponents, and the other minor characters, all form a web of relationships in which the narrative entangles the reader in order to make its impact. Careful analysis of all aspects of this web is needed. All characters need to be understood as well as possible in their own right, and then understood in terms of how they complement the other characters in the narrative.

In this model I proposed that the suppliant scenes play the very important role of forming a bridge from the 'story-world' into the 'real-world', because they themselves are 'real-world' people.

The suppliants and the real world

Many literary studies on Mark have devoted attention to the study of Mark's characters. This has usually been done as if they were simply 'literary', or 'staged', characters. After showing a great deal of interest in character study throughout the nineteenth and into the twentieth century, (non-biblical) literary critics began to lose interest in it in the nineteen-thirties and forties.[107] Nevertheless, they admit that character cannot be ignored, for 'individual readers will continue to respond to novels because their curiosity and their sense of common humanity is engaged by the portrayals of human beings which they find there'.[108]

As a result of the scholarly paradigm shift from 'history' to 'literature', history has sometimes been jettisoned. This dichotomy is proved false, however, by the fact that ancient writers of history were also interested in telling the story well. 'The didactic purpose of history went hand in hand with that other preoccupation of classical historians, the art of presenting it in attractive form.'[109] It is the same abiding interest in 'a common humanity' that makes the people in an ancient text like Mark continue to

---

[104] Tannehill, 'Narrative Christology', 67.   [105] Ibid.
[106] Tannehill, 'Disciples', 153.   [107] Stevick, *Theory*, 221–2.
[108] Ibid., 222.   [109] Judge, 'On Judging', 20.

have importance for the historian. History is 'a subjective encounter',[110] and 'we would do more justice to the nature of this encounter if we accepted that the process of understanding is essentially personal, and that unless we propose to dehumanise the dead, we owe them a personal response'.[111] Or again:

> History is not simple. It is as endlessly complex as we are our-
> selves. That is why it is a mistake to seek a total, objective
> explanation of history. We should not dare to impose on others
> explanations we would reject as artificial in our own case. Since
> we cannot explain ourselves – and who would venture to claim
> that before his own conscience – how can we pretend to explain
> the whole of humanity? Yet we must attempt to understand each
> other, for it is out of such communication that our human iden-
> tity is created. Its subjectivity is of its essence. It is by means of
> culture that we share and transmit our humanity.[112]

The people encountered in a historical work consist of a 'slice of life' through the world being described in the work. The discussion over 'characters' in Mark has tended to ignore the fact that the suppliants, whilst appearing in a narrative, also represent a 'slice of life' of the ancient world,[113] just as much as do the case studies in the Hippocratic corpus, for example.

Even the debate over characters in literature reflects a wider debate over the nature of persons, human beings and personhood.[114] Gill has suggested that 'the most obvious analogue in ancient philosophy for the modern concept of person was that of "human being" (*anthrōpos*)'.[115] It is a core issue in both ancient and modern philosophy as to

> whether we are to understand ourselves, essentially, as hu-
> man beings (with all that this implies, as regards our psycho-
> physical nature and our specific forms of shared life and
> self-understanding) or whether we are to identify ourselves
> rather with a certain set of mental capacities, conceived as

---

[110] Ibid.   [111] Ibid., 21.   [112] Judge, 'Ancient Beginnings', 482.

[113] Friedman, 'Point of View', refers to a narrative strategy of providing a 'slice of life', by which he means a narrative version of what a camera might provide. But the fact that Mark provides a slice of the real world of the day does not mean that he cannot tell his story with great narrative art.

[114] Gill, 'Introduction', 17.

[115] Ibid., 7. He develops this further in his contribution to the volume, 'Human Being'.

constituting our 'personhood' or 'divine' essence, which are
in principle shared by, and normative for, other forms of life and
intelligence.[116]

Despite the tendency to treat them as types, exemplars, or vehicles of
'traits', this is exactly how the suppliants in Mark are presented – as
anthrōpoi.

To enlist another of Gill's distinctions, the suppliants in Mark are not
treated as *characters* but as *personalities*,[117] a distinction which is also
aligned with that between *ēthos* and *pathos*. Gill uses the term *character*
in association with the process of making ethical judgements, but *personality* in association with: (i) an empathetic, rather than moral, response;
(ii) a concern with the unique individual, rather than with the bearer
of character-traits; and (iii) a perspective in which a person is seen as
psychologically passive, subject to forces beyond themselves.[118] Mark's
suppliants are presented in exactly this way, as personalities, who produce
in the readers 'the desire to identify oneself with another person [*viz*, for
Mark: the suppliant], to get inside her skin, rather than to appraise her
"from the outside".'[119]

Although the suppliants can be – and will be here – analysed in terms
of their being 'characters' within a story, they will also be regarded as
human beings from the first-century Graeco-Roman world. To the early
flesh-and-blood readers of Mark, these people would be recognised immediately as people from the real world to which they themselves belonged.
As such, there is more than 'an analogy' between the story and real-life.
Mark offers its readers an encounter with the real-life stories of other
human beings from their own world. Through the shared culture between
suppliant and flesh-and-blood reader, there would be a 'transmission of
their humanity'. In this capacity, these 'suppliants' provide the existen-
tial entrance for the early readers of the Gospel. The present study will
explore how this occurs through an analysis of the relevant scenes[120] and
their potential impact.

---

[116] Gill, 'Introduction', 17. The essays in the volume he is introducing contribute to this
question. Given Aristotle's influence on narrative analysis, it is significant that Gill argues
that he held a view of persons as 'human beings', i.e., as ethical-cum-empirical.

[117] Gill, 'Character-Personality'; 'Character-Development'; cf. Pelling, 'Conclusion',
257.

[118] Gill, 'Character-Personality', 2.   [119] Ibid.

[120] Dewey, 'Point of View', 106, also calls for a scene-by-scene analysis of the narrative
to test her theory of twofold identification (see her n. 15). The argument in this present work
suggests that the suppliants need to be factored into the equation.

Illness and death

For a modern reader to appreciate the early impact of Mark's healing/ exorcism stories, a first-century perspective on the illnesses concerned must be regained.

Illness

The distinction has already been made (above, p. 8) between disease, i.e., the product of some pathological causality, and illness, i.e., the social condition of being ill. Whereas the exact diagnosis of the diseases found in Mark would have only little value in terms of the impact of the narrative on its early readers, a better understanding of these conditions as illnesses has great value. Because 'illness and healing can be adequately understood only within the framework of a specific culture',[121]

> [u]nderstanding sickness as illness is, then, a cultural process. All cultures have patterns of perceiving, comprehending, explaining, assessing, and treating the symptoms of sickness. These patterns are influenced by personal and family perceptions, and through them by the cultural values of each society. The assessment of sickness takes place by a process of labeling symptoms and the sickness itself, as well as by expressing its significance for the individual and the group to which he or she belongs. In this way, the sickness itself takes on a precise meaning and is shaped according to certain patterns of behavior, being thereby transformed into a specific cultural form. That cultural form is what we call an illness.
>
> As a result of this process, the cultural construction of a sickness establishes (a) the way it is understood and explained; (b) the way it affects the status of the sick person; and (c) how to treat it, depending on the therapeutic strategies available.[122]

Ascertaining the social impact of an illness involves a range of questions such as: What did people think about the conditions? What was it like to suffer them? What were the anatomical/ physiological/ pathological understandings of these conditions? What were the fears they evoked? What was the usual approach to dealing with them?

It requires very little imagination to discern in the Hippocratic case studies, for example, the great distress and human misery accompanying

---

[121] Guijarro, 'Healing Stories', 103.   [122] Ibid., 105.

the progress of disease.[123] Those who died (approx. 60 per cent) endured
the disease for anywhere between 2 and 120 days, with an average length
of survival of 19.4 days; while those who survived had to endure the
disease for anywhere from 3 to 120 days and suffered an average of 34.8
days of illness.[124] Although it is not often done, Mark's healing/exorcism
stories can be regarded as another set of case studies which provide an
additional sample of life in this kind of world.[125] Given that the incidence
of illness in the first century was probably on the increase, and that the
overcrowded cities were 'pestholes',[126] Mark's sample would be all too
familiar. 'Not only was the Greco-Roman world periodically struck by
deadly epidemics, but illness and physical affliction were probably the
dominant features of daily life in this era.'[127]

The shadow of death

First-century people lived perpetually under 'the shadow of death'. Esti-
mating their average life expectancy is fraught with problems: no study
of mortality survives from that period, if one ever existed;[128] acquiring
accurate statistics is impossible, given that so much of what would be relevant evidence has not survived; and the evaluation of the evidence that

---

[123] For example, great pain in various parts of the body, violent and continuous headaches, ulcerated throats and suppurating ears, vomiting and diarrhoea, speech disturbances and deafness, paralysis, boils and abscesses, difficulty breathing, convulsions, delirium, rigor, coma, bleeding from various orifices, and so on, and all with no analgesics, antibiotics or other benefits of modern (post-war!) pharmacology.

[124] My calculations are based on the 42 cases in *Epidemics* I and III in which length of illness is specifically mentioned. Beyond these there is only one other case, which is declared to be beyond help. Combining both groups yields an average of 24.4 days of illness.

[125] There are other writers, such as Aelius Aristides, who are famous for describing their own illnesses. See Festugière, *Personal Religion*, ch. 6. Speculating about the conditions in first-century Palestine, Rohrbaugh, 'Introduction', 5, comments: '[F]or most lower-class people who did make it to adulthood, health would have been atrocious. Studies by paleopathologists indicate that infectious disease and malnutrition were widespread. By age thirty the majority suffered from internal parasites, their teeth were rotted, their eyesight gone. Most had lived with the debilitating results of protein deficiency since childhood.'

[126] Stark, *Rise*, 155: 'The Greco-Roman city was a pesthole of infectious disease – because it was always thus in cities. Indeed, it was not until the twentieth century that urban mortality was sufficiently reduced that the cities of western Europe and North America could sustain their populations without additional in-migration from rural areas.'

[127] Ibid., 154.

[128] Russell, 'Late Ancient', 5, bewails the fact that the Romans appear to have been uninterested in the things that interest population studies, i.e., length of life, migration, fertility, mortality.

has survived is not a simple matter.[129] Estimates have depended heavily on the evidence gleaned from extant tombstones, but this evidence cannot be relied upon to give a full and accurate picture.[130] Nevertheless, a working figure emerges from the discussion of the surviving tombstones that sufficiently illustrates the point to be made here. None of those discussing the inscriptional evidence puts the figure higher than 30 years of age, and some have worked with a figure as low as 20.[131] Wiedemann, for example, while stressing that figures must remain 'highly approximate', states that people in the first-century Roman world probably had an average life expectancy of around 20–25 years.[132]

Even those who are cautious about estimates based on tombstones alone come up with the same kind of figure. Despite applying a more rigorous method which utilized UN model life tables, and concluding that 'ancient inscriptions cannot be used as the basis for calculations of mortality, absolutely or even relatively',[133] Hopkins still agrees that 'life expectancy at birth was also probably under 30'.[134]

A low average life expectancy does not mean that some did not live into old age, for indeed the evidence clearly shows that there were those who did. In fact, their survival through the early years indicates a stronger constitution that may well have taken them through to a fairly grand

---

[129]   See ibid., 22–30, for a discussion of some of the problems and a careful assessment of the evidence. Although aware of the problems (pp. 28f.), he is happier to use the tombstones as a 'random sample' (p. 24), than are others (e.g., Hopkins).

[130]   For the key discussions, see Burn, 'Hic Breve Vivitur'; Russell, 'Late Ancient'; Durand, 'Mortality Estimates'; Hopkins, 'Probable Age Structure'.

[131]   Durand, 'Mortality Estimates', suggests the range 15–25 years for the Western Roman Empire in the first and second centuries, and 25 or 30 for the whole Empire.

[132]   Wiedemann, *Adults*, 14f. Agreeing that deriving statistical information from tombstones is fraught with difficulties, he refers to those from Roman tombs which suggest average life expectancies were 22 years for men and 20 years for women (p. 15). Egyptian tombstone studies suggest a life expectancy of *c*. 30 (*NewDocs* 3, **11**).

Pomeroy, *Families*, cautions that the Roman evidence should not be applied to Classical Greece. She discusses the complexities of the situation in chapter 3. Although it should be noted that 'age at death' figures are not the same as 'average life expectancy' figures, she refers to the estimates of Angel and Bisel that the age at death was 36.8 (females) and 44.1 (males); and of Gallant that men were 40 and women 38 when they died (p. 6, nn. 20–1). She also points out that figures taken from cemeteries need to allow for a female infanticide rate of about 20% and a lack of female burial in about 10% of cases (p. 121). At Olynthus, 30% of graves are infants, which is a 'reasonable reflection of actual mortality', and children make up another 21.4% (p. 121).

[133]   Hopkins, 'Probable Age Structure', 263.

[134]   Ibid. For the life expectation at birth of the Roman population he gives the range 20 to 30 years (p. 264). Russell, 'Late Ancient', 35, also agrees that the average length of life was about 30 years.

old age.[135] Instead, a low average life expectancy correlates with a high infant mortality. Infant mortality is itself difficult to estimate,[136] even from the tombstones, where infant deaths are underrepresented.[137] Burn and Hopkins suggest an infant mortality of above 200 per thousand,[138] and Durand assumes a 30 or 40 per cent death rate in the first year of life.[139] According to Wiedemann, only 50 per cent of children reached their tenth birthday and only 40 per cent of the population reached 20–25.[140] (For comparison, see tables 1–4).[141]

Illness was a part of the fabric of ordinary life and, without the advantages of modern medicines and health measures, it regularly brought the threat of death to the home. The fact that a regular part of the philosophers'

[135] Russell, 'Late Ancient', 22, 33, 35. He mentions (p. 33) Isidore's famous 'ages of man', which elaborates Tertullian (see Migne *PL* 2:746): Infantia (infancy) 0–7; Pueritia (childhood) 7–14; Adolescentia (adolescence) 14–28; Iuventus (youth) 28–50; Gravitas (maturity) 50–70; Senectus (old age) 70+.

[136] Russell, 'Late Ancient', 22, points out that this, in turn, makes it difficult to estimate average life expectancy, making it a rather unsatisfactory figure for use in population studies (see also pp. 34–5).

[137] Noted by Burn, 'Hic Breve Vivitur', 4; Russell, 'Late Ancient', 24; Durand, 'Mortality Estimates', 369; Hopkins, 'Probable Age Structure', 247. The same underrepresentation is found in Ausonius, *Parentalia* (See Russell, 'Late Ancient', 30). Alongside other possible reasons for this (Burn's 'infants were very rarely given tombstones' (p. 5) is more a description than a rationale) should be placed the practice of exposing unwanted infants, especially females, which was common (Russell, 'Late Ancient', 14), and there is also evidence to suggest that infants this young were not even properly buried. Wiedemann, *Adults*, 179, mentions children of less than 40 days old being buried under the threshold, or in a wall of the house. Jordan reported a find of the remains of over 100 newborn corpses in a blocked sewer. The fact that such corpses were highly sought after by magicians also may suggest they were easily obtained, and so not properly interred. These were the ἄωροι who were considered extremely powerful for magical purposes. See below, ch. 4, pp. 160–1.

[138] Burn, 'Hic Breve Vivitur', 14; Hopkins, 'Probable Age Structure', 263.

[139] Durand, 'Mortality Estimates', 371.

[140] These figures are based upon Ulpian's table (*Digest* XXX, ii, 68; 3rd c. AD), in comparison with Frier's population studies of Mauritius in the 1940s; see Wiedemann, *Adults*, 15; Frier, 'Roman Life Expectancy'. For Ulpian, see Russell, 'Late Ancient', 24.

[141] Cf. the discussion by Rohrbaugh, 'Introduction', 4–5 , drawing upon Carney, *Shape*: in the cities of the Roman period, about $\frac{1}{3}$ who survived their first year of life (i.e., those who survived infant mortality) were dead before they were six. 60% of these survivors were dead before they were 16. By 25, 75% were dead; by 46 90% were gone. Less than 3% of the population made it to 60. It was harder on the poorer classes. A poor person in the city of Rome in AD 1 had a life expectancy of 20 years. In a Palestinian peasant community infant mortality could have reached as high as 30%. Rohrbaugh comments that, 'at 32 or 33 years of age, if indeed he lived that long, Jesus would have been older than perhaps 80 percent of his hearers, who would have been ridden with disease, malnourished, and looking at a decade or less of life expectancy. Since few poor people lived out their thirties, we may also have to revise our picture of Jesus. He was hardly one who died in the prime of life' (p. 5).

Table 1 *Infant mortality and life expectancy in industrialised countries*

(Based on T. Wiedemann, *Adults and Children in the Roman Empire* (London: Routledge, 1989), p. 12.)

	Infant Mortality (per 1000)	Life Expectancy (years)	
		Males	Females
England and Wales (1979–80)	10.8	70.4	76.6
United States (1982)	10.9	70.8	78.2
West Germany (1980–2)	10.9	70.2	76.9

Table 2 *European countries with higher infant mortality and lower life expectancy rates*

(Based on T. Wiedemann, *Adults and Children in the Roman Empire* (London: Routledge, 1989), p. 13.)

	Infant Mortality (per 1000)	Life Expectancy (years)	
		Males	Females
Portugal (1975)	26.0	65.09	72.86
Romania (1976–8)	28.0	67.42	72.18
[former] Yugoslavia (1979–80)	29.9	67.72	73.15
[former] Soviet Union (1971–2)	27.7	64.00	74.00

Table 3 *Infant mortality rates in 'Third World' countries compared to industrialised European countries at the turn of the twentieth century*

(Based on T. Wiedemann, *Adults and Children in the Roman Empire* (London: Routledge, 1989), p. 13.)

	Infant Mortality (per 1000)
Turkey (1966)	153
Tanzania (1967)	160–165
Gabon (1960–1)	229
Zambia (1960)	259
Industrialised European countries (1900 $\pm$)	150–200

Table 4 *Comparative figures for 1999*

(Data source: 1999 *CIA* World Factbook; www.geographic.org)

	Infant Mortality (per 1000)	Life Expectancy (years)	
		Males	Females
Best	Isle of Man, 2.45	Andorra, 80.55	86.55
Australia	5.11	77.22	83.23
United Kingdom	5.78	74.73	80.15
United States	6.33	72.95	79.67
World Average	56	61	65
Worst	Afghanistan, 140.55	Malawi, 36.49	36.11

agenda was how to face death without fear, indicates that the fear of death was a feature of life that needed to be overcome.[142]

The very brevity of life would have made illness even harder to bear. Although it is not a particularly Roman-sounding sympathy, perhaps there would be those in the first century who would agree with the ancient *Prayer of Kantuzilis for Relief from His Suffering*:

> Life is bound up with death, and death is bound up with life. Man cannot live for ever; the days of his life are numbered. Were man to live for ever, it would not concern him greatly even if he had to endure grievous sickness.　　　　　　　(*ANET*[3], 400–1)

The treatment protocol

Although an older age – and perhaps its Stoic descendants – may have believed that 'there is no escaping disease sent by Zeus' (*Od.* 9.410), many across the centuries sought such an escape. Despite modern speculations that the inadequacy of first-century medical treatment would cause people to 'flock to faith healers and miracle workers',[143] the situation seems to have been a little more complex. The options available to the sick can be regarded as a 'health care system'.[144]

---

[142] I have explored the notion of life under the shadow of death in Bolt, 'Life, Death'. Also see below, on Suppliant 7.

[143] E.g., Meyer, *Who?*, 33.

[144] See Avalos, *Health Care*. The three sectors of a health care system can be listed as (a) the popular sector, family and friends; (b) the professional sector, physicians; (c) the folk sector, traditional healers (magicians). See also Guijarro, 'Healing Stories', 103, 104.

In his suffering, Kantuzilis prayed to the gods, '... grant me life. Would that my god, who for[sook] me, [might take] pity on me!' But the gods were not the only healing service available. There were the physicians – who in the first century would still be disciples of Hippocrates, 'that prince of medicine' (Pliny *HN* 7.51.171; cf. Apul. *Flor.* 19) – and there were magicians, and it seems that stiff competition prevailed amongst the various remedial agencies.[145]

Although it would be foolish to suggest that people turned to these various resources in exact sequence, the evidence suggests that there was a loose kind of protocol.[146] So, for example, a sequence is suggested in the report that, in the Athenian plague (431 BC), the physicians were no help, nor were prayers to the gods, nor oracles, so the people abandoned all these things (Thuc. 2.47).

The physician knew that he could only help in certain conditions.[147] In fact, part of the skill of being a good doctor – and so keeping one's reputation intact in the competitive environment that existed – was to know which cases properly belonged to the art and which did not. Although the physicians were certainly meant to provide what little assistance they could, a large part of their role apparently consisted of discerning the signs in the course of the illness which would enable them to predict whether the patient would live or die (cf. Hipp. *Prog.* chs 1; 20; 24; 25). This was an important task, because physicians' reputations depended upon the accuracy of their predictions.

When the physicians could not help, it was time to call upon the gods. Asclepius, for example, was a good second option,[148] since

> he often saves people after all medical efforts have failed to [liberate them] from the diseases binding them, if only they turn to him in worship, however briefly.
>
> (*P.Oxy* 1381 = Cartlidge, 122–4 (2nd c. AD))

[145] King, 'Bound', 115.

[146] 'Each culture establishes an implicit hierarchy which determines the way a sick person will pass from one sector to another in search of health,' Guijarro, 'Healing Stories', 104, although he 'supposes' that people would turn to magic first, then the physicians, if they had the means (p. 105).

[147] Gill, 'Ancient Psychotherapy', 317, points out that in Aristophanes, *Wasps* (*Vespae*), amongst the various remedies tried for Philocleaon's madness, 'nobody thinks of sending for a doctor. This seems to suggest that, as we would expect from other evidence, Greek doctors were associated primarily with the treatment of physical rather than mental illness.'

[148] Cf. Aristophanes, *Pl.*, 405–10: 'Bl. Had we not better call a doctor in? Chr. Is there a doctor now in all the town? There are no fees, and therefore there's no skill. [. . .] Chr. Why then, 'tis best to do what I intended, To let him lie inside Asclepius' temple A whole night long.' Votives and testimonies have survived from temples of Asclepius that testify to healing by his hand. See, for example, the famous inscriptions from the sanctuary at Epidaurus; LiDonnici, *Epidaurian Miracle Inscriptions*.

Through an oracle, the gods might also provide help with the all-important question of whether the patient would live or die. When the gods failed, the magicians could be of service:

> People with chronic diseases, when they have despaired of ordinary remedies and customary regimens turn to expiations and amulets and dreams. (Plut. *De facie* 920B)

They could provide additional assistance in predicting the outcome through some 'prognostic of life and death' such as Democritus' 'sphere' (see below, p. 82).[149] Magicians could help in other ways, for when 'an infection festered or a fever lingered, even the sternest critics of traditional or "superstitious" remedies turned to the application of amulets'. The cases of former critics turning to magic

> represent a plausible picture of competing cures and 'second opinions' as a disease worsens and seem to set the use of amulets squarely within the sphere of traditional beliefs.[150]

Even the physician Galen prescribed amulets as part of his regimen, although he denied the traditional explanation of their success.[151]

The magicians may have been especially useful if there was any suspicion that the illness had itself been caused by magic. If Pliny was right that in the seventies 'there [was] no one who [was] not afraid of curses and binding spells' (*HN* 28.4.19),[152] then this also implies that 'everyone' probably used amulets to protect themselves against the diseases inflicted by malevolent magic.[153]

Some kind of protocol can be discerned even within the Jewish Diaspora context. Ben Sirach's prescribed behaviour for the Israelite is clearly set against the normal procedures of the Greek (Sirach 38): they are to pray first, but then call the doctor and don't let him leave! The discovery of amulets on the fallen soldiers of Judas Maccabaeus (2 Macc. 12.34–39) showed that the practice had made inroads even amongst the Jews, whose law forbade such things, and magic was evidently familiar to those at Qumran. Josephus' comments on 1 Samuel 16 may even suggest that physicians called on the magician in difficult cases. When Saul's spirits caused him to be 'beset by strange disorders',

---

[149] Cf. the use of diagnostic 'wheels' in other circumstances. We know of other ancient prognostic calculations; cf. Brashear, 'New Texts', 210 nn. 1 and 2.

[150] Kotansky, 'Incantations', 107, referring to Pericles and Bion.   [151] Gager, 221.

[152] Cf. the question to the oracle, 'Am I under a spell?' (*P.Oxy* 1477 (3rd/4th c. AD)).

[153] Gager, 220.

> the physicians could devise no other remedy save to order search
> to be made for one with power to charm away spirits and to play
> upon the harp.   (*AJ* 6.166; cf. 168, 211)[154]

Does this reflect Josephus' knowledge of first-century (Palestinian) prac-
tices? If so, whereas the Greek protocol seems to have been: physician→
God→ magician, the Ben Sirach and Josephus texts suggest that the
Jewish protocol was: God → physician→ magician.[155]

The fact that physicians used magic, magicians used 'quasi-medical'
means, and priests also used magic in some quarters, would have eased
the patient's transition from one to the other.

Part of the legacy of nineteenth-century scholarship is the desire to distinguish too sharply between magic, science and religion,[156] or, 'magic,
medicine and miracle'.[157] Although attempts to make this tripartite distinction absolute, or to set it within some evolutionary framework, should
be eschewed, it is clear that it is not simply a product of the nineteenth
century since evidence for it can be found even in antiquity (e.g. Hipp.
Morb.Sacr. 4). There was certainly a great deal of overlap between the
three, but, nevertheless, when illness struck the home, there was a protocol
through which a patient could pass. There were those known as physicians, there were the gods, and – perhaps outside those more respectable
services – there were also those known as magicians.

Magic in first-century Graeco-Roman society

A magical renaissance

The study of ancient magic is currently enjoying a renaissance[158] as new
texts and better readings of old texts continue to emerge, which illustrate
ancient magical praxis stretching across centuries.[159]

Spells and curses have been gathered from the Ancient Near East, the
Graeco-Roman world, and from later Coptic Egypt. Discoveries have
also illuminated the role of magic within Judaism, where the previous

---

[154] David's musical abilities against *daimones* may lie behind the development of extra
psalms for this purpose; cf. 4Q510–511; 11QPsAp^a; 4Q560.

[155] We should also note that, even in Hellenistic settings, a dream (i.e., the gods) could
overturn the diagnosis of the physicians; Vallance, 'Medicine', 946.

[156] For a critical discussion of the distinction in nineteenth-century scholarship, see
Phillips, 'Occult' and 'Problems'.

[157] Cf. Kee, *Medicine, Miracle & Magic*.

[158] Meyer and Mirecki, *Ancient Magic*, 1. The scholars writing in their volume are
representative of this renaissance.

[159] Even Hull, *Hellenistic Magic*, ch. 2 mentioned 'new' discoveries and publications
when the floodgates were barely open.

conclusion that the era of the Second Temple was a magical time – drawn from a wealth of indirect evidence from later sources (such as the Aramaic Bowl Texts, Rabbinic sources, *Sepher ha-Razim*, *Harba de Mosheh*, *PGM* IV.3009–85; Hadrametum tablet)[160] – has now been endorsed from Qumran.[161]

Since several of the worlds represented in these sources overlap with that of the New Testament, even these cursory observations indicate that such discoveries are important for the study of its communication in its early environment. As the current renaissance continues to establish that magic was an integral part of ancient culture, it becomes increasingly important to ask how the hearing of the gospel message would have been affected by the magical conceptions which were a part of the mental register of Mark's readers.

Magic and Gospel studies

This renewed interest in ancient magic has made little impact upon NT studies in general and Gospel study in particular. Several problems can be identified.

Few studies

In 1974 Hull observed that 'the possibility of a relationship between magic and the early Christian tradition has never been fully explored,'[162] and then embarked upon an attempt to do so with respect to the Synoptic Tradition. There has been only the occasional example of such a study since his time.[163]

Unused sources

Another problem is that often the full range of magical sources was either unavailable to, or underutilised by, this small trickle of studies. The curse tablets, in particular, are conspicuous by their virtual absence, despite

---

[160] For an overview of Jewish magical sources, see Alexander, 'Incantations'.

[161] Cf. 4Q560, Penney and Wise, 'Power'; 4Q184, 4Q510–511, 11QPsAp[a], Burrelli, 'Psalm 91', ch. 1; Naveh, 'Fragments', 261.

[162] Hull, *Hellenistic Magic*, 1.

[163] J.Z. Smith, 'Demonic Powers'; Kee, *Medicine, Miracle & Magic*, ch. 4; Mills, *Human Agents*, and Twelftree, *Jesus*, both touch on magic; Garrett, *Demise*, on Luke; Arnold, *Ephesians*, on Ephesians. I know of no major work dealing with the Gospels of Mark, Matthew or John from a magical point of view. Malina and Neyrey, *Calling Jesus Names*, on Matthew is only an apparent exception, for this work employs modern sociological models with no reference to ancient magical texts. The commentaries make minimal reference to magic, although Gundry, *Mark*, is a recent exception.

being the best magical source in existence, attesting to magical practices throughout the Graeco-Roman world and across more than a thousand-year period,[164] and even though several collections have been available since the turn of the twentieth century (*DTA*; *DT*).

A focus on the historical Jesus

Operating within the paradigm of a previous age and using its methods, with the characteristic quest for origins and the subsequent source questions, previous studies have largely focused upon the relationship between magic and the historical Jesus. However, the recent shift of paradigms has led to approaches to the Gospels which have moved away from an interest in origins, to an interest in readers and their reception of whole texts. In line with this shift, the relationship between magic and the Gospel as a narrative whole is yet to receive attention.[165]

Magic and Graeco-Roman society

A widespread phenomenon

Commenting on excavations in Corinth and Athens, David Jordan recently spoke of 'more and more evidence, often from coastal cities with heterogeneous populaces, of a community of superstition in the *oik-oumenê* in the time of the Empire'.[166] The Egyptian magical papyri have been known for some time (= *PGM*), but recent discoveries are confirming that these do not simply represent an eccentric brand of late Graeco-Egyptian magic, but are, in fact, representative of magical practices on a far wider scale. The evidence is increasing that 'the medium through which details of such lore passed from one end of that world to the other was often the papyrus codex or scroll of magical recipes, of which we have dozens from Egypt'.[167]

This is an important finding, especially for NT studies in which the supposed eccentricity, and/or the late dates, of many of the papyri partly account for the reluctance to use 'magical sources' (by which authors

---

[164] More than 1100 have been recovered from all parts of the ancient world, dating from about 600 BC to AD 600. In addition, their existence and use are amply attested in the literary sources from Homer onwards; cf. the testimonies from Homer, Plato, Ovid, Tacitus, Apuleius, Plotinus, Eusebius of Caesarea and others which are conveniently collected in translation in Gager, ch. 8; and the originals in *DT*, cxvii–cxxv.

[165] Cf. Garrett, *Demise*, on Luke.   [166] Jordan, 'Sanctuary of Poseidon', 123.

[167] Ibid.; cf. Jordan, 'Notes from Carthage', 119.

usually mean only *PGM*). Although magical materials are extant in a variety of languages, the focus here will be on the Greek charms, for these provide closest contact with the vocabulary of Mark. Charms in other languages will be used either to plug a hole in the Greek materials, or to further illustrate what is found there.

A first-century phenomenon

The dating question is complex, but there are a number of factors which suggest that, with due caution, even later material can be used for first-century comparative purposes. In the first place, it is not true that all magical papyri post-date the NT era, even if most do. There are older magical papyri: a curse found in a metal box (6th c. BC);[168] a series of charms against headache and inflammation (*PGM* XX (2nd/1st c. BC)); and two love charms (PMonGr. inv. 216 = *GMPT* CXVII (1st c. BC); *SuppMag* 72 = *GMPT* CXXII (Augustan)); see also *SuppMag* 70 (2nd/1st c. BC), 71 (1st c. BC). The pickings from the 1st century AD are meagre,[169] but from then on the numbers begin to swell. The main problem with papyri is survival. Being an organic material, it is not surprising that the bulk of papyrus finds have come from Egypt, where the dry sands have ensured better survival of this material. But papyri have also been found elsewhere, sometimes inside metal containers, or, in one case, wrapped in a sheet of lead.[170] The more durable lead curse tablets testify in their own right to the existence of magic across a millennium spanning the NT period (600 BC to AD 600). They also provide evidence that some of the practices found on papyrus are much older than the papyri themselves, as do 'voodoo dolls' discovered from as far back as the 4th century BC, precisely made according to the recipe found in the much later *PGM*.[171] When this kind of artefactual evidence is placed alongside the presence of some older papyrus spells, there is little doubt that many more papyrus spells once existed.

---

[168] Jordan, 'Notes from Carthage', 123.

[169] 1st c. AD: *SuppMag* **52**, **73**; 1st/2nd c. AD: *PGM* LVII, *PGM* LXXII, *PHarris* **56** (= *GMPT* LXXXV); *SuppMag* **67**. The unpublished *PMich* inv. 1444 is said to be 1st to 3rd c. AD (see http:// www.lib.umich. edu/ pap/ magic/ agg.display.html). Brashear, 'Magical Papyri', 3491f., lists others assigned to the first century, but this dating is not without dispute: *PGM* XVI (Jordan: 2nd/3rd c. AD); CXI (*GMPT*: 3rd/4th c. AD); XV? (*GMPT*: 3rd c. AD); XXXa, XXXIb and XXXIa (oracular questions, excluded by *GMPT*).

[170] Jordan, 'Notes from Carthage', **5**. For fuller documentation of papyrus finds in the ancient world, see Crisci, *Scrivere*, and, for the near east, Cotton, 'Papyrology'.

[171] For example, *PGM* V.304; VII.394, 417; IX; XXXVI.1–35, 231; LVIII; Faraone, 'Agonistic Context', n. 5. For voodoo dolls see Faraone, 'Binding and Burying'.

Secondly, since the later papyri almost certainly represent collections of much earlier material, and since magical practices were conservative, or even reactionary,[172] it is not implausible to link such spells to the NT period.

Thirdly, the literary evidence provides ample testimony to magic being practised well before, and into, the NT period, as does the NT itself (cf. Acts 19.19).[173]

A wide-ranging phenomenon

Although not officially sanctioned, magic was practised everywhere and was a social phenomenon with a wide-ranging purview. The curse tablets, for example, were directed at a wide variety of situations of ordinary human commerce. Since they potentially affected people from all races, classes, occupations, ages and genders, they were universally feared. In the seventies Pliny could say, 'There is no one who does not fear to be spellbound by curse tablets' (Pliny *HN* 28.4.19). Similarly, the magical papyri confirm the many and varied reasons for which people would turn to the magicians, and, since these are magical recipes for the use of a professional magician, no doubt each one represents a market demand beyond an individual occurrence of a spell.

One of the interests of magic was illness, since illness and *daimones*,[174] medicine and magic, were closely related in the ancient world. The curse tablets often attacked people's health; the spells were often concerned to protect it, or to cure them once afflicted.

Magic and death

Although magic was used for a variety of purposes,[175] in the face of the natural fear of suffering and death, a major motivation to use magic was people's desire to stay alive. As Euripides so contemptuously put it:

---

[172] Possible evidence includes the continued use of lead, even when other mediums were available; retrograde writing, which may have become ' "petrified" in the ritual and henceforth assum[ing] greater significance,' Faraone, 'Agonistic Context', 7–8; and perhaps even the use of foreign words as if their efficacy depended upon their non-translation.

[173] A range of literary testimonies is conveniently collected in Gager, ch. 8.

[174] Although this can be exaggerated, e.g., Collins, 'Suffering', 47: 'virtually all health problems were ascribed to the influence of demons'.

[175] Cf. the list in Goldin, 'Magic', 117, the chapter headings in Gager, or the index in *GMPT*.

> I can't stand people who drag out their life
> with food and drink and magic spells,
> so that they might not die.
> Since they're no use to the world, they should clear off
> and leave it to the young.   (Eur. *Supp.* 1109ff.)[176]

People turned to magic as a desperate resort to stave off death – in all its forms. 'Magic [. . .] enticed the workaday person with a means of escaping a creation fraught with uncertainty and anxiety, a world that in the end could not itself provide a promise of health in its present society nor safety in the life to come.'[177]

As we shall see (chapter 3, Suppliant 1), magic also enlisted spirits of the dead to perform the various tasks assigned them by the magician. The world of magic was therefore intimately connected with death and with the dead. Both these connections will prove important for the potential impact of Mark on the early readers.

Caesar in first-century Graeco-Roman society

Ruler worship

By Mark's day, Roman rule had been firmly in place for many years. The structures shoring up the position of her chief man, such as the imperial cult, were gradually making inroads into the provinces,[178] assisting the task of subjugating the elite and, through them, the local populations.[179] The symbolism of the cult not only 'evoked a picture of the relationship between the emperor and the gods, but [it] was also structuring; it imposed a definition of the world. The imperial cult, along with politics and diplomacy, constructed the reality of the Roman empire.'[180]

Apotheosis

An important part of this 'construction of reality', which was gaining momentum at exactly the time when Mark was being first read, was the

---

[176] This translation is based on that of Garland, *Greek Way*, 123.

[177] Kotansky and Spier, ' "Horned Hunter" ', 329, adding, 'Magic and Gnosticism claimed they could do both.'

[178] For its remarkable growth from Augustus to Claudius, see Winter, 'Roman Religion'; Spawforth, 'Imperial Cult'; Winter, 'Imperial Cult'.

[179] It created a relationship of power between the subject and the ruler; it enhanced the dominance of the local elites over the populace, one city over another, and Greek over indigenous cultures. 'The cult was a major part of the web of power that formed the fabric of society', Price, *Rituals*, 248.

[180] Ibid.

apotheosis of the ruler after his death. Eventually it would reach such fulsome proportions and become so conventional that it was devalued, but in the middle decades of the first century, it was still a controversial issue. Julius Caesar and Augustus after him had become gods and the mythology surrounding Romulus' translation had been reissued in support (cf. Livy 1.16).[181] Claudius was the first to be granted divine honours since Augustus. Some idea of how this was received can be gained by Seneca's satirical mockery of it in his *Apocolocyntosis* in which Augustus himself asks, 'Is it for this I made peace by land and sea?' (10). In Mark's time, the apotheosis of the Caesars was still a debated issue.

Son of God, beginning of good news

Because Caesar had become a god, Augustus, and then Tiberius, were hailed as Son of God.[182] The Augustan poets used the phraseology to promote the fame of their leader.[183] Since the Augustan age was regarded as a turning point for the world,[184] the birthday of the divinised Augustus was proclaimed throughout the provinces in the calendar inscriptions set up by city officials[185] as 'the beginning of good news through him for the world' (ἦρξεν δὲ τῶι κόσμωι τῶν δι' αὐτὸν εὐανγελί[ων, *OGIS* **458** = EJ **98** = Braund **122** (9 BC)). As time went on this Augustan rhetoric became standard fare in the imperial propaganda, as the Caesars kept the 'Augustan Hope'[186] alive.

The ruler as the source of life

The propaganda associated with the ruler, repeated in the provinces as part of the imperial machinery, naturally set the ruler in a positive light. Augustus as 'the beginning of good news' evolved into subsequent rulers being viewed as 'the source of all good things' ([ἀρ]χὴ ὢν | πάντων | ἀγαθῶν, *P.Oxy* 1021.5–13 (17 Nov. 54, on Nero's accession)). Seneca spoke as if his ruler was the source of life for all:

> As long as [Caesar] is alive your dear ones are alive – you have lost nothing. Your eyes ought to be not only dry, but even happy; in him you have all things, he takes the place of all.
>
> (*Ad Polybium* 7.4)

---

[181] A.F. Segal, 'Heavenly Ascent', 1347.

[182] Cf. inscriptions from the West: EJ **100** = Sherk **7C** = *ILS* **112**.7 = *CIL* XII.4333 = L&R. II, pp. 62f.: Narbo, Gaul (AD 12/13).

[183] Cf. Wistrand, *Felicitas imperatoria*, ch. 6.   [184] Price, *Rituals*, 54.

[185] They therefore provide an 'upper-class' perspective, cf. Wengst, *Pax Romana*, 10.

[186] This phrase was inscribed on a coin on Claudius' accession (AD 41) (Small. **98** = Braund **209**).

When the imperial cult is properly understood as a social institution with broad social effects,[187] it can be seen how it would endorse the view of the ruler as the source of life.

Of course, such 'golden age' views were those of the elite, the pro-Romans, the collaborators who stood to gain from the Roman *imperium* – such as the Herods and the Jerusalem religious establishment. There was also a dark underside of Roman domination, and, despite Augustus, 'the poverty, misery and uncertainty caused by Roman economic exploitation',[188] especially in the provinces, continued, as did the long trail of blood left in the wake of the establishment and maintenance of the *Pax Romana*.[189] Roman 'advances' were not without their critics, but perhaps the voices of those critics were not as easily heard.[190]

The great Augustus had certainly improved the lot for some,[191] but for many the rhetoric outstripped the reality. It was said that he brought peace and security, but the *Pax Romana* was built on military might. It was said that he brought salvation from the ills of a now bygone day, and yet the ills of ordinary people's lives continued. It was even said that he brought life to a world on the brink of death.

Life from the dead

The inscriptions notifying calendar changes to allow for the greater celebration of the Augustan achievements proclaimed that:

> people would be right to consider this to have been the beginning of the breath of life for them, which has set a limit to regrets for having been born.[192]

Against the horrors of the previous century, the imperial propaganda proclaimed that Augustus had saved the world from inevitable destruction.

---

[187] Mitchell, *Anatolia*, 117. [188] Price, *Rituals*, 54.

[189] For a view 'from below', see Wengst, *Pax Romana*. Wengst generalises from Tacitus' comment: 'After that there had been undoubtedly peace, but peace with bloodshed' (*Ann.* 1.10.4), with the comment: 'Tacitus is thinking of the blood of the Roman nobility; other blood will have to be recalled' (p. 10 n. 19).

[190] One of the difficulties in understanding Augustus, for example, is that 'this emperor controlled every possible source of information. Not only is there nothing critical of his regime in our sources, but almost every reference to him is at least mildly eulogistic', Ramage, 'Response', 51. Cf. Johnson, 'Response', 39: 'There was genuine and, in some degree, valid criticism of A[ugustus], and we cannot get at it.' Johnson cites Ovid as a representative of the dissenting tradition, although his 'hostility' to Augustus needs further study.

[191] Deissmann, *Light*, 339, believed that the lot of 'the humble classes [. . .] had undoubtedly been on the whole improved by the Imperium'; cf. the sailors' praise of Augustus in Suet. 2.98.2. For a less positive analysis, see Wengst, *Pax Romana*.

[192] Translation: Price, *Rituals*, 55.

Given the perceived importance of the Roman *imperium*, when Seneca suggested a soliloquy for the young Nero, it was natural that he should stress the tremendous power that Nero had inherited from those before him:[193]

> Have I of all mortals found favour with heaven and been chosen to serve on earth as vicar of the gods? I am the arbiter of life and death for the nations; it rests in my power what each man's lot and state shall be, [. . .]   (*De clementia* 1.1.2)

> To give safety to many and to recall them to life from the very brink of death and to earn the civic crown through clemency – that is happiness. [. . .] This is divine power, to save life in mobs and states; but to kill many and indiscriminately is the power of conflagration and collapse.   (*De clementia* 1.26.5)[194]

In the second century, Aelius Aristides' view 'from above' praised the end of the controversies between cities brought by Rome as an escape from certain death, for

> as a consequence of their mutual discord and unrest the cities were already as it were on the refuse heap; but then they received a common leadership and suddenly came alive again.
>
>   (*Eulogy of Rome*, 155–7)

Mark's alternative

In contrast to this positive assessment, Mark was part of a movement which, in effect, proclaimed a new ruler.[195] According to this movement, there was now another 'source of life for the world'. Mark's Gospel proclaimed an alternative kingdom: the kingdom of God. It spoke of Jesus in terms associated with the Caesars, and, by so doing, proposed an alternative view of reality which offered an alternative set of hopes for the future. Mark's Gospel was subversive in that it undermined the claims of the *imperium* to be the source of life for the world and so joined forces with those critics who suggested that Rome had instead extended

---

[193] *De clementia* is a famous example of 'a well-known rhetorical device to praise a man for virtues that you hope he will practice', Wistrand, *Felicitas imperatoria*, 72. In *Apocolocyntosis*, Seneca may attempt to move Nero in the virtuous direction using a different genre.

[194] Cf. Ps-Seneca, *Octavia* 438–44, which has Seneca urging clemency against Nero's desire for blood.

[195] Deissmann, *Light*, 340.

the shadow of death across many nations. It proposed that the true source of life for the world was found in the gospel of Jesus Christ, and that he brought life to those who found themselves living under death's shadow.

Procedures

In an attempt to examine Mark's Gospel in terms of its potential impact upon its first-century readers, the study follows the narrative shape of Mark, commenting in detail on the thirteen healing/exorcism accounts of particular interest to this text–reader encounter, and more briefly on the narrative 'framework' within which they are embedded.

The text–reader encounter will be considered along two rather broad axes: (1) The Text to the (Implied) Reader; (2) The (Flesh-and-Blood) Reader to the Text. Hence, each healing/exorcism scene will be examined in two parts:

(1)   an exegetical/literary analysis demonstrates that the text aligns the implied reader with the suppliant;

(2)   a discussion of relevant Graeco-Roman material attempts to recover the perspective from which the particular suppliant's situation would have been viewed by Mark's early readers.

The comments on the remainder of Mark will be necessarily briefer, aiming to elucidate the framework of the story into which the readers are drawn by way of the healing/exorcism scenes. By this means, the study attempts to unfold the potential impact of Mark's message about Jesus' defeat of death on the early readers who were living in the Graeco-Roman world under the shadow of death.

2

THE BEGINNING OF THE GOSPEL (MARK 1.1–13)

Mark's title (1.1)

Although it is not the place to argue the point, it is most likely that Mark 1.1 functions as a title for the whole narrative.[1] Since τὸ εὐαγγέλιον would be familiar to Mark's readers as the basic (oral) message by which the Christian movement sought to persuade others,[2] Mark's work promises to show the foundation[3] of gospel proclamation by anchoring the message – and the movement spawned by it – in the events to be narrated.[4]

The title promises to make its impact upon the readers through engaging them in a narrative about 'Jesus Christ, [the Son of God][5]'.[6] Although the key words of Mark's title are firmly anchored in expectations generated by the OT,[7] the Graeco-Roman readers would recognise this language from

---

[1] For verse 1 as a title, see Kelber, *Mark's Story*, 15–16; Bryan, *Preface*, 85; van Iersel, *Reading Mark*, 31. Despite Guelich, 'Genre', and 'Beginning', 194–6, similar expressions in papyrus letters show that it is perfectly possible for the expression καθὼς γέγραπται (v.2) to begin a new sentence, and a work; see Deissmann, *Bible Studies*, 113f., 249f.

[2] Friedrich, 'εὐαγγελίζομαι', 35f.

[3] Cf. Lucian *Reviv.* 20, which uses ἀρχή for the 'foundation' of a philosophical position.

[4] So van Iersel, *Reading Mark*, 41.

[5] These words may not be original here, so Head, 'Text-Critical Study', although 'Son of God' is nevertheless an important title in Mark (1.11, 3.11, 8.38, 9.7, 12.6 (some include 13.32), 14.36, 61, 15.39).

[6] In terms of genre, the title already signals that what follows will be akin to 'biography'; cf. the thesis of Burridge, *What Are the Gospels?*. Nevertheless, Mark is best explained as 'history in the apocalyptic mode', with Collins, *Life?*, who rightly observes that Jesus is portrayed as a historical figure whose death changed reality (p. 35).

[7] *Gospel*: in a number of ways Mark's story presents Jesus' ministry as the fulfilment of the Isaianic promises (cf. Isa. 52.7; 61.1). His proclamation of the gospel of God (1.15) 'bears the stamp of Isa. 52.7', Stuhlmacher, *Gospel*, 20.

Son of God: The older designation of Israel as the 'son' of God (Exod. 4.22f.; cf. Hos. 11.1) became focused upon the Davidic king, and, through this association, gained a firm place in messianic expectation (2 Sam. 7.12–14; Ps. 89.4ff.; 1 Chr. 17.13; 22.10; 28.6; cf. Isa. 9.5; Ps. 2.7); Hengel, *Son of God*, 22f. These 'textual' expectations, i.e., they can be derived from the text, were also 'actual expectations', i.e., they demonstrably formed part of the expectations of real, historical people. This can be shown not only from the NT itself, but also from Qumran – 4QFlor. I.11f. transfers 'I will be his father and he will

its usage in connection with the Caesars. The Augustan phraseology, whose currency continued across the first century, proclaimed him to be Son of God,[8] and his birthday was proclaimed throughout the provinces in the calendar inscriptions set up by city officials[9] as 'the beginning of good news through him for the world' (ἦρξεν δὲ τῶι κόσμωι τῶν δι' αὐτὸν εὐαγγελί[ων, *OGIS* **458** = EJ **98** = Braund **122** (9 BC)). This notion evolved into the ruler's being viewed as 'the source of all good things' ([ἀρ]χὴ ὢν | πάντων | ἀγαθῶν, *P.Oxy* 1021.5–13 (17 Nov. 54, on Nero's accession)), a claim reinforced by the important social role played by the imperial cult. Graeco-Roman readers would immediately connect Mark's opening line with this kind of imperial propaganda. The oddity would be that it referred to someone other than a member of the imperial line.

Although it may well be true that the 'official, secular state religion was at best a negative stimulus, not a model',[10] Mark's provocative opening immediately makes claims for Jesus over against the imperial propaganda, raising a range of questions for the world which had supposedly benefited so much under Augustus and his successors. If the subject of Mark's story is also given imperial titles, what is the inevitable destruction from which this Son of God saves? In what sense will this Jesus be 'the beginning of the breath of life for them'?[11] Is this gospel about someone who also considers himself to be the 'arbiter of life and death for the nations' (Sen. *De clem.* 1.1.2)? Will his leadership make the world alive again (Aelius Arist. *Eulogy to Rome*, 155–7)? And, if so, how?

Like the rest of the NT, Mark speaks the language of its day.

> It is a popular and realistic proclamation. It knows human waiting for and hope of the εὐαγγέλια, and it replies with the εὐαγγέλιον [. . .] Caesar and Christ, the emperor on the throne and the despised rabbi on the cross, confront one another. Both are evangel to men. They have much in common. But they belong to different worlds.[12]

be my son' (2 Sam. 7.14) to 'the shoot of David', i.e., the Messiah (cf. Isa. 11.1). It also quotes Ps. 2, although the text breaks off before v.7 appears; 4Q246, in connection with Danielic eschatology, mentions the son of God who will reign in an eternal kingdom – and also the rabbis, in which 'the messianic reference of Ps. 2.7 and other similar passages is not completely lost', Hengel, *Son of God*, 44.

[8] Cf. inscriptions from the West: EJ **100** = Sherk **7C** = *ILS* **112**.7 = *CIL* XII.4333 = Lewis-Reinhold, pp. 62f.: Narbo, Gaul (AD 12/13). The Augustan poets used the phraseology to promote the fame of their leader; cf. Wistrand, *Felicitas imperatoria*, ch. 6.

[9] They therefore provide an 'upper-class' perspective, cf. Wengst, *Pax Romana*, 10.

[10] Hengel, *Son of God*, 30.   [11] Cf. the calendar inscriptions, Price, *Rituals*, 55.

[12] Friedrich, 'εὐαγγελίζομαι', 725.

The prologue (1.2–13)

Mark's 'prologue' offers the readers a 'panoramic view'[13] of events prior to Jesus' preaching in Galilee. It sets the story of Jesus against the backdrop of the prophetic expectation (vv.2–8). John comes as the fulfilment of the Isaianic expectation of the voice which would prepare the way of the Lord (Isa. 40.3); his baptism looks to (cf. εἰς, v.4) the coming of the forgiveness of sins; and he speaks of the coming stronger one who will baptise in Holy Spirit.[14]

The fulfilment theme continues with Jesus' baptism. The readers are privileged[15] to see with Jesus the heavens rent (cf. Isa. 64.1) and the Spirit descending upon him (v.10; cf. v.8, and Isa. 42.1, 61.1), and to hear the voice from heaven (v.11). Coming from God, this voice provides reliable commentary on the scene. This matches, in part, that of the narrator (v.1) and gains further reliability by alluding to Scripture passages declaring Jesus to be the messianic Son of God (Ps. 2.7) and the Isaianic Servant of the Lord (Isa. 42.1).[16] This scene commissions Jesus, i.e., provides him with the role which he is expected to fulfil in the course of the narrative to follow.[17]

Immediately after the baptism, Jesus is thrust into the desert by the Spirit,[18] where he is tested by Satan, in the presence of wild beasts, but served by angels (1.12–13). The function of this imagery is not easy to analyse precisely, for it is capable of neutral, positive or negative interpretations.[19] However, in view of the interest of this study, it can be noted that in the biblical tradition both the wilderness and the beasts can

---

[13] Such views are frequent at the beginning of narratives or scenes, Rimmon-Kenan, *Narrative Fiction*, 77. 'The prologue engages readers directly and gives them a vantage point from which they can appropriate the ensuing narrative,' Wegener, *Cruciformed*, 99.

[14] For an examination of Mark's forgiveness theme, see Bolt, 'Forgiveness'. The stronger one empowered with the Spirit is fulfilled in Jesus' role as Servant, see Bolt, 'Spirit', 46f.

[15] Cf. Kelber, *Mark's Story*, 19.

[16] The presence of scriptural allusions in a given text is often disputed, and here is no exception. There are several items in the Marcan context in favour of the Isaianic allusion: the expectation generated by the quotation from Isa. 40.3, since, in the flow of Isaiah, the Servant would follow the voice; the coming of the spirit upon him; the prominence of Isaianic themes in the remainder of the Gospel.

[17] Tannehill, 'Narrative Christology', 60–2.

[18] Despite Juel, *Master*, 39, finding this location inappropriate, it is exactly where the prophetic expectation would locate the Servant, whose ministry to Jerusalem was 'a new exodus [. . .] a new march on the promised land from the wilderness', Dumbrell, 'Servant', 106 (cf. Isa. 40.3–5).

[19] For the various options, see Bauckham, 'Wild Animals', 5–6.

connote death,[20] and that even the positive connotations (e.g., the beasts of Isaiah 11) draw some of their power by contrast with the connotations of death.[21] The threat of the beasts to humanity is a result of the fall, and the expectation is that a righteous man will rule over them still and that they will no longer be a threat in the eschatological age.[22] In addition, one traditional way of speaking about the resurrection presents both the wilderness and the beasts as 'places' from which the dead would be received back in the resurrection.[23]

First-century Graeco-Roman readers' knowledge of the conflicts between people and animals in the Roman amphitheatres would have also enhanced the sense of the wild beasts as a threat to human beings and a source of death.[24] It would be impressive that Jesus was 'tested' in this context, and yet he remained unscathed.

By providing the readers with privileged background information, the prologue begins to forge a close relationship between narrator and readers. Already Jesus is at centre stage, and, via reliable commentary provided by the narrator (1.1) and God himself (by both Scripture and a heavenly voice), the readers have been given an understanding of who he is and what he is expected to achieve. Already he is in a place of death, struggling with Satan, but being cared for by the angels. When this man emerges from this testing in the wilderness, what hope does he hold for others living under the shadow of death?[25]

[20] The various texts are discussed by Bauckham, ibid., 7–10. These connotations are exploited by van Iersel, who argues that Mark moves from wilderness to tomb, both locations of death. See van Iersel, *Reading Mark*, 20–1; *Mark*, 80–2.

[21] Bauckham, 'Wild Animals', 15–16.   [22] Ibid., 10–19.

[23] Cf. the texts discussed in Bauckham, 'Resurrection'. Although most of the texts are later than Mark, the tradition may have OT roots (Isa. 26.19; cf. esp. 4 Ezra 4.41b–43a; *b.Sanh.* 92a), p. 279, and it is attested in texts dated AD 50–150, which makes plausible the suggestion of its earlier representation.

[24] Cf. Bauckham, 'Wild Animals', 9. For the significance of the games in the Roman world, see Auguet, *Cruelty*.

[25] Cf. van Iersel, *Reading Mark*, 20–1, who draws together Mark's beginning in the wilderness and ending with the tomb.

3

THE KINGDOM IS NEAR (1.14–4.34)

The patterns and flow of the narrative suggest that the first major movement of Mark's story stretches from the call of the four fishermen (1.16–
20) through to the end of the parables discourse (4.1–34).[1] This first major
section is divided into four sub-sections each signalled by Jesus' presence
παρὰ τὴν θάλασσαν (1.16; 2.13; 3.7 (πρός); 4.1).[2] This division is reinforced by the occurrence of πάλιν in the second and fourth instance and
the presence of large crowds in the second, third and fourth sub-sections.[3]

In each sub-section, the seaside location introduces some kind of call:
Simon and Andrew and the brothers Zebedee (sub-section 1); Levi (sub-
section 2); the complete number of the twelve (sub-section 3). After this
threefold calling of disciples, the reader expects something similar when
the narrative returns to the same location for the fourth time, but what
occurs instead, through the vehicle of the parables discourse, is the general
summons for 'anyone with ears to hear' to hear.

The prologue has already begun to commission Jesus for his role in the
narrative. By the end of this first narrative section all major characters of
Mark's Gospel are assembled and commissioned.

The kingdom is near (1.14–15)

Text to reader

The announcement of John's 'handing over' indicates that it is time for
the one coming after him to arrive. Having been educated by the prologue

---

[1] This proposal crosses some structural barriers with long-established credentials, e.g.,
that 2.1–3.6 represents a collection of 'conflict stories'. The current increase in literary
awareness ought to re-open all such questions, for the movements of the story itself suggest
a different structure. Cf. Garland, ' "I am the Lord" ', 332, who, although allowing that the
latter may also be a part of the so-called controversy cycle, believes that 1.21–28 and 2.1–12
form an *inclusio*.

[2] Kelber, *Mark's Story*, 23, 25, 27, also notes the significance of this marker for the flow
of the story.

[3] Cf. ibid., 23, 27.

to think of Jesus in Isaianic terms, the reader is not surprised that Jesus now begins to go public with his message, nor that this message is styled 'the gospel of God' (cf. Isa. 41.27; 52.7; 61.1f.).

The narrator permits the readers to hear the content of this gospel for themselves by placing Jesus' message in direct speech (v.15). It contains a note of fulfilment (πεπλήρωται ὁ καιρός and ἤγγικεν), suggesting that all God had promised was coming to its conclusion, and also a note of expectation, for the announcement that the kingdom of God 'has drawn near' indicates that it has not yet fully and finally come, but that it is about to.

The call for his Galilean hearers to repent and to believe the gospel is a call to reorient their lives towards God, and to trust the promise about the future kingdom being near. Since this call is directed to no-one in particular and since the readers hear it in direct speech, it is as if it is addressed to them. Daniel's apocalyptic vision generated the expectation that God would set up his eternal kingdom over against the kingdoms of this world, and that he would give the authority in this kingdom to one like a Son of Man (Dan. 2.44; 7.13–14). The kingdoms of this world brought hostility, bloodshed and death (Dan. 7), but the kingdom of God would come through the resurrection from the dead (Dan. 7.22, 27; 12.1–3). Jesus' announcement has the effect of setting the whole of the following story within the framework of the expectation of the coming kingdom of God.[4]

Reader to text

Although Mark's Graeco-Roman readers may have known next to nothing about any Jewish expectations of a coming kingdom of God, the language of kingdoms would, of course, be familiar to them. In addition, the announcement of a coming kingdom would automatically raise the question of the relationship between it and the prevailing rule of Rome. The Romans frowned upon kings not appointed by their regime, and upon kingdoms not permitted by their own (e.g., Tac. *Hist.* 5.9). The gods had given the rule to them and, in fact, when the two great Caesars of the past

---

[4] The future βασιλεία τοῦ θεοῦ is a constant feature of Mark, setting the framework against which the events occur (cf. 1.15; 3.24; 4.11, 26, 30; 9.1, 47; 10.14, 15, 23–25; 11.10; 12.34; 14.25; 15.43). The clash of kingdoms, which is so much part of the apocalyptic perspective shared by Jesus (13.8–9), is played out in the clash between his own kingship and that of the human rulers. To this end, in the narrative Herod receives the title that he longed for in reality (6.14, 23, 25, 26, 27; cf. 13.9). But if there was a clash between Jesus, the one destined to be king in God's kingdom, and Herod, the puppet of Rome, then how much more severe will be the clash with Herod's masters. It is therefore no surprise that Jesus' kingship, which is latent in the title χριστός, is finally revealed when Rome has him crucified (15.2, 9, 12, 18, 26, 32).

had died, they had joined the ranks of the gods themselves, so what was this kingdom of God announced by Jesus?

Mark's title had announced Jesus in terms suggesting that he was an alternative ruler. Jesus himself now proposes an alternative kingdom to Rome. Readers would be well aware that to speak this gospel would be fraught with danger, for it would inevitably lead to conflict with imperial power.[5] If so, what would this entail for those who accepted Jesus' invitation to reorient their lives around this gospel of the kingdom?

To fish for people (1.16–20)

This scene provides another aspect of Jesus' narrative commissioning (cf. pp. 12–13). It is focalised through Jesus, who sees the brothers in the sea (v.16). The seeming redundancy of Mark's explanatory γάρ clause signals its significance.[6] Jesus' direct speech provides a command to 'come after me' and a motivation to do so in the promise that he will make them 'fishers of men'. The previous redundancy now enables the emphasis to fall on their new harvest: human beings. Their immediate response (v.18) adds to the sense of Jesus' authority. The scene is virtually repeated with the other brothers, although the readers are left to supply the content of Jesus' call (v.20) from before (v.17).

The first pair leave their nets to follow Jesus (v.18), the second, their father and the servants (v.20, cf. 17). As the four fall in behind Jesus, the movement of the story begins. His goal is the future kingdom of God (1.15), and he evidently seeks to take others with him on the journey towards this goal, requiring them to leave their ordinary lives behind. Since the narrative has commissioned Jesus to make something of these men, the readers now watch to see whether and how he will turn them into fishermen catching human beings.

Suppliant 1: a man with unclean spirit (1.21–28)

Text to reader: unclean spirits obey

Apart from the initial plural (v.21), the disciples are absent from the scene and cannot act as a 'role model' for the readers. Instead, the text aligns the readers with the man in need.

---

[5] Cf. Bryan, *Preface*, 165. The Roman authorities were concerned about Davidic descendants for a long time. Vespasian sought to eradicate the royal house, as did also both Domitian and Trajan (Euseb. *HE* 3.12, 19, 32). For Vespasian, this seemed to be simply in the wake of the AD 70 victory over the Jews, but Eusebius suggests that, for the two later Caesars, this sprang from some fear of the Christ.

[6] For explanatory γάρ clauses as explicit narrative commentary, see Fowler, *Let the Reader*, 92–8; cf. Gundry, *Mark*, 73.

The narrator introduces Jesus teaching (v.21), presumably the message spoken previously (1.15), and opposes the authority of his teaching with that of the scribes (1.22). The scene is focalised through a man in the synagogue by providing a description of his condition (v.23, ἐν πνεύματι ἀκαθάρτῳ) and his direct speech (v.24), which reduces the distance between him and the readers by 'showing' rather than 'telling'. Distance is further reduced when his insight into Jesus' origin and identity approximates to what they have learned through reliable commentary (cf. 1.1, 9, 11). Since the scene aligns the readers with him, he functions not as a 'type' providing the 'opportunity for Jesus to illustrate the authority of his teaching',[7] but as a realistic character whose tragic situation (possession) remains in focus throughout the incident (vv.23, 24, 25, 26).

By using unexpected plurals, his two questions suggest that his possession is worse than initially suspected: the first puts distance between Jesus and 'us'; the second asks whether Jesus has come to destroy 'us'. When the action switches to Jesus, the readers become observers. Reverting to the singular, Jesus rebukes 'him' and orders the spirit to be muzzled and to come out (v.25). It does so after attacking the man to the accompaniment of a loud cry (v.26). Since the narrator's description of the fulfilment echoes Jesus' order, the readers' perception of Jesus' authority is enhanced.[8]

The ensuing events reinforce this authority. The readers are drawn into the people's amazement and also, through the provision of direct speech, into their discussion (v.27) which functions like 'interior speech'.[9] The debate concerns the newness of the teaching which is further explained as having an authority which demands the spirits' obedience. Amazement will be a feature of Mark's account,[10] and this scene has effectively grafted the notion of Jesus' authority on to this emotion, all the more so because the narrator's comment has already highlighted this as the important feature (v.22). Thus, when the report about Jesus goes out everywhere (v.28), it issues from amazement at an authority which even commands the obedience of unclean spirits.

Although the demonstration of Jesus' authority is the burden of the scene, the character is not a mere type. The scene aligns the readers with him and Jesus does not exercise his authority in isolation from this victim of unclean spirits, but on his behalf. The crowd's amazement arises from

---

[7] J.F. Williams, *Other Followers*, 94.   [8] Fowler, *Let the Reader*, 75.
[9] This is another form of explicit commentary, ibid. 125.
[10] ἐκπλήσσω 1.22, 6.2, 7.37, 10.26, 11.18; ἐξίστημι 2.12, (3.21), 5.42, 6.51; ἐκστάσις 16.8; θαμβέω 1.27, 10.24, 32; ἐκθαμβέω 9.15, 14.33, 16.5, 6; θαυμάζω 5.20, 6.6, 15.5, [44]; ἐκθαυμάζω 12.17. Fowler, ibid., 122f., considers that amazement is Mark's desired outcome. Cf. Dwyer, *Motif*.

Jesus commanding these particular spirits, in this particular man. As such, this man 'introduces a new type of contact with Jesus. The possessed man is not called on to follow Jesus, but rather he is simply helped by Jesus.'[11] He is the story's first suppliant.

This first contact with a suppliant raises questions regarding Jesus' person (v.27, cf. 22) and his expected activity, which will abide throughout Mark's narrative. The unclean spirit(s) ask two questions (v.24), neither of which receives a definitive answer. The first suggests that Jesus and the spirits were on different sides. The second, and more important, question asks whether Jesus was going to destroy them. Jesus does not answer this question and the exorcism itself is not presented as their destruction, merely as their obedience (v.27).[12] The crowd's discussion opens the question of Jesus' identity: who is he, if he teaches with such authority? Because no answers are provided, this is 'not the direction of declarations, but the indirection of unanswered questions'.[13]

Questions play a very important role in the narrative's impact upon the readers. All questions provide implicit commentary upon the story,[14] but unanswered questions are particularly powerful, for they

> implicitly solicit a response by the reader at the level of discourse. They prod the reader to think about the question and to compose an answer of her own, or at least to begin to work toward that end.[15]

Being already privileged with information about Jesus' identity, the readers could answer the characters' question about Jesus' true identity (v.27). The question nevertheless engages the readers in the story, for they wish to see whether and how the characters discover the answer for themselves.

However, the spirits' questions are different. Although it is the first time these beings appear in the story, they already share the readers' insight into Jesus – to some degree at least. They apparently know who Jesus is, but do not know what he is going to do with them. Since the readers do not know the answer to this question either, they are even more powerfully engaged with the story because they too wish to find out whether it is his goal to destroy the spirits. This unanswered question adds to Jesus'

---

[11] See J.F. Williams, *Other Followers*, 94, who then argues that the reader does not identify with him for this reason.

[12] *Pace* Gundry, *Mark*, 76.   [13] Fowler, *Let the Reader*, 126.   [14] Ibid., 131–2.

[15] Ibid., 132. The danger with unanswered questions is that interpreters try to answer them immediately, and often from within the confines of the particular unit, instead of feeling their weight and waiting for the narrative to provide the answer in its own good time.

commissioning, since, having also opened up a gap in the discourse,[16] it 'hangs over' the narrative and awaits an answer: has he come to destroy them? If he has, how will he do it, and why? If he has come to destroy such beings, what difference will this make to the world? Here we need to understand what these beings would have implied to the Graeco-Roman reader.

Reader to text

The expression ἐν πνεύματι ἀκαθάρτῳ (1.23) introduces the readers to a description of a spiritual presence which occurs ten times in Mark,[17] but elsewhere only in biblical materials or in texts dependent upon them.[18]

Unclean spirits I

The fact that this expression is unattested in the Greek materials outside biblical influence indicates that it would probably be unfamiliar to Graeco-Roman readers. However, the spirits' fear of destruction (v.24b), their attempt to control Jesus by knowledge of the name (v.24ac), his word of command insisting they come under control and come out (φιμώθητι καὶ ἔξελθε), and perhaps the great cry as the spirit leaves (v.26b) can all be paralleled in magical practice (see below). This conceptual overlap would allow the Graeco-Roman readers to assimilate the unusual phrase 'unclean spirit' into their general framework. Since the 'spirits' involved in magical practice were usually called δαίμονες,[19] it would be natural

---

[16] 'Gaps' can be opened in both story and discourse levels. Here a gap is opened in both. For the importance of gaps, see Iser, 'Reading Process', and 'Interaction'. See also Fowler, *Let the Reader* (index).

[17] 1.23, 26, 27 (pl.); 3.11 (pl.), 30; 5.2, 8, 13 (pl.); 6.7 (pl.); 7.25.

[18] Apart from the NT occurrences, the expression is found in the following: LXX (Zech. 13.2, 1 Macc. 1.48א); TBenj. 5.2; Jub. 10.1 (= Ethiopic equivalent); 1QS 4.21–2 and 11Q5[11QPsᵃ] 19.13–15 (Hebrew equivalent); the Aramaic equivalent occurs occasionally in the Rabbis where it is associated with magic; TSol. 3:6; *PGM* P13, P13a (4th/5th c. AD); P10 (6th c. AD); P17 (5th/6th c. AD). Cf. also the ?Christian spell P.Fouad. inv. 123 (1st/2nd c. AD) which calls the addressee(s) ἀκάθαρτ[α], Benoit, 'Fragment'. Although unprovable, the two occurrences in medieval scholiasts (*Schol.Aeschin.* in or. 1.23; *Schol.Dem.* in or. 4.1b) probably represent biblical colouration from a Christian scribe. The cleansing of the land from the unclean spirit would accompany the arrival of messianic forgiveness (cf. Zech. 13.2). This proves to be an important link for Mark, see Bolt, 'Forgiveness'.

[19] It is doubtful whether the preference for δαιμόνιον in the NT, LXX, Philo and Josephus is a deliberate avoidance of the more 'loaded' term δαίμων so familar to the Greek world, (*pace* Foerster, 'δαίμων', 12), for they appear to be used interchangeably. Apparently Chrysippus also preferred δαιμόνια (so Brenk, 'Demonology', 2107).

for the readers to understand these 'unclean spirits' by what they already know about these more familiar beings. This assumption will be confirmed for them as the story proceeds, for Mark soon aligns the two (1.23, 26, 27; cf. 1.32, 34).

To introduce the discussion of these beings, the Capernaum exorcism can be compared with a formulary from a much later period (*PGM* IV.1227–64).[20] This appears in a 4th-century AD manuscript which contains Coptic insertions of some biblical names for God, 'Jesus Christ', 'Satan', and even 'unclean spirit'. However, if these can be regarded as late accretions and duly ignored, the Greek sections may be reminiscent of an original practice unsullied by Judaeo-Christian conceptions. This handbook instructs the exorcist to say:

> I adjure you, *daimon*, whoever you are (ἐξορκίζω σε, δαῖμον, ‖ ὅστις ποτ' οὖν εἶ), [. . .]
>
> Come out, *daimon*, whoever you are, and withdraw from so-and-so (ἔξελθε, δαῖμον, | ὅστις ποτ' οὖν εἶ, καὶ ἀπόστηθι ἀπὸ τοῦ δεῖνα), quickly, quickly, now, now. Come out, *daimon* (ἔξελθε, δαῖμον), since I fetter you with unbreakable adamantine fetters, and I hand you over into the black chaos into destruction.
>
> (*PGM* IV.1239–41, 1243–8)

The nature of the *daimon* to be cast out by this spell is hinted at in the phrase 'whoever you are'. Since this formula frequently occurs in the magical materials referring to the unknown spirit of a corpse, its use here suggests that the *daimones* dealt with in this ritual were regarded as ghosts of the dead. In fact, this is exactly what many Graeco-Romans would have thought of when they heard the term *daimon*.

Daimones *and the dead*

The more usual assumption in biblical studies, derived from the Jewish intertestamental material, is that these beings are some kind of fallen heavenly beings. Such a conception, however, would be foreign to the conceptual framework of the Graeco-Roman readers of interest to this study.[21] Instead of conceiving of the *daimones* 'from above', many of

---

[20] Due to the lack of earlier material, any comparative work on exorcisms in Greek writings must inevitably be done with material later than Mark.

[21] It may be comparable to Empedocles' and Plato's notion of the personal *daimon* given a soul at generation, and 'falling' with the soul to the bodily realm, but the differences are patent. Even if the comparison is valid, this would still provide a close link between the human soul and the *daimon*.

Mark's flesh-and-blood readers would have conceived of them 'from below'.

There was a very clear connection in the ancient world between *daimones* and the dead. With this conception in their repertoire, readers would recognise in Mark's stories of *daimones* the continued activity of the spirits of deceased people. For them, the *daimones* were not fallen heavenly beings; they were ghosts of the dead. Although surveys of NT demonology acknowledge this fact,[22] it is usually left to one side, and so has made practically no impact upon the explanation of NT passages relating to *daimones*. Since this study seeks to understand Mark against this ancient view of *daimones*, its virtual absence from NT studies justifies a rather lengthy survey of the supporting evidence. However, given the constraints of space, a summary of my previous findings will have to suffice.[23]

A vocabulary study of the δαίμων / δαιμόνιον family demonstrates that the *daimones* were connected with the dead in literary sources and magical practice, and that the term even finds its way into the literature most akin to Mark, i.e., that originating in a Jewish context, but written for Hellenistic readers.

Literature

This link is a persistent feature of the literary sources[24] from Hesiod (pre 700 BC; *Op.* 121ff.), through the tragedians,[25] and into New Comedy (last quarter 4th c. BC – 264/3), where Menander's notion that each man is guided by a *daimon*, whether good or evil,[26] logically precedes the *daimon* as the spirit of the departed. Despite Plato's elaborate daemonology,[27] he still allows Socrates to derive the notion of a personal *daimon* from the older understanding of the *daimon* as the spirit of the (heroic?) dead:[28]

---

[22] For example, Foerster, 'δαίμων', 6; Twelftree, 'Demon', 164. Cf. Sjöberg, 'רוּחַ', 374, who, after observing that Palestinian Judaism used רוה for spirits of the deceased, even for those who hang around tombs, asserts that there is 'no connection between this idea and the conception of demons'.

[23] See Bolt, 'Daimons'.

[24] It can be detected elsewhere, e.g., in the existence of places where souls of the dead could be consulted, and in grave inscriptions; Brenk, 'Demonology', 2071, 2143.

[25] Aesch. *Pers.* 620ff., 642, 630; *Cho.* 125; Eur. *Alc.* 1003, 1140; cf. 843–4.

[26] Cf. Plut. *De tranq. anim.* 474B. Plutarch disagrees in favour of Empedocles' notion of two forces mingled within each person.

[27] Plato uses δαίμων in four senses: lower divinity (*Apol.* 27c–e); departed soul (*Crat.* 397e–398c); intermediate spirit (*Symp.* 202d–203a; *Leg.* 4.713d; *Resp.* 617e; *Ti.* 40d, 42e); guardian spirit (*Resp.* 620d; *Phd.* 107d; cf. Socrates' *daimonion* and its importance in middle Platonism).

[28] Cf. *Phd.* 107D–108B; *Resp.* 469A, cf. 427B, 540C; *Leg.* 717B–718A.

[. . .] when a good man dies he has a great portion and honour among the dead, and becomes a *daimon*, [. . .]. And so I assert that every good man, whether living or dead, is daemonic (δαιμόνιον), and rightly called a *daimon* (δαίμονα).

(Pl. *Crat.* 398B–C)

While continuing the idea of the *daimones* as intermediate beings, both Xenocrates (head of the Academy 339–314 BC), and the greatly influential Posidonius (*c.* 135–51/50 BC), called the souls of the departed δαίμονες. A previous incarnation is implied by Xenocrates' notion of a 'survival' (Plut. *De defectu* 417B),[29] and, although the Stoics in general avoided the δαιμ- vocabulary, Posidonius apparently taught that 'if souls persist, the same souls become *daimones*' (Sextus Empiricus 9.74 = LCL III.I.74).[30]

In addition, according to Diogenes Laertius, the Stoics (?Posidonius) believed in *daimones* and heroes. Since the latter were 'the souls of the righteous that have survived' (τὰς ὑπολελειμμένας τῶν σπουδαίων ψυχάς, D.L. 7.151), this was probably also true of the former.

The evidence in Plutarch (AD 50⁻–120⁺) indicates that such ideas persisted in philosophical circles into and beyond the time of the NT. During the extended discussion of daemonological views in *De defectu oraculorum*, it is clear that the same connection is still known and debated, as it is in some of his other writings.[31]

In another place (*Dion* 2; cf. *Caes.* 49.11; *Brut.* 36–7), because of his regard for Brutus and Dion, Plutarch reluctantly commends[32]

that most extraordinary doctrine of the oldest times, that mean and malignant *daimones* (τὰ φαῦλα δαιμόνια καὶ βάσκανα), in envy of good men and opposition to their deeds, try to confound and terrify them, causing their virtue to rock and totter, in order that they may not continue erect and inviolate in the path of honour and so attain a better portion after death than themselves [the *daimones*].   (*Dion* 2)[33]

This ancient view clearly assumes that the *daimones* are spirits of the dead and vice versa, and suggests they are malevolently active in this world in

---

[29] Heinze, *Xenocrates*, 83.   [30] Ibid., 98.

[31] See *Symp.* III.7 655E; *Cons. ad Apoll.* 109C–D; *Parall. Graec. et Rom.* 308A; *Quaest. Rom* no. 51, 277A; *Apoph.Lac.* 236D. It is even present in the essays containing fairly elaborate daemonology: *De facie* 944C; *De gen.* 591C, cf. Hesiod, *Op.*, 121ff.; 591D–F, where the analogy with the retired athlete (593D–E) indicates 'once more that for Plutarch *daimones* seem primarily to be former souls', Brenk, 'Demonology', 2124.

[32] According to Brenk, ibid., 2128f., he disagrees with this view (from ?Chrysippus), cf. *Brut.* 37, but the language seems to indicate a tentative suggestion.

[33] Cf. Tatian *Or.* 16.1.

order to ruin the performance of the living so that their post-mortem lot is worse than their own.

Given the immense importance of Plutarch as a source for ancient daemonological views,[34] it is significant for the purposes of my argument that, alongside the presence of the *daimones* as intermediate beings, his writings also illustrate the connection between the *daimones* and the spirits of the dead and this may actually be his most basic belief.[35]

Magical practices

This connection was assumed by 'spiritistic'[36] magical practice, which used powers 'by which ghosts (*manes*) are made obedient' (Apul. *Met.* 3.15).[37] In this domain, the ghosts of the dead are used to achieve the magicians' ends. This is often clear from the context of usage: spells and curses often used corpses and graves in their rituals; they have been found in graves – even in corpses' mouths (*PGM* XIXa) or hands (SGD **1** and **2**) –, or other places connected with the underworld, such as chthonic sanctuaries, or wells.[38] This is not simply because such places were convenient 'openings' to the underworld deities, with the corpse being used like a 'pillar-box',[39] but, insofar as these spells are 'letters', many are addressed to the corpse,[40] either in an attempt to enlist help in gaining the power of an underworld god, or to enlist the ghost itself.

Many of the spells in the magical papyri show that the *daimones* manipulated by the magician were spirits of the dead.[41] Invoking the ghost of the corpse was such a standard feature of the magical procedures that, in time, the practice generated a special word. Many later spells are addressed to a νεκύδαιμον (*PGM* IV.361, 397, 368; IV.2031, 2060; V.334; XII.494; XIXa.15; *SuppMag* **49**;[42] cf. IV.1474f. τὰ εἴδωλα τῶν νεκύων; XVI.1, 9, 17f., 25, 34, 43, 54, 61, ?67, ?73). Peculiar to magical texts,

[34] Brenk, 'Demonology', 2082. He has played such a key role in daemonological studies that it is perhaps true to say that modern studies have not progressed beyond his own presentation. Morton Smith, *Magician*, 436, finds this remarkable.
[35] Brenk, 'Demonology', 2124f., 2127f.
[36] Its counterpart is 'natural' magic; cf. Langton, *Spirits*, 42.
[37] The Assyrians called the sorcerers 'raiser of the departed spirits', suggesting that this practice became their defining characteristic. Thompson I.xxxix also refers to an old Rabbinic tradition 'that the souls of the wicked when they die are the devils which are in this world'.
[38] See Jordan, 'Athenian Kerameikos', 231f.
[39] Garland, *Greek Way*, 6, 86, following Kurtz and Boardman, *Customs*, 217.
[40] Cf. Faraone, 'Agonistic Context', 4; Jordan, 'Athenian Kerameikos', 234.
[41] For details see Bolt, 'Daimons', 89–91. [42] Jordan, 'Love Charm Verses', 245–59.

this word makes explicit what other spells practise: they are addressed to spirits of the dead, i.e., ghosts.[43]

The curse tablets confirm that *daimones* were connected to the dead. The use of such tablets for cursing enemies, part of the malevolent magic mentioned in the literary sources (e.g. Pl. *Resp.* 364B), is attested for the first century,[44] as is the general understanding that these tablets were used in the attempt to enlist the forces of the dead (Tac. *Ann.* 2.69, in regard to Germanicus' death, AD 19).

In the earlier tablets, the corpse is not regarded as a power at all, but its very inertness is the key to the efficacy of the curses. But a change occurs in about the 4th century BC, and the dead become powers to be invoked.[45] About this time also the spirit of the dead begins to be called δαίμων (*DTA* **102** (4th c. BC);[46] *DTA* **99** (3rd c. BC)[47]), a usage which is amply attested in the later tablets.[48] As in the magical papyri, the later curse tablets also address the νεκύδαιμον,[49] the *daimon(es)* of this place[50] or those buried here,[51] or even '*daimones*, those roaming about in this place',[52] i.e., the grave or cemetery. Although occasionally the νεκύδαιμον is given a name,[53] i.e., that of the corpse, more frequently it is addressed as the *daimon*, 'whoever you are', i.e., the anonymous corpse.[54]

To sum up the magical evidence: the curse tablets provide evidence that the spirits of the dead were evoked as powers since the 4th century BC and at that time they were also called *daimones*. The tablets and the papyri show that this belief in the *daimones* as the dead eventually became enshrined in the term νεκύδαιμον. It is in the midst of this progression – which amounts to a strengthening of the same belief – that the Gospel writers spoke of Jesus casting out *daimones*.

---

[43] Jordan, 'Love Charm Verses', translates both νεκύδαιμον and δαίμον 'ghost' in *Supp-Mag* **49**.

[44] Claudia Pulchra was charged with using them against Tiberius (AD 26;Tac. *Ann.* 4.52), as was Servilia against Nero (*Ann.* 16.31); cf. Pliny, *HN* 28.4.19.

[45] For this paragraph, Bravo, 'Tablette Magique'.

[46] Ibid., 203.   [47] Ibid., 204f.

[48] See, for example, the 3rd-century AD tablets discussed in Jordan, 'Feasts', 131–43.

[49] *DT* **234, 235, 237, 239, 240, 242** – all 1st–3rd c. AD; SGD **152, 153, 160, 162**; BM1878.10–19.2 see Jordan, 'Sanctuary of Poseidon', 123 n. 22; *SuppMag* **42.**11f.; **46**.

[50] *DT* **22, 38** (= *SuppMag* **54**), **198**, cf. **234**.

[51] *DT* **25, 26, 29, 30, 31, [32, 33], 34, 35, 271**; *SuppMag* **45**.

[52] *DT* **38** (= *SuppMag* **54**) ll. 35f.: δ[αί|μο]νες οἱ ἐν τῷ τόπω τού[τω.] φοιτῶντες [. . .]

[53] *SuppMag* **37, 47, 50**; *PGM* XXXII and, for the formulary allowing such insertions, IV.2180.

[54] *DT* **234, 235, 237, 238, 239, 240, 242, [249]** – all 1st–3rd c. AD; AthAg **12** (mid 3rd c. AD).

Hellenistic-Jewish literature

The connection between the *daimones* and the dead and its exploitation in magical practices can also be discerned in the LXX, Pseudo-Phocylides, Philo and Josephus, all of which are similar to Mark, in that they stem from the Jewish milieu, but seek to communicate in a Hellenistic environment.

When the LXX uses the word-group, it associates idolatry with the worship of *daimones*.[55] It is also interesting to notice that idolatry is itself closely linked with the dead and with magic.[56] Isaiah 65 (esp. 3, 11), reflecting as it does necromantic practices, i.e., calling on the dead to aid the living, illustrates all three features in the one passage.

The *Sentences* of Pseudo-Phocylides (30 BC–AD 40) show a knowledge of magic,[57] and probably assume the connection when it warns:

> Do not dig up the grave of the deceased (τύμβον φθιμένων), neither expose | to the sun what may not be seen, lest you stir up the daemonic anger (δαιμόνιον χόλον). (PsPhoc. 100f.)

For the sake of his Hellenistic audience, Philo equates the angelic beings of the Jewish literature with the *daimones* (as intermediate beings) of the Greek literature. But the very fact that the *daimones* are also placed upon his continuum of souls indicates that they are related (*Somn.* 1.135–41; *Gig.* 6–12), if not explicitly equated (*Gig.* 16) to souls. The connection emerges very clearly when Philo reports that Gaius murdered his father-in-law 'after dismissing all thought of his dead wife's *daimones*' (πολλὰ χαίρειν φράσας τοῖς δαίμοσι τῆς ἀποθανούσης γυναικός). This incidental reference (*Legat.* 65) shows that the connection existed in Rome in AD 39–40 and, given the lack of either critique or explanation, that it was part of the repertoire of both author and audience.

---

[55] Deut. 32.17; Isa. 65.3, 11 (S δαίμων; A B δαιμονίῳ; MT ‏נד‎); Ps. 96 (LXX 95).5; 106 (105).37.

[56] All occurrences in Tobit (3.8, 17; 6.8, 15, 16, 17; 8.3) refer to the *daimon* Asmodeus, whose sole function is to kill, and whose 'exorcism' is achieved by magical means (for Tobit as a possible background to Mark 12.18–27, see Bolt, 'Sadducees'); Isa. 13.21, 34.14, Bar. 4.7, 35 (cf. Rev. 18.2) use the *topos* of a destroyed city being filled with *daimones*/ghosts; and Ps. 91 (LXX 90). 6 (Sm δαιμονιώδης) was appropriated by magical texts for centuries, cf. Burrelli, 'Psalm 91'. More generally, prohibitions against magical practices indicate that these were also part of things Canaanite, as was human sacrifice, thus connecting idolatry, magic, and *daimones*/ghosts.

[57] No. 149 explicitly refers to magic; but magical practices may also lie behind nos 100–2 (rather than grave-robbery for medical dissection) and no. 150, despite the fact that this has apparently not been canvassed previously, cf. Van der Horst, *The Sentences of Pseudo-Phocylides*.

Several passages in Josephus assume the connection between the *daimones* and the dead,[58] but on one occasion he actually defines the *daimones* as ghosts of the wicked, bent on human destruction (*BJ* 7.185; cf. *AJ* 8.45–9).

Summary of findings

It would be too much to claim that all people everywhere automatically connected the daemonic with the dead. In philosophical circles more elaborate daemonologies had emerged and were emerging in which the daemonic spirits were intermediate beings. However, it is clear that at the more popular level, as represented by the magical world, *daimones* were persistently identified with ghosts, and that this also protrudes into the literary sources, both Graeco-Roman and Hellenistic-Jewish. The involvement of ghosts in exorcisms is also attested in spells from Ancient Egypt, Ancient Babylon and Assyria, and in the second-century Greek writers Lucian (*Philops.* 16)[59] and Philostratus (*Vit. Ap.* 3.38; 4.20). Later readers apparently read Gospel exorcism accounts from this point of view, despite the Fathers' objections,[60] and perhaps this would have been automatic for many of Mark's earlier readers as well. In what follows, we will explore what such a reading would be like.

Unclean spirits II

Unclean souls

The clarification of the link between the *daimones* and the dead also suggests that the expression 'unclean spirits' may not have been as strange to Graeco-Roman readers as at first glance,[61] for it is similar to the

---

[58] The daemonic powers of the dead worked on the side of justice (*BJ* 1.82, 84; *AJ* 13.314, 317, 415–16, etc.), as vengeful ghosts (*BJ* 1.599, 607, cf. *AJ* 17.1) or as spirits of the blessed dead (*BJ* 6.47).

[59] W.D. Smith, 'Possession', 403–26, claims this as the first exorcism in non-biblical Greek literature. However, a fragment of a 5th-century BC mime may allude to an exorcism, Page **73**. See also n. 84 below.

[60] For example, Chrysostom, *Hom. on Matthew* 28, 3; *2Hom. on Lazarus* 6.235, 6. The critique of the *daimon*/ghost connection is at least as early as Tatian (*Or.* 16.1, referring to a lost work). Brown, 'Sorcery', 32, summarises: 'Where the teachings of the Fathers of the Church clash with popular belief, it is invariably in the direction of denying the *human* links involved in sorcery (they will deny, for instance, that it is the souls of the dead that are the agents of misfortune), [. . .]'.

[61] We should also notice Luke's linking of the two expressions with his πνεῦμα δαιμονίου ἀκαθάρτου, 'spirit of an unclean *daimon*' (Luke 4. 33).

Pythagorean notion of 'unclean souls'.[62] Clearly Pythagoras and those following him believed that a living man could possess either a 'pure' or an 'unclean' soul (Pl. *Leg.* 716e; Plut. *De lib.educ.* 12F, on Pythagoras), but what is of interest here is the fate of such souls in the afterlife.[63]

After the souls leave their bodies, Pythagoras held that

> the pure (τὰς καθαράς) are led into the uppermost region, but the impure (τὰς ἀκαθάρτους) are not permitted to approach the pure or each other, but are bound by the Furies in bonds unbreakable. The whole air is full of souls[64] (ψυχῶν) which are called *daimones* or heroes (δαίμονάς τε καὶ ἥρωας) [. . .]
>
> (D.L. 8.31)

These 'Pythagorean' notions evidently influenced authors such as Plato and Plutarch.

According to the *Phaedo*, at generation each soul receives a personal *daimon* as a guide. Whereas the 'orderly and wise soul' follows it,[65]

> the soul that is desirous of the body [. . .] flits about it, and in the visible world for a long time, and after much resistance and many sufferings is led away with violence and with difficulty by its appointed genius. (Pl. *Phd.* 108A–B)

> And when it arrives at the place where the other souls are, the soul which is impure and has done wrong (τὴν μὲν ἀκάθαρτον καί τι πεποιηκυῖαν τοιοῦτον) [. . .] is avoided and shunned by all, and no one is willing to be its companion or its guide, but it wanders about alone in utter bewilderment, during certain fixed times, after which it is carried by necessity to its fitting habitation.
>
> But the soul that has passed through life in purity and moderation (ἡ δὲ καθαρῶς τε καὶ μετρίως τὸν βίον διεξελθοῦσα), finding gods for companions and guides, goes to dwell in its proper dwelling.[66] (Pl. *Phd.* 108B–C)

---

[62] This helps to bridge the gap between the NT use of πνεῦμα and the Greek use of δαίμων identified by Brenk, 'Demonology', 2115. Cf. Schweizer, 'πνεῦμα', 336: 'By virtue of its related character as the breath or principle of life πνεῦμα is largely coterminous with ψυχή, and hence can easily be used in place of it.' Suda *s.v.*: πνεῦμα᾽ ἡ ψυχὴ τοῦ ἀνθρώπου; Arr. *Epict.Diss.* 3.13.14f.

[63] Contrast Philo, who certainly has the notion of the impure soul amongst the living (*Leg.* 3.8; *Det.* 103; *Deus.* 8; *Fug.* 81; *Migr.* 69; *Spec.* 3.209), but has no role for it in the afterlife and may even exclude the possibility (cf. *Spec.* 3.207).

[64] Cf. Philo *Gig.* 7–8.   [65] Cf. Philo *Deus.* 128.   [66] Cf. Pl. *Resp.* 517B.

In describing the various portions of the earth, Socrates then mentions the Acherusian lake where souls of most of the dead must await before being sent back into bodies (113A),[67] undergoing purification (καθαιρό-μενοι, 113D) and paying the penalty for any wrong done and rewarded for any good. But not all of the dead end up on these shores:

> Those who are found to have excelled in holy living are freed from these regions within the earth and are released as from prisons; mounting upward into their pure abode (ἄνω δὲ εἰς τὴν καθαρὰν οἴκησιν ἀφικνούμενοι) and dwelling upon the earth. And of these, all who have duly purified themselves by philosophy live henceforth altogether without bodies, and pass to still more beautiful abodes. (114B–C)

Plutarch's eschatological myth in *De sera numinis vindicta* echoes the same ideas. Immediately on death, some souls flit aloft (564A–B) and dwell 'above in the purity' (ἄνωθεν ἐν τῷ καθαρῷ, 564B), not requiring purgation. Those punished in the body by swift Poinê are dealt with comparatively gently, for she passes over 'many things requiring purgation' (πολλὰ τῶν καθαρμοῦ δεομένων, 564F), but those souls who come into the afterlife 'unpunished and unpurged' (ἀκόλαστος καὶ ἀκάθαρτος, 565A) begin to be tortured by Dikê's purification process which painfully removes each of the passions. The 'end of purgation and punishment' (καθαρμοῦ καὶ κολάσεως πέρας, 565C) arrives when the passions are completely smoothed away, although, before this can occur, some souls are carried off again into bodies (565E) because of their continued desire for the things of the passions (cf. 565F–566A, 567F).

Thus, according to the Pythagorean model, the pure souls return to their origin at death, becoming completely separate from the body 'wholly pure, even fleshless and sacred' (καθαρὸν παντάπασι καὶ ἄσαρκον καὶ ἁγνόν, Plut. *Rom.* 28.7).[68] On the other hand, the 'unclean spirits' would be the souls who require purgation, i.e., those still 'desirous of the body' (cf. Pl. *Phd.* 108A), passion-ridden (Plut. *De sera* 565B), and longing for the pleasures of the body (566A). These continue to hover in the air around the realm of the body. It is these 'unclean souls' who are manifested as ghosts.

---

[67] The relative state of uncleanness of soul also determines the reincarnated lot. In the *Timaeus*, Plato explains the water-dwelling creatures as the lowest forms of reincarnated men, 'seeing that they were unclean of soul through utter wickedness' (92b; cf. *Phd.* 81E–82A).

[68] Cf. the πνεῦμα doing the same: Dem. *Or.* 60.24; *Epict.Diss.* 2.1.17; *Epig.Gr.* 250.6; 613.6.

Such a soul is weighed down by this [desire for the body] and
is dragged back into the visible world, through fear of the invisible and of the other world, and so, as they say, it flits about
the monuments and the tombs, where shadowy shapes of souls
(ψυχῶν σκιοειδῆ φαντάσματα) have been seen, figures of those
souls which were not set free in purity but retain something of
the visible; and this is why they are seen.   (Pl. *Phd.* 81C–D)

It is difficult to say how pervasive these ideas were in Mark's world,
although from the first century BC Neopythagoreanism was in the ascen-
dancy, with a school centred in Rome, and would continue until it merged
into Neoplatonism, influencing people such as Nigidius Figulus (1st
c. BC), Philo (1st c. BC/1st c. AD), Apollonius of Tyana (d. *c.* AD 96–8),
and, later, Clement of Alexandria, Origen, Porphyry and Plotinus. For
any of Mark's Graeco-Roman readers with a Pythagorean legacy, the expression 'unclean spirit' would connote a soul still unpurged of the body,
which prefers to flit about where bodies still remain and which could
manifest itself as a ghost. This is virtually equivalent to the notion that
daimones are the souls of those who had already died.

Interfering unclean ghosts

Although the reference to 'unclean spirits' in the medieval scholia on
Demosthenes and Aeschines[69] may reflect Christian colouring, it provides
indirect support for the view argued here. These scholia explain that the
public assembly of Athens was cleansed through the sacrifice of a pig,
because formerly the assembly had been disturbed by 'unclean *daimones*
and spirits'. The coupling of the two beings is interesting in itself, but
also, since the pig was a chthonic sacrifice, this sacrifice indicates that
they were from the underworld. Although this does not require them to
be departed souls, it is consistent with their being so.

Some extant sacred laws indicate that such sacrifices may have been
thought to purify departed ancestors now in the underworld. The two-
staged rituals reflected in *LSSupp* **115** and the *Lex sacra* from Selinous
firstly purify the ancestor spirits, the *Tritopatores*, before making an offering to the spirits purified through the first rite. 'The impure *Tritopatores*
would appear to be the more abnormal and even dangerous figures,'[70]
akin to other vengeful spirits of the dead, *alastores* and the like.

Is this the kind of 'unclean spirit' in which the man in Capernaum was
existing?

---

[69] *Schol.Aeschin.* in or. 1.23; *Schol.Dem.* in or. 4.1b.
[70] Jameson et al., *Lex sacra*, 72.

A man 'in unclean spirit'

Although there is nothing in the account itself which specifically labels the 'unclean spirits' as ghosts, the links with the world of magic suggest this identification. Graeco-Roman readers would have no problem recognising this man, 'in unclean spirit' (ἐν πνεύματι ἀκαθάρτῳ, v.23), as a victim of a daemonic attack, or as someone under daemonic control. If the Pythagorean notion of unclean souls was also part of their repertoire, this would create a closer verbal link between Mark and their conception of the *daimones*. On this understanding, the Capernaum story would be read as Jesus being confronted by departed spirits and demonstrating his authority over them (v.27).

Jesus' authority

Daemonic fear (v.24b)

The magician attempted to gain control of the spirits by manipulating them with his knowledge of the higher powers who represented a threat for the spirits (cf. Lucian *Philops*. 16; Philostr. *Vit. Ap.* 3.38). The assumption of daemonic fear, which was so characteristic of magic, is a very ancient belief. It is found in an Orphic hymn which calls Zeus, 'he whom *daimones* dread, and whom the throng of gods do fear' (δαίμονες ὅν φρίσσουσι[ν], θεῶν δὲ δέδοικεν ὅμιλος) (in Clem.A. *Strom.* 5.14). The literature (e.g., James 2.19; TSol 6.8; *Vit. Ap.* 3.38; 4.20), spells (eg. Thompson "N".30; *PHarris* 55[71] (1st/ 2nd c. AD); *PGM* IV.3014ff.; XII.50ff., 117f.; LXXVII.5ff.; XXXVI.256–64 = Gager **130**; *Sepher ha-Razim* 2.40ff.; Isbell8.6–7, 8, 11; **43**.4; **55**.9; **54**.7) and curses (eg. Gager **28**; **27** = *PGM* IV.296–466) attest to the *daimones*' fear and to its being used against them.[72]

Sometimes the *daimon* is manipulated by a promise of a gift (Fox = Gager **134**), or an offering of some kind (εὐαγγέλια θύσω, *DTA* **109**), or of being left alone (ἐὰν τοῦτό μοι ποιήσῃς, ἀπολύσω σε, *SuppMag* **46**.27).[73] But the usual pattern was to threaten them, invoking one or many 'terrible fearful name'(s) (*PGM* VII.319–34). The magicians played upon their fear, whether of being harmed (e.g., the Augustan *SuppMag* **72** threatens the underworld gods with an intractable headache until the

---

[71] Powell, *Rendel Harris Papyri*. Cf. Gager **126**, where Israel's God is 'seated on the mountain of violence'.

[72] For other instances, see Wortmann, 'Texte', 73.

[73] See also SGD **173**, **54**, **109**; *DTA* 99; *SuppMag* 45.12–15; Gager **27**, **28**, **30**.

magician's purposes are fulfilled),[74] or tortured (Mark 5.7), or sent lower down in the underworld (cf. Plut. *Dion* 2; see discussion on Suppliant 6, below), or, as in Capernaum, of being destroyed (e.g., *PGM* IV.1247f.).

There was always the possibility that the magician's threats would backfire (cf. Acts 19.13–16),[75] but, in Capernaum, this does not happen. The *daimones*' perception of Jesus as a threat is clearly the recognition of his superior authority.

The muzzling (v.25)

The usual translation of φιμώθητι (v.25), 'be silent', although accurate, needs to be strengthened considerably. The verb is used for the muzzling of an animal (cf. 1 Cor. 9.9; 1 Tim. 5.18; cf. Deut. 25.4 = Philo *Virt.* 145), which implies control of its behaviour. When silence is required, additional words are often added (cf. Mark 4.39, σιώπα), such as in a wrath restrainer (4th c. AD): φιμώσατε τὰ στόματα | τὰ κατ' ἐμοῦ, 'control the mouths which are against me' (*PGM* XXXVI.164), or in a curse tablet (3rd c. AD): φιμώσατον δὲ τὰ στόματα πάντων 'muzzle the mouths of all' (*DT* 15.24),[76] but the basic idea of bringing under control is not compromised. It is similar to, but probably stronger than, καταδεῖν which is very common in the magical materials.[77] Jesus commands the spirit to 'be muzzled', i.e., to come under control.

This is endorsed by its use in contexts which show the magicians attempting to bring victims under control, e.g., 'muzzle, subordinate, enslave him [. . .] cause him to come under my feet (φίμωσον, | ὑπόταξον, καταδούλωσον [. . .] ποίη|σον αὐτόν ὑπὸ τοὺς πόδας μοι ἔλθῃ, *PGM* VII.965, 966–8 (4th c. AD); cf. IX.4–7, 9). The cognate adjective appears in the Cyprus curse tablets (3rd c. AD): 'I bind the aforementioned close in this "muzzling" deposit (φιμωτικὸν κατάθεμα)',[78] as does the noun (*DT* 25.14 δὸς φιμὸν τῷ θεοδώρῳ), and both the adjective and verb appear on a related selenite tablet.[79] The tablets clearly aim to silence opponents

---

[74] Unfortunately the text breaks off before these purposes are spelled out. Brashear, 'Zauberpapyrus', considers that it was the cure of the magician's own headache, in which case a series of charms associated with erotic magic ends with 'Heilszauber'. Although it is not uncommon to have lists of unrelated spells, in this case, it appears to me that the parts of this text can all be related to erotic magic and, on analogy both with other love charms and with other Helios invocations, I would speculate that the magician's goal was the drawing of the woman.

[75] Cf. the constant need for the magical spells to prescribe protective measures for the user.

[76] Gager 4 ignores the verb and translates '[. . .] the stomachs [*sic*] of all'.

[77] So Eitrem, *Notes*, 38.

[78] *DT* 28; trans.: Jordan, 'Feasts', 133. Cf. *PGM* VII.396; XLVI.4, 8.

[79] Jordan, 'Feasts', 136, 140.

at law,[80] but the related request that someone 'remain subject' the rest of their life may indicate that the silencing is also a sub-set of a bigger concept.

The rendering 'come under control' conveys an element of relationship that 'be silent' does not. Instead of simply being a command, this suggests that the spirit ought properly to be under the control of Jesus. Once again, in this relationship Jesus clearly has the upper hand.

The expulsion

Jesus' command (ἔξελθε) implies that he is dealing with a case of 'possession'. This needs to be asserted against the previous tendency of exegetes to explain away daemonisation by reference to epilepsy or madness.[81] The first-century Graeco-Roman world in which Mark was written knew of both these conditions and the vocabulary associated with them is not used here.[82] Mark's story opens with an account of an exorcism of a possessed person, not the cure of an epileptic, or a madman. Rather than reducing the account by way of a more manageable medical diagnosis, given its important position as the first of Mark's miracles, it is better to ask how this account functions in the narrative when it is read exactly as it is portrayed, i.e., as an exorcism.

Even on Palestinian soil, the number of demonstrable cases of exorcism should not be exaggerated,[83] still less the notion of 'possession' amongst the Greeks. Since the first extra-biblical Greek exorcism of someone 'possessed' is found in Lucian (*Philops.* 16; (2nd c. AD)), it is difficult to say whether this would be a familiar concept to the Graeco-Roman

---

[80] They ask for the victim's voice to be taken that they might become ἄφωνοι. Similarly, a red jasper from Afghanistan 'muzzles so-and-so', Jordan, 'Sanctuary of Poseidon', 124 n. 23 – the verb is φιμόω (D.R. Jordan, personal communication, 30/11/95). Isbell 61 muzzles someone in an anti-magical attack.

[81] Cf. Brenk, 'Demonology', 2108. Robinson, 'Problem', 93, complained of the tendency to reduce the exorcisms to healings.

[82] The vocabulary of epilepsy was used well before the first century (e.g., ἐπίληψις Hipp. *Coa praes.* 587, *Morb.Sacr.* 10, Arist. Pr. 960ᵃ18; ἐπιληψία Hipp. *Aph.* 3.22, Arist. *Fr.* 370), as was that associated with madness (e.g., μανία: Hdt. 6.112, Hipp. *Aph.* 7.5, Soph. *Ant.* 958; ἐξίστημι: Eur. *Or.* 1021, Arist. *HA* 577⁹12). The NT itself displays an awareness of the relevant vocabulary: Matthew uses σεληνιάζομαι (4.24; 17.15), which was later used of suffering epilepsy (Vet.Val. 113.10); and there are reports that various people had gone mad (Jesus: Mark 3.21, ἐξίστημι; John 10.20, μαίνομαι; a servant girl: Acts 12.15, μαίνομαι; Paul: Acts 26.24–25, μανία, μαίνομαι; the Corinthian church: 1 Cor. 14.23, μαίνομαι).

[83] Cf. 'exorcism was a common form of therapy in the ancient world', Meyer, *Who?*, 34; 'Exorcism is one of the most ancient and universal practices in the history of humankind. In first century Palestine it was widely practiced [. . .]', Rousseau and Arav, *Jesus*, 88, cf. 90. Twelftree, *Jesus*, 13–52, has a more sober assessment of the evidence.

readers at all.[84] However, whether or not 'possession' was a familiar term, expulsion of a daemonic influence was certainly known. Plutarch spoke of the μάγοι (probably meaning Persian specialists)[85] advising the daemonised (τοὺς δαιμονιζομένους) to recite the Ephesia Grammata (*Quaest.conv.* 706E). As well as in later charms (e.g., 3rd c. AD, *PGM* VII.215–18), these famous letters appear in spells much older than the New Testament.[86] They were used to avert evil, often in contexts suggestive of magic.[87] If so, then, by definition, they were also averting daemonic attacks.

The magical material contains spells which seek to avert daemonic attacks from a person. A malicious Latin tablet from Julius Caesar's time is a counter-curse (Fox = Gager **134**), as is a silver tablet, probably from the first century, which sought to turn away a curse – ὑπόθεσις, perhaps a reference to a curse tablet being deposited against her – and protect from poison (Gager **120**). Its location in a grave suggests that the conjurer was enlisting the dead, to protect against the dead (Cf. *PGM* I.195–222; IV. 86–7; 1227–64; 3007–86; V.96–172; VII.579–90; XII.270–350; XCIV. 17–21; *GMPT* CXIV.1–14).

The expulsion of the spirit by Jesus was the definitive demonstration of his authority. If he did not have the superior power, then he would not gain control of the *daimones* in this way (contrast Acts 19.13–16). The

[84] W.D. Smith, 'Possession', argues that it was not Greek at all, for Gods and *daimones* were thought to influence people by external means; cf. Brenk, 'Demonology', 2108. Although his argument has not gone without criticism, it is fairly persuasive. The fragment of Sophron's mime (Page **73**) is not necessarily an exorcism of Hecate, and it contains no hint of 'possession'; in Tobit, Sarah is not possessed by Asmodeus, so this is not an exorcism proper. [Arist.] *Mir.Ausc.* 166 mentions a stone from the Nile used τοῖς δαίμονί τινι γενομένοις κατόχοις, but the sayings in this collection were probably compiled from the 2nd to the 6th centuries AD, although the knowledge may be earlier. The ruse of Nicias (*c.* 214–211 BC; Plut. *Marc.* 20.5–6), certainly suggests that he had seen someone 'possessed' (by gods), in order to be able to do such a good job of its imitation. Cf. Hipp. *De morb.sac.* 4: 'When at night occur fears and terrors, delirium, jumpings from the bed and rushings out of doors, they say that Hecate is attacking or that heroes are assaulting.' For the Semitic origins of exorcism, see Kotansky, 'Demonology'.

[85] Cf. Pliny *HN* 30.2; Nock, 'Note XIV'; Morton Smith, 'O'Keefe', 306.

[86] They appear for example, in the unpublished lead tablet from Phalasarna (4th/3rd c. BC), and a similar older one in the Getty Museum, Jordan, 'Phalasarna'. Audollent, App. VII lists Ephesia Grammata in his collection of curse tablets, although including more than the classic six words. For a brief discussion and literature, see Jordan, 'Papyrus Love Charm', 257; Arnold, *Ephesians*, 15f.

[87] They were used to gain victory in a wrestling contest (Suda, *s.v.*; Eustathius, *Comm. ad. Hom.* on *Il.* 19.247, van der Valk, p. 171), in which they could have been a counter-charm. Menander, *Paidion* 371, reports them as 'evil-averting spells' for those getting married, i.e., counter-charms against separation magic? Anaxilis, 'The Harp-maker' (mid 4th c. BC) refers to 'wearing Ephesian charms in little sewed bags', as quoted by Athen. *Deipn.* 12.548c, which sounds like amulets against daemonic attacks.

cry from the *daimon* suggests that they did not go willingly, but they went nevertheless.[88]

The spirits' response

Daemonic knowledge

The spirits claim to know who Jesus is (v.24c), and, compared to what the readers already know from the narrative's reliable commentary, there is no reason to question the truth of their identification. 'Mark's audience would recognize that this unclean spirit has everything to lose by a false identification, which would insure a failure of the defensive maneuver.'[89] Their claim to know Jesus represents an attempt to gain the upper hand and so control him.

In magical manipulation of the underworld beings, it was essential to be well connected with those in power. Although it was perfectly acceptable to make use of the spirit of an unknown corpse, the magician needed to know the names of the powers to invoke so that that corpse could be released to his service. Although, having said as much, care was also taken that it was *only* the spirit of *this* corpse that was released (cf. *PGM* IV.369f. ἔγειρον μόνον σεαυτόν), for an unsummoned spirit could be a dangerous spirit. Thus, even the summoning of the anonymous *nekydaimon* was the summoning of a *particular* spirit, namely, the one associated with *this* corpse. But, in order to manipulate the higher powers, it was necessary to know the names. The long lists of names appearing in the various spells suggest that these invocations used as many names as possible (cf. Lucian *Philops.* 17) to enhance the chances of hitting on the correct spirit for the occasion.[90] A later bowl text shows the user attempting to get around the need to know them (*AMB* **Bowl 5**) by ordering the *daimon* to work, 'whether I know his name or not', and then bluffing that if he does not know the name, it was explained to him at creation or disclosed in the deed of divorce of Joshua ben Perahya (cf. Montgomery **8** and **17**).

This structure is reversed in the Capernaum story. Rather than Jesus attempting to gain control of the spirits in order to cast them out, it is the *daimones* who claim to know something about Jesus in an attempt

---

[88] Ghosts cry out (e.g., Scurlock **Presc 77**.14; Thompson **XV**.10; **"K"**.30; **"C"**.I.50ff. 'Behind me [howl] not, shriek not!'), and magicians respond in kind, cf. Lucian *Men.* 9.

[89] Gundry, *Mark*, 76.

[90] Thompson, *Devils*, II.xxviii comments on this phenomenon in the Assyrio-Babylonian spells, and the long lists of names in Greek magic suggest the same practice. Multiple names are also found in what is probably the oldest extant exorcistic spell (BMPap. 10685C, c. 1250–1100 BC; Egyptian), cf. Twelftree, *Christ*, 22.

to gain mastery over him. When the spirit says 'I know', at this point a
Hellenistic audience would think that the unclean spirit has gained the
upper hand and is about to adjure Jesus (cf. 5.7). Yet despite the attempt,
Jesus demonstrates his authority by gaining control (v.25).

The violence

In Capernaum, as a parting gesture, the spirit violently attacks this man.
Given the violence of the verb σπαράσσω (v.26), which was used to
mean 'tear apart, mangle', the customary translation 'convulse' sounds a
little tame.[91] The sense of violence is heightened by the spirits' great cry
as they depart.

A changed voice is often attested for people under the influence of a
spiritual presence. Nicias (*c.* 214–211 BC) adopted it as part of his ruse
that the Sicilian 'mothers' were afflicting him (Plut. *Marc.* 20.5–6), and it
was a feature of the exorcisms associated with Apollonius of Tyana (*Vit.
Ap.* 3.38; 4.20), although here the cry is 'a loud voice' (cf. *PGM* XIII.
242–4).[92] Both features are present in Plutarch's account of the Pythia
who died as a result of being forced to prophesy despite bad omens (*De
defectu* 438B). Her first responses were with an unusual 'harshness of
voice', which indicated she 'was filled with a mighty and baleful spirit'
(ἀλάλου καὶ κακοῦ πνεύματος οὖσα πλήρης). After finally becoming
hysterical, with a frightful shriek (μετὰ κραυγῆς ἀσήμου καὶ φοβερᾶς)
she rushed out and threw herself down and died a few days later.

Although all daemonic attacks may not be necessarily violent, this does
seem to have been one of their features.[93] The actions of *daimones* seem to
be violent[94] and bent on death,[95] such as the ghost possessing the boy who
would not come to see Apollonius, and threatened his mother 'with steep
places and precipices and declared that he would kill her son' (Philostr.
Vit. Ap. 3.38; cf. Mark 9.22). Other ghosts were just as violent, such as
that at Temesa (Paus. 6.6.8–11). One of Odysseus' sailors had raped a girl

[91] LSJ lists only Mark for this meaning. In the medical writings it is used for dry retching
(Hipp. *Coa Praes.* 546), or provoking sickness (Gal. 11.57). Luke 4.35 lessens the violence
of the scene by changing the phrase to ῥίπτω [. . .] εἰς τὸ μέσον. Cranfield, *Mark*, 79, asks
whether Matthew's omission of the entire story was due to this very detail which would
have been 'distasteful'; cf. his omission of Mark 7.31–37, 8.22–26.
[92] Sometimes the magician must respond in kind, commanding the *daimones* 'in a loud
voice', cf. *PGM* XII.160–78.
[93] So much so that Hull, *Hellenistic Magic*, 81 n. 29, has to apologise for its absence in
Mark 7.31–37, which he regards as a case of daemonic illness.
[94] Thompson V.iv.34; V.v.44 'knowing neither mercy nor pity'; "T".10 'they tear out
the heart'; "X" 'against the man angrily'; "Y" 'they have gone from the grave, angrily they
come' (cf. Ps-Phoc. 100f.)
[95] Robinson, 'Problem', 87–8.

in Temesa and was stoned to death. Odysseus sailed on, 'but the ghost (δαίμων) of the stoned man never ceased killing without distinction the people of Temesa, attacking both old and young' until they propitiated him with a temple and the yearly gift of the fairest maiden in Temesa as a wife. Another ghost was the Hero Eunostos, at Tanagra, who, having been killed by the machinations of a woman, would not tolerate any women to come near to his grave (Plut. *QuaestGr* no.40, 300D; cf. no.27, 297C; no.28, 297D; Hdt. 5.67; see also Paus. 9.19.38.3–6).

The violence of the daemonic is hideously portrayed in the counter-curse, mentioned above, which wishes the utmost torture and pain on the person who has previously cursed this client, before their eventual death.[96]

> Good and beautiful Proserpina (or Salvia, shouldst thou prefer), mayest thou wrest away the health, body, complexion, strength, and faculties of Plotius and consign him to thy husband, Pluto. Grant that by his own devices he may not escape this penalty. Mayest thou consign him to the quartan, tertian, and daily fevers to war and wrestle with him until they snatch away his very life. Wherefore, I hand over this victim to thee, Proserpina (or, shouldst thou prefer, Acherusia). Mayest thou summon for me the three-headed hound Cerberus to tear out the heart of Plotius, [. . .]
>
> Proserpina Salvia, I give thee the head of Plotius, the slave of Avonia, his brow and eyebrows, eyelids and pupils. I give thee his ears, nose, nostrils, tongue, lips, and teeth, so he may not speak his pain; his neck, shoulders, arms, and fingers, so he may not aid himself; his breast, liver, heart, and lungs, so he may not locate his pain; his bowels, belly, navel, and flanks, so he may not sleep the sleep of health; *his shoulder-blades, so that he may not be able to sleep well; his sacred part, so that he may not be able to make water; his buttocks, vent,* thighs, knees, legs, shanks, feet, ankles, heels, toes, and toe-nails, so he may not stand of his own strength. [. . .]
>
> May he most miserably perish and depart this life. Mayest thou so irrevocably damn him that his eyes may never see the light of another month.[97]   (Fox = Gager **134**)

[96] Although it is addressed to Proserpine, the agent of torture would no doubt be the *daimones* released to do her bidding.

[97] Fox, 206f. = L&R.II. **179** = *CIL* I.2520; = Gager **134**. * . . . * from L&R; omitted by Fox.

Similarly, erotic magic, which is one of the best attested kinds and is demonstrably earlier than the 1st century AD (cf. PMonGr inv. 216 (1st c. BC); *SuppMag* **72**,[98] (Augustan)), contains some particularly sordid examples of the violence of ghosts, which is what the conjurer uses against the victim. These spells frequently make use of the agency of a corpse-*daimon* to draw the intended lover to the client, using physical,[99] emotional and 'social'[100] violence.

The frequent provision in the magical recipes of protective measures for the user of the spells also testifies to the daemonic violence. Evidently, the practitioner himself was not immune from assault as he conjured the spirits, especially if he accidentally summoned one he, or his spirits, could not control (cf. *PGM* IV.369f.; Acts 19.13–16). If, as the curse tablets show, the ghosts were set free in order to fulfil curses which included severe bodily harm and a very painful death, then protection from such beings would be essential.

The spirits' question

The spirits' question may be due to their fear of annihilation, for, although the length of time that the *daimones* would live was debated, all were convinced that they would certainly die, because immortality belonged to the gods (Plut. *De defectu* 418E). They may have been afraid of being sent lower down in the underworld (cf. discussion on Suppliant 6, below), or of losing their influence in the upper world, which, given their propensity for the bodily realm, would be quite a punishment. Jesus could have been doing something akin to the various rituals for ridding households or communities of ghosts,[101] although, to account for the spirits' anxiety, perhaps something a little more permanent. The spirits recognise that Jesus has the authority to destroy them, but they are not sure whether he will. The readers are also led to ponder the question: has he come to destroy the ghosts of the dead?

What would this entail? Since the spirits of the dead were the agents of magic, their destruction would cut the heart out of it and impinge upon the huge influence of magic on society. All areas of life are represented in the charms and the curses. People were cursed in the name of business, or

[98] See n. 74 above.
[99] Love magic of all kinds was associated with death; cf. the male-directed aphrodisiacs that also tended to kill the intended, see Faraone, 'Sex'; 'Mistake'.
[100] They often entailed the separation of the intended from spouse and family. See further, Martinez, 'Love Magic'; Winkler, 'Constraints'.
[101] Cf. the festivals of Anthesteria and Genesia, Parentalia and Lemuria, as well as the rituals outlined in *LSSup* **115** and the *Lex sacra* from Selinous. In Rome the ghosts were allowed to emerge on 24 Aug.; 5 Oct.; 8 Nov.; Cumont, *Afterlife*, 71.

love, or success, or legal squabbles, or sport, or revenge, or because they cursed first, or merely because they were related to the wrong person. Such curses sought to damage every aspect of life: people's health, their relationships, their business, their reputation; and they often aimed to kill – but only after inflicting a great deal of suffering. In such an environment, any case of difficulty, be it sickness, or some other kind of suffering, would raise the suspicion that malevolent magic lay behind it. It is not surprising that in the seventies AD 'there [was] no-one who does not fear to be spellbound by curse tablets' (Pliny *HN* 28.4.19). On the other hand, magic could also be used to protect from daemonic attacks, from other spells, or from illness, in a desperate attempt to hang on to life and 'to ward off death' (Eur. *Supp.* 1109ff.). Along with the spells to counteract magic itself, there was even a charm to remove the fear of magic (*PGM* LXX.26–51).

Alongside this fear of magic went a fear of the dead by which it operated. This is obvious not only by the presence of the various protective charms within the magical materials themselves, but also in various other features of ancient society. The widespread fear of ghosts can be variously illustrated: from the ghost-ridding festivals and sacred ceremonies,[102] from certain features of 'secular' Attic law which can be explained in terms of the fear of ghosts,[103] and perhaps from the philosophers' need to speak against δεισιδαιμονία (eg. Philo *Gig.* 16; Plut. *De superstitione*). In a magical environment, the dead could suddenly arrive in a home, inflict great harm and seek to take family members with them to the underworld. If they succeeded, there was always the fear that the victims would also join the ranks of the ghosts, for the *daimones* aimed to ensure their victims had an underworld position no better than their own (Plut. *Dion* 2; cf. Tatian *Or.* 16.1).

The hostility of ghosts to humans, whether or not those ghosts had been set upon the victim by some magician (or his client), could have many unpleasant effects on ordinary life. The *daimones*' question raises the possibility that Jesus had come to destroy these beings. This would put an end to their manipulation by magicians and the resulting evil effects, thus breaking the fear of such influences and effects under which large segments of the populace were held. The question raises the exciting possibility that Jesus was about to unlock the stranglehold of the dead on the living. This could mean a whole new approach to life.

Jesus had won this encounter, the crowds were amazed at his authority, and the readers are left with the question: has he come to destroy the

[102] See previous note.   [103] Farnell, *Higher Aspects*, 89.

spirits, along with their reign of violence and death? In the spells, the end of a ghostly attack is occasionally described as being given life (Scurlock **Prescr 62**; Thompson t.IX.iv.208). This was exactly the experience for a man in Capernaum: he had lived under the influence of the dead, but now he had been given new life.

Imperial deliverance?

The framework of Mark's narrative sets Jesus against the backdrop of the Caesars. The imperial rhetoric proclaimed them as saviours who delivered the world from certain destruction. Some of them attempted to move beyond the rhetoric by establishing a reputation for themselves as miracle workers in a far more literal sense. Although Vespasian would later be credited with some miraculous cures (Tac. *Hist.* 4.81), amongst his Claudian predecessors, Gaius had attempted to fake some miracles,[104] and Nero devoted enormous wealth and energy in the pursuit of magic, before abandoning it, since his 'greatest wish was to command the gods' (Pliny *HN* 30.2).

But the Caesars' reputations were not really honed on their ability to perform miracles. Despite the rhetoric, the critics could point to the long trail of blood left in their wake.[105] Nero may have turned to magic to learn how to command the gods and manipulate the dead, but he was remembered because 'more cruelly behaving than any did Nero thus fill our Rome with ghosts' (Pliny *HN* 30.5). Rome's rulers would show themselves experts at creating ghosts, but they could do nothing to destroy them.

Significance in the narrative

Jesus' encounter with this first suppliant provides a brilliant opening to Mark's story. This is not a person who is merely playing with ghosts, or who fills the land with ghosts, but one who deals with ghosts. He rescued one of their victims and in such a way as to raise the question whether this event spells the end of the tyranny of the dead over the living.[106] Which of the Caesars could ever claim to have achieved such notoriety?

---

[104] Cf. Scherrer, 'Signs'.

[105] 'After [Augustus] there had been undoubtedly peace, but peace with bloodshed' (Tacit. *Ann.* 1.10.4). Tacitus was thinking of the blood of the Roman nobility, but as a lead-in to the rest of his book, Wengst, *Pax Romana*, 10 n. 19, adds that 'other blood will have to be recalled'.

[106] Robinson, 'Problem', 92, correctly recognised this scene as paradigmatic for interpreting the remainder of the conflict stories in Mark.

Suppliant 2: a woman with a fever (1.29–31)

Text to reader: raised from her bed

The narrative dynamics offer little support for the view that the main point of this encounter is 'to reveal the trust of Jesus' four followers'.[107] Although their presence in the scene provides continuity with the calling scene – and so with the ongoing movement of the narrative –, this will be their first encounter with a miracle. They were apparently absent from the synagogue,[108] which means that the first suppliant's story remains information shared between readers and Jesus, giving the readers a position of privilege over the four.[109] This places some distance between the readers and the disciples, whereas, in contrast, the scene closely aligns the readers with the suppliant.

The readers enter the scene with Jesus, coming from the synagogue (v.29), and the narrative comment immediately directs their attention to the fevered woman (v.30a).[110] The fact that, as part of her characterisation, she is a woman and is described relationally (πενθερά) increases the pathos, thus further binding the readers to her.[111] The revelation of the secrets of her condition (v.30a, κατέκειτο πυρέσσουσα) focalises the readers through her, and, because this occurs even before Jesus learns of it from the disciples (v.30b), the readers are given a position of privilege over all the characters. It is as if they have been placed in the woman's bedroom and now await the others to join them there.

This is Mark's first mention of illness. In terms of extraordinary abilities, the readers know only of Jesus' confrontation with the spirits of the dead (1.21–28). Even though the ancient world maintained a closer link between illness and malignant spirits, both for disease in general and fever in particular (see below),[112] there is no explicit mention of any spirits being involved in the woman's condition.[113] Nevertheless, as the

---

[107] J.F. Williams, *Other Followers*, 94; cf. 182 n. 1.

[108] Reading the singulars, ἐξελθών and ἦλθεν (1.29), which have strong external support, with, e.g., Swete, *Mark*, Cranfield, *Mark*, Taylor, *Mark*, *pace* Metzger, *Textual Commentary*, 75.

[109] They are therefore bound closely with the narrator and his perspective. For privilege, see Booth, *Fiction*, 160–3.

[110] Such explicit comments from the narrator are part of the 'stable backdrop of *direction* for the reader' essential for the rhetorical impact of a narrative; Fowler, *Let the Reader*, 81, who ignores Mark 1.30a.

[111] Characterisation can be simply through providing the gender of the character. See ch. 1, n. 87 on p. 19.

[112] So, for example, Kelber, *Mark's Story*, 21; Garland, ' "I am the Lord" ', 333.

[113] The expression ἀφῆκεν αὐτὴν ὁ πυρετός may suggest 'demonic activity' (so Garland, ibid., 335, following Weiss, 'πῦρ', 958), but it may be simply an expression for the

narrator supplies this information it raises the question: if Jesus can deal with the unclean spirits, what can he do with a woman already taken to bed with fever?

When the four inform Jesus about the woman (v.30b), there is no indication that the four expected that he would (or could) do anything for her, but they probably simply mention a matter of some concern for the household. Knowing about the synagogue events, the readers – still waiting with the woman – anticipate what Jesus may do and the surprise it will be for the disciples.

The readers then watch Jesus travel to the bedside (v.31). The absence of the four creates the sense that it is only the readers and Jesus who now stand there, which promotes an intimacy between these three parties, thus reducing distance. The finite verb supplying his action does not focus upon her healing *per se* (contrast, e.g., θεραπεύω, cf. 1.34, 3.2, 10, 6.5, 13; ἰάομαι, cf. 5.29), but on the fact that 'he raised' (ἔγειρεν) her – with some emphasis upon the verb, due to its position prior to its supporting participle (κρατήσας). This verb is used on several occasions in Mark with what seems to be a studied ambiguity. The usage of ἐγείρω and also ἀνίστημι appear generally to have overlapping semantic domains. Apart from instances denoting simply 'getting up' (from sleep: 1.35, 2.14, 4.27, 4.38; to move on: 3.3, 7.24, 10.1, 14.57, 60), or 'rising up against' someone (3.26, 13.8, 22, ?14.57, ?60), or to be 'raised' as a familiar spirit (6.14, 16),[114] the verbs are also used of the resurrection from the dead, whether in the case of an individual (Jairus' daughter: 5.41, 42; Jesus: 8.31, 9.31, 10.34, 14.28, 16.6), or to refer to the general resurrection that would usher in the kingdom of God (9.9–10; 12.23, 26).[115] The ambiguous usages of ἐγείρω all appear to describe a suppliant being raised up as a result of Jesus' activity on their behalf (1.31; 2.9, 11, 12; 9.27). As Mark's narrative proceeds, it is difficult not to see these 'raisings' as resurrection paradigms (see especially 9.26–27).[116]

---

passing of a fever (see also John 4.52). It is certainly an unusual expression, for I was unable to find it in any of the medical writers and Hippocrates, for example, used other expressions for the passing of a fever, e.g., γενέσθαι ἄπυρος, or ἄπυρος ἐκρίθη. The *daimonic* overtones which are 'indisputable' in Luke 4.39 (Weiss) are suggested by Jesus' posture and his rebuke of the fever (ἐπιστὰς ἐπάνω αὐτῆς ἐπετίμησεν τῷ πυρετῷ), perhaps not by the use of ἀφῆκεν.

[114] See chapter 7 for this explanation.

[115] Although I have followed the usual practice of discussing Jesus' resurrection and the general resurrection separately, it is likely that the passion-resurrection predictions would have been heard as speaking of the final resurrection at the end time (see Cavallin, 'Tod'; cf. Schaberg, 'Daniel 7, 12'). This also suits the NT picture of Jesus being raised as the first fruits of the resurrection to come (1 Cor. 15.20, 23).

[116] This is especially so if the full weight of the argument in the present volume is felt.

The stark narration of the consequence of Jesus' action conveys the sense that it was achieved with simplicity and ease (v.31b): καὶ ἀφῆκεν αὐτὴν ὁ πυρετός. Confirming that the cure was instantaneous and complete, the story ends with the woman, who had begun on her bed (v.30a), serving them (v.31b).

Despite all this happening, no response is reported. As the scene continues, those who had witnessed the events in the synagogue arrive, eager for more (cf. vv.22, 27f.), but the text is strangely silent about the reaction of the four when Simon's mother-in-law was raised from her bed. Since this is their first encounter with Jesus' abilities, their lack of response is deafening (contrast 1.22, 27–28). When the flood of people arrive at the door after sundown, it is as if the (unresponsive) disciples are already buried amongst many other people whose responses to Jesus are much more appropriate than theirs.

The scene does not focus upon the four disciples, but upon the encounter between Jesus and a woman with a fever. After being closely aligned with the suffering woman, the readers view the scene from her perspective. They learn that, despite her fever-stricken condition, Jesus raised her.

Reader to text

As the first healing miracle in Mark, the woman's raising has a position of some narrative significance. However, this miracle is probably one of the least impressive for modern readers convinced of the benefits of antibiotics and paracetamol! To appreciate the impact of this story upon Mark's early readers, their perspective on fever must be recovered. They would not regard the cure of Simon's mother-in-law as a minor matter, but as an instance of Jesus casting back the shadow of death itself.

Fever and death

Fever

Although not uninterested in underlying causes, the ancients tended to regard fever more as a condition than a symptom (e.g. Philo *Sobr.* 45). Simon's mother-in-law appears not as a case of 'malignant malaria, enteric or typhus' fever,[117] or of any other potential *disease*, but as a case of *fever*.

Fever was common in the ancient world. As well as appearing in two other cases in the NT (John 4.52; Acts 28.7–10) it appears constantly in

---

[117] Mastermann, *Hygiene*, 51, based on Luke's 'great fever' (4.38).

the medical literature. It is a feature of the Hippocratic corpus, whose
master had provided many of the classifications still in use,[118] it is the
most common item discussed by Celsus (*fl.* AD 14–37), and the need to
devote attention to fever had not abated by Galen's time (2nd c. AD),[119]
and, in fact, nor would it until the late twentieth century. The prevalence
of fever is confirmed by turning from the writings of the physicians to
the materials of the magical practitioners, who were also called upon to
deal with fevers.

Although mild cases obviously occurred, it must be stressed for the
benefit of those who live under the regime of post-war modern medicine
that fever was an extremely severe condition. It struck suddenly (Thompson"**O**".5: 'Fever, the evil disease which none can see'), taking an individual out of action (e.g. Thuc. 2.49; Joseph. *Ap.* 48); it was no respecter
of person, gender or age. Its severity was well-known: 'an attack of fever
is a disease not of a part but of the whole body' (Philo *Sobr.* 45);[120] being
likened to torture on the rack and wheel (Philo *Legat.* 206).[121] The second-
century woman mentioned in *P.Oxy* 1381 would no doubt have agreed,
having been afflicted for three years by a recurrent fever; as would her
son, who, after being cured by Asclepius of the same sickness, provided
a first-hand account of the distress:

> It was night when every living thing except those in pain is asleep
> [. . .]. An exceedingly hot fever burned me and I was convulsed
> with pain in my side because of constant coughing and choking.
> Groggy from suffering, I was lying there half-asleep and half-
> awake, being tended by my mother as if I were still a baby for she
> is by nature affectionate. She was sitting [by my bed] extremely
> grieved at my agony and not able to get even a little sleep [. . .].
> (*P.Oxy* 1381)

The distress here is both echoed and overshadowed by the Hippocratic
case studies, which provide detailed evidence of just how dreadful it was
to suffer 'fever' in an age without effective options for intervention. The
distress of the illness would be compounded by the extra suffering caused

[118] Weiss, 'πῦρ', 956.

[119] The Hippocratic corpus has over 1200 references to πῦρ; Galen, who devoted a
treatise to the subject (*De differentiis febrium libri ii*, Kuhn Vol. VII.273–405), over 2000.

[120] Cf. Thuc. 2.49 the plague 'spread through the whole body'; 2.50 the violence being
'too great for human nature to endure'; and the curse tablets which sought to insert fever
into all the members of the body (*DT* **51**; **74**; **75**).

[121] Cf. the use of μεγάλας βασάνους βασανιζόμενα 'tortured with great tortures' as a
reference to fever in *DT* 1; Versnel, 'Πεπρημένος', esp. 150; and 'Beyond Cursing', 73.

by relatives and neighbours, for diseased people were often isolated,[122] and, for conditions suspected of being contagious, sufferers were often left to care for themselves. Even the physicians felt no obligation to stay with their patients if they were at risk.[123]

The fear of fever

Given the prevalence and severity of the condition, it is not surprising to find indications that fever was feared. As indications of this fear, we can cite the variety of protective measures to which people resorted, whether gained from the physicians, for whom fever formed a large part of the case loads, or from the gods, such as Asclepius (*P.Oxy* 1381), or specialist fever gods,[124] or from the magicians. Many Greek charms against fever have survived,[125] as well as a few inscribed gems.[126] Although most of the Greek spells are later than the New Testament period, it is safer to assume that this is a matter of survival, than that earlier spells did not exist. Both the Philinna Papyrus (*PGM* XX (2nd/1st c. BC)) and the Augustan *SuppMag* **72** contain charms against headache, which shows that 'medical' magic was operative. This makes it rather difficult to believe that it was not used against such a common condition as fever. Since curse tablets used fever as one of their weapons against the enemy (see below), it is likely that there were magical counter-charms against such attacks. In any case, the Semitic materials demonstrate that magical protections against fever were certainly known in that context well before the first century.[127]

---

[122] Strubbe, ' "Cursed be he" ', 44. This is frequently attested: Versnel, 'Curious Formula', 254 with bibliography and Hasenfratz, *Die toten Lebenden*, for other cultures, esp. 14–24, 33–4, 38–41. Cf. Hipp. *Epid.* I. cases 6, 10, 13 and 14; III. cases 2, 3, 5, 8 and 12; III.17 cases 1, 2, 7, 8, 15; cf. Mark 6.56.

[123] Galen himself fled from the Roman epidemic in AD 180. For further discussion, see Stark, 'Epidemics', 168. To be fair, it is also true that many physicians during the Athenian plague stayed at the cost of their own lives (Thuc. 2.47, 51), but this does not seem to have been the norm. Stark argues that the contrasting attentiveness to the sick found in the early Christian movement was a major factor in its increase.

[124] Dunst, 'Fiebergott'. Febris also appears in Sen. *Apoc.* 6.

[125] A representative sample: fever amulets: 3rd c. AD: *PGM* VII.211–12, 213f., 218–21; XXXIII.1–25; *SuppMag* **2**, **3**, **4**, **79**; *P.Tebt.* 275; 3rd/4th c. AD: *GMPT* LXXXVIII.1–19; *SuppMag* **9**, **10**, **11**; 4th c. AD: *PGM* P5a (Christian); *SuppMag* **2**.10–14 (lead tablet), **12**; *GMPT* LXXXIX.1–27; 4/5th c. AD: *PGM* XVIIIb.1–7; *SuppMag* **19**, **21**, **22**, **29**; *P.Amst* 173 I (Christian); 5th c. AD: *PGM* XLIII.1–27; *PGM* P5b (Christian); *SuppMag* **23**, **25**; 5/6th c. AD: *SuppMag* **31**; 6th c. AD: *SuppMag* **35** (Christian; refers to the healing of Peter's mother-in-law); 7th c. AD: *SuppMag* **34**.

[126] Besides his own, Geissen, 'Amulett', cites only *SMA* 111. The 2nd/3rd c. AD gem against 'inflammation' of the uvula, Daniel and Maltomini, 'Gemma', could also be added, since it has the same grape-formation found in other fever amulets.

[127] Being on more durable material, these survived better than papyrus. For fever charms, see Thompson's volumes; e.g. 1.**III**.40, 117, 155, 163; "**K**".169 headache, shivering,

The use of such protective measures reveals that fever was not only undesirable, it was deeply feared. This fear is partly accounted for by the prevalence and severity of fever, and its sudden, mysterious nature. But the main reason for fearing fever was that it was a killer.

Fever the killer

Fever was a well-known killer (Thompson **XI**.3 fever is 'against his life'; **XII**.40 'it slayeth him'). Ancient physicians knew that the acute diseases, almost certainly accompanied by fever, 'kill the great majority of patients' (Cf. Hipp. *De diaeta in morb. ac.* 5). Infectious disease proper – which would also be 'fever' – 'was undoubtedly the single greatest threat to life in antiquity, with epidemics killing half or more of the populations of the world's larger cities'.[128]

Although not an infectious disease,[129] malaria was a major cause of fever, and it took its steady share of victims,[130] especially if accompanied

---

heartache; 286 'burneth [like] fire'; "**C**".ii.100 'noisome fever'; "**J**".5: 'The evil Spirit and Fever of the Desert; O Pestilence that has touched the man for harm'; cf. "**C**", 156, 173. The Ašakki marṣûti series has at least 12 tablets against fever.

[128] Zias, 'Death', 149. For a discussion of the known epidemics in antiquity, see Patrick, 'Disease', 238–40, 245–6. To a medical man, such as the famous second-century physician Galen, the word λοιμός (= Latin *pestis* and *pestilentia*) (cf. Luke 21.11; Mark 13.8 Σ *pc*) meant a severe disease attacking a large number of people at the same time, with a high mortality. But the word was also used in a more general sense for any calamity (cf. Acts 24.5), which makes it difficult to identify the 'plagues' of antiquity. At least five can be identified in the first three centuries: (1) that following the eruption of Vesuvius (AD 79); (2) the plague of Orosius (AD 125), which killed 30,000 Roman soldiers sent to defend the colony; (3) 'Galen's' (or Antoninus') Plague (AD 164–80); (4) Cyprian's plague (AD 251–66); (5) the smallpox epidemic of AD 312 (Patrick, 'Disease', 245).

Although it is difficult to identify the exact nature of these 'plagues', they were probably not bubonic plague, even though it is clear that bubonic plague did exist at the time. Rufus of Ephesus mentions contemporaries of Dionysius referring to a 'plague', seen mainly in Libya, Egypt and Syria, which was 'very dangerous to life'. His description is the only certain reference to bubonic plague in antiquity (ibid., 245–6).

Cf. Stark's discussion of the plagues in AD 165–80 and AD 251; 'Epidemics'; *Rise*, ch. 4, as well as that of Russell, 'Late Ancient', 37. Stark complains how little the impact of epidemics on history has been studied by classicists and historians of early Christianity (*Rise*, 73–4; 154). Following the lead of the fathers Cyprian, Dionysius, Eusebius and other church fathers, he argues that the disruption and demoralisation of the classical world wrought by such disasters was a major factor in the rise of Christianity ('Epidemics'; *Rise*, ch. 4).

[129] Cf. Ps-Arist, *Prob.* 7.8.

[130] The Hippocratic corpus shows that victims of malarial fever died; $\frac{1}{3}$ of the 'fever'–related deaths in Rogers' study were due to malaria, Rogers, *Fevers*, 200. 'Malaria, by reducing the health of even those to whom it was not fatal, caused many to die of diseases which normally they could have survived. Probably the very terrible mortality rates for Rome and Latium in classical times owe much to the prevalence of malaria in the area', Russell, 'Late Ancient', 40.

by tuberculosis (*Epid. I*, 24).[131] Tuberculosis, 'the white plague',[132] also killed after an episode of fever. This very serious illness appears to have had an epidemic character during Hippocrates' time, but indications in Celsus show that this had passed by the first century. When dealing with the signs of approaching death from the disease, Celsus indicates that the absence of a fever was a sign of recovery (*De med.* 2.8.8–9), and it does not appear to be as fatal as it was for Hippocrates.[133] Nevertheless, it was still a major killer. In Roman Spain, which had the best record of mortality of all the provinces,[134] it accounted for 11 per cent and 16.9 per cent of deaths of men and women between ages 15–19 and 20–24 respectively (cf. 3.21 and 3.25 for coloured women in the USA 1911–15).[135] This disease

> [. . .] places a heavier burden upon humanity than almost any other disease. It kills just when the long and expensive training for life has been completed, often before the patient has had a chance to contribute to the life of his society. Thus, a culture with a heavy mortality from tuberculosis carries a very heavy burden.[136]

The close association between fever and death is confirmed by non-medical sources, as far back as the Epic of Gilgamesh, which contrasts Enkidu's fate with two normal means of death: 'Fever did not seize him; [. . .] On the battle field of men he did not fall; the nether world seized him' (Tab. XII.51f.; *ANET*, 98). In the late first century, reflecting on the fear of death, Epictetus asks:

> What do the swords of the tyrants do? They kill. And what does fever do? Nothing else (πυρετὸς δὲ τί ποιεῖ; ἄλλο οὐδέν).
> (Arr. *Epict.Diss.* 4.7.26, cf. 27)

Here fever's ability to kill is proverbial, and, if the reality behind the rhetoric can be discerned, 'nothing else' implies that it exercised this ability extremely commonly, if not almost automatically. Lucian also hints at the frequency of death from fever, when Peregrinus is smitten 'by a very violent fever' before attempting his own apotheosis by burning himself alive. When his physician tells him that it may not be necessary,

---

[131] 'This indication of the fatality of those who combined tuberculosis with malaria is an important factor in the information about mortality', ibid., 38.

[132] Ibid., 36. It was probably the cause of the high death rate that prevailed amongst men from 20 to 30 (p. 35).

[133] Ibid., 38.   [134] Ibid., 39.   [135] Ibid.   [136] Ibid.

since 'Death had come to his door spontaneously', he replies, 'but that way would not be so notable, being common to all' (*Pereg.* 44).

This bringer of death, so 'common to all', had contributed to the deaths of several of the 'great ones' of human society: Alexander the Great; and, in Palestine, Alexander Jannaeus (*BJ* 1.106; 78 BC) and Herod the Great (*BJ* 1.656 (4 BC)).[137] The ability of fever to kill 'the great' would add extra 'glory' to its public reputation as a killer, as would the memory of times when it devastated populations, such as the great plague of Athens (Thuc. 2.47–52 (430 BC)).[138] Such epidemics would burn themselves into the collective memory, and increase the fear of this 'disease', which had rightly earned its reputation as a killer.

But the home was the context in which the devastation of fever-related death would be felt most severely. Within a matter of days, fever could remove a father or mother whose death would obviously have many on-going social consequences. The children of a home were even more likely to die than either of the parents, since they are less able to withstand high temperatures.[139]

Like the illness itself, fear of fever was both prevalent and chronic, for whenever a fever entered the house, it brought with it the potential death of parents, or of children, or – if it was the start of an epidemic – perhaps even of a major portion of the entire community.

The perception of the killer

It is also highly likely that the fear was exacerbated by the *perception* of fever as a cause of death being even greater than the reality. To illustrate from turn-of-the-(twentieth)-century India, Rogers[140] investigated the claim that 90 per cent of deaths in India were fever-caused. On his own analysis, fever accounted for $\frac{2}{3}$ of the deaths in a high-fever area, but 'the ignorant villagers' reported fever as the cause of almost all deaths. The fact that fever so often led to death clearly engendered such fear that they equated the two, thus inflating the reports. It is not unreasonable to suppose that the same would be true for the first-century Graeco-Roman world. Not only was fever a killer, but, in terms of public perception, its reputation probably even surpassed the reality.

[137] In AD 79 it would also take Vespasian (Dio 66.17).

[138] 'Galen's plague' (AD 165–80) and the outbreak of ?measles in 'Cyprian's plague' (AD 251), provide useful comparative data; Stark, 'Epidemics', 162.

[139] In Rogers' study, for example, $\frac{3}{4}$ of the malaria deaths were in infants less than 18 months old. The odds were against the ancient child as well, Wiedemann, *Adults*, 11–17.

[140] Rogers, *Fevers*, 200.

Fever: the shadow of death

With the onset of fever, the patient's life would hang in the balance for several days. Philo incidentally reveals the Hippocratic wisdom that the seventh day was the decider between life and death:

> Severe bodily sicknesses too, especially persistent attacks of fever due to internal disorder, generally reach the crisis on the seventh day; for this day decides the struggle for life, bringing to some recovery, to others death.   (Philo *Opif.* 125)

Although presenting a rather more complicated picture, the Hippocratic material attests to the kind of diagnostic procedures referred to here, in which a crisis was awaited to indicate whether the patient would live or die. If Philo is referring to generally circulated popular wisdom, then the expectation of potential death would be built into a case of fever and the person's life would be in the balance for at least the first seven days. Since 'the crisis' could be the moment when recovery began, if it did not come after seven days, this popular wisdom was even likely to increase the fear of death thereafter.[141]

Additional assistance in predicting the outcome might be sought by some magical means, such as a 'prognostic of life and death' like Democritus' 'sphere'. This consisted of numbers on two registers and was used as follows:

> Find out what day of the month the sick one took to bed. Add his name from birth to the day of the month and divide by thirty. Look up on the 'sphere' the quotient: if the number is on the upper register, the person will live, but if it is on the lower register, he will die.   (*PGM* XII.351–64)

Notice the significance of the day the patient 'takes to bed'. The sphere expresses the concept brought out by this translation (= *GMPT*), using ἀνέπεσε νοσῶν, 'lay back from sickness' (cf. Arr. *Epict.* 2.18.3). Mark's expression (κατέκειτο) is also regularly used to express the same thing. It is not unusual to find mention of a sick person lying down (κατέκειτο), whether in a temple (esp. of Asclepius, cf. Ar. *Pl.* 411), or elsewhere

---

[141] The actual Hippocratic case histories further complicate the matter: of the 16 patients in *Epidemics* I and III who recovered, the 'crisis' was reached on days 3, 5, 6, 11 (2x), 17, 20, 24, 27, 34, 40 (3x), 80 (2x), 120; only three (18.7%) had begun to recover during the first week; twice as many recovered after 40 days. In Thucydides' plague (430 BC) many died on the seventh or ninth day; in the plague afflicting the Carthaginians besieging Syracuse (probably smallpox; Patrick, 'Disease', 240), 'death came on the fifth day, or the sixth at the latest' (Diod. Sic. 2.14, 70).

(cf. Hipp. *Epid.* I. case 10, 13; III. cases 2, 3, 8, 9, 12; III.17 cases 1, 2, 3, 7, 8, 15. Cf. Hdt. 7.229), but it is a posture with negative connotations. The posture of a patient was important for the physician's diagnosis. If a patient was still 'standing upright' (Hipp. *Epid.* I.1, 5, 6, 10; III. case 13; III.17 case 9, 11, 13), this was a better sign than if he had 'taken to bed' (κατεκλίθη; III. cases 3, 4; III.17 cases 2, 3, 4, 13, 16).[142] The case studies occasionally comment on the movement from one state to the other as a sign of deterioration (III.17 case 13), as well as noting arising (ἀνισταμένη) to be a sign of improvement (I. case 11; III. case 2). The position in which a patient lay on the bed was also significant, so, for example, to lie on one's back was a bad sign (Hipp. *Prog.* 3) – exactly the posture taken by Socrates after drinking the hemlock (Pl. *Phd.* 117e).

The word group κατακλιν- is regularly used for this movement of a sick person to their bed (e.g. Joseph. *AJ* 4.277; Plb 31.13.7; *P.Ryl.* I.24.26 (1st. c. AD); *PGM* IV.2075 and 2496). Although this could occur for non-fatal causes, such as ποδάγρα, gout (Luc. *Trag.* 198), in general it appears to be a sign of a worsening condition, if not death itself. For example, when discussing consumption (φθίσις), Hippocrates (*Epid.* I.2) noticed that of those ailing from summer through the winter, many 'took to their beds' (κατακλίνησαν). He then adds, 'of those who took to their beds (τῶν κατακλινέντων), I do not know one who survived even for a short time.' Although some of those in the Hippocratic case studies who took to their beds survived, most did not.

The negative connotations of taking to the bed are confirmed by the fact that several magical curses seek to place the person on their bed (*DT* **155a**; *AMB* **Genizah 6** = Gager**113**; SGD **163**;[143] *PGM* IV.2075 and 2496; cf. Gager **13**, **106**), and the spell demonstrated to Hadrian boasted of having this effect in two hours, death in seven (*PGM* IV.2450–4). Once someone had taken to bed, it was a very real possibility that they would succumb completely to the 'incurable fevers' (cf. TSol 18.23) before which the physicians recognised their helplessness. Given the seriousness of this sign, it is understandable that at the very hour a sick person took to bed a horoscope known as the κατακλίσις (Gal. 19.529; Cat.Cod.Astr. 1.20, 8 [4] 57) was cast, such as the Sphere of Democritus mentioned above. Once

---

[142] Note the contrast drawn not only between ὀρθοστάδην and κατακειμένοισιν (I.6), but also ἐπὶ τῶν νοσημάτων (I.10).

[143] ἐξορκίζω ὑμᾶς χαρακτῆρα[ς κατα]κλῖνε (for -ναι) ἐπὶ κάκωσιν καὶ ἀε[ικίαν], 'I adjure you Characters to put to bed NN with? ill- and outrageous treatment' (near Hebron (3rd c. AD)). The *kharactērs* are special symbols which developed in magical writings, apparently to replicate the efficacious and symbolic roles of the ancient hieroglyphs; see Frankfurter, *Religion*, 255–6.

the person took to bed, the question became focused upon the outcome: will they, or will they not, die?

Fever and the dead?

Adding to the fear of fever would be the awareness that fever could be inflicted by magical curses.

Fever as curse

One of the oldest surviving *defixiones* may seek to inflict fever, since it uses the term πυριν (SGD **111** (*c.* 500 BC)).[144] An extremely fragmentary tablet from the first century (*DT* **246**) includes, presumably as part of its curses, ρυγοπύ [ρετος]. Two Attic *defixiones* (2nd c. AD) use the same formula to call upon the underworld powers to inflict someone 'with both shuddering and each day daily fever', before cursing the various members of his/her body (*DT* **74**; **75A**). Similarly, another asks them to

> [i]nsert grievous fevers into all the members (ἐνβάλλετε πυρε-τοὺς χαλε [πους εἰς] πάντα τὰ μέλη) of Game|tês, the daughter of Hugia Makrobios. Burn, O Chthonic ones (κατακαίνετε καταχθόνι[οί]), | both the soul and the heart of Gametês, [. . .]
> (*DT* **51** (unspecified date))

And a Latin curse against actors (c. AD 200) uses the word *pyra*, clearly borrowing from an earlier Greek model.[145]

Fever as ordeal

Other practices may have also wished fever upon people. Versnel[146] has related a group of lead tablets from the Demeter sanctuary at Cnidus (2nd/1st c. BC) to the confession texts from Lydia and Phrygia of the 2nd/3rd c. AD. In these texts, a culprit is driven to confession through πεπρημένος, which, in spite of the usual explanation (i.e., an Ionicising variant of πεπραμένος, 'being sold'), should be taken in its normal sense of 'burning/ burnt with fever'. Although Versnel suggests that this may relate to some kind of trial by ordeal, he does not exclude the possibility that it may still refer to the 'illness', fever. Perhaps the 'burning' in love spells (e.g. *DT* **270** = Grant, 241; *PGM* IV.2486ff.; XVI; LXVIII; CI. 1–53 = Wortmann, *Texte*) may have also been an attempt to inflict fever

---

[144] Versnel, 'Πεπρημένος', 148 (n.16, mistakenly as SGD **108**). Cf. SGD, 192f.

[145] Versnel, 'Curious Formula', 269.

[146] Versnel, 'Πεπρημένος', and 'Beyond Cursing', 73, 84f.

on a victim, on some principle of analogy as commonly utilised by sympathetic magic.[147]

The fear of fever-as-curse

An amulet on lead (*SuppMag* **2** (3rd c. AD)) probably illustrates the attempt to ward off fever as a curse. Since πράγματα may refer to magical actions (*PGM* IV.853, cf. 776; cf. *SuppMag* **54**.30f.), the amulet's request for protection ἀπὸ το <ῦ> πυρετοῦ καὶ παντὸς πραγμάτου [= πράγματος] suggests that the charm seeks protection against harmful spells directed towards the wearer, which, in this case, included fever.

Given that fever could be wielded as a curse, it is highly likely that many of the other amulets against fever, of which a large number have survived, were designed to give protection not only against the condition, but also (especially?) against the greater designs of people who may have enlisted the affliction as an instrument of their malevolent magic. Since everyone was afraid of being spellbound by curse tablets (Pliny *HN* 28.4.19), the onset of fever would have brought the additional fear that it might be the result of a curse from a rival in business or love, or an opponent at law, or another kind of enemy, perhaps even someone within the family.[148]

It is also clear that people feared the use of love charms against them. Ovid, for example, when he was unable to perform with a lover, asked:

> Has some Thessalian poison bewitched (*devota*)[149] my body, is it some spell or drug that has brought this misery upon me. Has some sorceress written (*defixit*) my name on crimson wax, and stuck a pin in my liver.   (cf. Ovid, *Amores* 3.7.27–30)[150]

Part of the fear was the belief that such charms could actually kill. A charm demonstrated to Hadrian (*PGM* IV.2441–621) 'evoked [one] in one hour, sickened and sent [one] to bed in two hours, killed [one] in seven' (ll. 2450–4). Another warns: 'Be sure to open the door for the woman who is being led by the spell, otherwise she will die' (*PGM* IV.2495ff.). Given the use of sleeplessness in these charms, *PGM* XII.376–96 may also be a love spell leading to death (cf. ll. 378, 396). The literary sources also illustrate the knowledge that love charms could kill (cf. Ovid *Ars. Am.* 2.

---

[147] For love's similarity to burning, see Meleager of Gadara (*fl.* 100 BC) in *AG* 5.160.

[148] Cf. the confession text from Asia Minor (AD 156/7), revealing that a mother-in-law was suspected of placing a curse on her son-in-law who had succumbed to a condition of 'insanity' (SEG 64.648; Gager **137**).

[149] *Devota* is a technical term used in relation to spells on curse tablets, as is *defixio*.

[150] Gager, 250, comments: 'The ease which Ovid considers this explanation suggests that the practice was well known at the time [i.e., 20 BC–AD 1].'

105–6; Plaut. *Truc.* 42–4).[151] If fever was one of the weapons wielded by these charms, then the onset of fever could indicate that someone was seeking to drag you to them for their own sexual pleasure, perhaps separating a person from spouse and family in the process, but certainly after inflicting all kinds of physical and mental anguish. Such fear would be all the worse if it was widely known that the 'fatal charm' of the *defigens* could be exactly that.

Fever as a counter-curse

If the fear of fever was not enough to turn a person to magical protection, the fear of fever produced by magic was sure to be. The counter-curse[152] secured by potential victims could itself wield fever as a weapon:

> [. . .] snatch away the health, the body, the complexion, the strength, the faculties of Plotius. [. . .] Hand him over to fevers – quartan, tertian and daily – so that they wrestle and struggle with him. Let them overcome him to the point where they snatch away his life.[153]

Although not all curse tablets actually sought to kill the victim,[154] this was clearly the intention here. After invoking fever upon Plotius 'to snatch away his life', the curse concludes:

> [. . .] so I hand over and consign Plotius to you, so that you may take care of him by the month of February. Let him perish miserably. Let him leave life miserably. Let him be destroyed miserably. Take care of him so that he may not see another month.
> (Fox = Gager **134** (mid 1st c. BC))

Fever's reputation as a killer was so firmly established that it could be enlisted to destroy an enemy. But the use of magical means to do so forges yet another link between fever and death.

Fever and the dead

Since the *daimones* manipulated by magic were the spirits of the dead, fever could be brought to the living by the dead. In the Semitic materials, fever was clearly associated with ghosts and the underworld.[155] One of the Greek curse tablets wishing fever upon the victim does so by calling upon

---

[151] See also Faraone, 'Sex'.

[152] See Gager, ch. 7 for some examples; cf. SGD, 197.   [153] Gager has 'soul'.

[154] It was rare in the early *defixiones*; Faraone, 'Agonistic Context', 8 n. 38. However, this would not always be the case, as in this instance. Cf. also SGD **163** (3rd c. AD) βάλεται (for -τε) αὐτὸν ἐπὶ κάκωσι<ν> καὶ θάν[ατον [. . .]

[155] For example, Thompson "C" ii.95ff. exorcises '[. . .] fever [. . .] evil Ghost'.

the dead (καταχθόνι[οι, *DT* **51**) to fulfil this wish. Other tablets which 'register' victims with the underworld gods (*DT* **74, 75**) may actually intend that these gods inflict the fever upon them through the release of a *daimon* from the underworld region.[156]

The closer the 'burning' in the love charms comes to being a real case of fever, the more clearly that fever is brought by the spirits of the dead. For the love charms patently use the spirits of the dead to bring about the distress in the 'intended'. Notice, for example, how *SuppMag* **54** calls upon 'the *daimones* who are in this place [i.e., the cemetery)' (l. 19: δαίμονες οἳ ἐν [τ]ούτω τῶ τόπω ἐστε), to constrain the victim; to 'hand [him] over by means of (or, 'to') the untimely dead' (l. 23: παράδοιτε ἀώροις), who were some of the most likely candidates to become ghosts. It is these '*daimones* who are roaming about in this place' (ll. 35f.: δ[αί|μον]ες οἱ ἐν τῶ τόπῶ τού [τω.] φοιτῶντες) who are called to complete the spell's transaction. From other charms it is clear that these *daimones* were to go to the victim's house, and draw her (usually) to the *defigens*. Although there is no reference to burning in this charm, its structure of operation and effects (ll. 22f.) are similar to other love charms, suggesting that fever could also be wielded by these *daimones* as one of the means to fulfil their task.

Even if all the connections are not made explicit in each individual charm, because the magical *modus operandi* was well known, so too would be the perception of fever as a force for death which could be wielded by the forces of the dead. Without doubt this connection with the dead would have increased the fear of fever. When fever entered a house, not only did it threaten to take the family to the underworld, but it might have been brought by the dead in an endeavour to swell the ranks of the shades below.

Raised from the dead?

During the Athenian plague, those who had recovered seemed to be immune from catching a fatal dose of the disease again. This experience apparently gave them a taste for immortality:

> They were not only congratulated (ἐμακαρίζοντο) by everybody else, but themselves, in the excess of their joy at the moment, cherished also a fond fancy with regard to the rest of their lives that they would never be carried off by any other disease.
>
> (Thuc. 2.51.6)

---

[156] This structure of operation is clear in other places, e.g., *SuppMag* **54**.

Noting the use of μακαρίζω, some have suggested that perhaps they were deemed to have risen from the dead and considered 'practically immortal'.[157] If so, 'fever' was such a killer that to be cured was on a par with rising from the dead!

The readers and the woman

For Mark's early readers, fever was no minor matter. Fevers were common, sudden, and extremely severe. Fear of fever drove people to a range of protective measures, perhaps especially to magic, for fever was a known killer and its reputation as a killer probably even exceeded the actual facts. A fever placed people under the shadow of death and their lives hung in the balance, especially if they had already taken to bed. Because fever could be caused by magical cursing, it would be suspected that a person with a fever had come under the influence of the spirits of the dead. To have a fever was to be so close to death that to be cured could even be regarded as having come back from the dead.

For early readers, Simon's mother-in-law would be at death's door. By the time they hear of her, she had already taken to her bed with fever (v.30a) which would raise the prognostic question: will she ever arise? Jesus had demonstrated his ability to deal with the spirits of the dead (1.21–28), who, in a magic-ridden world, might well lie behind a fever. The question had been raised whether Jesus had come to destroy such malignant spirits, and now he demonstrates his ability to cure death-dealing fever, which could well have been a consequence of their influence. He deals with this woman so effectively that she immediately begins to serve them. No longer under the shadow of death, she has rejoined ordinary life. Since the early readers would recognise that she has been brought back from the brink of death, Mark's description of Jesus' action – for those with eyes to see – may even contain a double entendre: 'he raised her'.

Jesus' fame expands (1.32–39)

The report of many more healings and exorcisms (vv.32–34) generalises what has occurred in the two scenes, so that the responses of Jesus to the possessed man in the synagogue and to Simon's mother-in-law become typical of his ministry to many.[158] Jesus' announcement that he will leave the crowds to preach elsewhere continues the narrative's sense

---

[157] Garland, *Greek Way*, 9, following Vermeule, *Aspects*.
[158] J.F. Williams, *Other Followers*, 95.

of movement towards a goal. This sense of a goal, and the reminder of the coming kingdom which is the theme of his preaching (cf. 1.15), tend to coalesce the readers' expectations. The expectation of the kingdom and the expectation of the goal of Jesus' journey are associated closely together.

Suppliant 3: a leper cleansed (1.40–45)

Text to reader

Since the disciples are entirely absent, the reader-oriented dynamics of the next scene arise solely from the interaction between Jesus and the leper. There is much to align the reader with both parties, although by virtue of the dynamics of the passage the readers are strongly aligned with the suppliant.

A leper's doubt (v.40)

The man who comes to him (v.40a), presumably during the Galilean tour, is characterised by reference to his being λεπρός. This description focalises the scene through him. The provision of his direct speech, supported by two participles (παρακαλῶν [. . .] λέγων), by 'showing' rather than 'telling', decreases the distance between him and the readers. The speech itself, expressing certainty about Jesus' ability, but some doubt about his willingness to cleanse him,[159] furthers the process of alignment by revealing the leper's inner doubts. Such 'inside views' are powerful reducers of distance, reducing to a distance of zero and thus powerfully aligning implied readers and characters.[160]

Having been aligned so strongly with the leper, the readers want to know, with him, whether Jesus is willing to cleanse him. This alignment enables the readers to see Jesus' actions and hear his declarations as if they themselves were the leper and to enter somewhat into the suppliant's feelings.[161]

---

[159] Despite the attempts to minimise his doubt (Taylor, *Mark*; Cranfield, *Mark*; Guelich, *Mark*; J.F. Williams, *Other Followers*, 96), the fact that Jesus assures him of his willingness is incomprehensible if there was no doubt present! It is a doubt about willingness, not ability. Hooker comments that it is hardly strange that he doubts Jesus' willingness, since this would involve Jesus coming near to him, a leper.

[160] For inside views, see Booth, *Fiction*, e.g., 5, 11–13, 17, 163–5, 245–9.

[161] J.F. Williams, *Other Followers*, 96–8, 103f., misses these dynamics and so denies any 'identification' of the reader with the leper.

Jesus' willingness (vv.41f.)

After drawing the readers into the leper's feelings, the story then reveals Jesus' feelings, the exact nature of which depends upon solving a textual difficulty. Despite σπλαγχνισθείς being the majority text, ὀργισθείς should be read.[162] It should be explained along with the participle ἐμβριμησάμενος (v.43) which continues the view into Jesus' emotions. The composition (ἐμ-) and usage[163] of this verb suggest a connotation of strength which is directed outwards, but forced inwards.

What sense can be made of Jesus' anger at this point in the story? It follows immediately after the leper's statement, and supplies the force behind Jesus' touch and expression of willingness. There is little to suggest anger at any infringement of the law, or the interruption of Jesus' preaching ministry; still less at some foreseen 'disobedience'.[164] A reaction to the foul disease or a connection with Jesus' assault on Satan are both possible, but they rely on assumptions that are not explicit in the text itself and difficult to prove from it. The most natural suggestion is that the deep emotion is aroused by the leper's doubts about Jesus' willingness; cf. the interpretation of Ephraem (4th c. AD), who wrote, 'Quia dixit: "Si vis", iratus est'[165]. Angry at the doubt, but in direct counterpoint to it, Jesus assures the leper of his willingness (θέλω), before issuing an imperative in regard to his cleansing (καθαρίσθητι).

The readers are placed in some tension by the supply of two very powerful inside views, drawing them towards the leper on the one hand (doubt), and Jesus on the other (anger). Jesus' reply evaluates the doubts, showing that they are groundless. Jesus' emotions are not evaluated, and they are emphasised through using two verbs expressing strong emotions (vv.41, 43). The dynamics of the relationships between narrator, readers and Jesus, coupled with the use of the powerful device of the inside view, makes the readers very reluctant to evaluate Jesus negatively.

The strong pull to both leper and Jesus creates a tension which seeks a resolution allowing for both emotions. The strong alignment with the

---

[162] *Pace* Metzger, *Textual Commentary*, with Turner, 'Textual Commentary'. It is the more difficult reading and the other variant is easily explained by scribal sensitivities to the attribution of a 'negative' emotion to Jesus.

[163] It is a fairly rare word (see Matt. 9.30, Mark 14.5 and John 11.33). There is but one occurrence prior to the NT in extra-biblical Greek materials (Aesch. *Theb.* 461), two in the LXX (Dan. 11.30; Lam. 2.6), and no examples in the non-literary material. Cf. the simple form in Lucian *Nec.* 20.

[164] So J.F. Williams, *Other Followers*, 97f.

[165] Cf. Turner, 'Textual Commentary', 157, '[. . .] perhaps because of his doubt of the will to heal'.

leper encourages the reader to adopt his situation, recognise his need and share in his doubt, and wonder about Jesus' willingness to cleanse. Since Jesus is shown to be angry at the doubt – in which the readers have been implicated –, the inside view of Jesus' emotions comes as a shock to the readers. His statement of willingness provides the negative evaluation of the doubt, but the strong emotion also adds a great deal of force against it. Because the readers have been aligned with the leper, the evaluation of the doubt is not from a distance, which would lead to the readers sitting in judgement over him, but from within, which leads them to also feel the need to correct the doubts by changing their picture of Jesus.[166] The strong emotion stresses the massive extent to which these doubts were wrong and this adds urgency to the need for change.

If this reading has cogency, then, perhaps strangely, the emotion that so often has been regarded negatively actually serves a positive narrative point. Jesus is offended at the leper's doubts: he is so willing to cleanse that the contrary suggestion arouses a 'righteous anger'. This leads directly to a touch, an expression of willingness, an imperative of cleansing, and an immediate result. The fulfilment of his command is narrated without much drama (v.42), affirming that Jesus' ability to cleanse was not the issue. At the same time his action has powerfully demonstrated that, whatever ability he may have had, he was certainly willing to use it.

Then, still 'holding in his emotion' (to paraphrase ἐμβριμησάμενος), even after the deed has been done, he threw the man out (v.43), telling him to hurry to the priests to get his proof of cleansing, not even stopping to tell anyone what has happened to him (v.44). The breathtaking flow of events, issuing from Jesus' strong emotional reaction to the man's request, underlines the point of the story: Jesus is willing – more than willing – to cleanse this man, and, duly certified, to get him back into his life anew.

Unofficial publicity (vv.43–45)

This also enables a better understanding of the leper's subsequent actions. After going out, the leper begins spreading abroad τὸν λόγον – presumably 'the matter', i.e., what had occurred. Although the leper does not follow Jesus' instructions, this is not evaluated negatively.[167] Jesus' 'command to silence' ought to be understood as an attempt to limit *when* he might tell others. Before speaking, he was to show himself to the priest

[166] See the similar explanation of the women's fear in Mark 16.8 offered by Boomershine and Bartholomew, 'Narrative Technique'.
[167] *Pace* the stress on his (and others') 'disobedience' in J.F. Williams, *Other Followers*, 98, 135.

in order to gain the necessary μαρτύριον for the people,[168] which, once given, would strengthen the proclamation of his cure. This suggests that the leper's eager proclamation (v.45) simply occurred *too early*. His actions are entirely consistent with positive narrative norms (1.27f., 32–34), and, in fact, it was the absence of such a response that seemed strange (1.31), not its presence. With nothing to encourage the readers' condemnation,[169] these previous textual norms and the readers' sympathetic alignment with the leper provide strong encouragement to share in his joyous reaction. The leper was so affected by Jesus' willingness to cleanse him that he was impelled to spread the news even before the appointed time, apparently causing great crowds to flock to Jesus even when he was hiding in the desert (v.45).

Impact

Williams, by effectively removing the leper's doubt and majoring upon his 'negative' characterisation of the leper (i.e., his supposed 'disobedience'), misses the factors strongly aligning leper and readers. He does identify two 'positive characterisations' (the leper's recognition of Jesus' authority and his confidence in Jesus' ability), but allows them insufficient strength to overcome the supposed negative characterisation. As a result of the positive characteristics, 'the reader is directed to recognize that this man and other suppliants like him are worthy of the compassion of Jesus and the sympathy of the reader'.[170] This is certainly true, but the statement sets the reader at some emotional remove from the suppliants: the reader is 'directed' to recognise, rather than simply 'recognising'; the leper is seen to be 'worthy' of 'compassion' and 'sympathy', rather than actually receiving compassion, and creating sympathy in the reader. In actual fact, the details of the paragraph strongly align the readers with the leper, leading them to sympathise with the leper, and so cause them to feel the compassion Jesus displays in this story.

Granted, the dynamics of the scene are complex. Several powerful devices decrease the distance between the readers and both parties and due

---

[168] αὐτοῖς is a dative of indirect object. 'The certificate obtained from the priest will serve as evidence to the people that the leper has been cured and is fit for readmission to society,' Trites, *Witness*, 70. Coupled with ἀλλά, as a contrast between the two commands, this indicates that Jesus wishes the man to have official confirmation of his cleansing before he starts talking. The 'command to silence' springs from an eagerness for him to gain this endorsement and return to normal life.

[169] This removes J.F. Williams' one item of 'negative' characterisation (e.g., *Other Followers*, 103).

[170] Ibid., 95f.

weight must be given to the complex effect of this interaction. The initial alignment with the leper and his doubt enables the readers to hear Jesus' statement of willingness from the sufferer's point of view. The strong expression of Jesus' emotion then adds great force to this willingness, which not only strengthens the willingness of Jesus (as described above), but also, by conveying Jesus' offence, offers a powerful critique of any doubts which pull in the opposite direction. By being aligned with the leper, the implied readers are aligned with his situation of need, but they then experience the powerful and confronting revelation of Jesus' willingness. This comes about, not through being forced to 'change shoes' and feel the emotions with him, but rather through a revelation that comes towards them in their (the leper's) situation of need. Any doubt they may have about Jesus' willingness is met with a powerful, overwhelming emotional expression to the contrary which immediately rules out such doubts in such a way as to intimidate the one who was foolish enough to entertain them.

After such an emotional engagement, the reader easily enters into the leper's actions subsequent to the healing. After doubt is removed by swift, concrete action, the resultant joy and the impossibility of keeping the tongue still even for a brief moment seem the most natural response in the world. Whether made official or not, this matter can only go public.

Reader to text

Leprosy and death

Leprosy

Although the precise diagnosis of λέπρα – clearly not Hansen's disease[171] – is difficult,[172] this does not inhibit understanding the condition as an *illness*. Unpleasant skin diseases would have affected quite a

---

[171] Cf. Lloyd Davies, 'Levitical Leprosy', 137; one of many articles seeking to prove this point. Hulse, 'Nature', provides a good discussion of the issues, as does Sandison, 'Skin', 449. Hooker, *Mark*, 78 intimates that Hansen's disease would, however, be included under the OT's Hebrew term. Hansen's disease was known as *elephantiasis* in the ancient world (cf. Celsus, *De med.* 3; Dsc. 2.70.3; Plut. *Quaest. conviv.* 8.9, 731A–B). For its known incidence, see Møller-Christensen, 'Evidence'. We should note, however, that λέπρα, as well as the later terms for leprosy, λώβη and κελεφία, can be found clustered together with ἐλεφαντίασις (e.g., *Cyran.* 1.4; 2.12).

[172] Patrick, 'Disease', 245. The Greek physicians applied the word λέπρα, not to tubercular conditions (i.e., those with nodes), but to scaly skin conditions. Leprosy in the Bible (λέπρα in both LXX and NT) probably consisted of a cluster of conditions such as simple vitiligo, eczema, psoriasis, alopecia, boils, myiasis and perhaps scabies.

substantial group of people. For example, one (admittedly high) estimate for a town, or tribe, of two thousand places 'about thirty unproductive members outside the camp'.[173] Λέπρα was a distressing illness,[174] probably consisting of a number of conditions, all producing a rough, scaly skin condition, which, whatever the personal discomfort entailed, clearly disfigured the skin so that the sufferer would stand out from the crowd and would engender disgust in others – cf. its categorisation amongst 'disfigurements rather than diseases' (ἀεικέα μᾶλλον ἢ νοσήματα, Hipp. *Aff.* 35; Theophrastus' Character 19, δυσχέρεια, 'Squalor' is described as 'Who goes around in a leprous and encrusted state, [. . .]' (οἷος λέπραν ἔχων καὶ ἀλφόν [. . .] περιπατεῖν)).[175] To capture both the information drawn from the various medical descriptions, as well as the consequent distress of the disease on the sufferer, Hulse suggests the translation, 'a repulsive scaly skin disease'.[176]

Leprosy and death

Unlike fever, λέπρα was not known as a killer[177] – although its listing amongst the diseases which are not fatal unless complications develop (Hipp. *Morb.1* 3) indicates that there was some risk of death. Illnesses presenting like λέπρα which resulted in death (Hipp. *Epid.* 5.9) would also associate the two in the popular perception.

Even if not fatal in itself, leprosy was suggestive of death. In the first place, it made the sufferer corpse-like (cf. καὶ νεκροῦ μηδὲν διαφέροντας, Joseph. *AJ* 3.258–64).[178] When the LXX has Aaron plead for Miriam μὴ γένηται ὡσεὶ ἴσον θανάτῳ (Num. 12.12), it is probably referring to her corpse-like appearance (cf. 'Do not let her be like a stillborn infant coming from its mother's womb with its flesh half eaten away'; NRSV, based on MT). Qumran's version of the Levitical regulations had the priest identifying cases of leprosy by noticing the amount of dead skin (e.g., 4Q272 [4QD^g] 1 I.1–20 = 4QD^b 9 I.1–12). Perhaps more importantly, leprosy was associated with death because in some nations, Israel included (cf. Lev. 13.45f.), it rendered the person unclean and liable to banishment from their community.

---

[173] Hulse, 'Nature', 100, based on the incidence of psoriasis.

[174] Emphasised by Hulse, ibid.; and Lloyd Davies, 'Levitical Leprosy'.

[175] Cf. the later term for λέπρα, or, at least for an associated condition, λώβη, which has connotations of being dishonoured, outraged, disgraced (Ps-Gal. 14.757). *Anon.Med.* 021 477 lists λώβη with αἰσχρὰ νοσήματα, 'shameful illnesses'.

[176] Hulse, 'Nature', 104.   [177] Just like leprosy proper, Pilch, 'Healing', 62.

[178] For a discussion of the link between the leper and the corpse in Judaism, see Maccoby, 'Corpse'.

Banishment

It appears to have been well known that certain 'barbarian' nations isolated λέπρα sufferers from mainstream society. Herodotus reported the practice amongst the Persians:

> The citizen who has leprosy or the white sickness (ὃς ἂν τῶν ἀστῶν λέπρην ἢ λεύκην ἔχῃ) may not come into a town or consort with other Persians. They say that he is so afflicted because he has sinned in some wise against the sun. Many drive every stranger, who takes such a disease, out of the country [. . .]
>
> (Hdt. 1.138)

But the most famous example, it seems, was the Egyptian banishment of the Jews. It was widely rumoured that the Jews originated from a group of lepers expelled from Egypt. In the 1st century BC, Diodorus Siculus (34/35.1–2), possibly drawing upon Posidonius, reported that when Antiochus VII Euergetes (who assumed the throne in 139/8 BC) besieged Jerusalem (cf. Joseph. *AJ* 13.236ff.) his friends had advised him to wipe out the Jews completely. They spoke of the ancestors of the Jews as

> having been exiled (πεφυγαδευμένους) from all Egypt as men who were impious and detested by the gods. For by way of purging the country all persons who had white or leprous marks on their bodies (τοὺς ἀλφοὺς ἢ λέπρας ἔχοντας ἐν τοῖς σώμασι) had been assembled and driven across the border, as being under a curse (ὡς ἐναγεῖς).

Pompeius Trogus, during the reign of Augustus (27 BC–AD 14), also recorded the story:

> The Egyptians, when they were suffering from scabies and skin-disease, on the advice of an oracle, to prevent further spreading of the plague expelled [Moses] along with the diseased from the frontiers of Egypt. So he became leader of the exiles [. . .]
>
> (Justinus, *Epitome* 1.10–2.16)

In the late first century, Josephus found it necessary to refute this rumour of Jewish origins at some length. His arguments surfaced in *Antiquities*, where he disputed in particular the view that Moses was a leper (*AJ* 3.265; cf. Exod. 4.6f.). Later, in *Contra Apion*, he disputed its various versions in Manetho (*fl.* 280 BC; *Ap.* 1.118–287), Chaeremon (1st c. AD; 1.288–92), Lysimachus (post 2nd c. BC; 1.312–20) and Apion (2.8–32), who was in

Rome under Tiberius and Claudius. Since Josephus found it necessary to dispute this opinion at the end of the century, and Tacitus (*Hist.* 5.3–5) repeated the rumour, apparently drawing upon Lysimachus, this ancient view of Jewish origins was evidently current and persistent in the first century – and beyond – and was perhaps particularly well known amongst the Romans.

Although Israel's (rather strange) laws were apparently widely known in general, especially those relating to dietary restrictions, circumcision and the Sabbath,[179] it is difficult to say just how widely known were their practices in regard to leprosy. Plutarch explains their well-known abstinence from pork[180] in terms of their abhorrence of leprosy:

> [. . .] because the barbarians above all people (μάλιστα πάντων) abhor the white disease on the skin and *lepra* (λεύκας καὶ λέπρας) and they think human beings are fed such sufferings by touch, and we observe on every pig *lepra* sailing up under the belly (ὑπὸ τὴν γαστέρα λέπρας ἀνάπλεων)[181] and scaly eruptions
> [. . .]   (*Quaest.conv.* 4.5, 670F)

Although μάλιστα πάντων indicates that other nations did not like these diseases either, evidently Greeks like Plutarch found such extremes of abhorrence rather odd. Elsewhere he reports that the Egyptians had a similar reason for regarding the pig as unclean (*De I et O.* 353F).[182] So, at least by Plutarch's day, it was possible to explain a Jewish/Egyptian dietary habit by reference to the fact that both were amongst 'the barbarians [who] above all people abhor the white disease on the skin and *lepra*'.

But although the Jews' abhorrence of λέπρα was known, as was the barbarian practice of excluding the leprous, no testimony apparently survives which clearly shows that the Jewish policy of banishing lepers was a matter of general knowledge. In fact, Josephus seems aware that his readers would regard the banishment practices as rather odd. In *Jewish War* he found it necessary to explain that lepers were not excluded just from the temple, but from the city altogether (5.226); and that they were excluded from the Passover sacrifice (6.426). The Jews' oddity in the ancient world

---

[179] Cf. the texts collected in Whittaker, *Jews*, pt 1.

[180] The question also bothered Caligula (Philo *Legat.* 361), Apion (Joseph. *Ap.* 2.13.137), and Epictetus (Arr. *Epict. Diss.* 1.22.4).

[181] Cf. the sought-after phylactery (for protection during use of its associated spell, *PGM* IV.3086–124) which specifies the use of a rib from a young pig, or 'from a black, scaly, castrated boar' (ἀπὸ συὸς μέλανος, λεπροῦ, ἐκτομιαίου); *PGM* IV.3115.

[182] Cf. Aelian. *NA* 10.16; Tac. *Hist.* 5.4.

is highlighted at this point by the fact that 'none of the many preserved sacred laws include the diseased among the polluted persons banned from entering a temple'.[183] In the *Antiquities*, as well as acknowledging how different Jewish practice was from other nations (*AJ* 3.265), Josephus had to explain why the four lepers lived at the gate (9.74; 2 Kings 7.3). The picture is a little ambiguous, however, for when he argued against the rumours regarding the Jews' leprous origins, he apparently assumed knowledge of Jewish leprosy laws. For, if Moses was himself a leper, he argued, then why would he create a law which excluded such people (*AJ* 3.265)?

Although the barbarians may have banished lepers, we have noted that Plutarch regarded the practice as part of a rather extreme abhorrence. Josephus knew that exactly the opposite scenario prevailed 'among many nations [where] there are lepers in the enjoyment of honours, who, far from undergoing contumely and exile, conduct the most brilliant careers, are entrusted with offices of state, and have the right of entry to sacred courts and temples' (*AJ* 3.265).[184] For sure, even the people of these 'sophisticated' nations would prefer to be free of the condition[185] and they were well aware that, if not λέπρα, then certainly associated diseases could be signs of the gods' displeasure.[186] But there was also an awareness that the threat of contracting the disease was minimal (Ps-Arist. *Prob.* 8, 887ª34) and the Greeks had long known of various remedies for it. With such knowledge available, it is not surprising that the barbarians' extreme abhorrence of the lepers' condition was regarded as odd. How much more strange would their banishment appear?

However, although odd, it was not completely without analogy. The sources already discussed show an awareness that λέπρα was associated with some kind of impurity and similar skin diseases were also regarded in this way by some in the Graeco-Roman world. The 'unclean' had the taint of death,[187] in which case banishment would be justified.

Exile itself became associated with impurity. In Homer the involuntary and even the 'justified' killer could be permanently exiled due to threat of revenge by the dead person's kin (*Il.* 23.85–8; *Od.* 22.27–32). In Attic law, such exile was associated with impurity; for the 'involuntary killer' incurred exile and could not return until he had been purified (Dem. 23.72).

---

[183] Parker, *Miasma*, 219. In fact, the diseased came to the temples in search of cure.

[184] According to Avalos, *Health Care*, 28, lepers were allowed into the temples of Asclepius, although he cites no evidence.

[185] Cf. Ar. *Av.* 151f. with Paus. 5.5.4–5

[186] For example, ἀλφός (Hesiod fr. 133 = *P.Oxy* 2488A), although the LXX distinguished λέπρα and ἀλφός (cf. Lev. 13.39). Cf. [Plut.] *Fluv.* 21.4.

[187] Parker, *Miasma*, 218.

In fact, exile itself was commonly regarded as a means of purification (Aesch. *Ag.*. 1419f, *Cho.* 1038, Eur. *Hipp.* 35, Pl. *Leg.* 865D–E; cf. Nic. *Dam.* 90 *FGrH* fr. 45).[188] Orestes, son of Agamemnon, was a famous exile (e.g. Aesch. *Cho.* 1ff., 115, 136, 181f., 332ff., 940, 1038; Soph. *El.* 601, 773ff., 1132ff.; Eur. *El.* 233, 236, 352, 587, 834), who, according to one version, was exiled due to the threat of 'leprous ulcers' at the hands of the *alastores* (Aesch. *Cho.* 278–96). Although it is impossible to say how widely this version circulated, wherever it was known it would have provided a further reference point for understanding the notions of a skin disease being a curse from the underworld, and entailing the 'death' of exile.

Several writers of the imperial period attempted to appraise exile philosophically, in order to console those enduring it. Since their endeavours 'protest too much', they speak eloquently of the terrors which exile evoked and of the need for the consolation they sought to offer. They realised that their approach was vastly different from that of the majority (Dio Chrys. *Or.* 13.2; Plut. *De exilio* 599F, 605F) for whom clearly exile was regarded as one of life's great calamities. *P.Berol.* 21198[189] (2nd/3rd c. AD), which predicts that someone 'will wander from place to place [. . .]', may endorse this picture gleaned from the literary sources, for it considers being separated from home an evil.[190] In the biblical tradition, the fear of this 'evil' is as old as the story of Cain (Gen. 4.12–16; cf. 1 Cor. 4.11 ἀστατέω).

Given these views of exile, it is not without significance that the story of the Israelite lepers being cast out of Egypt describes them as 'exiles' (Justinus, *Epitome* 1.10–2.16; Diod. 34.1–3; Tac. *Hist.* 5.1–13). No doubt in imitation of this tendency, when Josephus refers to the Israelite practice of banishing lepers, he also uses the language of exile (*AJ* 3.265).

So, whether or not the Graeco-Roman endorsed, or understood, the practice of banishing lepers, it was analogous to the well-known practice of exile. It would therefore not be difficult for them to realise that 'the biggest fear deriving from this kind of a situation is that the afflicted person may never be able to return to the community'.[191] For banishment was exclusion from the community, and so from life itself, with the terrible prospect of dying on foreign soil. In a very real sense, to be banished as a leper was to live under the sentence of death.

Although the philosophical writers tried to soften the blow of exile by recommending a change in nomenclature, so that exile was simply 'a change of place' (Sen. *ad Helv.* 6.1), the general populace was of a

---

[188] Further discussion in ibid., 114–18, 375–92.   [189] Brashear, 'New Texts', 2.
[190] Ibid., 213.   [191] Pilch, 'Healing', 63.

different opinion. For some it was a fate worse than death: 'I would rather be killed today than banished tomorrow' (cf. Arr. *Epict.Diss.* 1.1.26–7; Tac. *Hist.* 5.13), while others agreed with Polyneices, who, when asked whether exile is κακὸν μέγα 'a sore evil', replied μέγιστον· ἔργῳ δ'ἐστὶ μεῖζον ἢ λόγῳ, 'The sorest: In deed sorer than in word' (Eur. *Phoen.* 389).

Exile was not simply a problem for the upper classes, but was a fearful prospect for the nameless mass of people who, if defeated, could be sure of being taken away into slavery. Their exile, of course, was of far greater consequence than an enforced retirement to some island! Tacitus, for example, observed that both men and women were prepared to fight during the siege of Jerusalem, because 'should they be forced to change their homes they feared life more than death' (Tac. *Hist.* 5.13).

By the time of Epictetus, exile often appears in lists of misfortunes, alongside death (Arr. *Diss.Epict.* 1.4.24; 1.11.33; 1.29.6; 3.22.21; 3.24.29; 4.1.60; 4.1.172; fr. 21 = Stob. 3.7.16; 3.3.17; *Ench.* 32.3). He used these two potential disasters to bring life into proper focus: 'Keep before your eyes day by day death and exile, and everything that seems terrible, but most of all death; and then you will never have any abject thought, nor will you yearn for anything beyond measure' (Arr. *Ench.* 21).

So closely were they related that exile could be pictured as death. So, when Seneca sought to console his mother after his own exile he pictured himself as 'a man who was lifting his head from the bier to comfort his dear ones' (Sen. *ad Helv.* 1.3). He sympathised with his mother for, after burying so many others, she must now mourn the living (2.5), and consoled her with a sustained analogy between her, whose son was exiled, and that of other women whose sons had died (15–16).

Thus, even if leprosy itself was not explicitly connected with death, because it was known that barbarian nations banished the leper, and because banishment was feared as a living death, the Graeco-Roman reader would recognise that the banished leper is one of the living dead.[192]

Leprosy and the dead

Although it is conceivable that λέπρα was one of the skin diseases that could be inflicted through the workings of magic, i.e., through the influence of the dead, this is difficult to prove. Although λέπρα does appear

---

[192] This ancient belief is echoed in Shakespeare's *Romeo and Juliet*, when Romeo cries: 'Ha!, banishment! Be merciful, say "death"; For exile hath more terror in his look, Much more than death'; and again, '"banished" Is death mis-term'd; calling death "banished", Thou cut'st my head off with a golden axe, And smilest upon the stroke that murders me' (Act III scene iii).

in some broadly magical texts,[193] it is more difficult to prove a direct link between the dead and the disease by that name.

The Semitic magical material includes curses inflicting skin diseases. At least two Babylonian incantations seek to ward off a long list of skin diseases (Farber **4.1** and **4.5**[194]), which, through their allusion to the cooling waters of the 'daughters of Anu',[195] have invited comparison with the story of Naaman washing away his leprosy (2 Kgs 5).[196] A Mesopotamian incantation refers to what seems to be a skin disease inflicted by a ghost when it says, ' "They" consume all my flesh for me. [. . .] A ghost was set on me so as to consume me' (Scurlock **Prescr 63**).[197]

It may also be of relevance that the Persians believed a person to be afflicted with leprosy because 'he has sinned in some wise against the sun' (Hdt. 1.138). The leprous Jews were also said to have sinned against the sun, according to Lysimachus' version of the rumour (Joseph. *Ap.* 1.34.304–11). Helios was addressed in many magical spells as the god who releases the *daimones* from the underworld in order to bring about the magician's purposes. Although admittedly speculative, when read against Helios' role in magic, if λέπρα was a sin against the sun, could this illness also indicate that it had come about through daemonic activity?

Although I have not found λέπρα in the Greek magical curses or protective charms, there is the occasional reference to skin conditions. *SuppMag* **88**.1–5, a *logos* designed to combat the febrile skin disease erysipelas, is similar at a number of points to the Philinna papyrus (*PGM* XX (1st c. BC)),[198] whose rubric prescribes the spell πρòς πᾶν κατάκαυμ[α, which is 'an expression that can refer to a fever or a reddish, burning eruption or rash on the skin, such as shingles'.[199] In a curse (*IG* XII.9, **1179** = Lattimore, 116–17, Gager **86** (2nd c. AD)) protecting some baths, a Gentile who 'had learned from his contacts with Judaism [. . .] that the text of the Bible could be used as a source book for potent curses'[200] added some Deuteronomic curses to his model (cf. *IG* XII.9, **955**), including 'itch' (cf. Deut. 28.22, 28)[201] (cf. the bowl text including itch, *AMB* **9** = Gager **109**). A Latin curse threatens the *color*, 'colour, pigment of skin'

---

[193] The *Cyranides* (*ante* 1st/2nd c. AD) has several medico-magical remedies for λέπρα, but none with an association with ghosts (1.1; 1.2; 1.6; 2.12; 2.26; 2.36; 2.44; 3.37; 3.46; 4.14; 4.17; 4.68). The Egyptian medico-magical papyri describe an eruptive skin condition using a word (sbh) which is related to the Coptic word used to translate the biblical λέπρα; Møller-Christensen, 'Evidence', 304.

[194] See Farber, 299.

[195] These obscure women function 'as a sort of divine fire brigade' against eye troubles, skin diseases and inflammations; ibid., 302.

[196] Faraone, 'Mystodokos', 308 n. 32, on *PGM* XX.   [197] Cf. Scurlock, 91 n. 445.

[198] Cf. Faraone, 'Mystodokos', 297 n. 2.   [199] Ibid., 298 n. 4.   [200] Gager, 185.

[201] Jewish grave inscriptions also invoke Deuteronomic curses; cf. Gager **91**.

(*DT* **190**.5), which, if successful, would result in a condition close to skin diseases such as λέπρα, λεύκη and ἀλφός which made the skin turn white.

Although it is difficult to prove or disprove, perhaps curses against people's 'flesh' (σάρξ) were aiming to produce skin problems (*DT* **38**.23; **41** a.20; **155** b.14, 25; SGD **131**),[202] since the white skin disease threatened against Orestes at the hands of the Erinyes certainly ate the flesh away (Aesch. *Cho.* 278–96). However, I am inclined to understand σάρξ in the curses as being against what we would term muscle, i.e., the flesh between skin and bone (see discussion on Suppliant 4, below). Closer, perhaps, is the Latin tablet which curses a person's 'complexion' (Fox = Gager **134**).

So, although the pickings are sparse, it seems that skin diseases could certainly be part of magical curses, and 'leprosy' could well have been one of the options. If this was so, then the leper would represent a person who had potentially been afflicted by the forces of death. The ghosts of the dead could whiten and shrivel the skin so that it looked like a corpse; they could make the leper one of the living dead.

Jesus and the leper

When Jesus cleansed this man, his body went from being corpse-like, to being like that of any other person, and he was able at last to go home. Jesus sent him quickly to the priests for official confirmation, eager to get him back to life amongst the living. He had brought him from death to life.[203]

As part of a general increase in disease at this time, no doubt due to increasingly overcrowded cities,[204] the Western Roman world in the first century was experiencing an increase in disfiguring skin diseases. According to Pliny (*HN* 26.1–3), these new skin problems, 'so disfiguring that any kind of death would be preferable' (26.1), apparently began in the middle of the principate of Tiberius (26.3), and caused many physicians to come to Rome from Egypt (the 'parent of such diseases'), where they made their fortunes specialising in the treatment of this new plague.[205]

---

[202] Cf. Scurlock, *LKA* **84**.14, 17, cf. 20 = **Prescr 63**.

[203] Cf. the Rabbinic view that, because the leper was like a corpse (*AJ* 3.258–64), cure was akin to raising the dead (*LevRab* 16, interpreting Isa. 57.19; cf. *bSanh.* 47a). Leprosy was regarded as a punishment for sin, especially for slander; Garland, ' "I am the Lord" ', 337, referring to *b.Arak.* 15b, 16a and *bSanh.* 74a.

[204] Avalos, *Health Care*, 4–5.

[205] This is apparently despite the Romans being quite skilled in dermatology, as evidenced by the fact that Celsus wrote several chapters on skin diseases (*De med.* bks 3, 5, 6, 7). For a list of those that can be identified, see Patrick, 'Disease', 244, drawing upon Wilson, 'Dermopathology, 446, 465.

Despite the imperial rhetoric proclaiming Caesar to be 'Saviour', the source of life for all, what could he do about the ravages of such diseases? Mark's Gospel presents the story of a man doing some amazing things at exactly the same time as the Romans were labouring under this new plague. Mark shows how, on one occasion, Jesus dealt with a skin disease that caused its victims to join the living dead. Jesus didn't just get rid of the problem by banishing the victim with disease intact. On the contrary, he touched this exile and then sent him home. He brought the living dead back to life again.

Suppliant 4: a paralytic raised (2.1–12)

Text to reader: a paralytic raised

Jesus' return to Capernaum recalls the events which previously occurred there (v.1, πάλιν), raising the expectation that something similar might happen. The people of the town heard that he was 'in the house', presumably that of Simon and Andrew, and, once again, a huge crowd gathered in the house (v.2, cf. 1.32–34).

Once again, the disciples are absent, and the readers are focalised through a suppliant, this time a man in need and his friends.[206] Initially, the scene is focalised through the group carrying the paralytic (v.3). The readers are privileged to share in the sense of frustration at not being able to get through the crowd which motivates their digging through the roof (v.4). By slowing the tempo, the vivid detail focuses the readers upon this roof scene, further aligning them with this group and their cause. The readers feel the impediment posed by the crowd and the delight in finding a way around the problem. This produces a keen anticipation of the paralytic's ultimate arrival at the goal and his cure as Jesus deals with his problem. As the man is lowered through the roof, it is almost as if the readers travel with him.

Fowler comments that when Mark reports Jesus 'seeing' their faith (cf. ἰδών, v.5), he is using 'a figure of speech for [a] shrewd inference that is based upon observed behaviour'.[207] Even though Fowler still classifies this as an 'inside view of perception', if this is simply the narrator's figure of speech, then this should not, strictly speaking, be regarded as an inside view at all. Instead, ἰδών functions here in such a way as to leave the reader still in the category of observer. This means that it does not disalign the readers from the paralytic and his party, who hear Jesus' direct speech as

---

[206] J.F. Williams, *Other Followers*, 99f., 101.   [207] Fowler, *Let the Reader*, 121.

if they were the man. Since the scene has already created the expectation that Jesus will cure the man, his statement about forgiveness arrives with as much shock value to the readers as for the characters.

The scribes then appear in person for the first time in the narrative (v.6; cf. 1.22), and the narrator supplies an inside view of their reaction to Jesus' pronouncement. The narrative has already erected an opposition between Jesus' authority and theirs (1.22; cf. v.27), and now their internal questioning[208] revolves around exactly this question. The inside view aligns the readers with these men, especially since initially they voice the readers' question as well. After expecting Jesus to deal with the paralytic's physical problem and hearing instead an announcement about forgiveness, it seems perfectly appropriate to ask 'why is this man speaking in this way?' The scribes take it further, revealing that they consider Jesus to be blaspheming, for 'who is able to forgive sins, except one person, God?' Their rhetorical question provides the readers with one potential evaluation of Jesus' surprising statement. Since the authority of these men has been pitched against that of Jesus, their opinion may be suspect, but certainly their question joins that of the readers. Jesus' pronouncement and the scribal questions have opened gaps in the discourse which now await answers.

Next, the readers are supplied with 'an inside view into Jesus having an inside view'[209] – as Jesus immediately perceives by his spirit that the scribes were reasoning this way (v.8). Because the readers have also been 'in' their mind, pondering the questions they ponder, Jesus' inside view represents him knowing the readers' question as well! His question exposes opponent and reader at one and the same time: 'Why are you discussing these things in your hearts?' His ability to do so enhances his authority over that of the scribes.

After bringing everybody's question out into the open, he counters with one of his own (v.9). The question whether it was easier to forgive the man, or to raise him (ἐγείρειν) and send him home forces the realisation that both are equally hard, and probably imply the same thing: for God is both the one who forgives sins, and the one who heals. The purpose clause provides the explanation of the demonstration before it occurs,[210] and of Jesus' authority which has been on the agenda since the beginning of Mark's first major section. The authority which was demonstrated (1.16–20) and then recognised (1.21–28) is now explained as the authority

---

[208] For internal speech, see ibid., 125.   [209] Ibid., 75, cf. 123.
[210] This reads naturally as Jesus' speech, rather than the narrator's; *pace* Fowler, ibid., 102f., 131.

of the Son of Man (Dan. 7.13–14) and, with Isaiah, as having the purpose
of bringing the forgiveness for which the land (γῆ here referring to the
land of Israel)[211] has been waiting (cf. 1.4–5). The Servant who brings
forgiveness acts with the authority of the Son of Man, the one to whom
the kingdom of God will be given.[212]

Jesus does not say what he will do to demonstrate this authority, he
simply does it. He instructs the paralytic to rise, take up his mat and go
home (v.11), which he does (v.12a). By a flowback effect, this forces the
readers to answer the previous questions: if Jesus can do this, then he is
the Son of Man with authority to forgive sins on the land (v.10), and if he
can forgive sins, then what does this say about his relationship to God,
the only one who can forgive sins and heal? The scene ends with utter
amazement and a chorus of praise (cf. 1.27). Being so closely aligned
with the paralytic's cause, the readers are moved to join in the chorus.

Although the story does reveal the increasing conflict with Jesus' opponents, it primarily deals with another case of Jesus providing real help
to a person in need. The assertion that the 'portrayal of minor characters
in this section [i.e., 2.1–3.6] is subservient to his narration of the growing antagonism of the religious authorities against Jesus'[213] makes the
functionalist mistake of subordinating all to the plot and misunderstands
the important role the suppliants play in creating the total impact of the
narrative. This impact comes through the narrator's providing enough
characterisation to ensure that the reader is sufficiently aligned with the
suppliants' situation, in order to appreciate Jesus' impact upon it.

Reader to text

Paralysis

A paralytic

The adjective παραλυτικός makes its first literary appearance in the first
century (Dsc. 1.16 (*c.* AD 50); Mark 2.1–12, par. Matt. 9.2–8;[214] Matt.

---

[211] Since this is not the usual translation of this phrase, some further justification is
warranted. The word γῆ can be used to refer to the ground (Mark 4.26), a land in the
geographical sense, or the whole earth. The word was also used as a shorthand for the land
of promise, i.e., the land of Israel (cf. Acts 7.3 with Gen. 12.1; Heb. 11.9; Matt. 5.5 with
Ps. 37.11; Isa. 60.21). The translation decision in each individual instance is made upon
contextual grounds, as usual. My translation of Mark 2.10 arises from the consideration
of the biblical-theological context of the promises of forgiveness such as those already
canvassed (e.g., Zech. 13.1–2), and of the Marcan context in which it is the people of Israel
who are expecting the arrival of forgiveness (Mark 1.4–5 with Isa. 40.1, 9).

[212] See further, Bolt, 'Forgiveness'.   [213] J.F. Williams, *Other Followers*, 98.

[214] Luke 5.18, 24 has the participle παραλελυμένος. Cf. Acts 8.7, 9.33; Heb. 12.12.

4.24 and 8.6),[215] and, in the same period, finds its only documentary attestation in a fragmentary medical text referring to those suffering from epilepsy and paralysis: παθών οἷον ἐπιληπτικ[ῶν] | [- - - παρ]αλυτικῶν καὶ τῶν περὶ τὰ | [- - -] (Carlini 32;[216] cf. *NewDocs* III, **55**. 16–17). From what was this man suffering?

The conclusion of the scene suggests that the man had problems with his legs (vv.9b–12). This agrees with Galen's view of παράλυσις which was partial, in contrast to ἀποπληξία in which 'all the nerves together have been destroyed, both sensation and movement' (Gal. VIII.208; cf. Aret. *De causis* 1.6.11). However, this definition of παράλυσις is perhaps a little too 'modern', as is its counterpart in LSJ: 'the disabling of nerves'.

A condition of the nerves?

Although the two aspects of (nervous) paralysis – loss of sensation and of movement – had been recognised before him (e.g. Thphr. *De nerv. res.* 11.1 (4th–3rd c. BC)), the anatomical studies of Erasistratus of Ceos, who lived in Alexandria (3rd c. BC), led to the clear distinction of motor and sensory nerves. Following his lead (Galen VI.602), τὰ νεῦρα eventually provided the linguistic basis for our 'neurones'/nerves. Paralysis was recognised as the loss of sensation and strength by Rufus of Ephesus (αἴσθησιν καὶ ἰσχύν, cf. *De sat. et gon.* 47), physician under Trajan (98–117 AD), who had probably studied in Alexandria,[217] and certainly by Galen's time (Galen VIII.208) when Erasistratus' school flourished. In what was probably his most remarkable achievement, Galen himself conducted experiments showing the differing types of paralysis resulting from sectioning different levels of the spinal cord. His findings, however, were not developed and were not adequately appreciated until the nineteenth century.[218]

A condition of the sinews

However, before these ideas prevailed, τὰ νεῦρα were the sinews/tendons and παράλυσις was a descriptive term for what occurs when various parts of the body are 'loosened from the side, detached' (cf. παραλύω). The difference between the 'more recent' and the more ancient understandings can be demonstrated from two conditions mentioned in Greek only by Strabo (64/3BC–AD 21+). He explains στομακάκκη and σκελοτύρβη,

---

[215] Cf. Rufus of Ephesus (1st/2nd c. AD), *ap.*Orib.8.39.
[216] Could the text continue with a reference to νεῦρα (cf. Dsc. 3.78)?
[217] Edelstein, 'Rufus (4)', 938.   [218] Singer and Wasserstein, 'Anatomy', 60.

as being παράλυσις concerning the mouth and concerning the legs, respectively (16.4.24), but when Pliny describes them it is clear that they have nothing to do with (our) nerves, for they refer to a condition in which the teeth fall out and the use of the knee-joints fails (*HN* 25.20; cf. Heb. 12.12). In the first century, a variety of conditions could still be listed together with paralysis – including epilepsy[219] – because they were considered to be πάθη περὶ τὰ νεῦρα, 'afflictions concerning the sinews' (Dsc. 3.78; cf. ? Carlini **32**[220]).

Paralysis and death

Chronic or acute?

Although impossible to prove either way, the man's condition might not have been chronic, for paralysis could also occur in acute conditions (cf. Matt. 8.6). Generally speaking, it was the acute illnesses that caused the most deaths (Hipp. *Aff.* 13), which means that the more acute his case, the more his life was on the line. On the other hand, the more chronic, the closer he was to the 'living death' category.

Death from paralysis

Paralysis has a verbal link with death, in that παραλύω was used for 'releasing from life' (παραλύσαι ψυχάν, Eur. *Alc.* 118; παραλύσας ἑαυτὸν τοῦ ζῆν, Strabo 8.6.14, cf. Plut. *Ant.* 82). But the connection was more than verbal, for people actually 'died of paralysis', such as the Epicurean, Polyaenus (ἐτελεύτα δὲ παραλύσει; D.L. 10.25). One cause of life-threatening paralysis was drinking unmixed wine (Diod. 4.3.4–5), as in the case of Lacydes, whose 'death was a paralysis brought on by drinking too freely' (ἡ τελευτὴ δὲ αὐτῷ παράλυσις ἐκ πολυποσίας; D.L. 4.61; cf. *AG* 7.105 and 104).

Death invading the body

In a case of paralysis, death was already encroaching upon the person's body, even while alive. Hippocrates apparently regarded a paralysed leg as if it were that of a corpse (ὡς νεκρῶδες, Aret. *De causis* 1.7.2).[221] When Speusippus sent for Xenocrates to take over his school, 'already by paralysis even his body was corrupted' (ἤδη δὲ ὑπὸ παραλύσεως καὶ τὸ σῶμα διέφθαρτο, D.L. 4.3.3). The 'corruption' of death had already invaded his body.

---

[219] Dsc. 1.6, cf. Eup. 1.226; Dsc. 4.183; Carlini **32**; cf. Matt. 4.24.
[220] See n. 216.   [221] The saying is not in the Hippocratic corpus.

The sinews and 'the bonds of the soul'

This 'corrupting' process can be explained in terms of beliefs regarding the anatomical/physiological role of the sinews. Paralysis, i.e., the loosening of the sinews, placed the sufferer firmly on the path towards death, for death itself entailed such a loosening. For example, Odysseus' mother's shade instructed him that all people were like her when dead:

> For the sinews [here: ἶνες] no longer hold the flesh and the bones together, but the strong might of blazing fire destroys these, as soon as the life leaves the white bones, and the spirit, like a dream, flits away, and hovers to and fro.
>
> (*Od.* 11.218ff.; cf. *Il.* 23.97ff.)

This idea was echoed in Plato's cosmogony, where the 'loosening' of the soul from within the marrow took place in old age 'when the bonds of the triangles in the marrow[. . .] let slip in turn the bonds of the soul, and it, when thus naturally set loose, flies out gladly' (*Ti.* 81D). Although this refers to the natural decline of the body in the course of old age, the same occurs in death from disease, although, being against nature, in this case the release is painful and violent (*Ti.* 81E).

The relationship between a condition afflicting the sinews and death is illuminated by Plato's explanation of the construction of the body and the process of disease. When the demiurges constructed man,[222] they began with the soul and worked outwards (*Ti.* 69D). The four elements (earth, fire, water and air) were moulded into marrow, which acted as 'the bonds of the soul' (73B–C).[223] The immortal soul was placed in the portion of the marrow of the brain and the mortal soul in the marrow of the vertebral column and its offshoots (73D). For protection, this was encased with bone which was made from earth and marrow, dipped in fire and water so that neither could destroy it. The sinews and flesh were added to bind all limbs together and to protect the bone from heat and cold respectively (74B–C), and finally the skin (76A).

On such an understanding of the body, rooted in the older view that the soul is in the bones (cf. Hom. *Od.* 11.218ff.), the sinews are closely linked to the bodily components so essential to life. Thus, disease in the sinews is very serious. Since the body is compacted out of the four elements, one class of diseases arises from various imbalances amongst these. The sinews have a prominent place in a second class of diseases, in which a

---

[222] The creation of woman would occur later (cf. *Ti.* 76D).

[223] Cf. Pythagoras' statement (D.L. 8.31) that 'the veins, arteries, and sinews are the bonds of the soul' (δεσμά τ᾽ εἶναι τῆς ψυχῆς τᾶς φλέβας καὶ τὰς ἀρτηρίας καὶ τὰ νεῦρα).

reverse of the normal nutrition process occurs. In the order of nature, flesh and sinews arise from blood and produce a substance which nourishes the bone, and, in turn, the marrow (82D).[224] The severest diseases with the most dangerous results (82C) come from a reversal of this direction (82E). The decomposition of the flesh places products of corruption in the blood which unite 'with the air' (μετὰ πνεύματος), again in the blood, which leads to bile and phlegm. This destroys the blood, the nourishment, and, eventually, the body itself (83A).

When the flesh is being decomposed, if its bases remain firm, the force of the attack is halved (83E). But it is very severe 'whenever the substance which binds the flesh to the bones [cf. 82D] becomes diseased and no longer separates itself at once from them and from the sinews, so as to provide food for the bone and to serve as a bond between flesh and bone' (84A–B). Even more severe are the diseases of the bone, and the severest is when the marrow itself becomes diseased, 'for this results in the gravest of diseases and the most potent in causing death, inasmuch as the whole substance of the body [. . .] streams in the reverse direction' (84C).[225]

Such an understanding of anatomy, in which the sinews have a position just short of the marrow, the location of the soul; and of physiology, in which the sinews have a role in nurturing the marrow, the 'bonds of the soul'; and of pathology, in which a condition affecting the sinews, such as paralysis, is at the extreme end of the scale, provides a rationale for why such conditions could kill and why they were regarded as the presence of death's corruption even while a person was alive. The 'loosening of the sinews' (= paralysis) was but a short step from the loosening of the soul from the bonds which held it trapped inside the body.

While the various schools of Greek medicine agreed that disease was caused by an imbalance in the mixture of bodily constituents, they differed on what those constituents were.[226] Alcmaeon (*c*. 500 BC)[227] had dealt with opposite powers (δυνάμεις), amongst which the pairs hot/cold and moist/dry gained special prominence. The Coan school replaced the powers, which were considered philosophical intrusions (cf. Hipp. *VM* 1), with humours (χωμοί), which were said to be the actual bodily constituents which possessed the powers. Plato's theories were based upon an Empedoclean foundation in the four elements, rather than the four

[224] Cf. Pythagoras' view, D.L. 8.30.

[225] Cf. the murder of the doctor in Apul. *Met.* 10.26: 'meanwhile the [poison] raging through his intestines had been deeply absorbed into his marrow', and so he dies.

[226] This paragraph draws on Cornford, *Plato's Cosmology*, 332ff.

[227] Owen, 'Alcmaeon (2)', 38.

humours, which play a secondary role (*Ti.* 82B–83). His discussion of the diseases of the secondary tissues, bone, sinew, flesh and blood, is also reminiscent of Empedocles' notion that these tissues contain the four basic elements in differing proportions (cf. *Ti.* 73Bff.).

His view that disease is caused by the reversal of the normal process of nutrition from the marrow outwards, however, appears to differ from that of his predecessors.[228] So how influential would these views have been? Although it is beyond the scope of this study to answer this question fully, suffice it to say that the influence may have been considerable. The resurgence of interest in Plato's ideas, which commenced at the end of the 2nd century BC, was well under way by the beginning of the 1st century AD, and stretched on into the middle Platonists like Plutarch.[229] The *Timaeus* had an important part in this resurgence, playing a 'disproportionately great role [. . .] in supplying the fundamental doctrines of Middle Platonism',[230] and becoming Plato's 'most celebrated work', in fact, the 'Platonists' Bible'. The *Timaeus*, however, was not just for the philosophers, but 'its influence inevitably filtered down to men of letters and even those who had received only a smattering of learning'. As the most influential work of a philosophical nature in late antiquity, the *Timaeus* underwent 'intensive philosophical study and widespread cultural dissemination'.[231]

Although its anatomical, physiological and pathological views were not its main attraction, the success of the *Timaeus* ensured that they remained on the agenda and that they exerted considerable influence.[232]

Paralysis and the dead

Paralysis as curse

An Athenian curse from the mid-3rd century AD, actually using the language of paralysis (παραλελυμμένη; cf. Luke 5.18, 24; Acts 8.7; 9.33; Heb. 12.12), asks Mighty Typhon[233] to harm τὴν ἰσχύν, τὴν [δύνα]|μιν, τοὺς τόνους, τὰ νεῦρα, τὴν ψυχήν, τὴν [- - - τ]ὰ μέλη πάν[τα . . .

---

[228] Cornford, *Plato's Cosmology*, 336.

[229] Runia, *Philo*, 38–57, assesses the influence of Plato and of the *Timaeus* in particular, in the period up to Philo.

[230] Ibid., 49.   [231] Ibid., 57.

[232] 'The physiology of Plato's *Timaeus* proved a rich source of theory throughout the rest of antiquity', Vallance, 'Medicine', 948. Various ideas which enjoyed lasting influence, such as the idea of the body as the 'fetters of the soul' (e.g., Sen. ad *Helv.* 11.7), presumably also connoted the related anatomical/physiological ideas.

[233] For this underworld figure, see van Henten, 'Typhon', 1657–62.

('strength, power, tendons, sinews, soul,[234] - - -, all members') of one,
Tyche. After instructing him to 'Bind, twist - - - the strength, the capacity,
- - -, the joints, make her lungs disappear' the tablet follows the common
practice of comparing the names written on the lead with the desired
result for the victim:

> As I have written down these names and they grow cold
> (καταψύχεται), so, too, let the body and the flesh and the sinews
> and the bones ([αἱ σ]άρκες καὶ τὰ νεῦρα καὶ τὰ ὀστᾶ) and the
> members and the bowels of Tyche, whom Sophia bore, grow
> cold, that she may no longer rise up, walk around, talk, move
> about, but let her remain a corpse (μέ|νη νεκρά) pale, weak, paral-
> ysed, chilled until I am taken out of the dark air, rather let her
> grow exhausted and weak until she dies.   (AthAg **App**)

This curse illustrates not only the nature of paralysis, but that it was
regarded as a preliminary stage towards death, for the *defigens* wishes
that 'she may no longer rise up [. . .] but remain a corpse [. . .] until she
dies'. It is a useful starting point for discussion, first, because it actually
uses the language of paralysis; secondly, because it uses the language of
binding; thirdly, because it uses the language of 'chilling'.[235]

The language of paralysis is not often used in the curse tablets,
yet they have a special affinity with the condition. Their Greek name,
κατάδεσμοι, 'binding charms', deriving from the frequently used cog-
nate verb καταδέω, contains the notion of immobilising the victims,[236]
as does paralysis. Sometimes this is explicit, as in curses against ὁρμή,
'movement, motion' (*DT* **234**; **235**; **237**; **238**; **239**; **240**; **241**), and it
was also expressed by the use of 'voodoo dolls',[237] several examples of
which have survived in lead, bronze and terracotta,[238] but which were

---

[234] I have changed Jordan's 'strength, capacity, sinews, muscles, breath'. Ὁ τένων ὁ
τόνος was a species of νεῦρον, according to Galen (2.739; cf. 6.772). I have rendered the
other words in conformity with the Platonic anatomy, already outlined, according to which
Jordan's 'muscles' is a more suitable rendering of σάρξ than τὰ νεῦρα. The particular word
for muscle was μῦς (Hipp. *De arte* 10; Arist. *Pr.* 885ᵃ37; Theoc. 22.48), although the words
for sinew did service as well.

[235] A feature of the AthAg tablets (1st–3rd c. AD), see Jordan, 'Southwest Corner Athenian Agora'.

[236] Cf. Bravo, 'Tablette Magique', 191.

[237] See Faraone, 'Binding and Burying', for discussion and catalogue. Gager **107**, **108**
has sixteen found in Palestine (2nd c. AD). Pictures of bound figures are also drawn on some
tablets, cf. Carthage **3**.

[238] See *DT* **200–7**. See discussion in Faraone, 'Binding and Burying'.

also fashioned out of less durable material,[239] like wax (cf. SGD **152, 153, 155, 156**; cf. *PGM* IV.296–335;[240] Gager, figs 3, 11, 13, 14, 17, 23; cf. Pl. *Leg.* 933a–c; Theoc. 2.28–9; Virg. *Ecl.* 8.75–80; Hor. *Sat.* 1.8.30–3, *Epod.* 17.76). One such figure (4th c. BC) is inscribed with a curse illustrating that the rationale for such figures lies in a sympathetic relationship with the spells they bear:

> I register Isias, [. . .] Restrain her by your side! I bind (καταδ-εσμεύω) Isias before Hermes the Restrainer, the hands, the feet of Isias, the entire body. (SGD **64**)[241]

Thus, despite the fact that the actual παραλυ- vocabulary is rare, paralysis was an important goal in malicious magic, for the magical curses sought to bind their victims, in order to immobilise them in some way.

The desire to 'chill' the victim (καταψύχω) also has a peculiar association with paralysis, gaining extra force through sympathetic associations with the cold lead of the tablet, or the well, or the corpse. According to Theophrastus' Περὶ παράλυσεως (4th–3rd c. BC), the commonly given reason for the condition was 'chilling':[242]

> Since they say paralysis arises from chilling (ὑπὸ καταψύξεως), as appears to be the common report, [. . .]
> (Thphr. *De nerv. res.* 11.1)

Some say it is from too much 'air' (i.e., in the blood), and others by being deprived of 'air', for it is the 'air' that supplies both the heat and motion, and when the air is cut off, paralysis is associated with the chilling of the blood, or 'of the moisture' (τῆς ὑγρότητος). This understanding of paralysis probably undergirds Dioscorides' (1st c. AD) prescription of drugs with 'calorific' or 'heat-producing power' for its treatment (Dsc. 1.6). Thus, the desire to 'chill' (AthAg series; *DT* **155** = Gager **13** (4th c. AD)) a victim was tantamount to a wish for their paralysis.

Curses against bodily parts are well represented across several centuries straddling the New Testament period (SGD **3** (5th/4th c. BC); **51** (4th c. BC); **11** (late 4th c. BC); **69** (4th/3rd c. BC); **109** (?2nd c. BC);

---

[239] Faraone, 'Agonistic Context', 7. [240] Cf. Jordan, 'Love Charm Verses', 246–7.

[241] Translation: Faraone, 'Agonistic Context', 3. Cf. Sophronius' *Narratio Miraculorum Sanctorum Cyri et Joannis* (*DT*, cxxii–iii, translation Gager **165**); although late (6th c. AD), it is the only detailed narrative of a person's escape from a binding spell and it illustrates that the underlying assumptions about the paralysing but non-fatal effects of voodoo dolls were common knowledge, at least in the early Byzantine period; Faraone, 'Agonistic Context', 9.

[242] Pl. *Ti.* 46D talks of the 'auxiliary causes' of disease being 'cooling and heating, solidifying and dissolving' (ψύχοντα καὶ θερμαίνοντα πηγνύντα τε καὶ διαχέοντα).

Fox = Gager **134** (1st c. BC);[243] *DT* **74, 75a** (2nd c. AD); SGD **164** (4th c. AD)). They may speak generally of the limbs (τὰ μέλη: *DT* **38**; **51**; **241**; **242**; AthAg **App**), or itemise their various parts, as in a curse stemming from commercial rivalry which binds several people: 'I bind the soul, the work, the hands, and the feet; [. . .]' (*DTA* **87** = Gager **62** (4th c. BC); cf. SGD **150** (3rd c. BC)). Such body-part curses were particularly relevant in athletic rivalry,[244] such as the request to bind the 'sinews and members', in fact, all 365!

> Bind, bind | down the sinews, the members, the mind, the wits, | the intellect, the three hundred sixty-five | members.
>
> (*SuppMag* **53** = Gager **8**[245] (4th c. AD))

In Audollent's collection (= *DT*) alone, there are many curses seeking to damage the manifold parts of the leg: τὰ ἰσχία 'hips, hip joints' (**42b**), οἱ μηροί 'thighs, leg bones' (**42b**; **74**; cf. **135a** *femus*); or τὰ σκέλη 'legs from hips down, hams' (**239**; **240**; **241**; cf. *crus*, **135a**; **135b**; **190**); τὰ ἄρθρα 'joints' (**242**); οἱ πόδες 'the feet' (**15**; **47**; **49**; **50**; **64**; **66**; **77**; **85a**; **156**; **234**; **235**; **236**; **237**; **238**; **239**; **240**; **285**); ἄκρα ποδῶν δακτύλους 'the toes (at the end of the feet)' (**42b**); πτέρναι 'heels, feet' (**42b**); τὰ σφυρά 'ankles' (**15**). Curses against the tendons appear to be rare, although there is one from the 5–6th c. BC ([. . .] ἐνγράφω τᾶι τένον; SGD **99**), and the desire that the victim becomes ἄτονος could be overtranslated 'tendon-less' (AthAg **3**), cf. ἀπόδους 'without the use of their feet'[246] (*DT* **159**, **160**, **167**).

There is little to suggest a 'nerve' paralysis. Although two curses seek to harm the αἴσθησις, its presence in a string of words relating to the mind suggests it should be rendered 'perception' (*DT* **41a**; **242**) rather than 'sensation'. A couple of curses from the third century AD seek after ἀcθέν(ε)ια 'weakness' (Carthage **1**.15; Jordan, 'Sanctuary of Poseidon', **5**; Jordan, 'Notes from Carthage', **2**), cf. the protective charms against it (*GMPT* CXXI = Gager **128** (3rd/4th c. AD)).

Given their importance in sustaining life, it is not surprising that the sinews (τὰ νεῦρα) are attacked in vindictive magic. Such attacks are especially frequent in curses against charioteers – and their horses. Sometimes

---

[243] The oldest Latin *defixio* from Spain (late 1st c. BC) also curses body parts, Corell, 'Defixiones Tabella'. Williams and Zerves, 'Corinth, 1986', 31 report the discovery of MF-1986-44, which Jordan reads as a curse listing bodily parts from head to toe (n. 31), and compares with *DT* **74** and **75**, AthAg IL1722, MF-69-144, against an athlete, and SEG XXX.353 against a lover.

[244] AthAg 214 lists some against a *venator* (2nd or 3rd c. AD), runners (4th c. AD), and athletes and wrestlers (late Roman (1st–3rd c. AD)). Some 80 curses against athletes have been recovered, Jordan, 'Sanctuary of Poseidon', 117.

[245] His translation ignores τὰ μέλη.   [246] So Carthage, 130.

the agent is asked to 'de-sinew' (ἐκνεύρωσον) them (e.g., *DT* **234**; **237**; **238**; **239**; **240**); at other times the curse is against the charioteer's 'every limb and every sinew' (πᾶν μέλος καὶ πᾶν νεῦρον; *DT* **241** = Gager **12** (1st–3rd c. AD)); or it aims at 'the limbs, the sinews (τὰ νεῦρα), [. . .] heart, mind, wits [. . .] the whole of the limbs and sinews' (Carthage **1** (mid 3rd c. AD); cf. also *DT* **242**.50ff. = Gager **10**; MGP **4**.30–3 = SGD **167**).

But the sinews are attacked in other contexts as well, such as in the curse against a thief and those who had knowledge of the theft,[247] which curses the thief's brain, soul, sinews and hands, before cursing him inclusively from head to toenails (SGD **58**B (1st c. BC/1st c. AD)).[248] The sinews were attacked in the curse of the pantomimers (*DT* **15** = Gager **4** (3rd c. AD)), as they are in the erotic charm from the same time concerning two men, in which one is handed over to the 'untimely dead' (ἀώροις) '[. . .] in order that you will melt his flesh, sinews, members, soul' (*DT* **38** = *SuppMag* **54**.22f.; also MGP **2**).

There are also several curses which go the next anatomical step by cursing the marrow. Along with the (finger?)nails, the eyes (?), and the feet, a fragmentary text apparently curses the spine, the home of the marrow (SGD **80** (n.d.)). Another fragmentary tablet (?4th c. AD) aims at the marrow, along with the other components so essential to the body's health in the Platonic schema:

> O maidens, many-named maidens, damage and seize the soul, the heart, the innards, the marrows[249] and the sinews and the flesh (τοὺς μοιαλοὺς [for μυ-] καὶ τὰ νεῦρα καὶ τὰς σάρκας) of Akilatos, born of Akesamater, now, now, quickly, quickly.
>
> (SGD **131**)

Another from the same period also attacks these important substances, adding the bones as well, to conform the text exactly to the anatomy of the *Timaeus*:

> καὶ τὴν ψυχὴν καὶ τὸ ὀστέα καὶ τοὺς μυαλοὺς καὶ τ[ὰ] |
> νεῦρα καὶ τὰς σάρκας καὶ τὴν δύναμιν Καρδήλου [. . .]
>
> [. . .]and the soul and the bones and the marrow and th[e] |
> sinews and the flesh and the power of Kardelos [. . .]
>
> (*DT* **155**b.13f.)

---

[247] Cf. SGD **21** (1st c. BC).

[248] I have changed Jordan's rendering of νεῦρα as 'muscles'. For text, see Bruneau, *Recherches*.

[249] The plural may recall the two types of marrow, enclosing the two types of soul, cf. Pl. *Ti.* 73D.

The same curse also introduces the notion of chilling the victim:

καταψύξητε τ[ὴ]ν ἰσ-|
[χὺν] τοὺς μυαλοὺς [τὰ νεῦρα] τὰς σάρκας τή[ν δύναμιν, ἐν] |
ἡλικία Κὰρδηλον

chill the strength, the marrows, the sinews, the flesh, the power,
in the prime of life (for) Kardelos [. . .]   (*DT* **155b**.24–6)[250]

These malevolent curses aiming at paralysis certainly intended to cause
damage and suffering, but, since they even went as far as attacking the
bodily parts so close to the source of life, they were also aiming to kill.
In this context, an attack of paralysis would evoke the fear that it had a
magical cause and that the curser wished to kill.

Paralysis and the dead

Such curses bring the victim under the shadow of death, not only because
they bring an illness which is taking them towards the grave, or which is
bringing the presence of death into their body, but also because magical
practice operated by the agency of the dead. This was how magic in
general and the curse tablets in particular operated (cf. *PGM* V.304–
69; VII.429–58). Even though it may not always be explicit, there are
sufficient numbers of tablets in which the connection with the dead is
clear. So, e.g., a Latin curse against charioteers addresses an unknown
nekydaimon and asks for the rival drivers to be killed and mangled so that
they do not breathe again. In order to prevail upon the corpse-*daimon*, the
curser charges him by 'the one who set you free in his time, the god of
the sea and the air' (*DT* **286** = Grant, 241). This phrase reflects the belief
that the actual instrument by which the magician worked was the ghost,
but this ghost had to be released from the underworld (and/or threatened!)
by a higher power. Sometimes it is put from the opposite direction, as in
the curse which binds the god who has given the corpse 'the gift of sleep
and freed you from the chains of life', presumably so that the unknown
nekydaimon may then be sent back into active service for the curser (*DT*
242.30f. = Gager **10**). In other words, these curses against the charioteers
are designed to kill[251] by enlisting the powers of the dead.

The spirit of a dead person is directly addressed as the agent in several
curses against the sinews (*DT* **242** = Gager **10** [3rd c. AD]; *DT* **155b** =
Gager **13** (4th c. AD)), or to bind and chill (AthAg **12**). In addition *DT* **155b**

---

[250] Cf. AthAg **App**. A Syriac charm apparently also expels the spirit of lunacy 'from the
bones, the sinews, the flesh, the skin and the hair' (Thompson, 1, xl [n.d.]).
[251] Cf. *DT* **228A**, Grant, 242; *DT* **129**, Grant, 242; *DT* **155A**.

mentions some πάρεδροι (l. 20), i.e., ghostly assistants, and a garbled phrase 'who live in this place'[252] which locates the invoked powers in the cemetery. *DT* **38** = *SuppMag* **54** (3rd c. AD) calls upon δαίμονες οἵ ἐν [τ]ούτω τῷ τόπω ἐστέ (l. 19), and then hands the victim over to the untimely dead (ἀώροις, l. 22) in order to inflict the damage (ll. 22ff., see above). The voodoo dolls which depict being bound (?paralysis) so vividly were, according to a recipe for their preparation (*PGM* IV.296–466), probably also prepared for use by invoking Helios (435ff.) to arouse an unnamed *nekydaimon* from the cemetery (335–406).

Even the curses against horses could use a corpse for sympathetic magical purposes, 'Let him perish and fall, just as you lie (here) prematurely dead' (*DT* **295** = Gager **11**),[253] or invoke an unknown νεκυδαίμων ἄωρος (*DT* **234, 235, 237** = Gager **9, 238, 239, 240** (1st c. AD)). Even when there is no specific mention of a ghost when the charioteer is cursed along with his horses (e.g., *DT* **241** = Gager **12**), the similarities with other spells, and the specific mention of the use of a corpse in others, suggest that a ghost is assumed here as well.

Paralysis and the shadow of death

Given the above, the paralytic was well and truly under the shadow of death. Paralysis was a condition from which people died. With the sinews of the paralysed man loosened, death had already invaded his body. His condition could be under suspicion of being due to magical cursing, which would mean that somebody out there was using the dead to make him one of the dead. When Jesus 'raised' this man from his mat, Mark's vocabulary choice is significant (ἐγείρω): here was another example of someone who had been brought out from the shadow of death; he had been raised.

Lameness and the imperial power

In AD 69, while blockading Alexandria, Vespasian received a visit from a man who, according to Suetonius (8 (*Vesp.*).7), was lame.[254] Serapis (Asclepius) had told this man to ask the Roman general to touch his leg

---

[252] See Gager, 70 n. 96.
[253] The curse is Latin but the latter two words translate the Greek βίος θάνατος. Gager's translation follows a suggestion of D.R. Jordan (see p. 65 n. 70), which evidently takes βίος as βίας.
[254] In Tacitus and Dio (Tac. *Hist.* 4.81; Dio Cass. 65.8), the man had a withered hand. Cf. below on 3.1–6.

with his heel to cure it. Ascertaining from his doctors that it was curable, Vespasian did so, and the man was cured to the future ruler's greater glory.

This story indicates that at roughly the same time as Mark was being read, the tendency for Rome's (would-be) rulers to approximate divinity was on the increase, especially in somewhere like Alexandria.[255] Vespasian had performed a cure which the healing gods had apparently deferred to him. If such notions were present in Mark's readership, Jesus' abilities displayed in this scene would be impressive indeed.

Forgiveness enfleshed (2.13–28)

After opening with the call of Levi (2.13f.), the second sub-section shows Jesus modelling the forgiveness he has brought to the land by eating with sinners. In answering the scribal complaints, he likened the sick (οἱ κακῶς ἔχοντες) to sinners (ἁμαρτωλούς), and himself to a physician treating the sick (2.17) in order to summarise the goal of his ministry. This metaphorical meaning needs to be borne in mind when reading any of the healing stories. The last healing story explicitly connected forgiveness of sins with healing (2.1–12), and, as the story unfolds, there will be other miracles whose metaphorical meaning is made explicit by the story (3.4). But even when it is not explicit, Jesus' use of this metaphor in general connection with his ministry prepares the reader to watch/listen to the healing stories at more than a surface level, in order to discern the overtones which speak of Jesus' call to sinners.

As the controversy with his opponents continues, he likens the time when he is present with his disciples to a wedding feast, but, anticipating his own death, he hints that he will be snatched away (2.20). He insists that he brings something new (2.21f., cf. 1.27), and claims that the Son of Man – already introduced as the one who brings forgiveness to the land – is Lord of the Sabbath, which was made for the good of human beings (2.23–28).

Suppliant 5: life instead of death (3.1–6)

This scene is especially important for understanding Mark's healing stories, for it explicitly provides a metaphorical overlay in which healing is

---

[255] Alexandria was renowned for its attempts to give rulers divine honours. See for example, Philo, *Legat.* and the epistle from Claudius (*P.Lond.* 1912).

understood as a movement from death to life. Once again, the disciples are absent,[256] and the readers are aligned with a suppliant.

Text to reader: life on the Sabbath

When Jesus enters the synagogue again (πάλιν, v.1), it recalls the events of the Capernaum synagogue (cf. 1.21–28) and raises expectations that something similar may occur. The scene is focalised through another suppliant, characterised by his circumstances of need: he has 'a dried-out hand' (ἐξηραμμένην τὴν χεῖρα, v.1b). The readers learn the necessary background information that some people were watching Jesus to see whether he healed this man on the Sabbath – presumably the same opponents as previously, i.e., the scribes (2.6, 16) and the Pharisees (2.?18, 24). They have evidently made a decision about Jesus, for they seek a legal accusation against him (ἵνα κατηγορήσωσιν αὐτοῦ). Jesus' opposition to the scribes (cf. 1.22) has grown to such an extent that they are watching for a chance to remove him. Thus, from the beginning of the scene, this group is characterised negatively, which places distance between them and the readers.

The man's healing occurs in three movements. First, Jesus commands the man, 'rise (ἔγειρε) into the midst', making him the centre of attention, both in the scene itself and for the readers. Secondly, Jesus questions his opponents (v.4). Since this is in direct speech, the readers hear it for themselves and the question causes them to ponder an answer. It provides a metaphorical overlay to this illness and its cure, using two sets of contrasts. To heal the man is to do good, in fact to 'save a life' (ψυχὴν σῶσαι), whereas to leave the man unhealed is to do evil, in fact, to kill (ἀποκτεῖναι). Not to cure the man would be to leave the man in a state of death; curing him, on the other hand, would be to save his life.

The answer to the puzzle is quite obvious. The readers have already seen Jesus heal on the Sabbath (1.29–31; cf. 1.21–28). They know that he is the Lord of the Sabbath and that the Sabbath was meant for human good (2.28). They recognise the 'counter-trap' in Jesus' question: the opponents will have to say 'to kill' if they wish to prevent him from doing the good that is entirely appropriate on this day. Instead, they are silent (v.4b), refusing to choose life over death. Their silence is permission for Jesus to give life, which begins the third movement, the actual healing. Before it is narrated, the readers are focalised through Jesus (περιβλεψάμενος)

---

[256] Fowler, *Let the Reader*, 101, 'and so we cannot use them as role models, even if we wanted to'.

and given two views inside him revealing the emotions aroused by his opponents' silence (v.5): he looks with anger (μετ᾽ ὀργῆς), and he is deeply saddened (συλλυπούμενος)²⁵⁷ at their hardness of heart. Once before, Jesus was so willing to heal that he was angered by the mere suggestion to the contrary (1.41); now he is angered and grieved by these men who would prefer him to 'kill' than bring life on the Sabbath.

This also provides the second of two views into the opponents (cf. v.2) which both characterise them negatively. These inside views enable the readers to have the closest possible look at the motivations/thoughts of Jesus' enemies (cf. 2.6f.), while at the same time, the negatively evaluated revelation of their insides repels the readers from them. The readers first see a preference for 'death' and a desire to trap Jesus for 'saving life' (v.2), and then understand that this springs from a hardness of heart²⁵⁸ which makes Jesus angry and deeply saddened.

There is no chorus of praise as a result of this healing (contrast 1.27f.; 2.12) and no gathering crowds (cf. 1.32–34, 37; 1.45). Instead, the opponents – who are now identified as Pharisees –, having gained the evidence they were after, leave the synagogue and immediately they, along with the Herodians, 'gave counsel against him in order that they might destroy him' (v.6).

The contrast between Jesus' actions and those of the Pharisees reinforces the metaphorical overtones of the scene. Rather than kill on the Sabbath, Jesus 'saves life'. Because the Pharisees would have preferred him to leave the dead alone, they plan to destroy him. They find their reason to condemn him (cf. v.2) and, although they refused to answer his question with their lips, they demonstrate their answer with their actions. Their legal scruples about his healing on the Sabbath do not prevent their planning to kill a man on the same day. Jesus used the Sabbath to save a life; they use it to kill.

After those of Jesus (1.11; cf. 17, 24) and the disciples (1.17), this is the last of the three commissionings generating the plot. The gradually escalating conflict between Jesus and the opponents (1.22; 2.6ff.; 2.16; 2.18; 2.24) has reached a climax in their plan to kill him and this now becomes their narrative assignment. From this point on, their scheme to kill Jesus casts a dark shadow across the narrative, for it 'immediately raises the question of whether and how this intention will be realized'.²⁵⁹ This

---

²⁵⁷ συλλυπόμαι is a rare word, usually 'to mourn with', 'to sympathise', and this is apparently the only instance of the preposition having an intensifying force; cf. Cranfield, *Mark*.

²⁵⁸ Interestingly, D it syrˢ replace πώρωσις with νέκρωσις.

²⁵⁹ Tannehill, 'Narrative Christology', 66; cf. J.F. Williams, *Other Followers*, 28.

scene puts irrevocable distance between the readers and the opponents, who can never be regarded positively again.

However, although the scene is important for the generation of the conflict which helps to sustain the plot, the suppliant is not subordinated to a secondary position. The man's need was not merely the occasion for discussing Jesus' conflict with the opponents,[260] as if Jesus' 'saving his life' was an insignificant matter. Both elements are integral to the scene and an explanation must attempt to account for its complete dynamics. The 'great ones' (Pharisees) are prepared to use the needy person simply as an opportunity to further their purposes. They are so prepared to maintain his state of 'death' that they will kill in the process. Human need is simply confirmed by their system of law. On the other hand, Jesus cannot confirm the needy person in his state of death: he is prepared to die himself in order to bring life. Jesus was angered at the kind of hard-heartedness that would kill rather than give life and which would go to any length to prevent him from doing the reverse. But he would not let that stop him.

Reader to text

A withered hand and death

'Metaphorical' death
In one sense, there is no need for a detailed assessment of ancient views on withered hands, for the text itself explicitly provides a metaphorical understanding of the condition as a 'death' and its cure as the saving of a life. An understanding of the ancient views, however, shows that this metaphorical dimension is not simply an arbitrary overlay.

Paralysis and death
There is no need to repeat the discussion on paralysis, apart from indicating that it is of relevance here. Insofar as the hand was paralysed, it would be understood as a loosening of the sinews (cf. TSol. 18.11) and so as a serious condition in which death had already invaded the body.

Withering and death
The new feature of the story is in the description of the hand as withered, or 'dried out' (ἐξηραμμένη, v.1; ξηρά, v.3). As we have seen, moistness and dryness were important philosophical concepts with implications for

---

[260] Cf. Williams, *Other Followers*, 102.

medicine (Suppliant 4, pp. 107–114). As with other opposites, it was important to keep the balance between the two (cf. Hipp. *Morb. sacr.* 17). Moisture nourishes the all-important marrow (Pl. *Ti.* 77C),[261] but too much drying of the body leads to death (88D). Amongst Plato's first class of disease (problems with the elements), he lists the problem when 'particles that formerly were being cooled become heated, and the dry presently become moist, and the light heavy' (82B). When a hand is dried up, as here, something has gone seriously wrong, and, if possessing the appropriate moisture was to be healthy and full of life, then a dried-out limb is dead (cf. Hippocrates' saying in Aret. *De causis* 1.7.2).

These opposites also had importance in regard to the state of the soul in the afterlife, at least according to the Pythagorean schema. In the eschatological myth of Plutarch's *De sera numinis vindicta*, the moister the soul, the more fitting it is for the body (566A; cf. 1053B–C; Pl. *Resp.* 411B),[262] whereas the dry soul is prepared for the life above.[263] The myth suggests that the Dionysian mysteries 'liquefy' the soul and put it at risk of being reincarnated – cf. the 'Stele of Jeu the hieroglyphist in his letter' which also links the mysteries ('celebrated by Israel'!) with the revelation of 'the moist and the dry and all nourishment' (*PGM* V.108–17). Once again, this underlines the point that moisture is the natural state of bodily life, and so, as with a case of paralysis, a dry state already indicates the presence of death.

On this understanding of the body, Jesus is not speaking metaphorically at all. Although a withered hand might seem to be a long way from death for the modern reader, this was not the case in Mark's day. The body of this man in the synagogue had already been invaded by death, and, as Jesus pointed out, to leave him uncured is tantamount to killing, whereas to cure is to 'save a life'.

A withered hand and the dead

In the examination of paralysis, we have already seen that many curse tablets are directed at the body parts, including the limbs. Hands also

---

[261] Given the importance of the spinal marrow as the 'bonds of the (mortal) soul' it is not surprising that it was regarded as a severe disease (ὁ νοῦσος χαλεπή) when it 'becomes dry' (αὐαίνηται) (Hipp. *Aff.Int.* 3).

[262] See further, Vernière, 'Léthé'.

[263] It is a little more confusing in Heraclitus, who, although teaching that 'a dry soul is wisest and best' (fr. 74; from Plut. *Rom.* 28; Stob. 5.120; and Plut. *De esu carn.* 1.6 995E; *De defectu* 41; Pl. *Phd.* 73), apparently also said that 'it is delight for souls to become moist' (fr. 72). The latter saying may be explained, with the editor of the fragments, in terms of the soul in this world, 'perhaps because the change to moisture means death, and the rest of death is pleasant', i.e., the soul would find release.

received particular attention (4th c. BC: *DTA* **87** = Gager **62**; SGD **64**; 3rd c. BC: SGD **150**; 1st c. BC/1st c. AD: SGD **58B**; cf. SGD21 [1st c. BC]; 3rd c. AD: *DT* **15** = Gager **4**; 4th c. AD: MGP **4** [= SGD167]; cf. 6th c. AD: Sophronius, *Narratio Miraculorum Sanctorum Cyri et Joannis*).[264]

In addition, Audollent's collection contains curse tablets attempting to bind various other parts of the arm: ὦμοι 'upper arms, shoulders' *DT* **74**; **242**; the βραχίονες 'arms, shoulders': **74**; **156**, cf. *brac(h)ia* 'arm': **135ab**; **190**; οἱ ἀνκῶνες 'the elbows, arms': **242**; δάκτυλοι 'fingers': **42b**, cf. *diciti* (= *digiti*): **135ab**; **190**; καρπός 'wrist', **252**; **253**; **242**. Curses against αἱ χεῖρες 'the hands' themselves are particularly well represented (in addition to those already cited above: *DT* **47**; **49**; **50**; **64**; **85a**; **156**; **234**; **235**; **237**; **238**; **239**; **240**; **241**). There are also curses against the hand as a symbol of power, strength, and so ability: cf. SGD **106** (5th c. BC). An Aramaic bowl inflicts 'dryness', although to the legs, as a preliminary to death, asking 'that his legs may dry', as well as 'that he might die' (*AMB* **Bowl 9**). *Sepher ha-Razim* (2.95ff.) clearly shows that such dryness was under suspicion of a daemonic cause, when it provides a spell 'to heal a man with stroke and half of him has dried up, either by a spirit or by witchcraft'.

Once again, the point needs to be made that, since magic enlisted the dead as the agents of the curse – both generally, and also for curses against hands (e.g. *DT* **234–40**) –, then a case of a withered hand would be suspected of being caused by a magical – and so daemonic – attack, in which the forces of the dead bring death into a living person's body. When Jesus asks this man to stretch out his hand, not only is he removing the influence of death from him, but he is removing him from under the influence of the dead. He chooses not to kill, but to bring life.

Withered hand and the imperial power

In AD 69, while blockading Alexandria, Vespasian received a visit from a man who, according to Tacitus and Dio Cassius, had a withered hand.[265] Sarapis (Asclepius) had told this man to ask the Roman general to step on his hand to cure it. Ascertaining from his doctors that it was curable, Vespasian did so, and the man was cured to the future ruler's greater glory (Tac. *Hist.* 4.81; Dio Cass. 65.8).

This story indicates that at roughly the same time as Mark was being read, the tendency for Rome's (would-be) rulers to approximate divinity was on the increase, especially in somewhere like Alexandria. Vespasian

---

[264] *DT*, cxxii–iii; translation: Gager **165**.
[265] In Suetonius' version (8 (*Vesp.*).7), it was a lame man who was cured when Vespasian touched his leg with his heel.

had performed a cure which the healing gods had apparently deferred to him.

Life to the dead

In Mark's story, Jesus shows no reluctance at all, nor does he take medical advice, or act for the sake of better publicity – in fact, it is a choice which will lead to his death. He simply calls upon the man to stretch out the hand, and, when he does so, it is restored. Jesus has brought life to one who had been living under the shadow of death and under the influence of the dead. As a result, that shadow now falls across his own future. Like the great Asclepius, he is prepared to die himself, in order to bring life to the dead.[266]

The call of the twelve (3.7–19)

At the opening of the third sub-section, the echo of the previous pattern of events by the sea (v.7, cf. 1.16; 2.13) raises the expectation that another calling may soon occur. Jesus and his disciples are accompanied by a vast multitude from Galilee, Judea, Jerusalem, Idumea, across the Jordan, and the regions around Tyre and Sidon (7b–8a). They are coming to Jesus as they hear of the things that he is doing (8b).

This scene is filled with graphic language, conveying the forceful – even violent – nature of the events. Jesus ensures that a little boat 'might stay with him' (προσκαρτερῇ αὐτῷ), lest the crowd crush him (ἵνα μὴ θλίβωσιν αὐτόν). The reason for his fear is explained (v.10) by the fact that he had healed many, 'with the result that' (ὥστε [. . .]) the multitude, presumably, 'were attacking him' (ἐπιπίπτειν αὐτῷ) in order that he might touch as many as had afflictions. The attack was not simply from the living human beings, but the unclean spirits, whenever they saw him, 'were assaulting him' (προσέπιπτον αὐτῷ)[267] and crying out saying, 'You are the son of God.' Mark provides the reader with an 'inside

---

[266] As legend had it, Asclepius was killed by Zeus for raising someone from the dead, even if the exact identity of the person was disputed. Apollodorus (3.10.3–4) found six men raised by him: Capaneus, Lycurgus, Hippolytus, Tyndareus, Hymenaeus, Glaucus; see Cotter, *Miracles*, 24–30, for the discussion in the ancient sources. This promoted the idea that Asclepius was 'the god most loving towards humanity' (Ael. 8.12). Note, too, that Asclepius' action was regarded as 'saving humanity', cf. Hippocrates, *Ep.* 17: 'Let your ancestor Asclepius be a warning to you in that he was requited with a thunderbolt for saving humankind'.

[267] Although προσπίπτω τινί can mean 'to fall down at one's feet' (LSJ, item III), the violence conveyed by the use of θλίβω and ἐπιπίπτω in the preceding verse encourages a translation here drawn from the other end of its semantic range (LSJ, item I).

view',[268] revealing Jesus' desire to keep the lid on what was happening: he insistently rebukes (πολλὰ ἐπετίμα) them 'lest they make him manifest'.[269]

Then, in the call of the twelve, comes the call expected from the beginning of the sub-section. It is all the more significant now that it has been delayed, for it reads as a solution to the problem of the pressing crowds. Like some general gathering an army together for an imminent battle, Jesus designates twelve (v.13) 'to be with him in order that he might send them out to preach and to have authority to cast out the *daimones*' (v.14f.). These men are named and numbered (vv.16–19), indicating the closure of the group that Jesus began to assemble in 1.16–20. In final position, Judas' supplement brings an ominous note to the narrative: ὃς καὶ παρέδωκεν αὐτόν. The reader is now aware both of the plot to kill Jesus set in motion by the Pharisees and the Herodians (3.6), and of the means by which this will be realised: through the betrayal of one of these twelve men who are designated to be the closest of all to him (3.19). The shadow of his betrayal and death is rapidly falling across the narrative.

Jesus' source of authority (3.20–35)

The quest

In the opening segment of Mark's first intercalation, or 'sandwich',[270] Jesus' family seek to bring him home, thinking he has gone mad (3.20f.).

The accusation

In the middle section, he engages in controversy with the scribes from Jerusalem (vv.22–30), who were saying 'that he has Beelzebul, and that by the ruler of *daimones* he is casting out *daimones*' (3.22). This being, whom Jesus is supposed to 'have', is named and then given the function 'ruler of *daimones*'.[271] Later, Mark domesticates Beelzebul to the narrative by describing him in familiar terms, 'unclean spirit' (v.30).

---

[268] This is missed by Fowler, *Let the Reader*, and Boomershine, *Mark, the Storyteller*, whose classification of inside views ignores 'desires and intentions'.

[269] The clause is regarded as 'probably final' by Taylor, *Mark*.

[270] For Mark's well-known use of intercalations, or 'sandwiches'; cf. Edwards, 'Markan Sandwiches'; Shepherd, 'Intercalation', and *Markan Sandwich Stories*. For their function as implicit commentary see Fowler, *Let the Reader*, 143f.

[271] This would also be tantamount to the charge that Jesus was under the control of, or influenced by, if not possessed by, this being. Despite the magicians' attempts to control the spirits, it was a difficult and dangerous business – cf. the need for protective charms whilst engaged in summoning the underworld beings.

This is probably an accusation that Jesus was practising magic.[272] The magicians operated by gaining control of a *daimon*, by 'having' them under their authority, and Jesus is being accused of having one with a most important function.

Beelzebul, Prince of *daimones*

Beelzebul

The usual interpretations of the expression concentrate on the name, rather than the functional description. Because it is unattested apart from the Gospels and TSol.,[273] interpreters propose various etymological solutions.[274] The recent suggestion that Beelzebub should be read in an Aramaic incantation from Qumran (4Q560: בעל[דבב, Beel]zebub),[275] although possible, is far from certain, since it is a reconstruction and one which depends upon an etymological connection with the Aramaic expression 'to be an enemy, adversary' (דבב), which has not convinced many.[276]

The *Prince of the* daimones

In terms of its function in Mark's narrative, the explanatory expression is the more significant. Mark uses Beelzebul but once, but the *daimones* of which he is prince are constantly before the readers' gaze. The name

---

[272] So Kraeling, 'Necromancy?'; Morton Smith, *Magician*, 32ff. Cf. the later tendency for the Jews – probably reacting to the Gospel tradition, Meier, *Marginal Jew*, 97 – to explain Jesus' miracles as sorcery; cf. *bSanh* 43a; Justin's Jew, *Dial.* 69. This was also a charge that would gain currency amongst pagan writers, against both Jesus and his followers. It was perhaps adumbrated by Suetonius, who called the movement a 'new and criminal (*maleficus*) superstition', since *maleficus* can mean 'magical' (Wilken, *Christians*, 98; Morton Smith, *Clement*, 234; *Magician*, 45–67), and may lie behind Lucian's mockery of the Christians' gullibility before 'any charlatan and trickster' (*Pereg.* 13), but it is Celsus who first makes the charge explicit (Origen, *c.Cels.* 1.6). Arnobius (*Adv.Nat.* 1.43 (late 3rd c.)) and Lactantius (*Div.Inst.* 5.3 (late 3rd/early 4th c.)) also mention the opinion and it was still current in Porphyry's day (234–*c.* 305), although he himself denied it in favour of his belief that Jesus was a wise man (Wilken, *Christians*, 159–60). Eusebius wrote a treatise against Hierocles, governor of Bythinia, whose book had compared Jesus to Apollonius of Tyana (*Hierocl.* 1–2). It is also significant that Jesus' name was used by magicians in their incantations. Cf. Celsus' charge that Christians practised magic and that he had seen their books 'containing magical formulas' (*c.Cels.* 6.40).

[273] He appears frequently in TSol. This is probably an independent tradition to that found in the Gospels.

[274] For the various interpretations, see Lewis, 'Beelzebul'; Herrmann, 'Baal-Zebub'.

[275] Penney and Wise, 'Power'.

[276] Lewis, 'Beelzebul', 639; Herrmann, 'Baal-Zebub', 294.

was almost certainly unfamiliar to the Graeco-Roman readers, but the *daimones* were not. It therefore seems good sense to allow the familiar phrase to interpret the unfamiliar name.

Graeco-Roman readers may have recognised the link between Beelzebul and the Semitic name for a lord or god, 'Baʿal'.[277] This Semitic flavour – being foreign and oriental – in connection with the *daimones* provides a magical atmosphere. The magical curses and spells delighted to use foreign words, strange-sounding syllables,[278] different and unusual names of underworld beings, and the like. The accusation that Jesus was performing his exorcisms by the power of this being would be readily understood against the backdrop of magic, even if the name remained unfamiliar.

Beelzebul's function, however, would not be unfamiliar. On the understanding that the *daimones* are the spirits of the dead, Beelzebul is given the position of the 'Prince of the dead', the lord of the underworld. As such, the expression finds an abundance of analogies, both in literature and magic, as we shall see.

Some Semitic analogies can even be gleaned amongst the etymological approaches. In the Ugaritic epics, as well as being the ruler of the gods and of the earth,[279] Baʿal was also associated with the underworld through the defeat of Mot ('Death').[280] It has also been argued that Zeboul is related to the epithet *zbl bʿl arṣ*, meaning 'prince, lord of the earth [viz. underworld]' and referring to a chthonic god able to help in cases of illness.[281] If so, then both portions of Beelzebul's name connect him etymologically with the Lord of the underworld.

When Jesus reformulated the accusation for the purposes of his riddle (v.23), he introduced the figure of Satan (cf. 1.13; 3.23, 26; 4.15; 8.33). Although there is debate whether the OT presents 'Satan' as the same individual figure in each of the texts in which 'he' appears,[282] for our purposes it is enough to say that several of these texts associate him with death (Job 1–2; 1 Chron. 21; ?Zech. 3). In the NT, the connection between the accuser (Satan or ὁ διάβολος) and death is also well known (John 8.44, cf. 1 John 3.12; Heb. 2.14; 1 Pet. 5.8).[283]

---

[277] The name, as Βηλ, occurs only rarely in magic; cf. *PGM* IV.1010; Jordan, 'Sanctuary of Poseidon', **5** and 120 n. 17; *PGM* O2.7.

[278] Cf. the observation that anyone not knowing Hebrew would take it as a name; for anyone knowing Hebrew it would be a stumbing block! Gaston, 'Beelzeboul', 250, which may explain the change to Beelzebub in Syr and Jerome.

[279] For details, see Maclaurin, 'Beelzeboul', 158f.   [280] Gibson, *Canaanite Myths*, 81.

[281] Cf. Herrmann, 'Baal-Zebub', 295.   [282] Breytenbach and Day, 'Satan'.

[283] This connection between Satan and death was recognised by the Fathers, e.g., Origen identified the destroying angel of the Passover with Satan (*Princ.* 3.2.1; *cCels.* 6.43).

This identification also finds confirmation in the *Testament of Solomon*, the only other text in which Beelzebul appears. Although he certainly receives further elaboration here, one of the roles ascribed to Beelzebul is that of the one who binds people in Tartarus (TSol. 6.3). He is also called 'the ruler of the spirits of the air and the earth and beneath the earth [. . .]' (cf. Eph. 2.2), which may also indicate his rulership over the dead, since these are all 'eschatological' spaces in which departed spirits can dwell (TSol. 16.3).

Greek literature contains a wealth of analogies to Mark's phrase. The proem to the Orphic Hymns addresses 'O king of those under the earth' (καταχθονίων βασιλεῦ, *pr.* 12). Hades is often called the 'king of the dead below' (ἄναξ ἐνέρων Ἀϊδωνεύς, *Il.* 20.61; cited in Lucian *Men.* 10; *Hymn to Demeter* 357); or 'ruler of the dead below' (ἐνέροισιν ἀνάσσων, *Il.* 15.188f.); the 'ruler of the departed' (καταφθιμένοισιν ἀνάσσων, *Hymn to Demeter* 346); cf. inscriptions where he is god of the dead (Epig.Gr. 89.4; 26.9, 42.5 and 87.4). It is given to him (here Pluto) to rule the abyss (βασιλεύειν δὲ τοῦ χάσματος), and 'to rule those who have died' (ἄρχειν τῶν ἀποθανόντων, Lucian *Luct.* 2). Thanatos 'himself' – who is not often personified and never worshipped as a god – is also called 'king of corpses' (ἄναξ νεκρῶν, Eur. *Alc.* 843), and, in a phrase very close to Mark 3.22, he is also called 'the Lord of *daimones*' (ὁ κύριος δαιμόνων, *Alc.* 1040).

The magical literature has numerous underworld beings who can be manipulated to send up ghosts, although the picture is too complex to say that there is one who is *the* ruler of the shades below. The Aramaic bowl texts have a king of demons (Isbell **17**.5; **18**.4, 6; **19**.3; **20**.4, 7; **22**.2), who especially kills boys and girls, male and female foetuses (**19**.4; **20**.6, 7). An ἀρχιδαίμων appears in *PGM* IV.1349, in which his πάρεδροι, i.e., his assistants, are invoked by the magician, and who are also called 'rulers of *daimones*' (δαιμονοτάκτεϲ, 1374f.). Since the πάρεδροι are generally the δαίμονες of dead people,[284] this may suggest some kind of hierarchy in the underworld (cf. Plut. *Dion* 2). Osiris is also called the king of the underworld (e.g. *PGM* IV.10, in Old Coptic: ΠΕΡΟ ΝΤΗΠΝΗΒ etc., the king of embalming), and ?Anoubis is called ὁ κύριος τῶν χ<θ>ονίων ('the lord of the chthonians', *PGM* VIII.30). An unpublished lead tablet

---

Beelzebul is called the prince of death in *Christ's Descent into Hell* (5th/6th c.). Mac-Culloch, *Harrowing*, 346, 234, argues that, although Origen and possibly Irenaeus took the binding of the strong man to be the assault on Death and Hades, the Fathers did not entertain the notion of Satan being the Lord of the underworld (pp. 227, 229, 232f., 345–6). Huidekoper, *Belief*, argues to the contrary.

[284] Ciraolo, 'Supernatural Assistants', 284, 286.

in the Getty Museum also approximates Mark 3.22, when it invokes Bakaxichych (ὁ Βακαξιχυχ) as 'Prince of *daimones*' (ὁ τύραννος τῶν δαιμόνων).[285] The Cyprus tablets (*DT* 22– 36 (3rd c. AD)) mention the king of the deaf *demones* (βασιλεὺς τῶν κωφῶν δεμόνων – note spelling) and the lord of all the *demones* under the ground (δέσποτα τῶν ὑπὸ χθόνα δεμόνων, 25.12).

As time went on and the trend towards one universal god progressed, Helios took on an increasingly important role.[286] As the Lord of upper and lower worlds (*PGM* XXI; cf. XII.256) he was also the lord of the *daimones* of the dead. In this role, he was often petitioned at sunset at a graveyard, so that he might search for the *daimon* of the corpse, in order to send it up for the use of the magician (e.g. *PGM* IV.296–466).

The releaser of daimones

If Beelzebul is identified as 'the Prince of *daimones*', then he is being cast as the one who has the power to release or to restrain the *daimones* for magical ends in the upper world. Being the ruler of the *daimones* entails the receipt and release of the dead. Like Pluto,

> καταδεξάμενον δὲ αὐτοὺς καὶ παραλαβόντα κατέχειν δεσμοῖς ἀφύκτοις, οὐδενὶ τὸ παράπαν τῆς ἄνω ὁδοῦ ὑφιέμενον πλὴν ἐξ ἅπαντος τοῦ αἰῶνος πάνυ ὀλίγων ἐπὶ μεγίσταις αἰτίαις

> he receives them and takes them to hold them fast with in-escapable bonds, absolutely yielding the way above for nobody, except, in all time, a very few for most important reasons.
>
> (Lucian *Luct.* 2)

The ruler of the dead could send back the ghosts in his charge. So, for example, after Atossa's libation to Dareios, the chorus calls 'king of the dead, send forth to the light the soul from below' (βασιλεῦ τ᾽ ἐνέρων, | πέμψατι᾽ ἔνερθεν ψυχὴν ἐς φῶς, Aesch. *Pers.* 629–30, cf. 649–51). Magic assumed that if he *could* do it, then he *would* do it, if rightly 'persuaded'; cf. the curse tablet which promises the dead person, by way of incentive, that the curser will 'bind the god who gave you rest' (*DT* 242 = Gager 10), i.e., the one who sent him to the underworld, so that the ghost would be available to fulfil the magician's purposes.

---

[285] Kotansky and Spier, ' "Horned Hunter" ', 319. This name also appears on the gem that is the subject of their article. They refer to the explanation of the name as Egyptian for 'Ba ("Soul") of Darkness, Son of Darkness' (see p. 319 n. 15 for further details).

[286] Gordon, 'Helios'.

Jesus and the strong man

The Graeco-Roman readers would hear the scribes accusing Jesus of knowing magical secrets by which the prince of the underworld is bound so that the dead are temporarily released (cf. Lucian *Luct.* 2). Jesus' riddles present the scribes with an alternative explanation. The ruler of the underworld had to be persuaded in some way, i.e., 'bound', before the *daimones* could be released. The riddle suggests that he is binding the strong man in order to more permanently plunder his domain. It seems that he is planning, after all, to destroy the influence of the dead over the living (cf. 1.24). But, more than this, if the strong man is to be defeated, then those he holds in 'inescapable bonds' (δεσμοῖς ἀφύκτοις, Lucian, *Luct.* 2) could conceivably be freed from death's domain. What could this mean?

Some say Pluto (Hades), the Lord of the underworld, gained this appellative 'because of his wealth of corpses' (διὰ τὸ πλουτεῖν τοῖς νεκροῖς, Lucian, *Luct.* 2; from Cornutus). This would imply that 'his possessions' are the people held in his domain. This is also confirmed in the myth about Asclepius, in one reason given for Zeus striking Asclepius down with a bolt of lightning. Apparently, this was in response to a charge brought by Hades, that Asclepius was acting to the detriment of Hades' domain, for, he said, 'the number of the dead was steadily diminishing, now that men were being healed by Asclepius' (Diod. 4.71.1–3). On analogy, Jesus' activity amongst those who are still alive is also diminishing the number of the dead, thus plundering the possessions of the strong man. But there may be something bigger than this implied, as well. For if Jesus can successfully bind the strong man, in order to plunder his possessions, what will this mean for those who face the grave? Is he saying that, as the one who deals with the prince of *daimons*, he will also be the one who will even raise the dead?

Jesus warned the scribes against misunderstanding the nature of his authority. If they evaluate him incorrectly, they will be guilty of eternal sin (v.29), i.e., they will miss out on the forgiveness he brings,[287] and so they may miss entering the coming kingdom of God. The readers cannot help but feel the strength of this warning, which stresses the crucial nature of the question regarding Jesus' identity. If he is powerful enough to deal with the prince of the underworld, then it would be a big problem to mistake his identity.

---

[287] According to Zech. 13.1–2, the cleansing of the land from the unclean spirit accompanied the arrival of forgiveness of sins. If Jesus is the one who casts out Beelzebul, then he is the one who brings forgiveness too. See further, Bolt, 'Forgiveness'.

The resolve to keep going

The close of the sandwich (3.31–35) is usually explained as a lesson for true discipleship. Instead, it should be explained as another story about Jesus. The call from Jesus' family (3.21, 31, 32) is a call to return home to where it all began (1.9). As such, it is a call for Jesus to leave the course upon which God has set him (1.11), and the calling which God has given him. When he looks at those around him and talks of those doing the will of God being his family, this should be primarily understood in terms of the implications for him, not for them. He is the one being called, therefore his statement that he is staying with those who wish to do the will of God and not returning home amounts to a choice to do the will of God. Since the outside of the 'sandwich' is to be interpreted together with the inside, the intervening debate with the Pharisees informs the reader of the content of this phrase. For Jesus, the Servant of the Lord, the will of God will apparently involve the plundering of the underworld.

The sandwich provides the readers with some distinct options for Jesus' identity and his authority. Is he mad (3.21), or is he doing the will of God (3.35)? Is he manipulating the *daimones* by their prince (3.22), or is he binding him in order to plunder the underworld on a more permanent basis (3.27)?

Listening for the kingdom (4.1–34)

Jesus' return to the location by the sea (4.1) introduces the 'parables discourse' as the climax to Mark's first main section. The well-established pattern erects the expectation of another calling. When it arrives, it moves beyond the call of the disciples (1.16–20; 2.13f.; 3.13–19) to a general invitation issued to anyone who has ears to hear.

The parable of the soils is separated from its explanation by a quotation from Isaiah 6.9f., which plays a key role in the elucidation of the parable and of Jesus' ministry. In the Isaianic context, the hardening of Israel was only temporary, for the purposes of allowing God's judgement to fall (vv.11f.), and to provide the context for the gathering of God's remnant, the 'holy seed' (v.13). Jesus' use of this citation suggests that he finds himself amongst a hard-hearted Israel, with a similar task to Isaiah, to gather in the 'holy seed'.

As Jesus explains the parable of the soils, the emphasis falls upon the need to listen (Mark 4.3, 9, 15, 16, 18, 20, 23f.) to the word being sown (v.14). Presumably this word is the gospel of God concerning the imminence of the kingdom (1.15). The key to becoming part of 'the harvest' is to hear the word of the kingdom with acceptance (v.20).

The parables of the kingdom set the eschatological horizon as still future to the story, teaching that the coming kingdom will arrive suddenly (vv.26–29), and when it does it will encompass the world, like the 'world-tree' of the prophets (vv.30–32; cf. Ezek. 17; Dan. 4).

By linking the image of the harvest with the expectation of the coming kingdom, the two halves of the parables discourse are closely related, producing the combined effect that the key to entering the coming kingdom harvest is to hear the word of the kingdom with acceptance.

When Jesus introduces the Isaiah citation, he tells those around him that they have been given the mystery of the kingdom. In a world in which the mystery cults promised a 'better hope' (Marcus, in Cicero, *Leg.* 2.14.36) through initiation, this language would be recognised as coming from this conceptual pool. Jesus' 'better hope' is the kingdom of God which will come suddenly and encompass the world, and those around him have been given the 'mystery', i.e., the way in, to that kingdom. Initially, the readers are not fully aware of what this mystery is, which is perfectly in line with the usual secrecy surrounding such things. But then Jesus immediately opens the secret to 'anyone who has ears', by explaining that the key to entering the kingdom is to hear the word he is speaking, and accept it. This is the mystery that will take a person into the better hope of the kingdom of God.

4

JESUS AND THE PERISHING
(MARK 4.35–8.26)

'Master of land and sea'

Text to reader

The second main section of Mark's narrative is broadly structured around three sea journeys (4.35ff.; 6.45ff.; 8.10ff.).[1] Each occasion in the boat is a significant moment towards the unfolding of Jesus' identity. Since the readers are privileged to share these moments of revelation, they develop a greater bond with Jesus and also a degree of sympathy with the disciples, even though the negative evaluation of the disciples also introduces some distance.

Since this section contains six of the thirteen suppliant passages, it plays a crucial role in making contact with Mark's readers.

Reader to text

The sea

Mark's use of θάλασσα in connection with lake Gennesaret has evoked surprise from early days.[2] Porphyry's criticism of this feature (Mac. Mag. Apoc. 3.6, cf. 4) finds good precedent in Luke's more exact use of λίμνη in both his special material (Luke 5.1) and material drawn from Mark (8.22, 23, 33).[3] Like Josephus (who always uses λίμνη for Palestine's inland waters, including Gennesaret; e.g., *BJ* 2.573; 3.463), 1 Maccabees

---

[1] Recognised by, e.g., Tannehill, 'Disciples', 146; Kelber, *Mark's Story*, 30 (although he breaks the section after 8.21); Petersen, 'Composition', 194–6; van Iersel, *Reading Mark*, 89–98; J.F. Williams, *Other Followers*, 45; Juel, *Master*, 72. 6.31–33 and 8.10 are not sea crossings, but simply changes in location on the shoreline (Kelber, *Mark's Story*, 35, 40).

[2] For discussion see Theißen, ' "Meer und See" '. Van Iersel, *Mark*, 37–9, offers a critique of Theißen's view.

[3] He retains only two of Mark's nineteen (17.2, 6).

(in which Gennesaret is τὸ ὕδωρ τοῦ Γεννησάρ, 11.67), and the secular Greek writers (e.g., Homer, Herodotus), Luke appears to reserve θάλασσα for the Mediterranean.[4]

There is little point in correcting Mark's usage,[5] which may be explained in terms of its Semitic background, or of local practice.[6] Whatever the background, it remains true that the use of θάλασσα would more naturally evoke in the Graeco-Roman readers something larger than an inland lake. The potential confusion is exacerbated by the fact that Mark only occasionally specifies which 'sea' is in view (1.16; 7.31), which raises the question whether this is a studied ambiguity in order to enhance the impact of the message. For, in fact, the mastery of the sea was something attributed to the Caesars.

Caesar as 'master of land and sea'

The phrase 'land and sea' was enlisted in the rhetoric praising Augustus' achievements. Philo's *Embassy to Gaius* waxes lyrical on this theme, describing Augustus' entrance on the scene when Europe and Asia were 'waging grievous war all over sea and land, battling on either element'.

> This is the Caesar who calmed the torrential storms on every side (ὁ τοὺς καταρράξαντας πανταχόθι χειμῶνας εὐδιάσας), who healed the pestilences common to Greeks and barbarians (ὁ τὰς κοινὰς νόσους Ἑλλήνων καὶ βαρβάρων ἰασάμενος), [. . .] This is he who not only loosed but broke the chains which had shackled and pressed so hard on the habitable world (οὗτος ἐστιν ὁ τὰ δεσμά, οἷς κατέζευκτο καὶ ἐπεπίεστο ἡ οἰκουμένη, παραλύσας). This is he who exterminated wars [. . .] cleared the sea of pirate ships and filled it with merchant vessels. [. . .] reclaimed every state to liberty, who led disorder into order and brought gentle manners and harmony to all unsociable and brutish nations, [. . .] made a new Hellas and hellenized the outside world [. . .], the guardian of peace, [. . .]
>
> (Philo *Legat*. 145–7)

The phrase may have been part of the Roman self-image for a long time prior to Augustus, for, according to Plutarch, after Cato's victorious triumph, the people of Rome were filled 'with the proud feeling that it was

---

[4] Theißen, ' "Meer" und "See" ', 9–13.   [5] Cf. NRSV translating 'lake'.

[6] Theißen, ' "Meer" und "See" ', 6–9, 21–4. The LXX also uses θάλασσα of an inland lake, including Gennesaret (Num. 34.11; Josh. 12.3; 13.27).

able to master every land and sea' (Plut. *Cato Ma.* 14; cf. *Pomp.* 70.2–3).
But with Augustus, it seemed as if they had achieved their destiny. His
own record of achievements used the phrase to refer to the doors of Janus'
temple being ordered closed 'whenever there was peace, secured by
victory, throughout the whole domain of the Roman people on land
and sea' (*RG* 13; see also 3, 4, 25, 26), adding that they had been
closed only twice before his birth, but three times during his principate. Inscriptions praised Augustus as 'overseer of every land and sea'
([πάσης] γῆ[ς κ]αὶ θ[α]λάσσης [ἐ]π[όπ]τ[ην], Pergamum No. 381).[7] The
Augustan poets also used the phrase as part of their repertoire (cf. Virgil,
Georgics 1.24–35).

Just as other Augustan phraseology became the stock of imperial propaganda, so too, did this phrase. The conquest of Britain (AD 43) further
enriched the phrase, since the island 'at the world's end' had fallen under Roman sway.[8] Tacitus alludes to the phrase in a speech placed in the
mouth of the Briton Calgacus. Britain faced an assault from 'these deadly
Romans, whose arrogance you cannot escape by obedience and self-
restraint. Robbers of the world, now that earth fails their all-devastating
hands, they probe even the sea' (Tac. *Agric.* 30.3–4; 31.2.; cf. Aelius Arist.
Eulogy of Rome 28). In his satire of the deification of Britain's conqueror,
Seneca has Augustus cynically ask whether it was for the apotheosis of
Claudius that he 'made peace by land and sea' (Sen. *Apoc.* 10). Mastery
over land and sea is evidently an Augustan 'trait', to which his successors
may aspire, but to which they may not be equal. In his appeal to Nero,
Seneca also used the phrase, alluding to the prevailing peace on land and
sea (*De clem.* 4). Nero's coins echoed the Augustan language (AD 64–5),
showing the door of Janus closed and the inscription 'with peace obtained
by land and sea he closed Janus by decree of the senate' (Small. **53** =
Braund **247**), as did his bestowal of freedom and immunity from taxation:
'I reward your gods, whose constant care for me on land and sea I have
enjoyed' (Small. **64** = Braund **261** (AD 67); cf. Suet. 6 (*Nero*).24.

Given its role within the propaganda, it is understandable that the phrase
was also used by the critics of the *imperium*. The rhetoric praised Augustus
for 'filling the seas with merchant ships' (Philo *Legat.* 146); the critics
used it to expose the insatiable gluttony of Rome for further conquest
(Plut. *Pomp.* 70) and plunder. 'The conquering Roman now held the

---

[7] From Deissmann, *Light*, 347, fig. 64.

[8] As Julius Caesar's 'failed victory', the conquest of Britain played a significant part
in the imperial rhetoric. Even though Augustus never sailed against Britain, the Augustan
poets spoke of him as about to conquer 'the last people on the earth'; see Griffin, 'Augustus',
198 (Horace), 206 (Propertius), 212 (Virgil).

whole world, sea and land and the course of sun and moon. But he was not satisfied. Now the waters were stirred and troubled by his loaded ships [. . .]' (Petronius *Sat.* 119.1–3, cf. 4–18, 27–36; cf. Plut. *De fort. Rom.* 325D–E; cf. Aelius Aristides, *Eulogy of Rome* 11; Sen. *Ep.* 60.2, 89.22; cf. *ad Helv.* 10.2–7; *De vita beata* 11.4). For the mastery of Rome 'on land and sea' was achieved at great human cost. It was clear from the beginning that it came through war, destruction and violence, for it 'was peace, *secured by victory*, throughout the whole domain of the Roman people on land and sea' (*RG* 13, my italics). The mastery of the *Pax Romana* was 'the political goal of the Roman emperor and his most senior officials and [was] brought about and secured by military action through the success of his legions'.[9] As Tacitus had Calgacus say: 'To plunder, butcher, steal, these things they misname empire: they make a desolation and they call it peace' (Tac. *Agric.* 30.5).

One of the critics of Rome's 'belligerent policy leading to and maintaining the position of a world power and the urban luxury based on it'[10] sought to put things into perspective:

> Now o'er such wide seas are we tempest tossed; we seek out a foe and pile fresh war on war.   (Propertius 3.5.10–12)

This came about through avarice and the one who went after plunder in war was pursuing a vanity in the face of death:

> Yet no wealth shall you carry to the waves of Acheron: naked, you fool, you shall be borne to the ship of hell. There victor and vanquished shades are mingled in the equality of death.
>   (Propertius 3.5.13–15)

'Master of land and sea': Jesus?

Since the use of sea and land is so prominent in Mark, can the journeys of Jesus be understood in the light of this well-known phraseology? As Jesus goes backwards and forwards across 'land and sea' he too shows his mastery, yet it has a different character from that of the Roman *imperator* ('commander').[11] Whereas Augustus' mastery over the storms was metaphorical, Jesus' is presented as real. Whereas the Roman *imperium*

---

[9] Wengst, *Pax Romana*, 11. Cf. Ign. *Rom.* 5.1 (AD 117).

[10] Wengst, *Pax Romana*, 44.

[11] The use of 'imperial' language should be carefully tailored by the appropriate usage of the period. Not to do so runs the risk of importing later and anachronistic models of 'empire'. See further, Judge, *Augustus and Roman History*, 211; 'Second Thoughts'.

(command) over land and sea cost lives and brought plunder and death, Jesus' authority leaves no trail of blood. On the contrary, wherever he finds death, his command brings life.

Journey 1: the question raised, 'Do you not care that we are perishing?' (Mark 4.35–41)

In the previous section, Jesus rescued five people out from under the shadow of death. In the next series of scenes, beginning with the first sea journey, death is even more prominent[12] and Jesus' rescue even more powerful.

Text to reader

The story asks three unanswered questions which continue to guide the reading of the narrative. The significance of two of them has often been recognised; but the importance of the third is generally overlooked. The Christological question ('Who then is this?'; v.41) maintains the readers' interest in Jesus' identity. Since the question is not answered, it opens a gap at the discourse level which forces the readers to seek for an answer. In this way, it guides the reader to think Christologically about the narrative to follow.[13]

Jesus' question to the disciples ('Why are you afraid? Do you not yet have faith?'; v.40) functions in a similar fashion. While coupling their fear with their lack of faith, it also provides an expectation that this faith will come (cf. οὔπω, 'not yet'). This question guides the readers to watch to see if Jesus' analysis of the disciples' state is true, and/or to wait for faith to emerge.

The third question provides the context for the other two. Like them, it too remains unanswered and guides the reading of the next section of the narrative. It is a question about mortality ('Teacher, do you not care that we are perishing?'; v.38). This question reveals that the disciples' fearful lack of faith is focused by the prospect of their death. Since Jesus is surprised by the disciples' fear, it seems that they should have believed that he could do something about their perishing. Thus the three questions are integrally related.

[12] The severity of the circumstances of people in this section is often acknowledged, e.g., J.F. Williams, *Other Followers*, 108; Fisher, 'Miracles', 13f.
[13] Juel, *Master*, 65, 72–3, notes how the following three miracles answer this question, although he overlooks the narrative significance of the other two.

At the discourse level, any question becomes that of the readers and these are no exception. As we have seen, unanswered questions are extremely powerful devices for engaging the reader, since they make the questions of the narrative become the readers'. Here, the more the flesh-and-blood readers are aware of their own desperate fear of perishing, the more this question would become their own. Since the world of Mark's early readers was a perishing world, the heart-felt cry of the disciples would no doubt strike a chord with many readers and the questions would then encourage them to read on in search of answers to the Christological question, the faith question, and the mortality question. It is not surprising that the sequence of miracles which follows reveals something about Jesus and faith in the face of death.

Reader to text

Perishing at sea

For Graeco-Roman readers, Mark's use of the term θάλασσα would evoke images of Mediterranean sea travel. Although Augustus may have cleaned up the danger from pirates (*RG* 25), sea travel had other intrinsic dangers. Shipwreck was always a possibility ('Pity the shipwrecked, for navigation is unsure', Ps-Phoc. 25), since 'in a moment the sea is moved to its depths' (Sen. *Ep.* 4.8).

Death at sea was 'above others a cause for grief',[14] for, as Hesiod said, 'it is a terrible thing to die among the waves' (Hes. *Op.* 687). One of the major problems with drowning at sea was the forfeiture of a decent burial (*Od.* 5.308–12). The fear of drowning and not being properly buried – whether buried by strangers, if your body was found washed up on some foreign shore; or not buried at all, if your body was lost at sea – is expressed in the many surviving epitaphs from tombs erected for shipwrecked bodies buried by strangers and also from the many cenotaphs (κενοὶ τάφοι, 'empty graves') erected for those lost at sea.[15] Without a proper burial, the shipwrecked person, being one of the ἄταφοι, also ran the risk of becoming a ghost, who would then be manipulated by magicians (cf. Apul. *Met.* 3.17, Pamphile's workshop contained 'remains of shipwrecked vessels'; *PGM* VII.465f. calls for a nail, and *PGM* V.54–69 for some water from a shipwreck).

---

[14] Lattimore, 199.   [15] Cf. Bolt, 'Mk 16.1–8', 30f.

Fear at sea

It is not surprising, then, that a storm at sea engendered great fear. To be on the sea in a storm was to be staring your death in the face and, since it was filled with more than the normal share of terrors, this was a terrible death indeed. When Theophrastus presented the character 'Cowardice' (*Characters* 25: δειλία, cf. Mark 4.40; = ὕπειξίς τις ψυχῆς ἔμφοβος (*sic*)), the only arena from which he illustrates, alongside military service, is sea travel and it is portrayed as a fearful thing indeed. Not surprisingly, sailors were counted amongst the brave, as in the anonymous literary papyrus attributed to Moschion (1st c. AD):

> Look at sailors – constantly up against every difficulty! Storm, gale, rain, mountainous seas, lightning, hail, thunder, seasickness, [. . .] darkness! And yet every one of them awaits the gleam of Hope and despairs not of the future. One takes hold of the ropes and watches the sail, another prays the Samothracian gods[16] to assist the pilot, hauls the sheets in [. . .]
>
> (Page **61**; cf. Lucian *Pereg.* 43)

Fear was perfectly understandable, as was the need for rescue. Sailors could pray to their various national gods (e.g., Jonah 1.5f.), but there were also certain gods who specialised in sea rescues, e.g., the Dioscuri (cf. Acts 28.11) and the Samothracian gods. Although the mystery religions were concerned with the fate in the afterlife, the Samothracian initiates were also promised safety in this realm. Just as Lucius was told that Isis would lengthen his life (Apul. *Met.* 11.6), these initiates apparently believed that they had special protection against shipwreck and drowning.[17] Indeed, according to Theophrastus, the coward, 'when a wave hits, asks whether anyone on board has not been initiatied' (καὶ κλύδωνας γενομένου ἐρωτᾶν εἴ τις μὴ μεμύηται τῶν πλεόντων, *Characters* 25.2).[18]

Sailors could also seek magical protection. If magic could cause storms (Hipp. *Morb.Sacr.* 4; cf. 'Seth who makes the sea boil', AthAg, pp. 245ff.), it could also calm them. Apparently Orpheus had the power to 'lull to sleep the howling winds and the hail, and the drifting snow, and the roaring

---

[16] Cf. Ramsay **289**: 'having been saved at sea' (σωθεὶς κατὰ θάλ[ασ]σαν) by the Samothracian gods.

[17] Faraone, 'Mystodokos', 324f. One of the epithets of Isis was 'the pilot', *POxy* 1380.iii.69 Isis = Tyche? (*PWisc.* 1 13.16; *POxy* 491.19); and of Zeus, *POxy* 105.16; 646.

[18] The editors take this as a reference to the Samothrace mysteries, referring to Burkert, *Ancient Mystery Cults*, 13–14.

sea' (*AG* 7.8), so perhaps it was hoped that his art would continue in the songs of the sailors which were probably magical charms ensuring safe passage (e.g., Page **98** = *PGM* XXIX (3rd c. AD).[19] There were also spells which promised the ability to calm the sea: 'Let the earth be still, let the air be still, let the sea be still; let the winds also be still, and do not be a hindrance to this my divination' (*PGM* VII.320ff.; cf. *Sepher ha-Razim* 2.111f. and 4.30ff.).

When Jesus stands and orders the sea to 'be muzzled', he uses a word familiar to magical incantations (φιμόω; cf. 1.25).[20] Is he using some kind of magic to calm this storm, and to keep his friends safe? Or is there some other reason that the sea grows calm? Who then is this?

The fear of death

The fear of death was a recognised problem which the philosophers sought to combat. 'Most men ebb and flow in wretchedness between the fear of death and the hardships of life; they are unwilling to live, and yet they do not know how to die' (Sen. *Ep.* 4.6). As well as counselling that death ought to be seen as just another part of life, Stoics like Seneca also regarded death as one of the evils which they attempted to surmount through anticipation, through the practice of *praemeditatio futurorum malorum*, 'preparation for future evils'.[21] According to Gill, this involved two things:[22] (1) 'a studied anticipation of future possible disasters'; and (2) 'an insistence on the radical distinction between external contingencies [. . .] and our state of mind and character'. In view of our present passage, it is of interest that this latter distinction was frequently expressed in terms of 'calm within a storm' (Cic. *Off.* 1.83, cf. 69, 72–3; Sen. *Tranq.* 14, esp. 10; Plut. *De tranq. anim.* 475B–476D, esp. 475e–476a).[23] Seneca praises Julius Canus, approaching his own death, for exhibiting 'calm in the midst of a storm and a mind worthy of immortality' (Sen. *Tranq.* 14.10). For Plutarch, the wise man's disposition (*diathesis*) can bring calm in physical and emotional storms (Plut. *De tranq. anim.* 475d–476a). The best protection against fear of death is an understanding of the nature of the psyche and a realisation that death is a change to the better or at least to nothing worse, so that, if things are externally bad, 'the harbour is near' and we can 'swim away from the body as from a leaky boat' (Plut. *De tranq. anim.* chs 17–18, esp. 476a–c).[24]

---

[19] Pythagoras also was said to calm winds and seas; cf. Porphyry, *Vit.Pl.* 29.
[20] Cf. *PGM* VII.396; VII.966; ?VII.347; IX.4; IX.9; XLVI.4; ?LXI.27.
[21] Gill, 'Panaetius', 335; cf. 344–9.   [22] Ibid., 344.
[23] Cf. ibid., 344, 347.   [24] Cf. ibid., 348.

The disciples' fear of dying is aroused in the very specific context of sea travel, a fear in which Graeco-Roman readers would readily share. But, since sea travel was often used as a metaphor to depict human frailty in the face of death, this particular fear also arouses the more general fear of death, endemic to Mark's world.

> The popular entertainment literature of the first century [shows] an abundance of sea-storm stories in which the hero shows his character during a sudden threat to his life. In the first century, such stories serve as metaphors, the sea representing the uncertainty of life in the sublunar region [– i.e.,] the sector of the cosmos where one found famine, disease, war and death.[25]

This being so, as this scene aligns the readers with the disciples in their fear, it begins to say something about the more general fear of dying. Who then is this, who deals with this most basic of fears?

The ruler of the waves

For those familiar with the Old Testament, it was YHWH who could not only silence the winds (Ps. 107.25–30; Prov. 30.4; Job 38.25; Amos 4.13; Nahum 1.3f.), but also subdue the waves (e.g. Pss 33.7; 65.7; 77.16; 107.28–32). Hellenistic culture also knew of rulers who had the divine ability to master the waves.[26]

Figures in the ancient myths were given power over the waves, such as Euphemus (Ap. Rh. 1.179–84; Schol. Pindar: Drachmann **106**; Schol. Lycophron: Scheer **287**), Orion (Apoll. *Bib.* 1.4.3; Ps-Erat. *Catast.* fr. 32), Abaris (Porph. *Vit. Pythag.* 29; Iamblichus *Pythag.* 136; cf. Hdt. 4.36), and Heracles (Sen. *Herc. fur.* 322–4; Julian *Or.* 7.219D). By the fifth century BC, such power was also granted to rulers. Xerxes' crossing of the Hellespont received such a mythical overlay (Hdt. 7.35, 56). His power to 'walk dryshod over the sea' was apparently still believed by enough people in Dio Chrysostom's day to warrant his refuting the claim (3.30–1).[27]

Power over the sea belonged to the fantastical stuff of later satire (Lucian *Ver. Hist.* 2.4), or of dreams (Dio 11.129). Nevertheless, such a dream would be a good omen for a ruler:

---

[25] Cotter, 'Cosmology', 119, 121.

[26] The following discussion draws upon Collins, 'Rulers' and Cotter, 'Cosmology'. I was unfortunately unable to consult Cotter's thesis, 'The Markan Sea Miracles: Their History, Formation and Function' (PhD dissertation, University of St Michael's College, 1991).

[27] Collins, 'Rulers', 218–19.

> For all those who earn their living from crowds, for statesmen,
> and popular leaders, it prophesies extraordinary gain together
> with great fame. For the sea also resembles a crowd because of
> its instability.   (Artem. *Oneir*. 3.16)

Despite its being humanly impossible, magical writings portrayed the
power over the sea as possible to those who know the correct magical
means (*PGM* XXXIV>.1–24; cf. *Sword of Moses*, Gaster 1.331). As
an image of what is humanly impossible, the motif was applied to the
arrogance of a ruler aspiring to empire (cf. 2 Macc. 5.21, of Antiochus
IV Epiphanes).

But the motif had been utilised in the service of a prestigious array of
rulers, not just Xerxes. It was used of Alexander the Great. Eustathius
(12th c. AD) refers to Homer's description of Poseidon: 'Then gambolled
the sea beasts beneath him [Poseidon] on every side from out of the deeps,
for well they knew their Lord, and in gladness the sea parted before him'
(*Il*. 13.27–9), before quoting Callisthenes (*c*. 356–323 BC), the biographer
of Alexander: 'It [the sea] did not fail to recognize its Lord, so that arching
itself and bowing it may seem to do obeisance' (comment on *Il*. 13.29).[28]
Here Callisthenes is saying that the sea recognised Alexander's divine
empowerment and that 'he is not to be impeded in his fulfilment of his
heavenly mandate as Lord of earth and sea '.[29] Menander also alluded
to Alexander's speaking of the necessity 'to tread a pathway through the
sea' (διελθεῖν διὰ θαλάττης πόρον τιν', frg. 924K).

Similar imagery is enlisted in support of Augustus. A gem carved in
31 BC to celebrate his triumph at Actium pictures Octavian as Poseidon
pulled by four horses across the waves,[30] showing that

> Augustus has been granted authority over the cosmos, including
> the sea. The sea recognized Augustus's heavenly authorisation
> and would not obstruct his war plans. Thus nature demonstrates
> its subservience to the one chosen by heaven to guide the destiny
> of the world.[31]

Gaius Caligula, who wished to be named a god in his lifetime, may have
also tried to imitate this feature of divine authorisation by the construction
of the five-mile bridge across the Bay of Baiae out of ships lashed together

[28] See Pearson, *Lost Histories of Alexander*, 37; Jacoby, *Fragmente*, II.B.650.
[29] Cotter, 'Cosmology', 123.   [30] Hadas, *Imperial Rome*, 69.
[31] Cotter, 'Cosmology', 124. Cf. Virgil *Georg*. I.24ff., where Augustus is spoken of as a god who is yet to choose his domain. One option is that he becomes a sea god and marries a mermaid, giving her as dowry all the waves.

(Dio 59.17.11). Because the sea remained calm while he rode across, he was convinced that Neptune feared him. 'In effect, using artificial means Gaius could boast that he had ridden across the water dryshod. Neptune's subservience to his plan was interpreted to mean that he too recognized him as Lord.'[32]

This theme is part of the Augustan legacy that Philo uses to call Caligula to adopt his proper role. In his *Embassy to Gaius* (144–5), he praises Augustus in similar terms, using the metaphors of a man ordering calm to a storm and healing a pestilence without a petition to a deity. 'This is the Caesar who calmed the torrential storms on every side, who healed pestilences common to Greeks and barbarians, pestilences which descending from the south and east coursed to the west and north sowing the seeds of calamity over the places and waters which lay between them.' Thus, this evidence surrounding Caligula shows that 'the idea of a hero calming a storm on his own is already "alive" from the 40s of the first century'.[33]

The theme of Caesar calming a storm reappears in a poem by Calpurnius Siculus (*c.* AD 50–60) in Nero's honour. Here a shepherd says:

> Do you see how the green woods are hushed at the sound of Caesar's [Nero's] name? I remember how, despite the swoop of a storm, the grove, even as now, sank sudden into peace with boughs at rest. And I said, 'A god, surely a god, has driven the east winds hence.'   (*Eclogue* 4.97–100)

Mark's account gives to Jesus literally what Philo grants to Augustus metaphorically.[34] Both Augustus and Jesus are credited with the salvific activity reserved for God (cf. Ps. 107.28–32). This, at the least, would signal his divine authorisation, and perhaps even his own divine rule, on a par with Alexander, and the great Augustus.

Who then is this?

Crossing the sea could be for commerce or for conquest – both well-known Roman pursuits. Even in the early days of the *imperium*, Propertius offered a quiet protest. Because of Roman avarice they found themselves 'now o'er such wide seas [. . .] tempest tossed; we seek out a foe and pile fresh war on war' (Propertius 3.5.10–12). He attempted to put the imperial project of seeking wealth through war into perspective: 'Yet no wealth shall you carry to the waves of Acheron: naked, you fool, you

---

[32] Cotter, 'Cosmology', 127.   [33] Ibid., 124.   [34] Ibid., 125.

shall be borne to the ship of hell. There victor and vanquished shades are mingled in the equality of death' (3.5.13–15). Rome was braving the uncertain enterprise of sea travel for the sake of plundering the earth. In the exercise of their *imperium* they were taking people to the Acheron and this very early critic of the eternal city was asking, what for?

One of her early representatives, Julius Caesar, smuggled himself into a boat in pursuit of Pompey. When he detected the pilot was changing course because of heavy seas, he unveiled himself and said 'Go on, good sir, be brave and fear nothing! But entrust your sails to Fortune and receive her breeze confident because you bear Caesar and Caesar's Fortune.' Plutarch comments:

> Thus firmly was he convinced that Fortune accompanied him on his voyages, his travels, his campaigns, his commands; Fortune's task it was to enjoin calm upon the sea, summer weather upon the winter-time, speed upon the slowest of men, courage upon the most dispirited [. . .]   (Plut. *De fort. Rom.* 319C–D)

The disciples display a thoroughly normal response to the storm. The storm signalled to them that they were probably about to perish and a miserable death at sea was filled with even greater terrors than normal. With a word of command, Jesus calmed the sea, displaying the same confidence in 'Fortune' as Caesar. But although Caesar did nothing except give the order to the pilot to go on, Jesus gave the orders to the storm and it responded. What kind of Fortune is that?

The Fortune of the Romans helped them to cross land and sea seeking 'glory' through the plunder of the nations. Augustus had stilled the storms of a troubled world. Jesus' 'fortune' had kept them safe at sea and he had literally stilled the storm. But why was he crossing it? What plunder was he seeking?

> In the Stilling of the Storm, Jesus' command to the wind and the sea would suggest to a first-century audience that he is Lord of the sea. Metaphorically, since the sea symbolizes life's unsettled and dangerous character, Jesus' authority as Lord of the sea signals to the attentive listener that just as surely as he commands the elements such as wind and sea, so too he has control over life-threatening events.[35]

In reality and in mythology, the sea represented the waters of death. Jesus had previously riddled about plundering the realm of the prince of

[35] Ibid., 127.

daimones. Now his first sea crossing issues in a series of events which are nothing other than an assault on the underworld.[36]

Suppliant 6: out of the tombs (Mark 5.1–20)

Text to reader

Apart from the initial plural verb (v.1) the disciples are absent and cannot play a role towards the readers. Instead, the readers are strongly aligned with the man from the tombs.

The man from the tombs

This 'man from the tombs, in unclean spirit' met Jesus after he crossed the lake (vv.1f.). The scene is focalised through the man, since he is the subject of the verb while Jesus is referred to with a personal pronoun (v.2b). A lengthy and detailed description of his plight creates sympathy with him (vv.3–5). Interrupting the flow of the action (v.2: action begins; vv.3–5: description; v.6: action resumes), this evidently provides information which is essential for the proper understanding of the scene.[37] The extensive detail slows the pace, keeping the readers' attention on him to create the illusion that they are themselves viewing the man's plight.[38] All this decreases the distance between the readers and the man.

Although he is 'in unclean spirit' (v.2), more interest is initially shown in his circumstances. That he dwelt amongst the tombs is especially emphasised – through being reported twice in the key initial position (vv.2f.) and then resumed in final position in the description (v.5). This characteristic is explained by a second, that he was so strong he could no longer be bound, despite many attempts (vv.3f.).

Despite these features, the description does not encourage fear (contrast Matt. 8.28b), but arouses sympathy. The details are filled with pathos: he came from the tombs (v.2b); in fact, he lived in the tombs (v.3); this was a home of last resort, for many times people had tried to bind him, unsuccessfully (vv.3bf.); now he spent his nights and his days amongst the tombs, crying out and cutting himself with stones (v.5).[39] This is a picture

---

[36] For a similar argument, see Kotansky, 'Jesus '.

[37] It acts as explicit commentary, cf. Fowler, *Let the Reader*, 105, 101.

[38] For tempo and time manipulation, see Licht, *Storytelling*, ch. 5; Rimmon-Kenan, *Narrative Fiction*, 51–6; cf. Chatman, *Story*, 62–84.

[39] The overtones of death are sustained all the more if this is a 'continuous mourning ritual', Derrett, 'Legend', 68. Cf. McVann, 'Destroying Death', 126–7.

of a human being in great distress, who, although alive, lives amongst the
dead.

The clash of the spirits

The scene continues to powerfully focalise the readers through the man
(v.6), using an inside view of perception (ἰδών),[40] and the reader trav-
els with the man 'from afar' towards Jesus. His cry recalls the man in
Capernaum, with whom the reader had been aligned. His recognition of
Jesus as Son of the Most High also creates sympathy, since it sounds like
the opinion of Jesus expressed by previous reliable commentary (1.1, 11;
3.11), even if it raises the question of how the man could be so discerning.
The direct speech maintains the sense of closeness to this character, as
does the pathos of the content (v.7). When the cry is initially heard, it
is heard as that of the man himself, adding to the sense of his desperate
situation: having been so alienated from all normal human intercourse,
he is so filled with fear of being harmed further by this new stranger that
he resorts to a strong adjuration to prevent Jesus from torturing him.

The narrative then provides a mini-flashback which forces the reader to
re-read the man's cry. The narrator explains the cry (γάρ)[41] by reference
to information which has so far been withheld. Jesus had previously been
saying,[42] 'Come out, O unclean spirit, from this man' (v.8). The verbal
similarities in the flashback[43] recall the scene in Capernaum where the
unclean spirit spoke through the man. This encourages the readers to view
the cry of the Gerasene similarly. Once the readers realise that the spirit
is addressing Jesus directly, the insight into his identity is understandable
(cf. 1.24; 1.34; 3.11).[44] The revelation of the true source of his cry, in
turn, continues to promote sympathy with the man, for now his degraded
condition is explained by the presence of these spirits (cf. v.2b).

The question about his name reveals that the spirits are multiple,
as in Capernaum (1.24), which is emphasised by Legion's explanatory
gloss 'for we are many' (v.9). At this moment, when the source of the
man's remarkable strength and living death becomes clear, the readers'
sympathy with him reaches its peak.

It is here that the contest between the spirits and Jesus also becomes
central. The man fades from view and the spirits speak directly to Jesus.

---

[40] Cf. Fowler, *Let the Reader*, 121f.   [41] This acts as explicit commentary, ibid., 92.

[42] So the imperfect, cf. Zerwick, *Biblical Greek*, §290.

[43] J.F. Williams, *Other Followers*, 109.

[44] The cry acts as implicit commentary, confirming previous reliable commentary
(1.1, 11), Fowler, *Let the Reader*, 131.

The readers are now assigned the role of observers. As the spirits desperately beg Jesus not to send them out of the region (v.10), the readers sense their fear and, with Capernaum in the background, their imminent demise.

The spirits into the sea

By providing the necessary background information regarding the large herd of pigs nearby (v.11), the narrator aligns the readers with himself, enabling them to continue to observe the action from a more detached vantage point. They hear the spirits' request to enter the pigs (v.12) and Jesus' permission (v.13a). The dramatic details give the impression that they actually observe the spirits entering the pigs, the herd rushing down the slope into the sea, and the two thousand being drowned in the sea (v.13). The double reference to the sea reinforces the importance of this location. Since they enter the underworld through this watery portal, the swine are portrayed as meeting the fate from which the disciples were rescued in the previous scene.

The aftermath

From a distance, the readers observe the swineherds' flight and hear of their widespread report drawing the crowds to 'see' what had happened (v.14). Although the visual verbs (ἰδεῖν, θεωροῦσιν) briefly allow the reader to see the man who had previously been daemonised sitting clothed and in his right mind (v.15) through the perception of the crowds,[45] the rapid change of subject works against any sustained alignment with them. By specifically mentioning that the man was the one who had had the legion, the narrator does not permit the readers to forget the events just described. This reminder underlines the enormity of what had happened to this man. Against this memory, the reaction of the Gerasene populace comes as a shock: they were afraid. Since this recalls the disciples' reaction to Jesus' amazing deed on the boat (4.41), the natural presumption is that they were afraid of Jesus, the one who had calmed the man whom no-one had been able to bind and who had dwelt amongst the tombs.

The report that the swineherds reiterated the events they had witnessed (v.16) encourages the reader to recall the scene for the second time, and, once again, the reaction of the crowds comes as a shock: there is no Capernaum amazement (1.27; cf. 2.12), and no marvelling crowds

[45] Ibid., 121f.

(1.28, 32–34, 37, 45; 2.13; 3.7–12, 20, 32; 4.1), but, instead, the Gerasenes beg Jesus to leave their region (v.17).

The report

As Jesus steps into the boat, the man who had been daemonised becomes an actor. His request that Jesus allow him 'to be with him' (ἵνα μετ᾽ αὐτοῦ ᾖ, v.18) recalls the calling of the twelve (cf. 3.14), which indicates that this man, wittingly or unwittingly, is asking to be one of Jesus' closest companions.[46] Although this group has already been closed (3.13–19), when Jesus called them to be with him it was an intermediate step towards being sent out to continue his mission (3.14f.). Although refusing to allow the Gerasene man into this closed number (v.19), Jesus nevertheless sends him on a mission. He is told to go home and tell what the Lord has done for him and how he had mercy on him.

As the fulfilment of his mission is reported it contains two subtle changes for the readers' ears only. Instead of going to his home, he goes throughout the Ten Cities and instead of proclaiming what the Lord has done, he proclaims what Jesus has done (v.20). This should not be taken as a case of 'disobedience'[47] which 'prevents the reader from completely identifying with this character',[48] for this runs counter to the narrative's previous strong alignment of the readers with the character. In addition, there are absolutely no negative judgements upon him. Instead, his actions are read more naturally as an abundance of obedience: so overwhelmed was he by what had occurred that he was apparently convinced that Jesus could be equated with the Lord and he went even beyond the bounds of his mission. The end of the story is consistent with this reading for it is only at this point that we hear of the amazement that was previously expected but not delivered (vv.15, 17). As the readers hear that 'everyone was amazed', they too are able to enter into this choral ending and rejoice with this man.

The significance for the narrative

This incident constitutes the supreme exorcism in the Gospel of Mark. Jesus' unanswered riddle to his opponents had suggested that no-one can plunder the strong man's house, 'unless he first binds the strong man' (3.27). The narrative stressed the strength of the man from the tombs, by saying that 'no-one was able to bind him any longer' (οὐκέτι οὐδεὶς

---

[46] J.F. Williams, *Other Followers*, 111.
[47] Ibid., 111f., 126, 135, 154.   [48] Ibid., 126.

ἐδύνατο αὐτὸν δῆσαι, v.3), for 'no-one was strong enough to conquer him' (οὐδεὶς ἴσχυεν αὐτὸν δαμάσαι, v.4). By means of these allusions to 3.27, the subjugation of this unbindable strong man suggests another dimension to the readers: Jesus' riddle is finding an answer and *the* strong man is being subdued. As Jesus banishes the legion of *daimones* and delivers the man from the tombs, the 'prince of the *daimones*' suffers a major defeat.

The scene stresses the radical change in the man's circumstances. As a result of the Legion being cast out, he was rescued from the graves and sent back into ordinary life. He went from crying out in distress day and night, to preaching far and wide. He was brought from death to life and this issued in his proclamation of God's mercy. When Jesus defeated the strong man, a man who had been his victim walked out from amongst the graves and began to live again.

Reader to text

Living with the dead

Living in the tombs, the man is clearly amongst the dead. The readers may recognise this as a case of the exclusion of a 'madman', as practised by some barbarian nations (Hdt. 1.138.1). The legion of *daimones* is easily identified as a horde of ghosts, since tombs were their natural location. In addition, 'madness' was believed to be caused by the souls of the departed,[49] and the man may also be seen as someone who had practised magic himself, but had lost control of the spirits who now controlled him. The man's self-destructive tendency (v.5) also fits the scenario of his being plagued with ghosts, who were known for violence directed towards injury and death (cf. *BJ* 7.185; *Vit. Ap.* 3.38). He is living with the dead and the dead are living with him.[50]

Unable to be bound

His strength

Graeco-Roman readers would recognise the man's exceptional strength as a sign of the supernatural. A story of Dionysus being captured by pirates who thought him a king's son (pre-3rd c. BC) provides a nice parallel:

[49] Baroja, 'Magic', 77.
[50] At least one commentator has recognised that the *daimones* possessing this man are the spirits of the dead – even speculating that they are the ghosts of those who fell in battle with the Romans! Theißen, *Miracle Stories*, 89 n. 21; 255 n. 58.

148   *Jesus' Defeat of Death*

δεσμοῖς ἔθελον δεῖν ἀργαλέοισι. τὸν δ' οὐκ ἴσχανε δεσμά, λύγοι
δ' ἀπὸ τηλόσε πῖπτον χειρῶν ἠδὲ ποδῶν

They sought to bind him with rude bonds, but the bonds would
not hold him, and the withes fell far away from his hands and feet.
(*Homeric Hymns* 7.12–14)

The inability to bind him issues in a discussion about which supernatural
being they have detained. The source of the exceptional strength of Mark's
man from the tombs is not a divinity, but the spirit(s) from the tombs with
which he is afflicted.

The attempts to bind

The many attempts to bind him may have been motivated by self-
protection (cf. Matt. 8.28), but it is also possible that they sprang from
more noble motives. Celsus, the first-century Roman physician, prescribed, amongst other things, that some patients suffering from mental
illness were to be treated brutally, including using fetters when the patient
is violent.[51] Exorcisms operated upon assumptions of what is commonly
called 'sympathetic magic', but better termed 'persuasively analogical'
practices.[52] So, for example, some lead curses hoped that the victim would
become as cold, inert and silent as the lead of the tablet; the use of bound
or pierced voodoo dolls of metal, clay or wax imitated the binding of the
spell; water (and spittle) was poured on the body so that the spirit/disease
would imitate its flow away from the body; or an animal was treated in
a way corresponding to the desire of the spell. One of the very ancient
practices associated with exorcism which operated on such principles was
the binding of the victim.

The influence of the spirit upon the victim was itself regarded as a
binding. This was sought by malevolent curses (e.g. *PGM* IV.296–326;
330f.; 350; [372, 376]; 380), often used in conjunction with figures of
wax, clay, or metal, bound up and pierced in gruesome fashion. An illness
or affliction could therefore be considered the result of the spirit binding a
person, possibly as a result of some curse. This language is even detected
in the language of sickness (*P.Oxy* 1381: 'healed the diseases binding
them', τὰς κατεχούσας αὐτοὺ[ς] νόσους ἔσωσεν). Somehow the illness
has itself become unbound: 'Headache, though bound in heaven, hath

---

[51] Moss, 'Mental Disorder', 716; Gill, 'Ancient Psychotherapy', 319. The use of bonds
in cases of mania evidently continued, for it was condemned by Caelius Aurelianus (4th or
5th c. AD) (*On Chronic Diseases* 1.144–52 and 1.183).
[52] Faraone, 'Agonistic Context', 8, referring to the anthropological work of Tambiah,
'Form', and Lloyd, *Magic*.

escaped on earth' (Thompson ṭ.**IX**.147). The magician would seek to release the person bound, by rebinding the forces loosed against them: 'May he not be held in bondage, May his fetters be loosened' (Thompson **1. III**.124–5); '[Who]lly bound and sealed and tied in knots and chained (are you) that you [g]o away and be sealed and depart from the house' (Isbell **10**). On the principles of sympathetic magic, such a procedure may have included some kind of binding procedure, whether the tying of knots (*PGM* IV.331); or binding of a figure (*PGM* IV.296ff.); or even drawing a bound figure.[53] It may also have involved the binding of the patient (Thompson ṭ.**IX**). Now, if the many attempts to bind this man were actually noble attempts at exorcism, then their failure signals the extremely powerful nature of his spirits and it is no surprise to find they are so numerous that they use the name 'Legion'.

This name may also indicate why the previous attempts were futile. The exorcist had to name the spirit. Although this required knowledge, it did not have to be exact, so the spells tended to list numerous names of spirits and more were always being added (such as, later, the name of Jesus; see Acts 19.13–16; *PGM* IV.3020; ?Isbell **52**.3). By this 'shotgun' approach, the magicians hoped to name the spirit concerned and gain mastery over it. But, here in the Decapolis, if there are enough spirits to warrant the name Legion (i.e., perhaps up to 6000),[54] no exorcist could hope to gain control.

The clash of spirits

The encounter between Jesus and the man has a number of features reminiscent of magical practice. The use of ὁρκίζω and its compounds is frequent in magic, although here it is in reverse: the spirits adjure Jesus! The *daimones*' plea, 'do not torture me' (μή με βασανίσῃς), uses another word from the magical texts,[55] and illustrates the fear in which the *daimones* existed and by which they were magically manipulated. The request for the name (v.9) is necessary in order to gain control (cf. *PGM* XIII.425ff.); and the great cry is also reminiscent of ghostly behaviour (v.7). These features combine to make the story a clash between two great

---

[53] Cf. Isbell **8** and p. 36 n. 8.   [54] Gealy, 'Legion'; Watson and Parker, 'Legion'.

[55] Eitrem, *Notes*, 24f. See Versnel, 'Beyond Cursing', 73, for the requests for the gods to use such judicial torture. The love charms often request that the victim be tortured by their thoughts of the interested party, occasionally with this word, e.g., *DT* **242**, **271**. *PGM* II.51?; IV.1407, 1412f., 1766; XIII.289; XIXa.50f.; XXXVI.201. *SuppMag* **72** (Augustan) threatens the underworld gods with intractable headache until the magician's (probably erotic) purposes are fulfilled.

powers. The man who could not be bound (v.4) attempts to bind Jesus (v.7) – as if Jesus is the superior *daimon* and the *daimon* is the magician! Nevertheless, Jesus proves to be the master.

Into the sea

The fear of a changed location

A special feature of this story is the *daimones*' request that Jesus would not send them 'out of the region' (ἔξω τῆς χώρας, v.10). This seems difficult to account for,[56] if their fear is simply of being sent outside the region of the Gerasenes (cf. v.1), or even the region of the tombs, even on the theory that *daimones* are geographically limited.[57] Instead, they are probably referring to an underworld space.[58] In the spells invoking Helios, the region of the dead is the realm in which the *daimones* are recruited by him on his nightly underworld journey to be released for the use of the necromancer in the upper world.[59] A silver phylactery may provide a rationale for their fear in its threat to remove them from this region, to regions 'below the springs and the abyss'.[60]

The springs were also a feature of the underworld. They appear on the 'Orphic' gold leaves at the entrance to the underworld and are the

---

[56] If the request is simply about a local geographical region, then Jesus' permission, if genuine, constitutes a departure from normal exorcistic common sense. He himself would acknowledge that the *daimones* would look elsewhere for another home (Luke 11.24–26). Cf. Gordon, on the theory that the Aramaic incantation bowls were used to trap the *daimones* within them: 'the last thing the ancients wished to do was to trap on their own property the demon which might subsequently escape and work mischief on the spot', cited in Isbell, 8.

[57] Hooker, *Mark*, 143. I am not sure that the evidence usually assembled proves the existence of this belief. Luke 11.24–26 hardly warrants it and the frequently asserted view-point that *daimones* preferred deserts and ruins is derived from spells which sought to cast them into these places, for the very reason that they were uninhabited. This may partly lie behind their fear here (see Gundry, *Mark*, 251f.). If this view has anything going for it, the *daimones* would be asking to stay around these particular tombs, for spirits naturally inhabit graveyards.

[58] The 'region' (χῶρος) of the dead appears several times in the magical papyri (*PGM* IV.446, 1967; VIII.80; VII.268).

[59] Cf. also the *defixio SEG* VI.**803** (3rd c. AD) which asks Helios to send 'the wailing of the violently killed' upon an opponent, presumably by bringing their *daimones* up with him. Helios is invoked in the Augustan *SuppMag* **72** = GMPT CXXII. For this same pattern of the *daimones* being called up by the sun and appearing in human form, see *AMB* **Bowl 13**. A late Coptic charm describes Helios as the Father of 'those in the abyss', Mirecki, 'Hoard', 458.

[60] Jordan, 'Phylactery Beirut', 61–9 = Gager **125**. See also *PGM* IV.1247f., where the *daimones* are bound with fetters and delivered into 'the black chaos in perdition' εἰς τὸ μέ|λαν χάος ἐν ταῖς ἀπωλείαις. For the abyss, see *PGM* I.343; III.554; IV.512, 1120; 1148; 1350; 2835; 3064; VII.261, 517; XIII.169, 482; XXXV.1; XXXVI.217; LXII.29, 31.

source of the refreshing waters from which the initiates receive their 'cool water' in order to forget the bodily world and enter into the realms of afterlife bliss.[61] But here, the *daimones* are being sent below these springs, i.e., far away from the entrance, and below the abyss, which is in the direction of Tartarus, i.e., the realm from which they may never return. The combined picture is that they are being threatened with expulsion from the underworld regions which still allowed some traffic with the world of the body, for, once banished to 'below', their potential for harm has ceased. Does the fear of such nether-nether regions lie behind Legion's question?[62] If so, this has implications for understanding the result of this clash with the ghosts.

The pigs into the sea

The pigs being sent into the sea is not simply a conventional feature of such stories, providing the demonstration necessary to prove the exorcism successful (cf. *AJ* 8.42–9, a bowl turned over; perhaps *Gen. Apoc.* 20.21, 'the king arose and spoke';[63] *Vit. Ap.* 4.20, a statue moves; Lucian *Philops.* 16, a *daimon* departs as smoke; *ActsPeter* 2.11, Caesar's statue is kicked to pieces), but it is an integral part of the help Jesus provides for the man.

Given the *daimones'* fear (v.10), it is difficult to say what occurs when Jesus allows them to enter the swine to plunge into the sea. It may be that the sea is a natural home for the *daimones* (e.g., *AMB* **Am6**.14 has a demon from the sea), but this is because the sea is an underworld location, or, at the least, a portal into the underworld. After all, it was the way so many sailors entered this realm, and, not being properly buried, the potential for becoming ghosts was high (cf. Mark 6.49). So Jesus could be sending the dead back into the underworld.

But have they simply returned to the 'region of the dead', or have they gone to a region further below? If the former, the upper world is afforded only temporary relief – until the next time they are summoned forth by magic. But, given their fearful question and the narrative's previous suggestions that Jesus has come to deal decisively with underworld beings who still operate above (1.24; 3.27), the readers may well suspect that he has 'destroyed' them, i.e., permanently removed them from any further influence in the upper world. A Latin curse against charioteers (*DT* **286** = Grant, 241 (3rd c. AD)) indicated that the *daimon* it was enlisting to kill them had been set free by 'the god of the sea and the air. [. . .]'.

---

[61] See Harrison, *Prolegomena*, 574–86, text I and II; Zuntz, *Persephone*, 368f.

[62] Luke takes it this way (8.31) and in Matt. 8.29 the fear of torture before the appointed time may indicate that it is then that they will be sent into the Abyss (cf. 25.41).

[63] Duling, 'Eleazar Miracle', 5, calls this a 'mild demonstration'.

Jesus has demonstrated himself to be the 'god of the sea' (4.35ff.) and no matter who had permitted them to enter the upper world, Jesus now rescinds this freedom.

The pigs are often taken as a signal that this incident took place in non-Jewish territory. The Jews' avoidance of the pig was certainly known in the Graeco-Roman world, even if the reasons for it were little understood (Plut. *Quaest. conv.* IV.5 669E–671C). However, instead of reading with Jewish eyes, the Graeco-Roman readers are more likely to understand the significance of the pigs according to their own cultural framework.

Although pigs could also be sacrificed to Zeus as a purification rite,[64] they were the standard sacrifices offered to the chthonic gods. Julian refrained from pigs because they 'are coarse, earthly, vile creatures, only offered to the chthonic gods' (*Or.* 5.175–7). They were apparently used in Athens as sacrifices to dispel unclean spirits (*Schol.Aeschin.* in or. 1.23; *Schol.Dem.* in or. 4.1b) and five Latin curse tablets from Rome (mid 1st c. BC) promised Proserpine and Pluto the offering of 'dates, figs, and a black pig' if the curse is completed by March (Fox = Gager **134**). Once Augustus added his genius to the Lares (7 BC), a pig was sacrificed to the Lares Augusti.[65]

Faraone has suggested that the sacrifice of the pig is one of 'the recurring patterns [which] suggests that the *praxis* of Assyrian or Babylonian rituals reappears as part of the plot of Greek myths and legends'[66] (e.g., Aesch. *Eum.* 283; Ap.Rh. 4.698ff.; and vase paintings in which the god stabs a small pig over a youth's head). He refers to an Assyrian cuneiform tablet, which instructs that a piglet be dissected over the head of a patient so that the blood is spread everywhere (i.e., Thompson **"N"**.ii.40ff.). Such rituals as these suggests a clue to the meaning of the pigs entering the sea.

The sea was in itself involved in purification sacrifices. For example, the Achaeans were told by Calchas to 'wash off their pollution and throw the pollution into the sea' (*Il.* 1.314). This anticipates the practice of the purifiers in Hippocrates' *On the sacred disease*, who 'bury some of (the polluted remains) in the ground, cast some in the sea, and carry others to the mountains' (*Morb.Sacr.* 4.43–6). But, in the Greek world, impurity could also be absorbed by a variety of substances (eggs, fleeces, mud, bran mash), and, as in the Ancient Near East, by animals.[67]

[64] The sacrifice to Zeus of a piglet, in the context of a meal to purify from *elasteroi*, is also found in the *Lex sacra* from Selinous (Col. B, l. 5), see Jameson et al., *Lex sacra*, 17, cf. the Kyrene inscription *LSSupp* **115**. If the offering to Zeus is to stay the wrath of the Erinyes (cf. Ap.Rh. 4.698ff. and the sacrifice of an Athenian manslayer on return from exile, Dem. *Or.* 23.72, 73) then the chthonic associations are not so far away.
[65] Huzar, 'Emperor Worship', 3117.   [66] Faraone, 'Aphrodite's ΚΕΣΤΟΣ', 240.
[67] Parker, *Miasma*, 230f.

This brings us back to the ancient Semitic practice of the transfer of disease to animals. The tablet illustrating practices which, according to Faraone, may lay behind the Greek use of pigs – which, incidentally, involves both a pig and water from the sea – explains the ritual in substitutionary terms:

> Give the pig in his stead and Let the flesh be as his flesh, And the blood as his blood, And let him hold it; Let the heart be as his heart (Which thou hast placed upon his heart) And let him hold it; . . . [That the] pig may be a substitute for him . . . May the evil Spirit, the evil Demon stand aside!
> (Thompson "N".iii.10ff.; cf. 30ff.)

In the cultural framework of the Graeco-Roman readers, the pigs are the usual chthonic sacrifices; they are involved in purificatory rites; and they act as a substitution for a person in order to rid them from the influence of the *daimones*. If so, these pigs moving from the man into the sea could be seen as a sacrifice to the underworld gods, which draws off the unclean spirits for the cleansing of the man.[68]

Jesus cares for the perishing

Several unanswered questions had opened gaps in the discourse, guiding the reading of what follows. The disciples had asked, 'Do you not care that we are perishing?' (4.38) and, 'Who then is this that even the winds and waves obey him?' (4.41). The questions begin to find answers in Gerasa, where Jesus not only demonstrates that he does care for one who is perishing under the evil and destructive influence of the world of the dead, but also that he is the one who can liberate people from such beings. The story is cast as a contest between Jesus and the power(s) of death.[69] The man leaves the tombs and once again enters ordinary life. Once again, Mark has presented the story of this suppliant as a resurrection paradigm.[70] The 'dead' has come to life again.

The next two suppliants, whose stories are intercalated, both, in their own way, reinforce Jesus' ability to deal with death. Although the

[68] Derrett, 'Legend', 68, therefore takes this as 'a taste of the Passion'.
[69] Robinson, *Problem*, 87–8, rightly noted the sharp contrast between death and life (5.15, 19, cf. 2f., 5), as does Gundry, *Mark*, despite according it a secondary status.
[70] '[The Gerasene] represents death at large amongst men, and Jesus' act is a triumph over death. It is a resurrection scene', Derrett, 'Legend', 68; cf. McVann, 'Destroying Death', 126–7.

disciples are present, they act either negatively or neutrally, which hardly promotes engagement with the readers, who are once again strongly aligned with the suppliants.

Suppliant 7a: the synagogue ruler (Mark 5.21–24a)

Text to reader: life from the brink of death

After Jesus crosses the lake and a large crowd gathers (5.21), the narrator mentions that Jesus was παρὰ τὴν θάλασσαν. This appears rather unnecessary and so stands out as a deliberate reuse of the phrase from Mark's first major section (1.16; 2.13; cf. 3.7; 4.1), which evokes the well-established pattern and erects the expectation that a call to follow Jesus is about to occur. However, instead of this, Jesus is summoned to follow someone else.

A man comes who is described in terms of his position in the synagogue – as he will be throughout the account (vv.22, 35, 36, 38), despite the fact that his name could have been used (v.22). Although part of the religious establishment, the story will show that he is not opposed to Jesus,[71] but because of his need he has been drawn towards him. Apparently he had found his own religious system, being dead at heart (3.5), to be impotent before his affliction and had decided to go elsewhere.

The scene is focalised through this man by naming him[72] and providing an inside view of visual perception (v.22b, ἰδών).[73] The incongruity of a synagogue ruler falling at Jesus' feet may suggest that he recognises Jesus' authority (cf. [1.40]; 5.6), but it certainly indicates his desperation, as does his repeated begging and his actual request. The direct speech enables the readers to hear his words for themselves. He begs Jesus to come and lay his hands on his 'little daughter'. This description adds much *pathos* to the account: she is female; she is relationally described; and her father uses the diminutive, which stresses his endearment for her.[74] His dear one is at the point of death (v.23, ἐσχάτως ἔχει),[75] and

---

[71] Cf. Malbon, 'Jewish Leaders', 157–9; cf. J.F. Williams, *Other Followers*, 113.

[72] For naming as a verbal indicator of focalisation, see Rimmon-Kenan, *Narrative Fiction*, 82f.

[73] Fowler, *Let the Reader*, 121f.

[74] Recall the discussion in the Introduction, p. 19. It should be noted that it is impossible for the girl, being dying and dead in this account, to offer a model for the ἦθος of Mark's narrative. She is described in terms of her dire need, her state of life, rather than her character.

[75] Cf. Diod. 10.3.4; Hdt. 7.229 (ἐς τὸ ἔσχατον).

he wants Jesus to touch her 'in order that she might be saved and live' (v.23b).

When Jesus leaves with him, the readers also embark on this journey to bring life to the dying daughter (v.24). The switch of subjects begins the process of dis-alignment, restoring the readers to the role of observers. They are accompanied by a large crowd, crushing in upon him (cf. 3.9–10). But before they come to Jairus' daughter, the narrator interrupts the journey to tell of an afflicted one (cf. μάστιξ,[76] vv.29, 34, cf. 3.10) in the crushing crowd (vv.27, 24, 31, cf. 3.9) who wishes to touch Jesus (vv.27, 28, 30, 31; cf. 3.10) so that she might be saved. The readers are forced to hear her story, before they hear what happens to the girl.

Reader to text

The situation

Whatever the exact medical reason for the girl's condition, she has reached the point of death. Although medicine had its prescribed remedies for children (e.g. Pliny *HN* 20.114, 191f.; 28.39, 114, 257–9; 30.135), it was too late, for Jairus is already seeking help beyond the profession. What help was there now?

Plutarch reports and explains a Pythagorean allegory which applied to those reaching this point in life:

> 'Do not turn back on reaching the borders': that is, when about to die and seeing the border of life (τὸν ὅρον τοῦ βίου) is near, to bear it calmly and not be disheartened.
>
> (Plut. *De lib.educ.* 12F)

Many other philosophers attempted to calm people's fears in the face of death, which in itself indirectly testifies to such fears and to how difficult it must have been to attain this calm. But what about when a child reaches this point of no return?

Death and the child

Expendable children?

If the people in the Roman world had an average life expectancy of between 20 and 25, and only 40 per cent of the population reached that

---

[76] The connotations of this word, 'scourge', would not be lost on Mark's readers. Scourging was a horrendous punishment to endure.

age, and every child had a 50 per cent chance of reaching the age of 10, the mortality rate amongst children was extremely high.[77] This kind of mortality produces a definite pattern in the population: half of the population would be less than 18–22, one third less than 14; and a negligible proportion would be over 70. This pattern can be described in terms of the toll felt by a family:

> If a family had six children it would have to expect that the first would die as a baby, the second by twenty, the third by thirty-five to forty, the fourth by forty-five to fifty, the fifth by sixty and the sixth later. However, this was under the best of conditions: in time of plague the children disappeared much faster. It would require about six children for the family to replace the dead under good conditions. In time of plague it required at least nine.[78]

With such high losses, it is sometimes suggested that people were hardened towards the death of children,[79] in which case, Jairus would be something of an oddity. The Stoic resignation to fate perhaps came closest to this attitude, epitomised in Marcus Aurelius. Although renowned for being fond of his children (cf. Gal. 14.3), believing that childhood illness must be accepted as a natural event, he refused to pray, like unphilosophical parents, 'How may I not lose my little child'. Instead, he prayed for himself: 'May I have no fear of losing him' (M.Ant. 9.40).[80] He found solace in a saying from Epictetus, that

> when you kiss your child, you should say 'Perhaps it will be dead in the morning'. Ill-omened words these! 'Not ill-omened', says he, 'but referring to a process of nature. Otherwise it would also be ill-omened to speak of the corn being harvested.[81]
>
> (M.Ant. 11.34; cf. Epict. 3.24.88)

Writing to his wife when their two-year-old daughter had died while he was away, Plutarch commended her for responding in a similar manner – so fitting for one married to a philosopher (*Cons. ad ux.* 608B–609D)!

However, even this evidence suggests that such an attitude had to be deliberately cultivated, which is a far cry from the suggestion that parents

---

[77] Wiedemann, *Adults*, 11–17.

[78] Russell, 'Late Ancient', 35.   [79] So Wiedemann, *Adults*, 6f.

[80] Cf. his counsel to stick to the immediate impressions: 'I see my child is ailing. I see it, but I do not see he is in danger' (8.49).

[81] Cf. 7.40: 'Our lives are reaped like the ripe ears of corn, And as one falls, another still is born'; = Eur. *Hypsipyle*, Frag. 757.

were unmoved by the death of their children. Why is it, for example, that child mortality is one of the few contexts in which Marcus Aurelius actually meditated upon children? Since he lost four of his own children as youngsters, each before the next was born, perhaps his meditation, as well as his 'more philosophical' prayer, stands as indirect testimony to his own pain. Certainly his philosophy did not prevent him from prohibiting his daughters to be taken outside at night, for fear the wind would do them harm, or speaking of their illnesses in his correspondence. Or again, it must have been regarded as a tragedy for Cornelia to lose 10 out of 12 children (Sen. *ad Helv.* 16.6), in order for Seneca to parade her as an example of womanly bearing in grief. Plutarch's advice to his wife assumed that she would be grieving, even if this grief was to be expressed in a controlled fashion. Since his letter is but one of many other consolations on the death of a child (cf. *P.Oxy.* 115), it seems clear that, just as childhood death was a common feature of ancient life, so too was parental grief.[82]

It is also clear that the philosophical approach was not the only one adopted. Even as part of Plutarch's advice to his wife, he must warn her against others who weep and wail in, what is to him, an unseemly fashion (*Cons. ad ux.* 610B–C). The evidence from grave stones, as unrepresentative as it may be, should not be dismissed too quickly as one way of accessing parental grief.[83] The overrepresentation of children between 1 and 9, and of youths between 10 and 19, on the extant tombstones[84] must surely testify to the fact that their departure was a blow to their parents. The inscriptions themselves provide a sample of opinions, at least, and they include many indications that the loss of a child was regarded as a grievous tragedy. This would especially be true because the illness to which they succumbed was often so horrendous, as in this epitaph recorded by Martial (*c.* AD 40–104) of a child's death from the now unknown disease *cancrum oris*, a spreading gangrene which erodes away the face before killing its victim:[85]

---

[82] The information in this paragraph is drawn from Wiedemann, *Adults*, 6, 8f., 96f.

[83] 'The evidence of inscriptions is far too scanty and too atypical to function as some sort of opinion poll of what parents thought about their children,' ibid., 42. Although Garland, *Greek Way*, xi finds the epitaphs of little value, he recognises that they do testify to 'the sense of loss [the deceased] bequeathed to his relatives'. To prove the same point, Shelton, *As the Romans Did*, 26, points to Quintilian's grief over the loss of his two sons (*Or.* 6. Pr. 6–13), as well as inscriptional evidence (*CIL* 6.19159 (*ILS* 8005)). Cf. Cicero's grief over the death of his 30-year-old daughter (*Att.* 12.46).

[84] Hopkins, 'Probable Age Structure', 246.

[85] Patrick, 'Disease', 243. Patrick comments, 'I never saw a recovery. I should doubt if they are seen now.'

Aeolis' daughter, Canace, lies buried in this tomb, a little girl
to whom a seventh winter came as her last. 'What a crime,
what a villainy!' Traveller hastening to weep, you must not here
complain of life's short span. Sadder than her death is the manner
of her death. A hideous corruption stole her face and settled
on her tender mouth, a cruel disease ate her very kisses and
mutilated her lips before they were given to the black pyre. If
fate had to come in so precipitate a flight, it should have come
by a different path. But death hurried to close the channel of her
sweet voice, lest her tongue should prevail to sway the pitiless
goddesses.   (Martial 11.91)

Burying your children

Parental grief would be real, even if the reasons for it are judged to be
rather 'selfish' by the more child-conscious standards of a later day. The
death of a child represented the death of the family's hopes for the future:
'Here Philippus laid his 12 year old son, Nicoteles, his great hope' (*AG*
7.453).[86] Part of these 'hopes' concerned the parents' own future. The
loss of a child was mourned as a loss of a natural harvest (cf. *AG* 7.467),
which left the parents with no-one to care for them in old age or to bury
them properly.[87]

The inscriptions testify to parents' disappointment at children prede-
ceasing them, as if 'cheated of the return that was due to them'.[88] But,
alongside this thoroughly reciprocal view of the child–parent relationship, other evidence shows that the tragedy was also felt on behalf of the
child. For example, the tombstone of a seven-year-old complains: 'I did
not know what it is to enjoy the life of a man' (1st or 2nd c. AD); and
another: 'what great hopes would there have been, if the fates had allowed
it; when I was a boy, the Muses gave me the gift of eloquence'.[89] The
pathos of the epitaphs is also increased by the fact that they give the children's age fairly precisely – even occasionally to the hour![90] In addition,

[86] For the child as 'an investment in future security', see Wiedemann, *Adults*, 39–43.
Cf. 'I have become childless and without hope. I keep watch at the grave of my son' (TSol.
20.20).
[87] See Wiedemann, *Adults*, 9, 39–43. These twin ideas are enshrined in the duty of
ΓHPOBOΣKEIN in the law of Solon and Plato *Leg.* 913A–938C (Bk. 11), and expressed
elsewhere, e.g., *Il.* 4.477f.; Hes. *Op.* 187f.; Eur. *Med.* 1032; *Rhe.* 980ff.; Ar. *Ach.* 688ff.
Cf. Plato's ideal life: 'to be rich, healthy, honoured by the Greeks, reach old age, and, after
burying one's parents well, to be laid out well by one's own children and buried mag-
nificently (μεγαλοπρεπῶς)', *Hp.Ma.* 291D–E.
[88] Wiedemann, *Adults*, 40.   [89] Both from ibid., *Adults*, 41f.
[90] Cook, *Greek Inscriptions*, 29.

it is not clear that some of the supposedly 'selfish' reasons ought to be condemned so harshly. The necessity for someone to care for the aged and eventually bury them, as a reality in a community without social services, should not be minimised.[91] But it is difficult to see that this motivation exhausts the sense of tragedy in the frequently occurring sentiment that something seems awry in parents burying their children, when it ought to be the other way around (*AG* 7.261, 361, 466, cf. 468, 638).

Dying young

Dying young was a tragedy because it meant that bitter fate had cheated the person of life before they had reached their allotted span. For female children,[92] this is frequently expressed in terms of dying unmarried,[93] which is particularly pertinent for Jairus' daughter, who, at twelve, would be recognised as entering marriagable age.[94]

Amongst the twelve-year-olds mourned on the tombstones in the *Greek Anthology* Bk 7 (cf. 467), we find one who was a bride-to-be (547) and another 'an unmarried maiden' (604). Many other inscriptions mourn unmarried girls (486; 487, aged 14; 488; 489; 490; 491; 507B; 515; 527; 568, aged 14), some who died on their very wedding night (182, 183, 188, 298), still others who died within a year of marriage (566, aged 16; 567, aged 16, 'mourned by her husband and father'). Sometimes this is accepted philosophically: 'A. He knew not wedlock. B. Nor the pains of wedlock' (603; cf. Plut. *Cons. ad ux.* 611C, cf. 115E–F), but,

[91] As Wiedemann, *Adults*, 42, admits.
[92] Although this is not exclusive to females, cf. *AG* 7.515.
[93] Wiedemann, *Adults*, 41. Cf. the unwedded girls, brides, and young bachelors listed amongst the dead (*Od.* 11.34 ff.; Virgil *Aen.* 6.297–332). This tragedy also finds expression in various myths in which 'girls die specifically when ready for marriage', Dowden, *Death*, 13.
[94] Based on tomb inscriptions from Rome, Harkness, 'Age' (followed by Russell, 'Late Ancient', 14, 18), suggested that men married at 26 and girls at 18, marriages lasted about 24 years, and about 39–44% of the population would be married. Considering Harkness 'thorough, and yet misguided' (p. 309), Hopkins, 'Age', argues that it is better to speak of the 'modal' age, which would have been 12–15, although many were married a lot earlier (p. 326). Even on Harkness' figures, many Roman girls were married by 15 (of 171 in the tombstone sample: 67 (39%) were 10–14; 60 (35%) 15–19; 26 (15%) 20–24; 4% 25–29; 4% 30–34; 1% 35–39). For some examples, see *CIL* 13.1983 (*ILS* 8158): 15 years; *CIL* 1.2.1221 (*ILS* 7472): 7 years; Quintilian (6 Pr. 4–5): his wife died at 19 after already bearing two sons.
    Plutarch commented disapprovingly that the Romans married their women at twelve or less (*Comp.Lyc. et Num.* 4.1; cf. Dio Cass. 54.16.7). Greek women in the classical period married at 14–15 (Xen. *Oec.* 3.13, 75), which was considered to be the age of menarche (Soranus, *Gyn.* 1.4.20).
    Although the rabbis spoke of 13 being the ideal age for a Jewish girl to be married, Ilan, *Jewish Women*, 65–9, finds it difficult to prove from known literary examples that this was so in practice.

on the whole, the sense of parental grief is patent. This is underlined by their sheer helplessness, despite their position or their possessions (cf. the inscription on the tomb of a son who died at 15 years and 24 days which mourns 'neither your grandfather's high office helped thee, nor the riches of thy father', 602).

Dying young in a magical environment

The magical materials certainly enhance the feeling that the loss of a child was a tragic event for parents. The curses against the family show that losing children was undesirable and the spells seeking protection against child-killing *daimones* show that it was feared.

The Assyrio-Babylonian spells speak of the spirit which 'draweth up the little one like fish from the water' (Thompson **"X"**.15; cf. **"C"**.135); or those which 'snatch the child from the knees/loins of a man' (**IV**.25f.); or 'slay the [offspring?]' (**"K"**.60); or 'lay low the maiden, the little ones like a leek they tear in pieces' (**"T"**.10). A charm in *Sepher ha-Razim* (2.124) drives off the spirits causing the death of children. An Aramaic bowl text seeks to remove the 'smiter and burner of boys and girls, male and female foetuses(?)' (Isbell **22**); others mention the 'king of demons' (Isbell **17**.5; **18**.4, 6; **19**.3; **20**.4, 7; **22**.2) who especially kills boys and girls, male and female foetuses (**19**.4; **20**.6, 7), and ghosts who devour sons and daughters (**19**.9). In another, the *daimones* called up by the sun urge each other on to further human destruction: 'let us sweep away the children in the market places, let us chase them in their bodies, let us chase them in their roads' (*AMB* **Bowl 13**).

Dying young and the fear of ghosts

Magical practices also raise a special cause for concern in regard to the death of a child. Those who died before their allotted span (ἄωροι)[95] – sometimes further specified as the unmarried, the youths and the maidens – were believed to be barred from full entry into the underworld (cf. Plautus, *Mostellaria*, 499–500) and so to have a special propensity for becoming ghosts and being potent agents of magic.[96] In the magical spells they are frequently summoned to perform the magicians' bidding. Since the Romans widely believed that witches would even kill small children in order to use them for their spells (Cic. *Vat.* 6.14, Hor. *Epod.* 5

---

[95] The scanty references to the ἄωροι in the literature suggested the theory that they were those who died young. This now seems supported by archaeological evidence, wherever the age of the skeleton in a grave can be tested; cf. SGD, 152–3.

[96] Although the Twelve Tables forbade burial within city walls, children under 40 days were buried under the threshold, or a wall of the house, Wiedemann, *Adults*, 79, which presumably made their graves quite accessible to those with magical plans.

and Petr. *Sat.* 63.8), this was an additional source of parental fear, as reflected in the epitaph of a slave-boy, not yet four:

> The cruel hand of a witch has snatched me away, while she remains on earth to harm people with her skills.
>
> Parents: watch carefully over your children!
>
> (*CLE* **987** (1st c. AD))[97]

Given the magical power of such youthful victims of death, they may have also been liable to post-death mutilation. Pliny spoke of the practice of 'tearing to pieces for sinful practices the limbs of still-born babies' (*HN* 28.20.70). Whereas the curse tablets were deposited in graves simply in order to make use of the corpse and/or the corpse-*daimon*, some of the magical spells actually made use of parts of bodies in their rituals (*PGM* I.247f., the eye from a corpse of a βιαιοθάνατος; IV.296–466;[98] IV.2645ff., including 'a young boy's heart';[99] Gager **29**; cf. Ps-Phoc. 101–3, 149f.; Apul. *Met.* 2.20–30; Pamphile's workshop contained 'many limbs of dead and buried men', 3.17).

Adding to all the fear associated with death and especially the death of a child, the prospect that a beloved child might be entering an in-between existence, in which they would be manipulated for all kinds of nefarious purposes, was hardly comforting.

Death and the dead

Curses and the family

Many curses were often directed not only at the person in view, but also their offspring and family.[100] This was sometimes with the intent to kill them, as in a curse against a number of people:

> All of these I consign, (inscribed) in lead and in wax and in water (?) and to unemployment and to destruction and to bad reputation and to (military?) defeat and in tombs – both these and all the children and wives who belong to them.
>
> (*DTA* **55** = SGD **105** = Gager **64** (4th c. BC))

---

[97] Translation: Wiedemann, *Adults*, 79.
[98] Cf. Gager, 96.   [99] See Henrichs, *Phoinikika*, 32–7.
[100] Cf. SGD **91** (*c.* 450 BC); SGD **15** (4th/3rd c. BC) which curses οἰκία, household?; *DTA* **78**, **102**; one in which a man, his wife, chattels, and bodily and mental parts are cursed (SGD **3** (5th/4th c. BC)); *DTA* **77** = Gager **24**; SGD **170** (1st c. BC, see Bravo, 'Tablette Magique', 192); *DT* **4** = Gager **89** (1st c. BC); another (*DT* **208**; 3rd c. AD) wishes enmity upon a man and his whole household (οἰκία ὅλη); and more. Curses against the family are also common in funerary imprecations, see Strubbe, 'Cursed be he', 43.

If prominent people in a society were especially singled out for curses in general, and this kind of curse in particular, Mark's readers may have recognised this synagogue ruler as belonging to a category particularly at risk from this kind of cursing. Was his daughter at the point of death, simply because she was related to the wrong person?

Love magic gone wrong?

The fact that Jairus' daughter was of marriageable age raises the possibility that another dark cause lay behind her demise. Amongst the magical materials can be found a distinct class of spells known as 'love charms',[101] or – since the contents of the spells are far from 'loving' – better, 'drawing charms', which seek to draw the victim to the *defigens*, for erotic purposes. If the victim already had a partner, these charms sought to separate them from their loved ones, thus they can also be called 'separation charms'.[102]

As previously noted, people feared the use of curse tablets, in general (Pliny *HN* 28.4.19), and love charms, in particular, against them. Ovid, for example, when he was unable to perform with a lover, asked:

> Has some Thessalian poison bewitched (*devota*)[103] my body, is it some spell or drug that has brought this misery upon me. Has some sorceress written (*defixit*) my name on crimson wax, and stuck a pin in my liver.   (Ovid, *Amores* 3.7.27–30)[104]

Such 'erotic magic' was dangerous. Just as aphrodisiac potions were known to walk a fine line between being effective and being fatal,[105] these drawing charms were also known to be risky to the victim.

The spells worked by calling up a ghost to draw the victim to the *defigens*.[106] The love charms clearly operate through raising the spirit

---

[101] For discussions of erotic magic, see Winkler, 'Constraints'; Martinez, 'Love Magic'; and Faraone, 'Aphrodite's ΚΕΣΤΟΣ'; 'Sex'; 'Mistake'; Petropoulos, 'Erotic Magical Papyri'. Two love charms on papyrus are extant from the first century, in fragmentary form, i.e., *P.Mon.Gr.* inv. 216 and Supp.Mag. 72.

[102] Faraone, 'Agonistic Context', 13, distinguishes two different kinds of amatory curse: (1) the separation curse; and (2) the aphrodisiac or erotic curse, in which only the beloved is mentioned. Faraone lists fifteen Greek separation curse tablets published at that stage: *DTA* **78, 89, 93**(?); *DT* **68, 69, 85, 86, 198**; *SGD* **30–2, 57, 154**; and refers to two 'divorce curses' announced by Miller, 'Excavations' (although this is not Miller's term). The papyri also have examples of separation charms.

[103] *Devota* is a technical term used in relation to spells on curse tablets, as is *defixio*.

[104] Gager, 250, comments: 'The ease with which Ovid considers this explanation suggests that the practice was well known at the time [i.e., 20 BC–AD 1].'

[105] Cf. Faraone, 'Sex'; Winkler, 'Constraints', 220–2.

[106] For a discussion of these assistants, see Ciraolo, 'Supernatural Assistants'.

of a dead person to bring about the distress in the 'intended'. Notice, for example, how *SuppMag* **54** calls upon 'the *daimones* who are in this place [i.e., the cemetery]' (l. 19: δαίμονες οἳ ἐν [τ]ούτω τῷ τόπω ἐστε), to constrain the victim; to 'hand [him] over by means of (or, 'to') the untimely dead' (l. 23: παράδοιτε ἀώροις), who were some of the most likely candidates to become ghosts. It is these '*daimones* who are roaming about in this place' (ll. 35f.: δ[αί|μον]ες οἳ ἐν τῷ τόπῷ τού[τω.] φοιτῶντες) who are called to complete the spell's transaction. These *daimones* were to go to the victim's house, and draw her (usually) to the *defigens*.

Through the instrument of these underworld assistants, the charms sought to draw the intended lover through inflicting all kinds of suffering. We have already noted that some sought to inflict a fever on the victim, perhaps to provoke the 'burning' of love for their tormentor (chapter 3, Suppliant 2). But this was not the only intended suffering. Charms demand that, e.g., 'NN should be able neither to drink, nor eat, nor show affection, nor have strength or health, nor get sleep apart from me, NN' (*PGM* IV.355; cf. *P.Mich.* 757.12–13 and 23–4). Robbing the victim of sleep is common: 'Take sweet sleep away from her, let her eyelids not touch and adhere to each other, let her be worn down with insomniac anxieties focused on me' (*PGM* IV.2735–9; cf. IV.2767; VII.888–9; XXXVI.142, 147–52). In another, the *nekydaimon* is invoked, 'Go to her and seize her sleep, her drink, her food, and do not allow Matrona [. . .] to have love or intercourse with any other man, except Theodoros. [. . .] Drag Matrona by her hair, by her guts, by her soul, by her heart until she comes to Theodoros' (SGD 156 ll. 48–62; cf. SGD 152, 153; *PGM* IV.367ff.; Jordan, 'Love Charm Verses'). In another, commissioned by a woman, the command is to 'melt his heart and suck out his blood in his love and desire and distress' (*PGM* XVI).[107]

Part of the fear of erotic magic was the belief that, as well as causing suffering, these charms could actually kill. A charm demonstrated to Hadrian (*PGM* IV.2441–621) 'evoked [one] in one hour, sickened and sent [one] to bed in two hours, killed [one] in seven' (ll. 2450–4). Another warns: 'Be sure to open the door for the woman who is being led by the spell, otherwise she will die' (*PGM* IV.2495ff.). The 'charm to induce insomnia' (*PGM* XII.376–96) is also a love spell, for it seeks to make the woman 'lie awake until she consents'. The spell informs the reader that 'the woman will die for lack of sleep, without lasting seven days. This charm cannot at any time have an antidote.' The literary sources

---

[107] See Jordan, 'Papyrus Love Charm', 237.

also illustrate the knowledge that love charms could kill (cf. Ovid *Ars. Am.* 2.105–6; Plaut. *Truc.* 42–4).[108]

If they are intended to draw a potential lover, why would these charms seek to kill their victims? We have already noted that love magic, in the form of aphrodisiac pharmacology, always bore the risk of fatality, so there could have been the perception of a risk by association. But, in addition, this outcome may also be explained by the fact that the spells asked for their intended to be bound to them for the rest of their days, or until they were parted by death (e.g., *P.Mich.* 757.28; *SGD* **156**; cf. *PGM* IV.381f.). Presumably, if the lover was not drawn, then the only alternative was for them to suffer long and hard, and then for them to die.

Was Jairus' daughter, just ripe for marriage, sought after as a potential lover? Had somebody used a curse to inflict this suffering upon her, in the hope that she would be drawn away from her home and into his arms? Was she the victim of a ghostly attack? And had the love magic gone too far; had the underworld caused such suffering that she had now 'reached her last'? Were the dead about to claim her as their own?

Curses and death

Curses aiming at the death of the victim were not so unusual. Judging from the rarity of the verb ὄλλυμι, familiar to cursing formulae, Faraone has argued that the death of the victim was rarely the goal of early *defixiones*.[109] Coincidentally, his two secure examples also curse family members: *SGD* **104** (5th c. BC) 'May they be utterly destroyed, they and their kin', followed by a list of names; 'May they be destroyed with their families' (3rd c. BC).[110] *PGM* XL (4th c. AD)) also uses this verb in a curse against 'my daughter's father [who] robbed [her] of the funeral gifts and tomb'. The curse asks, 'may he be destroyed badly (κακῶς ἀπολ-λύοιτο), both by land and sea'. Despite the rarity of this verb, the aim to kill the victim, however, is by no means rare as time goes on. Gager **117** reports a series of spells (1st c. BC) which may be death spells, or they may concern admission to life. Another series of Latin curses (2nd c. AD) speaks of spilling the blood of the victim (*DT* **212** = Gager **95**), cf. Gager **96** and **97** (4th c. AD), and Gager **100** asks that they might pay with blood and life (1st/2nd c. AD). Death ('τέλος') is one of the things protected against in Gager **128** (3rd /4th c. AD), which may imply a curse wishing it.

---

[108] See also Faraone, 'Sex'.

[109] It appears only five times in published *defixiones*, three times in tentative restorations (*DTA* **75a** (*bis*); SGD **75**); Faraone, 'Agonistic Context', 8 n. 38.

[110] From Faraone, 'Agonistic Context' n. 38.

In terms of public perception, as time went on 'death was quite frequently considered to be the result of witchery, and such beliefs were not confined to any one sector of society'.[111] To take a second-century literary example, Apuleius' *Metamorphoses* contains a story which clearly shows malevolent magic aiming at (and achieving) a man's death. The magician manipulated the ghost of a murdered woman (9.29), who possessed him and took him down to the underworld (9.31), apparently via prompting him to suicide. Although curse tablets are not mentioned in this incident, they are known to the wider story (3.17). Such practices must have been sufficiently well known to the second-century audience for Apuleius to expect verisimilitude, and this was magic which aimed to kill. For a historical example, we can cite the incident in AD 19, when curse tablets were discovered in the floor of the house after the popular Germanicus had died unexpectedly (Tac. *Ann.* 2.69, cf. 3.13; Suet. 4 (*Gaius*).3; Dio Cass. 57.18).

A number of extant tablets show that the aim to kill was not unique to Germanicus' enemies. Several times we have had recourse to the vindictive counter-charm from the time of Julius Caesar, for example, which not only aimed at the death of the victim, but in the most painful of possible ways: '[. . .] take care of him by the month of February. Let him perish miserably. Let him leave life miserably. Let him be destroyed miserably. Take care of him so that he may not see another month' (Fox = Gager **134**).

In addition, occasional idiosyncratic phrases imply the destruction of the victim: 'I bind these men in tombs' (*DTA* **55**, **87**); 'I do away with him (ἀφανίζω) and bury him under (κατορύττω)' (*DT* **49**; cf. SGD **48**, **49** and AthAg).[112]

The desire to kill is clear in a new text from Carthage (imperial):

III .c.2   δόται ἀcθένιαν |τη Αἰ. [. . . I have discontinued the citation]
5   ἤδη, ταχύ | [κ]αὶ θάνᾳτον
IV. b.1   Δὸc θάνατον
V.1   Αλ|αcιc

'give debility to A, [. . .] now, quickly, and death. Give death to A., [. . .]'.[113]

[111] Baroja, 'Magic', 73.
[112] 'Restrain him until he comes down to Hades' (*DT* **50** (late?)), may also be relevant. Although it certainly means 'for the rest of his life', Faraone, 'Agonistic Context', n. 38, this does not exclude the possibility that death is also included in the curse's desire, cf. AthAg **App**, discussed below.
[113] Jordan, 'Notes from Carthage', **2**.

Carthage has yielded a number of curses against charioteers which seek to inflict great damage on horse and rider, if not death. This is explicit in a Latin curse against charioteers from Hadrametum:

> I charge you, *Daimon*, whoever you are, from this hour, this day, this moment, torment and destroy the horses of the Green and White; kill and mangle the drivers Clarus, Felix, Primulus, Romanus; let them not breathe [again].
>
> $\qquad\qquad\qquad$ (*DT* **286** = Grant, 241 (3rd c. AD))

In addition, if the arguments of this study are valid, then many more of the tablets seek death for the victims, even if vocabulary specifically related to death or destruction (such as ὄλλυμι) is not mentioned, by virtue of the fact that they curse crucial bodily parts and use vocabulary of physiological/pathological significance. For example, although some have denied that the use of graves and the comparison with the lead is a sympathetic magical technique indicating a desire to destroy the victim,[114] the use of 'chilling' in the AthAg tablets seems to be exactly that. Given the role chilling has in theories of disease (see above, on Suppliants 4 and 5), it seems likely that these tablets are actually seeking after the person's death.[115] In fact, this is explicit in one of them:

> As I have written down these names and they grow cold, so, too, let the body and the flesh and the sinews[116] and the bones and the members and the bowels of Tyche, whom Sophia bore, grow cold, that she may no longer rise up, walk around, talk, move about, but let her remain a corpse, pale, weak, paralysed, chilled until I am taken out of the dark air, rather let her grow exhausted and weak until she dies (γένοιτο μέχρι θανάτου).
>
> $\qquad\qquad\qquad\qquad\qquad\qquad\qquad\qquad\qquad\qquad$ (AthAg **App**)

Malevolent magic used the dead to bring about people's deaths. When a child was at the point of death, this could raise the suspicion of magic.

---

[114] Faraone, 'Agonistic Context', 8–10.

[115] The desire to chill the soul, impulse, charm, mind, knowledge, reckoning, when read against the physiological understandings of (some of) these terms, sounds rather final, as does wanting them to take on all the characteristics of the corpse: deaf, dumb, mindless, harmless. The use of underworld language (e.g., 'unilluminated air of oblivion') may reinforce this point, although this refers to the underworld abode of the one invoked. ἀφανίζω is also used, which Faraone, ibid. n. 38, translates 'I do away with [. . .]'.

[116] In view of the arguments above on Suppliant 4, I have changed Jordan's rendering of νεῦρα as 'muscles'.

This, in turn, would raise the fear that the dead were about to take the child into their number, for the dead were the agents who fulfilled such curses (cf. *DT* **286** = Grant, 241).

Jesus and death

It seems that the greater loss of children simply made for a greater sense of loss. Jairus, displaying no philosophically appropriate decorum, falls at Jesus' feet and begs him to touch his daughter. His distress at his daughter's coming to the point of death would arouse the sympathies of the Graeco-Roman readers (whether philosophical or not) and cause them to be aligned strongly with his situation as he begs Jesus to come and save his daughter by bringing her back from the point of death.

The Augustan rhetoric which proclaimed the Caesars to be the source of life for all would issue in Seneca's suggested soliloquy for Nero, that his role was 'to give safety to many and to recall them to life from the very brink of death' (*De clementia* 1.26.5). In the second century, Aelius Aristides' glowing praise of Rome proclaimed that the cities 'were already as it were on the refuse heap; but then they received a common leadership and suddenly came alive again' (*Eulogy of Rome*, 155–7). But in our story, this synagogue ruler did not turn to his own religious system, nor did he turn to Rome. Out of his desperate need, he turned to Jesus of Nazareth, begging him to save his little daughter from death.

Suppliant 8: the bleeding woman (Mark 5.24b–34)

Text to reader: a woman saved

Despite a brief appearance in this scene, the disciples are evaluated negatively since they act in opposition to Jesus. This prevents their being strongly aligned with the readers, who are, once again, aligned with the suppliant.

Jesus' journey to save Jairus' daughter on the brink of death is suddenly interrupted by a very powerful description of a woman in desperate physical and social circumstances (vv.25–26). This description works to produce πάθος: she was a woman; she had existed with a flow of blood for the last twelve years; she had suffered much at the hands of doctors and lost all her means; and instead of being made better, she had only become worse. Despite her major physical need, this suppliant had been thoroughly exploited by the ones from whom she had sought help. Although in a different sense, she, like Jairus' daughter, had also been brought to the end of her life. The reason why this detailed description of this woman is introduced becomes clear when the narrator reveals that she was in the crowd pressing around Jesus as he headed for Jairus' home.

The scene is focalised through the woman. Already her description has privileged the readers with information above that of the characters, and, by being oriented towards πάθος, it has strongly aligned them with her situation. As the action begins, an inside view of aural perception[117] continues the alignment (v.27, ἀκούσασα), by explaining how the woman came to be in the crowd. The readers are already located in the crowd (v.24) and now they travel with the woman as she emerges from the crowd to (secretly) touch Jesus' garment from behind (v.27b). Their alignment is completed by the explanation of her motives (v.28),[118] which, as a report of the woman's interior speech, powerfully reduces the distance between them. The extremely close alignment is continued by giving the readers the privileged information that she was cured (v.29a) and yet another inside view revealing her perception of her cure at the moment it occurred (v.29b).

At this point, where the previous narrative expectations may suggest that some response is appropriate (1.27, 31–34; 1.45; 2.12; 5.20), a sudden change of perspective occurs. So far, because the readers have been so strongly aligned with the woman, Jesus has been relegated to a figure on the edge of their vision; someone who is approached from behind. Suddenly the narrator changes the perspective by providing an inside view of Jesus, so that the woman's action can be viewed from his perspective (v.30): he had experienced it as a drain of power.

This new perspective does not dis-align the reader from the woman, however, but simply promotes further understanding of what had happened to her, as well as launching the quest for the one who touched him. Rather than being 'granted Jesus' perspective as he turns in the middle of the thronging crowd and asks who had touched him',[119] the readers have been so closely aligned with the woman that, when Jesus turns in the crowd, they are not realigned with him, but it is as if he is now looking for the readers as well! His question (v.30b) indicates that there is some distance between him and the readers, for they know something that even Jesus does not know and Jesus is seeking after exactly this information.

---

[117] Fowler, *Let the Reader*, 121.
[118] The γάρ clause provides explicit commentary; ibid., 95, cf. 92.
[119] Ibid., 69.

This scene gives the readers a view of the action shared only with the narrator.[120] This means that the solution to the various tensions in the story resides in the readers, who must await both Jesus and the woman discovering each other in order to discover what the readers already know. Given these dynamics, the disciples' declaration that the quest is impossible (v.31) functions as a blockage to the successful resolution of the story. This creates distance between the readers and the disciples, who now represent an obstacle to be overcome. The disciples' statement reveals their utmost ignorance of what is going on around them. They 'have not the slightest idea of what is happening in their midst, but [the readers] understand completely'.[121] So on this rare occasion when the disciples are actually present in a healing/exorcism story, they are at the opposite end of the spectrum to the readers: they know nothing, Jesus and the woman know some things, but the readers know it all. There is absolutely no 'strong identification' forged between the disciples and the readers; the strong alignment is reserved for the suppliant.

This alignment continues as the woman's confession is reported in a series of inside views (v.32) showing her emotions (fear and trembling), and a reminder of her knowledge that she had been cured (v.33). The readers travel with her to the moment of truth in which the narrative tension is resolved by Jesus and the woman finding out the information the readers already know. This forges the links between the three and the readers then become observers, hearing Jesus' final pronouncement to the woman (v.34). For twelve years nothing has come to this woman for free, but this time things are different.[122] The woman has been saved by her faith and she is dismissed in peace, henceforth to be healed from her affliction.

The significance in the narrative will only finally be known when the final part of the narrative sandwich reveals what happened with Jairus' daughter. But already the intercalation suggests various points of comparison between the woman and the synagogue ruler. He was a prominent leader who approached Jesus and asked him to come and touch his daughter that she might be saved and live. The woman, from the other end of the social scale – thanks to her exploitation by others –, comes from behind and touches Jesus so that she too might be saved (v.28). She is 'saved' and told that this is because of her faith. This pronouncement becomes significant in what follows, for she becomes a paradigm against which the readers will evaluate the synagogue official in matters of salvation.[123]

---

[120] Ibid., 126.   [121] Ibid., 94.   [122] Kahl, 'Jairus', 71f.   [123] Ibid., 75.

Reader to text

Bleeding and death

The illness
The woman clearly suffered a chronic bleeding disorder, but, once again,
precise diagnosis of its cause is not as important as gaining a greater
understanding of the effects of her illness upon her life. Unlike modern
commentators, the narrator does not mention the issue of purity at all.[124]
It is also probably inaccurate to talk of her bleeding as if it were menstruation, although I have continued this practice on the assumption that the
ancient writers were even less likely to make 'proper' modern medical
distinctions and her disorder would have been at least placed in the same
category. She would also be regarded as barren.[125] In addition, the long
period of suffering, her worsening condition, and the poverty brought
about by the many attempts to treat the condition, receive particular emphasis from the narrator.

Bleeding to death?
The Hippocratic doctors (Hipp. *Morb.I.*3) regarded 'a haemorrhage in
a woman' (γυναικὶ ῥόος αἱματώδης, cf. v.25) amongst those diseases
considered 'to be inevitably long' (μακρὰ τάδε ἀνάγκη εἶναι), and those
which were 'uncertain with regard to mortality' (ἐνδοιαστὰ τὰ τοιάδε
ἀπολλύναι τε καὶ μή). Twelve years was a long time to live with an uncertain mortality, especially since copious menstruation was also supposed
to lead to other diseases (*Aph.* 5.57). Menstrual blood was accorded negative properties, including some ability to kill, which may have 'made
it all the more attractive to magicians',[126] although it makes a rather

[124] See ibid., 66f. The discussion of purity draws upon Jewish regulations in regard to
menstruation. If purity were an issue in Mark's story, it could be exploited in terms of being
yet another 'living death'. However, it is almost certainly misguided to draw upon such
data to understand this story. In the first place, it was menstrual blood that defiled, and this
is not in view here. In addition, in cases of long-term bleeding, the sage or the physician
could examine the woman and pronounce the bleeding clean (*tNidd.* 4.3–4; *yNidd.* 3.2,
50c; *bNidd.* 22b; *mNidd.* 8.3; cf. Ilan, *Jewish Women*, 100–5). Given the long-term nature
of this woman's problem, and the fact that she had been seen by countless physicians,
the presumption would be in this case that it was a non-defiling bleeding condition. The
discussions about purity tend to overlook the real problem, i.e., the condition of life to which
her illness has brought her.
[125] Cf. Aubert, 'Wombs', 434. Ilan, *Jewish Women*, 112, notes that a man could divorce
his wife after she had been barren for ten years, so this woman may have also lived with
the additional social difficulties of being on her own.
[126] Aubert, 'Wombs', 431, citing ancient literature. Cf. Pliny *HN* 7.63–7, 11.44, 17.266,
19.176, 28.78–80.

minor appearance in the actual spells (*PGM* XXXVI.321–32 (4th c. AD);
LXII.76–106 (3rd c. AD), see below). To the degree that the woman's condition was regarded as menstrual, she may have been regarded as being
some kind of 'carrier' of death, but this is admittedly speculative in the
Greek context.[127]

Her barrenness is easily associated with death, by virtue of its being the
death of the line, and, because it does not produce life, the barren womb
is naturally described as being dead, or destroyed (cf. Eur. *Andr.* 157f.,
διόλλυται). Her bleeding for twelve years had effectively killed off her
progeny.

Bled to death

Being a female, she was likely to progress right through the 'protocol'
(physician: gods: magician) for gynaecological problems were particularly difficult. Greek medicine excelled at external medicine, e.g., the
setting of fractures and the healing of wounds, but became less sure of
itself as it moved towards internal medicine, especially when dealing with
the hollow organs such as the womb. When the doctors failed, women
could turn to gods such as Isis,[128] or Asclepius,[129] but we also know that
their problems were of great interest for the magicians.[130]

By the time the woman came to Jesus, many doctors had already failed,
making her condition even worse. This represents, not just a 'well-known
literary motif' (cf. 9.18),[131] but the harsh reality of the ancient world

[127] It is certainly Semitic, for menstrual emissions were 'synonymous with the loss
of the life force within the woman's body. Blood is, after all, the *nefesh* (Deut. 12.23)',
Feldman, *Defilement*, 37. Fear of menstrual blood as a polluting force was not a strong
feature of ancient Greek culture, only appearing in late sacred laws of non-Greek cults,
Parker, *Miasma*, 101f.

[128] Isis was especially regarded as the one in charge of sexual relations, length of pregnancy, and birth (*IG* XII.5 739.36–9 (1st c. BC); *I.v.Kyme* 41.18–20 (1st c. BC/AD); *IG* XII.5
14.17–21 (2nd/3rd c. AD); *SEG* XII.316, XXXIV.622, 626f. (imperial period)).

[129] Cf. *P.Oxy* 1381 (2nd c. AD). Gynaecological conditions, together with eye complaints,
are the most frequent amongst the Epidaurus miracles, which were generally chronic conditions which the doctors had not been able to cure; see *NewDocs* II.11–23.

[130] See the convenient discussion in Aubert, 'Wombs'. Magic could be enlisted in the
attempt to cure bleeding disorders; e.g., the late Coptic spells (*PDM* xiv.953–55; 961–5;
970–7; 978–80; 981–4); and the engraved stones ACBM **73, 76, 24** cf. *SMA* pl. 6, 135;
ACBM **27, 26, 28** and MES **38**.

[131] It is Theißen's motif 8, Theißen, *Miracle Stories*, 51f.; cf. John 5.5; Lucian *Abdic.* 7;
D.L. 8.69; *AJ* 1.166–9 (contrast 1 Sam. 16.14–23, see Duling, 'Eleazar Miracle', 4f.); *Gen.
Apoc.* 20.18. Failed medicine was a reality: 'It is doubtful whether medical care helped
very much in the battle against disease. [. . .] After all, the doctors could only diagnose the
disease and prescribe simple remedies based, for the most part, upon quite wrong premises.
They did not know what caused diseases, let alone how to cure them. [. . .] Thus medicine
had little more effect than that of bolstering the confidence of patients'; Russell, 'Late
Ancient', 35.

(cf. *P.Oxy* **1381**). The physicians may have simply failed to check the normal course of the disease, but the description suggests that her worsened condition resulted from their attempts at healing. It is hardly surprising that the medicine of the day had the potential to make things worse for patients. Many of their remedies are now known to be useless and many downright dangerous. Women were apparently overrepresented amongst the patients treated with drugs,[132] and since there was (and still is) a fine line between a drug and a poison, this may have been an additional factor in the woman's decline.[133]

The ancient doctors were aware of the tendency of their profession to create a bad image amongst the laymen (cf. Hipp. *De diaeta in morb.ac.* 8) – sometimes the profession was explicitly cursed.[134] In acute diseases, the physicians were not prepared to take the blame when 'the patient is overcome by the magnitude of his disease', but only if 'the physician treats either incorrectly or out of ignorance' (Hipp. *Aff.* 13). As for this woman's chronic condition, the writer of *The Art* would probably argue that the physicians should not have been treating her at all, for incurable conditions did not belong to the physician's art – which was, by definition, to cure the curable (Hipp. *Arte* 3, 8)! But she had evidently fallen into the hands of a series of unscrupulous physicians who kept treating her to the limit of her financial resources. Some readers may have agreed with Heraclitus (fr. 58) that it was questionable to earn money from medicine anyway, but all would recognise that, in this case, the physicians had gone too far.

Although the text says nothing about her use of magicians, the Graeco-Roman audience would also know that many of them would gladly join the physicians in assisting her towards financial ruin. Philostratus mentions that athletes, merchants, and especially lovers used magic, whether or not it was successful, and in the process they were relieved of vast sums of money, without its helping at all (*Vit. Ap.* 7.39; cf. Pl. *Leg.* 884–910D (Bk. 10)).

This woman had been brought to economic ruin in her endeavour to find salvation. She could say to her 'helpers' what the poor man could say when his patrons charged him what they thought was a just return:

---

[132] As Singer and Wasserstein, 'Anatomy', 662f., conclude from the fact that most of the 300 pharmaceuticals listed in the ancient works are in works on the treatment of women.

[133] Cf. male-directed aphrodisiacs which had the unfortunate side-effect of paralysing or even killing the lover, Faraone, 'Sex'.

[134] SGD **124** = Gager **81** (4th/3rd c. BC) curses 17 physicians, perhaps a Pythagorean medical practice.

'This is sport to you, but death to me' (Arist. *EE* 1243ª20). This woman was not only bleeding to death, but had been bled to death. Unscrupulous men had exploited her need, left her in her living death, and brought her to economic death.

Bleeding and the dead

Rather surprisingly, the woman's precise condition scarcely receives representation in the curse tablets, although in general terms, curses against women were a substantial part of ancient magical practice.

> In a society in which survival was a day-to-day struggle, with a high infant mortality rate and a short life expectancy at birth serving as a constant reminder of the precariousness of life, the reproductive functions of women were highly valued; all sexual and physiological dysfunctions were considered threats to society. In this context, the womb was viewed as a potential target of undesirable influences from occult powers, against which it needed the protection of specific gods and demons.[135]

This receives endorsement from 'the abundance of prophylactic material, spells, and amulets that make up the bulk of our evidence for uterine magic',[136] on the assumption that what is magically protected was magically attacked, as well as from hints in the literature.[137]

Although 'uterine magic' is represented in the sources (for example, in spells against the moving of the womb; e.g., *PGM* VII.260–71), as far as I am aware, there are no *defixiones* specifically causing female bleeding disorders. Perhaps bleeding would be a result of the first-century AD curse (*DT* **42b**) against various parts of a body – possibly female, since breasts are also cursed –, which includes an attack on the pudenda (αἰδοῖον). In addition, the numerous curses against a victim's family, or their wife (e.g., *DT* **190**), sought some condition causing barrenness, such as this, as is sometimes made explicit (SGD **21**).[138]

There is also one spell (3rd c. AD), however, which should be regarded in the same category as the *defixiones* because it explicitly seeks a bleeding episode.

---

[135] Aubert, 'Wombs', 425f.   [136] Ibid., 426.

[137] *Od.* 4.230, 10.394; Eur. *Andr.* 32f., 157f., 205, 355f.; *Med.* 717f.; Cic. *Clu.* 31; Pliny *HN* 25.25.

[138] Barrenness has a long history as a curse, Aubert, 'Wombs', 441, and is also a feature of funerary imprecations, Strubbe, 'Cursed be he', 43.

'Let the genitals and the womb of her, NN, be open, and let her become bloody by night and day.' And [these things must be written] in sheep's blood,[139] and recite before nightfall, the offerings (?) . . . first she harmed . . . and bury it near a sumac,[140] or near . . . on a slip of papyrus.   (*PGM* LXII.103–6)

Although the spell could be a cure for amenorrhea, it is possible that it was a malevolent spell, either to cause menorrhagia, which would be bad enough, or, because the Greek medical writers thought that a return of the menses or a menorrhagia would terminate a pregnancy, to cause an abortion.[141] Such a curse would be used to deprive an enemy of progeny.[142]

On the basis of such slim evidence it is impossible to show that curses inflicting bleeding disorders (if more than one existed!) used the agency of a ghost for their implementation.[143] But the protective charms show that the fear of magical attack would also lie behind gynaecological problems. Since these attacks normally enlisted the agency of the spirits of the dead, as did curses against the family, this woman's condition may also mean that she would be seen to be under the sway of the dead.

Turning to someone new

The ongoing social consequences of her condition (her ill-treatment at the hands of many; the loss of all her resources; the persistent lack of any cure) must have made this woman's distress almost unbearable. In such a situation, when medicine had failed so dismally, it would be perfectly natural for her to turn elsewhere for help. She had heard of a man doing marvellous things for those who were suffering like her (v.27) – magical sounding things. She could not afford any more fees – for physician or for magician – and so, she came to Jesus to do what so many others were doing. She simply pressed on to him from the crowd (cf. 3.7–12), hoping that she would be saved at last.

Her touch of Jesus' garment brought instant knowledge of success; the source of her flow had been stopped. Her living death was over: she had been saved from death. If her scourge (μάστιξ, v.34) was due to some

---

[139] A better reading is αἰσχρῷ αἵματι, 'with menstrual blood'; cf. Aubert, 'Wombs', 430 n. 14, improving *PGM*.
[140] 'Ροῦς could mean either 'flow, stream' or the fruit 'sumac', which was recognised to have pharmacological applications as a cure for various gynaecological ailments; ibid., 433f.
[141] So ibid., 434.   [142] Ibid., 435.
[143] *PGM* LXII.76–106 has some 'chthonic' features: the use of blood; recitation before nightfall; the burial of the charmed papyrus.

magical attack, it too was now over: she had been saved from the clutches of the dead. Her faith in Jesus had brought life, where once there was only death.

Suppliant 7b: the synagogue ruler (Mark 5.35–43)

Text to reader: a daughter raised from the dead

Three disciples are present in this scene (v.37) but they are treated neutrally and no textual devices encourage any strong identification with them. At the most, the readers are their fellow-travellers, but even here this is because the disciples travel with the suppliant with whom the readers are still aligned, as in the first part of the scene.

The juxtaposition of Jesus' words of compassion to the woman and the news of the girl's death (v.35) causes a mixture of emotions. After such strong alignment with the woman, when Jesus makes her secret healing public and so heralds her return to public life, the expected response of joy or amazement, which had been delayed once already (v.29) and is expected again (v.34), is displaced by the arrival of the bad news. This causes a re-reading of the woman's story, for her good news has become the cause of bad news for Jairus:[144] her interruption of the journey home caused the delay which has now led to the child's death. This mixture of joy turned to sadness fills the scene with even greater poignancy and the news of the child's death with greater tragedy, all of which promotes even greater sympathy for the synagogue ruler's desperate situation.

The tragedy is reinforced by the rhetorical question at the conclusion of the message, voicing ordinary common sense: 'why trouble the teacher any more?' (v.35b). The readers recall that, even when the girl was at the point of death, there was hope. Now that Jesus has shown the ability to cure an illness the physicians had found incurable (5.24b–34), the readers have no doubt that he would have been able to cure her too. But now she is dead, all hope is superfluous. This question offers a potential closure for the scene: death is the end of all hopes and even Jesus can do nothing.

The focus then falls upon Jesus: he is the subject of almost all the remaining verbs and there are two reports of his perception, one aural (v.36, παρακούσας [. . .]), one visual (v.38, θεωρεῖ) – although, since he 'sees' a tumult, it is also aural. Neither is a full-blooded 'inside view'.[145] The first comes after the news from home is reported to Jairus. After the readers

---

[144] Kahl, 'Jairus', 72, observes that what is life for one is death for the other.

[145] *Pace* Fowler, *Let the Reader*, 114, 121.

are permitted to overhear, it is then reported that Jesus also overheard. Instead of moving the readers inside Jesus, this has the opposite effect of moving him towards them, enabling him to overhear what they have already overheard. In other words, they are still focalised with Jairus which enables them to hear Jesus addressing his situation as if it were theirs. The second is another example of a description of a person's reaction to external circumstances also obvious to the observer. The tumult in the house was public knowledge and obvious as soon as Jesus and his companions entered. To say that Jesus 'saw' it is not necessarily providing an 'inside view'. Especially since the verb used has connotations of gazing upon a spectacle, when the narrator says that 'he looked upon a tumult' (v.38, θεωρεῖ θόρυβον), it is probably an external description indicating that Jesus (paused and) gazed upon the scene before he acted.[146] It seems likely that the readers are still focalised through the suppliant, not through Jesus. Despite the *focus* of the action being upon Jesus, the readers nevertheless remain *focalised* through the suppliant, observing what Jesus does on his behalf from his vantage point.

To return to the scene, in response to the message from home, Jesus speaks to the synagogue ruler (v.36). Jairus was present when Jesus told the woman from the crowd that her faith had saved her (v.34). He had wanted Jesus to save his daughter (v.23), but the opportunity to do so has passed by. His daughter has died, what can be done now? Jesus tells him to 'stop fearing' (μὴ φοβοῦ) and to 'keep on only believing' (μόνον πίστευε), even in the face of death. The contrast between fear and faith recalls the scene on the boat (4.40) when Jesus suggested that if the disciples had had faith they would not have been afraid of the imminent prospect of death. Here Jairus is told to keep exhibiting the faith that brought him to Jesus in the first place, even though death has removed all hope.

Initially, the reader had expected another call for someone to follow Jesus, but Jesus had been called to follow someone else. This call has now been revoked and, seizing the initiative, Jesus issues the expected 'call', allowing a select group of people to follow with him (v.37, μετ' αὐτοῦ συνακολουθῆσαι). Jesus' limitation on the number of companions

---

[146] This classical meaning of θεωρέω cannot be automatically assumed for NT texts. However, the data are insufficient in Mark to demonstrate that it does the work for tenses of ὁράω not represented, as it does for some NT authors; and it is not used as a synonym for other verbs of seeing (not even in 5.15f., *pace* Michaelis, 'ὁράω', 345). Contextual considerations suggest that Mark retains the classical sense, which is admitted for 15.40 (ibid., 346); most likely for 5.15, 38; 12.41; 15.47 and 16.4; but less certain in 3.11, where it depends upon the immediacy of the spirits' action.

(v.37) increases the readers' sense of privilege, for they will also take the journey. When the group arrives at the house, the scene is focused upon Jesus, who 'gazed on a tumult' (θεωρεῖ θόρυβον, v.38), consisting of 'much crying and loud shouting' (κλαίοντας καὶ ἀλαλάζοντας πολλά). The visual and aural images enhance the vividness of the scene, enabling the readers to enter into the shock of the tumult inside Jairus' home. All this noise is not so much a celebration of death, as one writer put it,[147] but adds to the deeply tragic emotions so far in the scene. Human beings are distraught. This is so readily understandable in the face of death that Jesus' question as to why they are causing such a tumult and weeping – the direct speech enabling the readers to hear his question for themselves (v.39) – stands out as something of an oddity. Jesus does not seem to have given up hope, for he then baldly states that the girl has not died, but is merely sleeping. The contradiction between this statement and the drift of the scene so far is striking, but the strong sense of sympathy with the suppliant and positive regard for Jesus prevents the readers from reacting like the mourners. Their laughter (v.40a), implying that Jesus is a fool,[148] repels the readers. Jesus removes them from the house and so from the story. Narrowing the group heightens the readers' sense of privilege at being able to accompany Jesus (cf. v.37), his select group, and the parents into the girl's room as observers (v.40).

Once inside, Jesus does exactly what Jairus originally desired and seizes her by the hand (v.41; cf. v.23). His command is preserved in the original tongue, adding an atmosphere of mystery.[149] The rendering into Greek is cast as Jesus' direct speech: 'little girl, I say to you, arise'. Given the circumstances, this is nothing other than a command to rise from the dead. There is immediate success: the girl arose (v.42, ἀνέστη) and walked around. A γάρ clause explains her ambulation in terms of her age. It is only at this point that a clearer picture of the girl emerges, whereas previously she has been defined in terms of her relationship to Jairus, i.e., she was his affectionately regarded daughter.

Having expected a response for so long, the readers also join the utter amazement which results (v.42b). Jesus insistently commands that no-one know of what happened, which increases the readers' sense of privilege, and that the girl be given something to eat (v.43), which suggests that she has been returned to ordinary life.

Jairus receives a miracle even after all hoping had stopped. The woman's faith led to her salvation. Jairus was told to have faith and

---

[147] Kahl, 'Jairus', 74.   [148] J.F. Williams, *Other Followers*, 63.
[149] Cf. Fowler, *Let the Reader*, 108f.

he received salvation for his daughter of a kind even greater than asked for. He had hoped that Jesus might save her and make her live when she was at the point of death. Jesus saved her and made her live, even when she had crossed that final border.

However, once Jesus encouraged him to keep on believing even in the face of death, the narrative made no more comments about Jairus' faith, which makes it difficult to say that the story is primarily about his being an exemplar of faith.[150] This is certainly an important secondary theme, but, primarily, the story shows Jesus at work; giving life, even to one who had died. Initially, the readers were identified with Jairus in order to have sympathy *with his situation* and the emotions it aroused. When switched to the role of observer, they saw what Jesus did on his behalf, even when the situation had grown much worse. The combined impact of this dynamic encourages the readers to be drawn towards Jesus as the one who can deal with their worst tragedy: he can bring life to the dead. What does this say about his identity?[151]

Reader to text

Death: the end

For Homer real life was above the ground and death was a travesty: 'Say not a word in death's favour; I would rather be a paid servant in a poor man's house and be above ground than king of kings among the dead' (*Od.* 11.487ff.). Implacable death was a harsh and obvious fact of life:

> Hades, I ween, is not to be soothed, neither overcome, wherefore he is most hated by mortals of all gods.   (*Il.* 9.158–9)

Across centuries to come, literary (e.g., *Il.* 21.106ff.; Aesch. *PV* 235ff.) and inscriptional (οὐδεὶς ἀθάνατος, 'no-one is immortal')[152] testimony proclaimed that death was the end for all. Even in the second century AD, Lucian's mockery shows that the general population had not moved too far from the ancient hatred:

> [. . .] these things and others still more ridiculous are done at funerals, for the reason that people think death the greatest of misfortunes.   (Lucian *Luct.* 24)

---

[150] So Williams, *Other Followers*, 112.

[151] In the Jewish world, God was the one who could raise the dead. See Bauckham, 'Resurrection'; Petterson, 'Antecedents, 1 and 2'.

[152] The inscription is on literally hundreds of tombstones across centuries.

People were completely helpless before death. Even the gods could not protect them (*Od.* 3.236ff.) – 'Why sigh we for our dead sons, when not even the gods have power to protect their children from death?' (*AG* 7.8) – and they abandoned them (Eur. *Hipp.* 1473f.; *Alc.* 22).[153] Not surprisingly, this bred the kind of resignation which said, 'truly there is nothing anyone can do in the face of such things' (*P.Oxy* 115 (2nd c. AD)). This comfortless consolation is just like that offered Jairus when he heard the news of his daughter's death (5.35). They were too late: she had gone, and all hope had died with her.

The tragic end of pain

In Tragedy, the pain of life makes death a welcome relief. The craving after a long life is despised as folly, for it simply leads to more misery:

> Until at last the Deliverer comes
> Who sets things right for everyone,
> When the messenger of Hades extends an invitation
> To a wedding without music or dancing
> Death is the end.
> Never to have been born at all:
> None can conceive a loftier thought!
> And the second-best is this: once born,
> Quickly to return to the dust.
> Youthful folly passes away,
> And already distresses have begun;
> Trouble and pain,
> Envy, strife, struggle, war,
> And slaughter, until at last
> The worst of all appears,
> Helpless old age, unaccompanied
> By praise, by love, or by friends,
> The wretchedness of the world one's only guide.
>
> (Soph. *OC* 1213ff.)

Given the pains of life 'Birth should be lamented, death rejoiced over' (Eur. *Cresphontes* fr. 449), especially when a loved one has already died, 'For death is sweetest so With dear dead to lie low' (Eur. *Supp.* 1000–8). The tragic nature of human life made it difficult to see anything better:

---

[153] Cf. Garland, *Greek Way*, 18, 44.

> The life of man is all suffering, and there is no rest from pain
> and trouble. There may be something better than this life; but
> whatever it be, it is hidden in mists of darkness.
>
> (Eur. *Hipp.* 189)

This perspective also made its way into Comedy:

> Everyone says that so-and-so is *makaritēs*, he's passed away,
> gone to sleep. He's a *eudaimōn* (fortunate) fellow because he no
> longer feels any pain.   (Ar. *Tagēnistai*)[154]

Pliny's *Natural History* shows the sentiments were still current in the
first century, when he says, 'Nature has granted man no better gift than
the shortness of life', and again, 'Most miraculous and also frequent, are
sudden deaths (this is life's supreme happiness)' (*HN* 7.50 and 53). On
such views, Jairus' daughter would be deemed fortunate to have avoided
the full extent of pain that could have been hers.

This sense of 'death as deliverer' probably lies behind Socrates' famous
last words: 'Krito, we owe a cock to *Asklepios*. See that it is paid' (Pl. *Phd.*
118A), which 'are perhaps intended to signify the philosopher's belief
that death was a cure for life, since Asklepios was the god of healing'.[155]
But the philosophers, as is only proper for those who ought to study
'nothing but dying and being dead' (*Phd.* 64A), also took the discussion
into questions of the afterlife.

Philosophical views of death

Although Lucian mocked those who thought that death was 'the greatest
of misfortunes' (*Luct.* 24), Socrates had been more agnostic, saying that
'no-one knows what death is, not even whether it is not for man the
greatest among all goods' (Pl. *Apol.* 29A). His logic led him to recognise
death as 'one of two states: a dead person is either the same as nothing,
not having any kind of sensation of anything, or, death is the removal and
relocation of the soul from here to another place' (*Apol.* 40C). These two
views were represented by the Epicureans and Stoics on the one hand,
and the Platonists on the other.

Death as nothingness
As far back as Democritus, who spoke of the soul perishing along with
the body, there were those who drew the sting of death by proclaiming it
to be a natural event at the end of life.

---

[154] Translation: ibid., 9.   [155] Ibid., 20 n.

An Ephesian inscription (2nd c. AD) from an Epicurean meeting hall says that during life they were given release from concern about death.[156] This derived from Epicurus' teaching that the human body dissolved into its component parts and disintegrated at death, and so, in the end, death does not affect a person (D.L. 10.139). If so, then it was eminently sensible to enjoy life while it lasts: 'eat, drink, and be merry, for tomorrow we die'. Although this sentiment is ancient, cross-cultural and long-lasting, it was especially linked with Epicureanism.[157]

For the Stoic, although the soul survived for a short time after death, it was eventually absorbed into the impersonal life-force of the universe.[158] The virtuous man is absolutely brave, because pain and death are not evils, and he does not 'eat, drink, and be merry', because pleasure is not a good. The Stoics urged people to detach themselves from life, possessions, and even spouse and children, in order to be able to bid them farewell easily when it came time to die (Epict. *Ench.* 7).

The two groups' scepticism about immortality echoed throughout the Roman world in the first centuries BC and AD. A number of epitaphs show their influence extended beyond the schools: 'we are mortals, not immortals' (*CIL* 11.**856**); 'when life ends, all things perish and turn to nothing' (CLE **420**); 'We are and were nothing. Look, reader, how swiftly we mortals pass from nothing to nothing' (CLE **1495**); 'I was not, I was, I am not, I don't care' (a recurrent formula). These sentiments may have been 'exceptional',[159] but they were nevertheless a part of the world to which Mark wrote (cf. Acts 17.18, 32), and they represent a self-conscious rejection of anything beyond the grave and an embrace of the resultant nothingness of life, albeit in two distinct forms.

Death as the relocation of the soul

Not everyone was content with death being the end of life. The alternative was to propose that, at death, true life was just beginning. Euripides had allowed the possibility of something more, if only to close it down promptly (Eur. *Hipp.* 189). The middle comic Antiphanes was more positive:

---

[156] See Horsley, 'Inscriptions', 152f.

[157] See the references collected in Bolt, 'Sadducees', 381 n. 36 (on Tob. 7.10f.); to which can be added Gilgamesh Epic, Tablet X.III.1ff. = *ANET*, 90; Aesch. *Pers.* 840–2; Eur. *Cyc.* 345f.; Plaut. *Most.* 64f.; Philo *QG* 2.12; Plut. *De I. et O.* 357F (cf. Hdt. 2.78); and the epitaphs: 'play, have a good time, live; you have to die' (*Epig.Gr.* 362.5 (2nd–3rd c. AD); for more texts see Lattimore, 260–3); 'Drink up!, you see what you will come to' (Peek, *GV* **378**); cf. ζήσας καὶ τρυφήσας ἐν τῷ βίῳ κ[αθ]ὼς εἰδὼς ὅτι ἀπ[οθ]ανεῖν δεῖ, Ramsay **206** (n.d.). Cf. Isa. 22.13.; 1 Cor. 15.32.

[158] Toynbee, *Death*, 36.   [159] Ibid., *Death*, 34.

We should not mourn overmuch for those who are dear to us.
They are not dead; they have only gone before upon the road
that all must travel. Some day we too shall come to the same
way, to spend the rest of time in their society.

(Antiph. *Aphrodisius*; Kock fr. 53 = Stob. 124.27)

But it was the Pythagoreans like Plato – so often mocked by the middle
comics – who elaborated the possibility. The words of a deceased Orphic
initiate[160] not only express the view that the pain of life was over, but
also hint that he had gone to another place: 'I have flown out of the
sorrowful weary wheel'.[161] Similarly, Pindar (fr. 131 = Plut. *Cons. ad
Apol.* 120D) said that our bodies follow the strong call of death, but our
εἴδωλον αἰῶνος survives death, for that alone is of divine origin. With
such notions in mind, Socrates was tempted to agree with Euripides'
question, 'who knows whether to live is to be dead, or to be dead to live?'
(*Gorg.* 492E),[162] before discussing the idea of the body (σῶμα) as tomb
(σῆμα), in which the soul is trapped until released by death.

We have already had cause to mention the Pythagorean notions of the
soul being released from the body, with good souls flying to the upper
realms and those attracted to the body being purged and/or reincarnated,
or simply hovering around the bodily realms, which can be traced through
Plato's elaboration, on to Plutarch (see above, on Suppliant 1). The death
of Socrates proved a great inspiration for such views. He affirmed that
'when death comes to a man, then what is mortal about him, it appears,
dies, but what is immortal and imperishable withdraws from death and
goes its way unharmed and undestroyed' (Pl. *Phd.* 106E). Hopefully, a
good man's soul might then ascend to live 'altogether apart from the
body' (ἄνευ τε σωμάτων [. . .] τὸ παράπαν) in celestial bliss (114B–C).
This is 'the great hope' (ἡ ἐλπὶς μεγάλη, 114C), which, for the person
who has filled his life with the proper pursuits, readies a man for death
(cf. 63B–C). At this, Socrates says it is time for his friends to go so he
can take a bath before he drinks his poison.

Although 'this philosophical teaching was widespread in the ancient
world and afforded comfort to many people',[163] Fronto (AD 100–66) later
expressed doubts at the helpfulness of the doctrine of the immortality
of the soul when it comes to the death of a child: 'If the immortality
of the soul should ever be proved [. . .] it will not be an answer to the
grief felt by parents' (Haines II.226). Plutarch, however, shows that it

[160] For Orphism, see Rohde, *Psyche*, ch. 10; Nilsson, 'Orphism'.
[161] Harrison, *Prolegomena*, 589.
[162] Cf. Heraclitus, in ClemA. *Strom.* 3.3; S.E. 3.230.
[163] Kaiser and Lohse, *Death*, 95.

was certainly enlisted by its supporters[164] in exactly this context. When his little daughter died while he was away from home, Plutarch wrote to his wife with a range of advice for her comfort (*Cons. ad ux.*). Alongside such practical advice as avoiding those who mourn without decorum, he reminded her of various beliefs that should help her cope with the disaster before them: the hopes that they had gained from the mysteries (611E); the notion that their two-year-old had 'passed to a state where there is no pain' (εἰς τὸ ἄλυπον ἤκουσα, 611D; cf. Ps-Plato *Ax.* 327A), gained from the philosophical tradition. But his parting words returned to the cluster of ideas associated with the Pythagorean notions of the soul in the afterlife. Because his daughter was only two, she had not grown accustomed to the body and so was more likely to escape to the upper regions, than to be reincarnated in the cycle of rebirth (611E–F).[165]

If a belief in the dissolution of the body led to a greater focus upon the things of this life, the belief in the transfer of the soul promoted the opposite. Itemising the three features of present-life enjoyment which would later become associated with Epicurus, Socrates considers that the philosophical man does not care much for 'the so-called pleasures, such as eating and drinking [. . . or] the pleasures of love' (*Phd.* 64C). By rising above the body to concerns of the soul, death could be faced without fear (64Eff.; cf. Epicharmus fr. 22 (Diels-Kranz) = ClemA. *Strom.* 4.170). Excessive love of the body caused a soul to be led away to the underworld 'only with violence and difficulty' (*Phd.* 108F), but a pure soul, such as that of Socrates, put up no such resistance (115C) and could calmly 'run the bath' before ending it all.[166]

Since not many would have attained to such philosophical heights,[167] presumably most people did not die without a struggle. For them, perhaps the mysteries offered a better alternative.

The mysteries

Also promising a relocation of the soul, the mysteries were a source of hope for people facing the pain of their own death, or the death of their

---

[164] The immortality of the soul was the one thing which held together the Middle Platonist school, see Atticus in Eus. *Prep.Ev.* 15.9.2; Young, 'Middle Platonists'.

[165] Cf. Menander: 'He whom the gods love dies young' (Plut. *Cons. ad Apol.* 119E).

[166] Garland, *Greek Way*, 66, detects a change in Plato, yielding a more cautious attitude: compare *Phd.* 63C: 'I am hopeful that there is something for the dead, and, as men of old have declared, that it is something better for the good than for the wicked'; with the more tentative *Apol.* 42A: 'But now the time has come to leave, I to die and you to live, but which of us goes to a better lot is unknown to anyone except God'; cf. *Phd.* 115A. The nature of the change depends upon the relative order of the dialogues.

[167] Garland, *Greek Way*, 19.

children (cf. Plut. *Cons. ad ux.* 611E). The promise of a better lot in the afterlife (Pl. *Resp.* 364E–365A) was a great attraction for some of the Romans:

> [. . .] nothing is better than those mysteries. For by means of them we have been transformed from a rough and savage way of life to the state of humanity, and have been civilised. Just as they are called initiations, so in actual fact we have learned from them the fundamentals of life, and have grasped the basis not only for living with joy but also for dying with a better hope.
>
> (Marcus, in Cicero *Leg.* 2.14.36)

The basis of this hope was not so much a belief as an action, for, like Orphism,[168] it was based simply upon being initiated.[169] Although the mysteries are shrouded in secrecy,[170] this apparently consisted of a quasi-death which may have been actually life-threatening (Apul. *Met.* 11.21). Lucius explains what occurred during the rite:

> I went to the very boundary between life and death. I crossed the threshold of Proserpina. And after I had passed through all the elements, I returned once again. At the very hour of midnight I saw the sun shining with its bright light:[171] I beheld the lower and the higher gods face to face, and I worshiped them in their presence.
>
> (Apul. *Met.* 11.23)[172]

The so-called Mithras liturgy also shows that people turned to the mysteries because they 'request immortality' (cf. *PGM* IV.475ff.):

> [G]ive me over to immortal birth and, following that, to my underlying nature, so that, after the present need which is pressing me exceedingly, I may gaze upon the immortal beginning with the immortal spirit, [. . .] that I may be born again in thought.
>
> (*PGM* IV.502ff.; cf. 645ff.)

Here too the rite is recognised as a death-like experience:[173]

---

[168] Cf. Pl. *Resp.* 11.364C; Plut. *Quom. adol. poet.* 21F = Soph. fr. 753.

[169] Cf. Meyer, *Ancient Mysteries*, 12–13.

[170] For example, Eur. *Bac.* 469ff.; Livy 39.10, 13; Diod. 5.48.4, 49.55f.; Plut. *Symp.* IV. no. 6.1 671D; Paus. 4. *Messenia* 33.5; Apul. *Met.* 11.23; Lucian *Salt.* 15.

[171] This would be in the underworld, where the sun is on its nightly journey.

[172] Meyer, *Ancient Mysteries*, 158, comparing the Egyptian *Book of the Dead.*

[173] Cf. also Plut. fr. 178 = Stob. 4.52.49.

> O Lord, while being born again, I am passing away; while grow-
> ing and having grown, I am dying; while being born again from
> a life-generating birth, I am passing on, released to death – as
> you have founded, as you have decreed, and have established
> the mystery. (IV.719ff.)

Isis promised Lucius:

> You shall live blessed. You shall live glorious under my guid-
> ance; and when you have travelled your full length of time and
> you go down into death, there also, on that hidden side of earth,
> you shall dwell in the Elysian Fields and frequently adore me
> for my favors. For you will see me shining on amid the darkness
> of Acheron and reigning in the Stygian depths.
>
> More, if you are found to merit my love by your dedicated
> obedience, religious devotion, and constant chastity, you will
> discover that it is within my power to prolong your life beyond
> the limit set to it by Fate. (*Met.* 11.6)

Since the fate in the afterlife depended on initiation, it is understandable
that some initiates apparently obtained a 'pass' to ensure their just deserts
in the underworld. A number of gold leaves (i.e., literally) have been discovered in corpses' mouths, in order to identify initiates to Persephone.[174]
These indicate that Dionysus, who crossed so many boundaries himself,
'aids in the crossing of what for the classical Greeks was the greatest of
all divisions, the barrier of life and death and between the human and
divine'.[175]

The will to live

It seems difficult to erase the basic will to live. Strangely, it can be discerned behind the longing for a short life, the 'eat, drink and be merry'
attitude, and even amongst the more resigned philosophers' care for their
children, or their promotion of the 'healthy' lifestyle, as much as it can
behind people turning to immortality of the soul, or to the mysteries for
'a better hope'. But it screams out loud and strong in the fact that people
turned to gods, doctors and magicians in the desperate attempt to stave off

---

[174] Cf. Dickie, 'Mysteries'; Merkelbach, 'Goldtäfelchen', 'Zwei neue Totenpässe' and
'Die goldenen Totenpässe'; C. Segal, 'Dionysus'; Zuntz, *Persephone*, 275–393; Harrison,
Prolegomena, ch. 11, esp. 575ff.; Graf, 'Eschatology'.
[175] Segal, 'Dionysus', 418f.

death. When it came to death, if the gods could not help (*Od.* 3.236ff.), and medicine would not (cf. Hipp. *Arte* 3, 8), then the magicians were left the market. People turned to them in the attempt to 'drag out their life with food and drink and magic spells, trying to keep death out of the way' (Eur. *Supp.* 1109ff.). They may have turned to purpose-built charms like the 'Stele that is useful for all things; it even delivers from death ([. . .] ῥύεται καὶ | ἐκ θανάτου)' (*PGM* IV.1167–1226). But, in one sense, all remedies had this aim and the use of magic should be seen against a general will to live in a world where everything seemed to be against this most human of desires.

Hope

Although Philo may have felt that hope was the 'one thing which is naturally capable of consoling human life' (Philo *Flacc.* 20.176), the Greeks and Romans did not regard hope as at all trustworthy. The Greeks knew that humanity was perennially 'tormented by the two grimmest tyrants: Hope and Fear'[176] (cf. Lucian *Alex.* 8; *Charon* 15; *Demon.* 20). The tragedians recognised the vanity of hopes and despised them as the very things which prevent human beings from seeing their own mortality (Soph. *Aj.* 473ff.; Aesch. *PV* 250, 253; cf. Pl.*Gorg.* 523D). Hope was suspect, since it could so easily be revealed as false and empty.[177]

However, as Jairus had discovered, the two tyrants seem to travel together. His daughter had died and Jesus told him not to fear, only believe. Jesus asked for Jairus' trust, but what was the hope he could offer in the face of death? At this point was not any hope as empty as any other, no matter which of the two standard options now lay before him? Should he recognise that he has to live with the pain of his daughter's end, and either live it up before he dies too, or Stoically seek to lay aside the pain even before his end comes, because this is in line with some supposed divine reason? Or should he embrace Socrates' 'strong hope' that his daughter's soul is immortal, and, sooner or later, it may, perhaps, return to its origins and Jairus, if all goes well, may one day attain to the same regions where his soul will reunite with that of his daughter? Does Jesus offer some different hope to Jairus, and, through him, to the Graeco-Roman readers? A hint in this direction comes when Jesus ignores the advice to stay away. On either of the usual scenarios, this advice was completely sound, for any comfort he may have had in regard to the afterlife could be offered

[176] Bickermann, 'Symbolism', 151.
[177] For a similar Roman distrust of Hope; cf. Clark, 'Images', and Walsh, 'Spes Romana'.

at a distance (cf. Plut. *Cons. ad ux.*). But instead, Jesus tells Jairus to continue to believe and then sets out for the house of mourning.

At this point, the Graeco-Roman reader would have run out of options. Although the mythology of the ancient poets had a few cases of resuscitations, the idea of resurrection for real, historical people was not seriously entertained.

Resurrection?

The denial of resurrection

'Resurrection' is most commonly found in non-biblical Greek literature in a statement of the impossible: the dead are not raised.[178]

> Thou, hapless queen, fret not thine heart away Without avail. Menelaus hath his doom, And thy dead husband cannot live again.   (Eur. *Helen* 1285–7)

However, despite this impossibility, there were a number of exceptions in the form of resuscitations, i.e., restorations of the dead to life on this earth, followed by eventual death.[179] Pliny was also aware of reports of people coming back from the dead. However, since he mentions them in the context of a discussion on the signs of approaching death (*HN* 7.51) to illustrate that 'in the case of a human being no confidence must be placed even in death' (7.52), he evidently considers the diagnosis of 'death' to be mistaken, despite the time taken for it to come out. He also knows of 'cases of persons appearing after burial' but does not discuss them because his subject is 'works of nature, not prodigies' (7.52).

The eschatological myths of Plato (*Resp.*10.614B) and, following his model, Plutarch (*De sera* 563ff.) have characters who undergo a 'resurrection' which enables them to speak of their other-worldly journeys – with precedent in the various under-worldly journeys in older literature. So temporary restorations to life were 'not completely alien even to the

---

[178] Wedderburn, *Baptism*, 181. Cf. Hom. *Il.* 24.551, 756, cf. 21.56; Aesch. *Eum.* 647f.; cf. *Ag.* 565ff., 1361; Soph. *El.* 138f.; Hdt. 3.62.3f.; cf. 2 Sam. 12.22f.; Ps. 88.10–12; Aristotle uses it in a *reductio ad absurdum* (*De anima* 1.3.406^{b}3–5), not even allowing the theoretical possibility. Despite the claim by Porter, 'Resurrection', 53, that the Greeks had a 'significant tradition of bodily resurrection', the nearest case to resurrection that he demonstrates is that of Alcestis, who is a mythological character rather than a historical person. Such an example would not have been taken seriously by Plutarch, who would have regarded it as the stuff of the poets and their mythology (*Quom. ad. poet.* 16A–17F; cf. Pl. *Euth.* 5E–6C), for resurrection is 'against reason' (cf. *Rom.* 28.7–8).

[179] Wedderburn, *Baptism*, 181–3 for examples of restoration of life to this world.

Greeks',[180] even though these are mostly not strictly 'from the dead' for they have not been buried and so have not entered the realm of the dead.[181] Thus, although it would be deemed unusual, Jesus' raising of the girl to a temporary existence before she died again would certainly be within the conceptual boundaries of the Graeco-Roman readers.

Magical resurrection?

After putting out a distinctly 'unphilosophical' group of mourners, who may have genuinely felt the tragedy of the occasion,[182] Jesus arrives at the girl's bedside. The foreign words 'Ταλιθα κουμ' add a magical atmosphere (v.41), since the magical spells overflow with 'foreign-sounding, meaningless names and poly-syllables' (βαρβαρικά τινα καὶ ἄσημα ὀνόματα καὶ πολυσύλλαβα, Lucian *Men.* 9).[183] So, is Jesus using magic to raise the dead?

The traditional wisdom said that this would be highly unusual, if not impossible. In fact, as the case of Asclepius showed, it was forbidden by the gods (Aesch. *Ag.* 1010ff.; cf. *Eum.* 647f.). Yet this did not prevent the magicians from trying. In the second century, Apuleius told of an Egyptian who reanimated a corpse (Apul. *Met.* 2.28–30) and Mark will soon report a well-connected suspicion that Jesus had done the same thing with John the Baptist (6.14–16). A number of spells have survived which call upon the corpse to 'rise' (cf. ἔγειρε, v.41b),[184] so is this what Jesus is doing here?

---

[180] Hengel, *Judaism*, 2, 131 n. 575, referring to Pliny *HN* 7.124; Apul. *Flor.* 19; Philostr. *Vit. Ap.* 4.45.

[181] Wedderburn, *Baptism*, 165, making an exception for Lazarus, Alcestis and Eurydice.

[182] Plutarch's reference to the wailers (*Cons. ad ux.* 609E–F) seems to indicate that this was normal, as opposed to philosophical, rather than false/artificial as opposed to genuine.

[183] ταλιθα actually entered into the magicians' usage; see Jordan and Kotansky, 'Two Phylacteries from Xanthos', 1 (3–4th c. AD), pp. 162, 167.

[184] 2nd c. AD: *DT* **198**.10 ἐξεγέρθητι; <3rd c. AD: *SuppMag* **46**.6f: διέγι|ρέ μοι σεαυτὸν νέκυς δαίμων; 3rd c. AD: *SuppMag* **39**: δ<ι>εγείρω [τὸν] | δαίμονά σου; *SB* 4947: ὁρκίζω σε, νεκυδαῖμον, καὶ δ' ἐγείρω [τὸν] | δαίμονά σου, in which the name of the person is addressed; *DT* **16** I 15: ἐξεγ(ε)ίρ(ε)ῖς; *DT* **22**.3, 43, **26**.3, 31, **29**.29, **30**.35, **31**.28, **37**.29: ἔγ(ε)ιρον δὲ μοι σύ; 3/4th c. AD: *SuppMag* **49**: ἔγειρέ μοι σεαυτόν; 5th c. AD: *SuppMag* **45** ἐξορκίζω ἐγείρεσθαι δέμονες, addressed to corpses; *SuppMag* **72** also has ἔγειρε, but this is probably addressed to the lover.

See also: *PGM* IV.1468, 1475, 1479, 1480, 1494, 1495: 'Send up the phantoms of the dead', Jordan, 'Feasts', 137; with the naming of the person addressed: *SuppMag* **44** = GMPT CVII (3rd/4th c. AD), a named ἄωρος; *SuppMag* **47** Antinous, but probably not Hadrian's favourite; Cf. 'he can get there' *PGM* IV.52f.; *PGM* IV.2215 he will come to life, i.e., one of the untimely dead; *PGM* XIII.1076 to call phantoms; *PGM* XII.201–69 to call for helpers; *PGM* XVIIb.1–23? rouse again; *PGM* VIII.64–110 send up a prophet from the realm of the dead.

In actual fact, these cases are not so much 'resurrections' as reanimations, or the recalling of the corpse-spirit in order to provide a daemonic assistant to do the magician's bidding. So, for example, the Egyptian prophet in Apuleius invokes the Sun to release the spirit of the man for just long enough to allow justice to be done, and the corpse speaks about what had truly happened. Other spells also allowed corpses to be questioned (*PGM* IV.1990ff.; 2140–44).

However, the occasional charm may ask for something more:

> Resurrection of a dead body (ἔγερϲιϲ ϲώματοϲ νεκροῦ). I conjure you, spirit coming in air, enter, inspire, empower, resurrect (διαέγειρον) by the power of the eternal god, this body; and let it walk about this place, for I am he who acts with the power of Thayth. (*PGM* XIII.278–83 (AD 346))

What was desired here? Διαέγειρον [*sic*] may indicate it is simply another reanimator of the corpse-*daimon*, and, since it asks for the body to walk around the room, it may even be simply interested in a magical performance, rather than a restoration to life.[185] One of the Aramaic bowl texts (*AMB* **Bowl 4**) provides another ambiguous example. Admitting that the meaning of the lines is obscure, the editors suggest that it may be a spell protecting a tomb (cf. ll. 1–3, 8).[186] However, since the spell seeks 'to make his body alive' (l. 8), it could be a spell desiring to bring one who had died back to life again. Neither of these spells give any hint about how they were used, or their efficacy, but they may well testify to magicians who were well aware of the great tragedy of death and, not content to provide spells merely to stave it off, offered charms to bring someone back from the dead.

Raised from the dead

Since the time of Alexander, the Greeks had been fascinated by things Oriental – the Magi, the Chaldeans, the Indians, and even the Jews. Plutarch was well aware of the Chaldean expectation of some kind of future new world, in which 'those who are resurrected require no food and cast no shadows' (Plut. *De I et O* 370C), even if he considers such views as rather fabulous. His Pythagorean notions of the soul being captive in the body and real life being that of the soul above prevented him from fully appreciating such views. For him, it was the pure souls above who cast no shadows, those who have been liberated from the body

---

[185] For other magical 'gimmicks', see *PGM* VII.167–85; XIb.1–5.   [186] *AMB*, 152.

(cf. *De sera.* 564D), not resurrected bodies in a renewed earthly situation. He could see no sense in taking the body to heaven (*Rom.* 28.7f.).

However, when Jesus stood at the bedside of the girl, he orchestrated the reanimation of a person, not just of her voice or her corpse-*daimon* – or even her body in some bizarre spectral performance. Once she had been raised, two things occurred. First, she got up and walked around (v.43). This is certainly not the action of a corpse (contrast: 'that she may no longer rise up, walk around, talk, move about, but let her remain a corpse, [. . .]' AthAg **App**), but it is conceivable that it may still be read as a powerful reanimation of the body. But this possibility is dismissed when Jesus orders some food for her, for neither ghosts, nor dead bodies – even if given the ability to dance around a room –, needed to eat (cf. Luke 24.39–43). She was raised, a person, i.e., a human being: twelve years old, in a family, whose bodily nature insisted on being fed. The girl had rejoined bodily life. She had been raised from the dead.

Impact of the narrative

The bleeding woman scene has taught the reader that faith saves, but here the call to follow Jesus is into a situation beyond all hope, into the jaws of death itself. What can faith do in the face of the grave?

The previous main section (1.14–4.34) had shown several significant miracles in which Jesus brought people out from the shadow of death. Then, as the waves pounded their boat, the frightened disciples had asked whether Jesus cared that they were perishing (4.38) and he had demonstrated that he did. He then brought a man out from the tombs and sent him back to a new life (5.1–20). Now he had actually raised a dead girl to life. The accumulating picture is that Jesus brought people out from the shadow of death; back from a living death; back from the brink of death; back from amongst the dead; and now back from death itself. Mark's story shows him plundering the domain of the prince of *daimones*. He is defeating death.

Galilean leadership (Mark 6.1–7.23)

Throughout Mark 4.35–8.26, the question of Jesus' identity is kept on the agenda by presenting a variety of different answers to the question 'who then is this?' (4.41). The question is asked in a slightly different form in Nazareth (6.2) and the answer is supplied in terms of the very human background that Jesus left in order to do the will of God (1.9; 3.20f., 31–35). The report of the townsfolk's lack of faith issues in the enigmatic statement that Jesus could not do any miracles, apart from some healings. This suggests that (mere) healings were not considered 'powers' in the same sense as the miracles just prior to this scene, i.e., those which explicitly and powerfully demonstrated his power over the dead. After starting with an exorcism and then some healings, the narrative has moved to encounters with death itself, which are what the healings were pointing to anyway (3.4).

The account of John the Baptist's death (6.14–29) has been regarded by interpreters as something of an oddity at this point in the narrative. A key towards its proper understanding, however, arises from the observation that it is actually cast as an extended aside to the question of Jesus' identity. This suggests that it is not simply added for its own sake, but in order to supply further insight into Mark's main character.

The mission of the twelve (6.7–13) causes Herod to ask questions about Jesus (vv.14–16). This leads into the story of Herod having John killed (vv.17–29).[187] When he hears of the mission, he explains the powers at work in Jesus (NB ἐν αὐτῷ, v.14) in terms of John having been raised from the dead. The 'demise of John' story is then provided as an explanation (γάρ) of Herod's opinion about Jesus.[188] The story sketches the background of Herodias' hatred of John and her desire to kill him (vv.17–20), before telling the events of the fateful dinner-party when she seized her opportunity (vv.21–28). The narration of the grisly events focuses upon the removal of John's head: the girl asks her mother about her reward and is told to ask for the head (v.24b); she does so (v.25); the king sends the *speculator* to bring John's head (v.27a); he beheads him in the prison (v.27b); brings the head on a plate to the girl (v.28a); and the girl gives it to her mother (v.28b) to complete the revenge sequence. Herodias' hatred for John had found its opportunity and Herod had been manipulated into killing John, by removing his head. This sequence of events, somehow, provides the explanation (NB γάρ, v.17) for Herod's suggestion that Jesus' powers exist because John has been raised (v.16).

Despite the fact that so few have noticed it,[189] and so many have ignored it, it seems that the narrative is saying clearly that Herod considered Jesus to be a magician who had raised John's spirit in order to capitalise upon its power.[190] This is why the focus is upon John's beheading. A beheaded

---

[187] Cf. Gundry, *Mark*, 303.   [188] So, too, ibid., 304.

[189] See Kraeling, 'Necromancy?'; Morton Smith, *Magician*, 33f.; cf. Aune, 'Magic', 1541f. The declarations that the view is 'improbable' (Twelftree, *Jesus*, 208), or 'too subtle' (Gundry, *Mark*, 315), are hardly decisive critiques.

[190] The distinction between Jesus having control of the dead man's spirit and *being controlled* by that spirit is a fine one. If Jesus had John's ghost under his power, then it

man, as a βιαιοθάνατος, would make a powerful ghost and would be highly sought after by the magicians. An ἀκέφαλος may have been an additional sub-category of useful ghosts.[191] When Herod suggests that Jesus has 'raised' John, he uses language that regularly appears in the magical material for the summoning of the ghostly *daimon* from its rest in the underworld in order to do the magician's bidding.[192] Herod thinks that Jesus is a magician who has done this and is effectively using John's spirit in his territory. Mark, however, very subtly puts this theory to rest by his mention of John's disciples properly burying his corpse (v.29). John may have been an ἀκέφαλος but he did not remain an ἄταφος. His proper burial would be seen as a ghost-removing activity, indicating to the readers that, in the narrator's opinion, Herod was mistaken. Jesus was not a magician operating by the powers of the dead.

The correct evaluation of Jesus is provided in the conclusion of the mission of the twelve into which the Herod account was intercalated (vv.30–44). Jesus looks at the multitude and describes what he sees using an Old Testament phrase. Like Israel of old, they were 'like sheep without a shepherd' (v.34; cf. Num. 27.17; 1 Kgs 22.17 = 2 Chr. 18.16). Whereas Micaiah was told that Israel were to be sent home, because 'they have no master', here Jesus doesn't want to send them home (v.36). Instead, he teaches and feeds them, implying that he is the master who steps into the breach when Israel's leadership has failed.

The sheep–shepherd relationship was a long-standing kingship image in the Ancient Near East, applied to both gods and human rulers. In the Old Testament it is used of YHWH and of his future Messiah.[193] It was also an image that was deeply embedded in Greek culture. By the time of Homer the image of the ruler as a 'shepherd of the peoples' (ποιμὴν λαῶν) had already acquired a customary meaning (e.g., *Il.* 2.75–109; *Od.* 3.156). It is an image that can be found from the poet, to the tragedian (Eur. *Supp.* 191; *Helen* 1479–94), to the philosopher (Pl. *Resp.* 342–3 (esp. 343A–B), 345; *Plt.* 266–72B) and one that was still current at the end of

could also be said that he was *under its power*. Thus, Herod could have been saying that Jesus *is* John. Note, however, that there is a clear distinction between the statements about Elijah and the prophets (v.15, ἐστιν) and those about John (vv.14, 16). The powers are at work in Jesus (v.14b) because John the Baptist has been raised (vv.14a, 16), viz. by Jesus.

[191] Headless *daimones* appear in the spells; see Preisendanz, 'Akephalos'. Cf. the finds of decapitated figurines (3rd c. BC), Faraone, 'Binding and Burying', fig. 7, pl. 5.

[192] See on Suppliant 7b, pp. 188–9.

[193] See Jeremias, 'ποιμήν'; Vancil, 'Sheep'. The image continued to be applied to the Messiah beyond the OT; see Pss.Sol. 17.23–46; Zad.Frag. 16.1–3 (Barrett, *New Testament Background*, **232**); 2 Esdr. 2.34.

the first century in Epictetus (Arr. *Epict.Diss.* 3.22.34, of Agamemnon) and Plutarch (*De virt. mor.* 452C, citing Hom. *Il.* 15.262; see also *Reg. et imp. apoph.* 201E, of Scipio, conqueror of Carthage (147–146 BC); and *Agis.* 1.3.1 where Sophocles' lost saying about shepherds being slaves to their flocks (cf. *TGF*, 249) is applied to 'public men').

Although the Roman form of government had little use for such a symbol in the early days, it became important from the mid first century AD when Roman attitudes began to be affected by eastern/Greek ideas of kingship. Writers such as Philo, Seneca (*De clem.*) and Dio Chrysostom (*Or.* 1–4) described the duties of the Roman chief man in terms derived from Hellenistic kingship theory.[194] When doing so, Philo and Dio drew upon this ancient image of the ruler as shepherd.

On several occasions Philo harks back to the Homeric phrase in order to draw upon what would be recognised as a stock image of rule. 'So full of dignity and benefit has the shepherd's task been held to, that poets are wont to give to kings the title of "shepherds of peoples" (ποιμένας λαῶν)' (*Agric.* 41; cf. *Vit.Jos.* 2; *Vit.Mos.* 1.60ff.). When attempting to sway Caligula to more clemency towards the Jews, Philo appealed to this image, indicating that it must have also been recognisable to Rome of the Caesars:

> For it is not to be thought of that the sovereign of earth and sea (τὴν ἡγεμόνα γῆς καῖ θαλάττης) should be overcome by a song or dancing or ribald jesting or anything of the kind, instead of always and everywhere remembering his sovereignty, that he is as a shepherd and master of a herd (καθάπερ ποιμένα τινὰ καὶ ἐπιστάτην ἀγέλης) [. . .]   (Philo, *Legat.* 44.)

With Homer, Dio argues that the ruler is to be a 'shepherd of the people' (ποιμένα λαῶν) (2.6). He reports Socrates' view (3.41, imitating Xenophon *Mem.*): 'if he lacks even the quality of a good shepherd, who takes thought for the shelter and pasturing of his own flock, and, besides, keeps off wild beasts and guards it against thieves; nay, if he is the very first to plunder and destroy them [. . .] never should I style such a ruler either emperor or king, but he would be a tyrant'. The difference between a shepherd and a butcher is the difference between monarchy and tyranny, for, once again alluding to Homer, 'the shepherd's business is simply to oversee, guard, and protect flocks, not, by heaven, to slaughter, butcher and skin them' (4.44). The ruler should become 'indeed a guide and

---

[194] Murray, 'Kingship', 807.

shepherd of his people, not, as someone has said, a caterer and banqueter at their expense' (1.13; cf. Pl. *Resp.* 421b and 345c).[195]

Herod was not a properly constituted king, for Augustus had not seen fit to grant him this title, and his request that it be granted led to his dismissal and exile in AD 39 (Joseph. *AJ* 18.240–56). If this was known to Mark's Graeco-Roman readers, then the usage of the title would be a bitterly ironic reminder of the power of Rome. Behind this 'shepherd' lay Caesar, the 'shepherd and master of a herd', namely, the precious herd of humanity (cf. Philo, *Vit.Jos.* 2; *Vit.Mos.* 1.60ff.). Also, when read against the stream of Old Testament tradition, Israel really had 'no shepherd' in the person of 'King' Herod. His was a travesty of leadership, for it simply led to the death of God's prophet as dinner-party entertainment. He was one of a long line of rulers who had not brought life to Israel, but had brought an experience that could be described in terms echoing that of the Psalmist: 'Death shall be their shepherd' (Ps. 49.14). The Psalmist placed no trust in anyone's ability to redeem the situation, for only God could ransom life from the grave (v.15). During the exile, Ezekiel indicted the leaders of Israel for plundering the flock of God and promised that God himself would act as their shepherd. He would not plunder the flock, but would care for it and feed it (Ezek. 34–36) before the resurrection of the dry bones of Israel occurred (Ezek. 37). In this scene Jesus plays the role of the expected good shepherd. No-one in the leadership has helped Israel – not the Roman puppet Herod, nor the religous leaders in Jerusalem, nor the one who granted them their power: Caesar himself. Israel still lives under the shadow of death. Jesus does not send the crowds of Israel away, but provides for them in their need.

Journey 2: the heart problem (Mark 6.45–8.10)

The second sea journey begins without Jesus who follows later 'walking on the sea', intending 'to pass them by' (v.48). Both these phrases are reminiscent of language used of God in the OT in a famous theophany (Exod. 33.19, 22; 34.6). Being at sea in a storm, the disciples sensibly evaluate what they see and conclude that Jesus is a ghost (φάντασμα, v.49). Mark says their resultant cry was because they all saw the same thing and were thrown into confusion (ἐταράχθησαν, v.50). In an action also reminiscent of YHWH, Jesus tells them not to be afraid (e.g., Isa. 41.14) and then, continuing the impression that this scene is a theophany, he uses 'ἐγώ εἰμι', YHWH's self-address (Exod. 3.14). When he climbs

---

[195] For further uses of the image, see Dio 1.17, 1.28, 56.2.

in the boat, the wind ceases and the disciples are astounded. Mark's narrative commentary (vv.50, 51b–52) stresses the lack of progress made by the disciples since the first sea crossing, for they were afraid in both storms. The first occasion they cried out 'Who then is this?', but this time they apparently should have known. Mark explains their astonishment as being due to the fact that they had not understood the significance of the loaves, but their hearts, like Israel's, were hardened. If they had understood the loaves, then they would not have been afraid when they saw Jesus acting with the prerogatives of YHWH. Presumably this means that Jesus' multiplication of loaves also has some theophanic significance. Instead of plundering the flock of God and bringing death, like the false shepherds, as the good shepherd, Jesus feeds the flock of God and brings life from the dead.

Previously, the storm at sea scene (4.35–41) had raised the question, 'Who then is this?' Both Jewish, Greek and Roman traditions would raise the same question for Mark's early readers. That Jesus can still the storm, or walk a pathway through the waves, indicates that the power over the sea motif applied to mythological figures, as well as to great rulers such as Xerxes, Alexander and Augustus, has now been applied to him. The Old Testament traditions spoke of YHWH being the one who trod down the waves and stilled the waters of chaos and death (e.g., Job 9.8; cf. Ps. 74.12–17; Isa. 51.9–11).[196] The theophanic portrayal of this scene is now suggesting that Jesus is a ruler who can tread down the waves, because he is the great 'I AM'.

When they land, the narrative's final summary statement (6.53–56) tells of amazing events which provoked overwhelming responses to Jesus wherever he went. People were flocking to benefit from his leadership. After σώζω has acquired overtones of being saved from death (5.21–43), the readers would also hear them echoed here when many who touched Jesus found that they were 'saved' (6.56).

After the poverty of the leadership offered by the political Herod has been depicted in the previous sub-section, the poverty of the leadership offered by those holding religious positions in Jerusalem is now exposed (6.45–8.10). But it must be remembered that these religious leaders also held political positions. Under Roman administration of Palestine, those holding 'religious' positions did so by the grace of Rome, and, as with the administration of the imperial cult in other provinces, the religious leadership of Israel had been political for some time.

---

[196] Cf. Collins, 'Rulers', 212–13.

Jesus disputes with the religious leaders from Jerusalem, using Isaiah to expose the hardness of heart (7.6f.) which had led them to nullify the word of God (v.13). As he explains this to the disciples, a further word to the crowd stresses how significant the heart problem was (vv.14f.,19). His explanation also indicts the disciples in the same problem suffered by Israel and her leadership: 'thus are you too lacking in understanding?' (οὕτως καὶ ὑμεῖς ἀσύνετοί ἐστε; v.18). By recalling the parables discourse, this underlines the serious nature of the charge. For there the hardening prevented people from receiving forgiveness, and lack of understanding through not listening prevented access to the coming kingdom harvest. The 'kingdom' of Herod led to the death of God's prophet and the 'kingdom' of the religious leaders led to the nullification of God's word and of basic human decency (vv.9–13), resulting in every known human evil (vv.21–23). If the disciples are still a part of such hard-heartedness, then they have a long way to go before they are ready for the coming kingdom.

Suppliant 9: exorcism of a Greek (Mark 7.24–30)

Text to reader: a *daimon* leaves a Greek

The disciples are completely absent from this scene and the readers are drawn towards a Greek woman who acts on behalf of her daughter.

The readers accompany Jesus in his movement from the previous location into the region of Tyre (v.24a) and on into a house. They are supplied with an inside view of Jesus' wishes:[197] he wanted no-one to know (v.24b). Being in the house raises the motif of the insider versus the outsider.[198] Jesus' desire for absolute secrecy, in effect, makes all potential visitors into outsiders. But his secret is out when a woman comes to him (v.24c).

Ἀλλά introduces a strong contrast with the preceding, indicating that the details about Jesus' whereabouts and desire for secrecy are background to the woman's story. The scene is then focalised through this woman, beginning with an inside view of aural perception[199] (ἀκούσασα, v.25; cf. 5.27), followed by a relative clause introducing extra detail about her circumstances: she has a (beloved? – note the diminutive, θυγάτριον; cf. 5.23) daughter with an unclean spirit. The fact that she is a woman, that the one in need is described in relation to her, and that the diminutive is used, all add to the *pathos* of the scene.[200] Further alignment comes by

---

[197] Fowler, *Let the Reader*, 123f.   [198] Ibid., 211.
[199] Ibid., 121.   [200] See discussion above, Introduction, p. 19.

recollection of the scene where two 'daughters' had previously gained help from Jesus (cf. 5.23, 34, 35). This woman bursts into the privacy of the house, frustrating Jesus' desire for secrecy, and falls at his feet. Despite the intrusion, the readers are already on her side.

The narrator suspends the action with the woman on the floor to introduce a piece of information about her. Although introduced by a δέ parenthesis, one of the weaker signals of explicit commentary,[201] this proves to be extremely important for her story (v.26a): the woman was Greek, or, more particularly, Syrophoenician by race. This is not so much a comment upon her religion, i.e., that she was a 'pagan',[202] but upon her cultural orientation. This explicit comment to the reader hints that the proper understanding of the story will be connected with the woman's Greekness. A Greek was now seeking Jesus out.

When the action resumes, it continues to be narrated from her point of view. However, since her request is given in reported speech, a degree of distance from the readers is introduced (v.26b), beginning to shift them towards the role of observers. Jesus' reply is in direct speech – a 'showing', enabling the readers to hear Jesus' words as the woman would have done (v.27). Given the narrative portrayal of Jesus so far, his reply comes as something of a shock and forces the issue of ethnicity. Since parables were his preferred medium for outsiders (4.11), even the form used speaks of rejection.[203] The readers are aware that Jesus, as the true shepherd of Israel and in contrast to the established leadership which had failed, has already fed the people with bread (6.30–44; cf. 6.34). They have been informed that the disciples' continued state of fear and amazement was due to a lack of understanding of the bread miracle, which was, in turn, due to their hardness of heart (6.52). The image of 'bread' encompasses not only Jesus' teaching, but all that he has to offer – as illustrated here, where the request for exorcism is encompassed by the metaphor. The narrative has been one long description of how Jesus was supplying bread to those in need, but now, when the Greek woman asks for help, he reveals that the 'bread' is for the children (presumably Israel) and it should not be thrown to the dogs (presumably Greeks like her). Jesus saw his prime role as removing the unclean spirits from amongst Israel, rather than from amongst the Greeks. Since the readers have already been aligned with many other suppliants like this woman and have observed Jesus supplying their needs, his reply is shocking. It places distance between him and the reader, which causes some tension and at the same time aligns

---

[201] Fowler, *Let the Reader*, 116f.   [202] So Taylor, *Mark*.
[203] J.F. Williams, *Other Followers*, 119.

them further with the woman. Although the woman managed to penetrate into Jesus' secret location, she seems to have little chance of penetrating further to receive the help that she needs. Since his reply speaks of a denial of access which ensures that the outsiders remain outsiders, this distance also moves the readers – who have been so well aligned with the woman – towards the status of outsiders (cf. 4.10–12, 33).

Despite the harsh insult, the woman persists, indicating that her need must be great indeed. Without contradicting Jesus' statement, her reply (also cast vividly in direct speech), uses his figure of speech to her advantage by suggesting that she only wants some crumbs from the table (v.28) – perhaps reminding the readers of the crumbs that were left over at the feeding miracle.[204] After being shocked by Jesus' remark, the readers cannot help but be impressed by the woman's reply. It not only highlights their own lack of insight, relative to hers, but, because it is so attractive and helps the readers out of their own puzzled state, it also maintains their alignment with her. It also seems to express an insight which is entirely suitable for the view of Jesus being presented by the story so far. He is the one who brings bread for the needy; even though she may be a 'dog', she is prepared to accept the crumbs.

Her reply also impresses Jesus, who expressly makes it the basis of the fulfilment of her request and announces the *daimon* has left her daughter (v.29). This statement encourages a reassessment of his previous remark that caused such consternation. Since he eventually fulfils the woman's request, this re-reading reapplies the positive regard for Jesus built up across the course of the narrative to this scene, leading the readers to view his initial statement not as a rejection of the woman, but as a means towards eliciting the required response.

The account ends still focalised through the woman. The readers join her in the discovery of her daughter lying on the bed, no longer troubled by the *daimon* (v.30). Jesus had cast out a *daimon* even from a Greek.

Reader to text

The woman's race

Although the woman is a Syrophoenician by race, which in the eyes of some may exclude her from true Greekness (cf. Lucian *DeorConc.* 4), the text emphasises her cultural orientation as a Greek. Any of Mark's readers who knew their own Greekness would stand even more firmly

---

[204] The vocabulary is different: κλάσματα (6.43); ψιχία (7.28).

with this woman and her need – as would plenty of Romans, since they were increasingly impressed with things Greek as time went on.

The child and death

Since the child is offstage for the entire incident, it is difficult to say much about her problem, although, given the mother's evident concern and persistence, her situation seems serious. The *daimones* are known to be violent and bent on destruction; and the girl is already on her bed, suggesting a serious condition, perhaps even life-threatening.[205]

The child and the dead

Once again, readers would consider the *daimon* as a ghost of the dead. The question would arise whether it had been set upon her by some magical curse. This could have resulted from a curse upon the family, or, since she is a female and if she is approaching marriageable age, she, like Jairus' daughter, could be a victim of the frequent erotic magic (see on Suppliant 7a). In this case someone would be seeking to draw her to himself by torturing her with a *daimon*. These spells could pin her to her bed in great suffering, e.g., 'Lay Allous low with fever, with sickness unceasing, starvation, and madness' (*PGM* O2 = Gager **35** (2nd c. AD)). As we have seen, they were particularly vindictive and closely aligned with death. Counter-curses could be taken out to protect the women of the family from these kinds of spells (e.g., Gager **125**). Whatever the cause, she is under the power of the dead and her mother is concerned for her. But Jesus casts out the spirit, even at a distance.

Jesus and the Caesar

Jesus' assistance even for a Greek may be another small item setting Jesus in parallel with the Caesars. It was said of Augustus that he was the Caesar 'who healed the pestilences common to Greeks and barbarians' (Philo *Legat.* 145). Since Philo was a Jew, who would be classed as a barbarian by the Graeco-Romans (cf. Plut. *Quaest.conv.* 4.5, 670F), he apparently cites a piece of standard Augustan rhetoric in an endeavour to move Caligula to emulate his noble predecessor.[206] Augustus' 'healing'

---

[205] See the comments on being bed-ridden above, on Suppliant 2. That she is on her bed is implied by v.30, even though this verse is a statement of her final state of cure.

[206] I have not been able to find the thought elsewhere, however.

was purely metaphorical, but Mark's account is of something actually happening to a real person. If this rhetoric was well known, perhaps the readers would recognise Jesus, in Augustan fashion, moving from the barbarians to the Greeks. Jesus could break the bondage to the dead even amongst the Greeks.

Suppliant 10: a deaf man with difficult speech (Mark 7.31–37)

Text to reader: a deaf man healed

Consistent with what is by now the normal pattern, the disciples are absent from the scene and the readers are aligned with the suppliant. Returning to the Decapolis (v.31) recalls the encounter with Legion, whom Jesus had sent on a mission to this region (5.20). An undefined group (cf. 2.3; 8.22) bring a κωφὸν καὶ μογιλάλον for Jesus to lay hands upon (v.32).

The double description of the man's condition aligns the readers with this man in his desperate situation. The man is deaf (κωφός), but it should not be assumed that this was a congenital condition. He could have gone deaf later in life, and, indeed, it is not even clear whether his condition is chronic or acute.

He is also μογιλάλος. This word signifies that he was not completely voiceless (i.e., ἄφωνος, Hipp. *Epid.* III.17 Case 3), but had some difficulty with speaking. The use of ἄλαλος (v.37) 'speechless' certainly could imply that he was mute, but it could equally refer to being without articulate speech. The man's difficulty in speaking is also hinted at in the description of his cure, where a problem of articulation is hinted at (v.35, ἐλύθη ὁ δεσμὸς τῆς γλώσσης αὐτοῦ) and the result is given as 'straight talking' (cf. ἐλάλει ὀρθῶς). Evidently he had some difficulty with his speech. There were other words for being a stammerer in speech (e.g., παφλάζω τῇ γλώσσῃ, 'spluttering in tongue', Hipp. *Epid.* II.5.2; τραυλός, 'mispronouncing letters, lisping', *Epid.* II.6.1; ψελλός, 'faltering in speech, like a child', *Epid.* II.6.14), that are not used here, so can we be more precise about the difficulty?

Besides its occurrences in the LXX,[207] μογιλάλος is used on only one occasion prior to our passage, in Ostanes (5th c. BC) when referring to cures occurring 'through this lovely and divine water' (διὰ τοῦ ἐρασμίου καὶ θείου ὕδατος τοῦτο) which

---

[207] Isa. 35.6; Aq.: Exod. 4.11, Isa. 56.10; Sm. Th.: Exod. 4.11; Quint.: Ps. 55 [56].1.

πᾶν νόσημα θεραπεύεται. Ὀφθαλμοὶ βλέπουσι τυφλῶν, ὦτα ἀκούουσι κωφῶν, μογιλάλοι τρανῶς λαλοῦσιν.

heals every disease. The eyes of the blind see, the ears of the deaf hear, the MOGILALOI speak distinctly.   (Frag. 2.261)

In derivation, μογιλάλος means 'speaking with toil/pain' (cf. μόγις), which could denote a hoarse voice. The textual variant μογγιλάλος (B³LWD et al. f^{13}) – also in existence for LXX Isaiah 35.6 – points in the same direction (cf. μογγός, LSJ: 'with a hoarse, hollow voice', *PLond.* 3.653.16 (4th c. AD); Hippiatr. 14; Paul. Aeg. 3.24). Perhaps in an endeavour to avoid demonic overtones to the scene, some commentators have attempted to give the two words distinct meanings, but it is more likely that it is simply a variant in spelling.[208] The 'hoarse voice' need not indicate a demonic overlay, although this becomes more likely when it is combined with other features of the passage (see below).

The similarity of the introduction of this scene to others involving suppliants[209] further assists in aligning the readers with this sufferer. The readers are privileged observers of the private interaction between the man and Jesus (v.33a). Jesus performed a series of actions (vv.33f.): he put his fingers into the man's ears, spat, touched the man's tongue, looked up to heaven, sighed, and said a word requiring translation.[210] The man's hearing was restored and 'the bond of his tongue was released and he spoke straight' (ἐλύθη ὁ δεσμὸς τῆς γλώσσης αὐτοῦ καὶ ἐλάλει ὀρθῶς, v.35).

Jesus commanded the wider group (αὐτοῖς, v.32) not to tell anyone, but the narrator stresses that their opposite response was in proportion to his commands: 'as much as he commanded, the more they were more excessively proclaiming' (v.36). Rather than this being a disobedience which would prevent readers from identifying with the suppliant,[211] this is a delightful example of Mark's irony and tongue-in-cheek humour.[212]

Jesus' dealings with suppliants have often issued in speech rather than silence (1.44–45; 5.19–20; 7.36; 10.48), which 'creates the expectation that minor characters will speak freely when they are confronted by

---

[208] Cf. Suda: Μογγιλάλος = μόγις λαλῶν. The Fathers oscillate between the two in their explanations of Isaiah and Mark.

[209] Cf. J.F. Williams, *Other Followers*, 121f.

[210] Translation adds an exotic flavour, see Fowler, *Let the Reader*, 108.

[211] So Williams, *Other Followers*, 122, 123, 126.

[212] For irony in Mark, although not particularly helpful for this passage, see Booth, *Irony*; Camery-Hoggatt, *Irony*; and S.H. Smith, *Lion*, ch. 6.

the miraculous power of Jesus'.[213] This textual norm – especially when the previous occasions have also been expunged of any suggestion of 'disobedience' – makes it difficult to evaluate the speech negatively on this occasion. In addition to these textual norms, the scene ends with a description of the crowd's emotion, thus creating further sympathy. So too does their positive evaluation of Jesus, for it is offered as an explanation of their persistent speech. When a weakness is explained, it promotes sympathy, not judgement. Because the crowd has been acting on the side of the man in need, it seems so appropriate that the story ends with much speech, that, far from sitting in judgement on these intractable talkers, the readers are entirely sympathetic to them. In tune with Mark's famous irony, this is a touch of subtle humour: the more Jesus sought to silence them, the more they spoke! The narrator indicates that the movement had acquired such momentum that even Jesus could not stop it.

The irony of this verse speaks strongly against any interpretation that majors upon this being a disobedient act. Whereas a negative judgement such as 'disobedience' introduces distance between the reader and the person so judged, irony actually aligns the readers all the more strongly with the implied author – and so with any character with whom the implied author is aligned:

> [T]he building of amiable communities is often far more important than the exclusion of naive victims. Often the predominant emotion when reading stable ironies is that of joining, of finding and communing with kindred spirits. The author I infer behind the false words is my kind of man, because he enjoys playing with irony, because he assumes *my* capacity for dealing with it, and – most important – because he grants me a kind of wisdom; he assumes that he does not have to spell out the shared and secret truths on which my reconstruction is to be built.[214]

If there is an excluded 'naive victim' in this account, it is, in fact, not the 'disobedient' crowds, but Jesus himself, who seems to be the only one who doesn't want his deeds to be noised abroad. But even this 'victim' is eventually included, for his deed is the source and motivation of the proclamation and his greatness is its content. If it is true that 'every irony inevitably builds a community of believers even as it excludes',[215] here the 'excluded' (Jesus) is bound together with the community (the

[213] Williams, *Other Followers*, 54. He fails to draw the implications of this statement for his view of suppliant disobedience.
[214] Booth, *Irony*, 28.   [215] Ibid.

characters and the readers) by the very irony in which Mark engages! In addition, through the use of irony Mark 'builds a larger community of readers than any possible literal statement of his beliefs could have done', for it can be shared by anyone in whom the man's story has aroused any sympathy.[216]

The final statement gives the readers insight into the people's overwhelming amazement at what had occurred and provides direct speech so the readers can hear for themselves (v.37). Their positive evaluation generalises beyond this one incident (καλῶς πάντα πεποίηκεν) enabling the readers to recall all the marvellous events so far and presenting the healing of this man as something of a climax to the series, for Jesus 'even makes the deaf to hear and the speechless to speak'. In this way it acts as an explicit commentary on this incident and on Jesus' ministry in general. The clear allusion to Isaiah 35.5–6 also supplies implicit commentary from the OT for those with eyes to see. As another stroke of irony, these people from the Graeco-Roman Decapolis (whether knowingly or unknowingly) proclaim that Isaiah's promises to Israel are being fulfilled in their midst. The crumbs falling beyond the borders of Israel are being snatched up with great excitement.

The symbolic dimension of this miracle is regularly noticed. Defective hearing is an established Marcan metaphor for the inability to understand (4.12 = Isa. 6.9; cf. 7.14, 18). Jesus called upon people to hear (4.3, 9, 23, 24; cf. 7.14, [16]), using a parable stressing the various types of hearers (4.15, 16, 18) and recommending that the word of the kingdom be received (4.20). This was a call for Israel to join the remnant, in order to be a part of the coming kingdom harvest. The opponents, and even the disciples (7.17f., cf. οὕτως καὶ ὑμεῖς [. . .]; cf. 6.52), have not performed well in terms of hearing and understanding, and even a Greek woman had been more attentive (7.25, 28). Since this man had an inability to hear and yet he was healed by Jesus, the readers are given hope that the 'metaphorically deaf' will be healed by him too.[217]

But this metaphorical dimension must also be understood within the wider framework of the expectations of the kingdom. Entry to the kingdom comes through understanding Jesus and this comes through hearing well (4.20). This scene suggests that as Jesus is the one who opens the ears of the deaf, so he will also be the one to equip them to enter the resurrection harvest.

---

[216] Ibid., 29. Here I am applying Booth's comments on the crucifixion account.
[217] J.F. Williams, *Other Followers*, 123.

Reader to text

The suppliant and death

Being deaf and having difficulty in speaking did not, in itself, place a person at risk of death. It should be noted, however, that in a pre-antibiotic world ear disease was also a killer,[218] so this man may have been regarded as in danger (if the condition was acute), or as a 'survivor' (if the condition was chronic, following some previous illness). Nevertheless, deafness, like blindness (see on Suppliant 11), was regarded as a quasi-death. The senses of hearing and seeing were often coupled together, for they represented the means by which sense information was gained. Like sight, hearing was connected with understanding, and deafness with its lack.[219] Conversely, once the mind and wits are bound, a person will cease speaking (Gager **115**; Philo *Det.* 168). Because the soul is nourished through the intellect, i.e., through this epistemological process, then to be a deaf man with difficult speech is to have a poverty-stricken soul. Just as the blind were already living in the darkness of the underworld (as we shall see), so, too, the deaf were living in a realm as silent as the grave. When Oedipus plucked out his eyes after discovering what he had done, he wished he could do more:

> Had I known a way to choke the springs
> Of hearing, I had never shrunk to make
> A dungeon of this miserable frame,
> Cut off from sight and hearing; for 'tis bliss
> To bide in regions sorrow cannot reach.   (Soph. *OT* 1386–90)

Being deaf and mute made a person like a corpse; cf. the term of abuse 'You deaf and dumb corpse!' (Apul. *Met.* 8.25). Several curses draw a comparison between the desired silence/deafness and the corpse with which the tablet was deposited, as in the separation charm:

> As the dead man who is buried here can neither talk nor speak,
> so let Rhodine who belongs to Marcus Licinius Faustus be dead
> and unable to talk or speak. As the dead is welcome neither
> to gods nor men, so shall Rhodine who belongs to Marcus

---

[218] See, for example, the Predynastic Egyptian skull indicating that 'the individual probably died from the extensive inflammation in the ear region', McKenzie and Brothwell, 'Ear Region', 470.

[219] Qumran and the rabbis connected the deaf-mute with the imbecile (4Q267 [4QD^b]); Rabinowitz, 'Deaf Mute'.

Licinius be as welcome and just as precious as this dead person
who is buried here. Dis Pater, I commend to you Rhodine, that
she may be ever hated by Marcus Licinius Faustus.

(*CIL* I.2.1012 = Grant, 240f. (1st c. AD))

Sometimes the wish seems to be that the victim actually becomes
deaf/dumb like the corpse – as a preliminary to being dead themselves:
'let her no longer rise up, walk around, talk (μὴ λαλῆσαι), move about,
but let her remain a corpse, pale, weak, paralysed, chilled' (AthAg **App**).
The illnesses in a first-century BC Roman counter-curse are intended to
fill the time before the victim's eventual death with horrors: 'I give thee
his ears, nose, nostrils, tongue, lips, and teeth, so he may not speak his
pain [. . .]' (Fox = Gager **134**). A burial inscription from North Africa
(AD 212⁺), which bears testimony to the tragedy of being on the receiving
end of such a curse, shows that muteness could be attributed to a *defixio*
and a step towards death. Here a Roman tribune laments over his wife,
in her late twenties, who had 'long [lain] mute' before she died. 'She did
not receive the kind of death she deserved – cursed by spells (*carminibus
defixa*)' (*CIL* 8.2756; Gager **136**).

Although not absolutely clear, an undated inscription to Good Fortune
from Apollonia ad Rhyndacum in Mysia may illustrate that deafness was
regarded as a living death. It tells of the dedication of the 'ears' of an altar
in thanks for the recovery of hearing:[220]

> ταῖς ἀκοαῖς τῆς | θεοῦ | Ἑ[ρ]μιανὸς ΟΚΙ - - | ζήσας ἀπέδωκεν |
> εὐχαριστήριον | τὰ ὦτα καὶ τὸν βω|μόν

> For the hearing of the goddess, Hermianos | having lived . . .
> rendered the ears and altar as a thank-offering

(*NewDocs* III **22**)

Although ζήσας may simply introduce an age note, if it can be translated
in a causal sense (cf. Ps.[LXX] 118.37; 1 Thess. 3.8, νῦν ζῶμεν), then the
cured man would be referring to his healing as 'having come alive'. If
deafness was like being dead, hearing again would be life from the dead.

The suppliant and the dead

It has long been recognised that, of all Jesus' healing stories, this one has
the clearest links with magic, even if commentators have been reluctant

---

[220] The dedication of votives in response to healing often took a form relevant to the
cure. See, for example, the discussion of those at Epidaurus, Corinth and Athens; LiDonnici,
Epidaurian Miracle Inscriptions, 41–4.

to acknowledge its presence fully.[221] Jesus performs privately, puts his fingers in the ears, spits, touches his tongue, looks to heaven, sighs, utters a word of command, in a foreign tongue, and the man is healed instantly, with the bond of his tongue being loosened.[222] These actions are not merely symbols of Jesus' mercy and power,[223] or part of a medical healing ritual,[224] but suggest a magical framework. If the Graeco-Roman readers recognised the healing's connections with magic, this would increase the probability that they would suspect that the illness was also magically caused. In this context, because magic operated by and against the *daimones*, the suggestion that this man was suffering from a daimonic attack would be a very real possibility for Mark's early readers, even if there is no explicit mention of a spirit.[225]

Attacks on the ears and the tongue were a particularly frequent kind of magical assault. A curse on the tongue was the bane of the legal advocate and orator, who would suspect a curse if performing badly. So when Aristophanes alludes to the sudden paralysis of the orator Thucydides during a trial, the scholiast, preserving some fourth century BC Attic source, suggests his tongue had been magically bound[226] (*Vesp.* 946–8; see also Cicero *Brut.* 217; *Orat.* 128–9; Libanius[227] *Orat.* 1.245–9).

Curse tablets were clearly one way such attacks upon the talking class were implemented. Amongst their numerous attacks on various body parts, often named with a precision similar to that of Mark 7.32ff., the organs of hearing and speech are well represented. The ears are cursed in the tablet from Julius Caesar's time which we have already noted above (Fox = Gager **134**); another curses the hearing organs (ἀκοαί, *DT* **41**a = Gager **85** (1st/2nd c. AD); cf. Mark 7.35). Several curses aim at making

---

[221] Deissmann, *Light*, 304ff. (cf. *New Light*, 84ff.), discussed Mark 7.32–37 in the light of the binding conception in ancient magic. This was one of the oldest discussions of the impact of magic on the New Testament. Until the twenties, however, magic received only the barest of mentions in the commentaries; Hull, *Hellenistic Magic*, 75 n. 13. Although Hull says that it is 'mentioned often' in those thereafter, his comments indicate that it is 'often mentioned' only to be rejected (cf. n. 14) and, since his time, magic is still regularly overlooked.

[222] Hull, *Hellenistic Magic*, 73; Bonner, 'Traces'.

[223] This was the normal 19th-century view, revived by Hunter, *Mark*. For a critique, see Hull, *Hellenistic Magic*, 73f.

[224] For a critique, see ibid., 74f. See also: Martial 1.47; 5.9; 8.74; Pliny *HN* 29.8.16–18.

[225] Several commentators have dismissed the suggestion of Deissmann, *Light*, 304–8, that the expression ὁ δεσμὸς τῆς γλώσσης αὐτοῦ indicates a binding through demonic influence (cf. Luke 13.16), by reference to the absence of an explicit reference to a spirit (e.g., Taylor, *Mark*, 355; Gundry, *Mark*, 390).

[226] Faraone, 'Agonistic Context', 15, and Faraone, 'Accusation'.

[227] Cf. Bonner, 'Witchcraft', and, more generally, for the continuation of such charges in late antiquity, see Brown, 'Sorcery'.

a person deaf (κωφός), usually in combination with the loss of speech. For example, the AthAg tablets (3rd c. AD) 'chill' their victims so that they become 'deaf, dumb, without mind, without heart' (κωφός, ἄλαλος, ἄνους, ἀκέραιος; SGD **23**; AthAg **2, 4, 8, 9, 10**), or, 'hearing nothing' (μηδὲν ἀκούων, AthAg **3, 6, 8, 9**; cf. SGD **164** = Gager **77**[228]).

As for speech, the 'silencing charm' must be one of the oldest and most frequent magical curses.[229] The context for these silencing curses is readily understood. The wish that the words of an enemy may be disregarded or silenced is natural, especially if there is some kind of legal battle going on, although it would not have always been the innocent party engaged in the use of a *defixio*,[230] such as that requesting the underworld powers, 'bind them with the fetters [. . .] so that they will be speechless; pervert their speech; in their place hobble and tie them' (McCullough **E**). The binding of the tongue was in order to stop the words of opponents (*DTA* **75** = Gager **65** (4th c. BC)) by making them ἄφωνοι (e.g., *DT* **66** (4th c. BC)). An ancient curse (older than 5th c. BC) seeks 'a twisted tongue for incapacity' (γλῶσα ἀπεστραμέν᾽ ἐπ᾽ ἀτ<ε>λείαι, SGD **99**), and another curses the tongues and souls of more than twenty men and women (SGD **1**; cf. SGD **75** (n.d.)). Such curses can be found from the third century BC (SGD **150**), through to the third or fourth century AD (SGD **169**).[231] Silencing is a prominent part of the Cyprus tablets (*DT* **22, 24, 25, 26, 29, 30, 31, 32, 33, 35**; (3rd c. AD)) which use numerous expressions amounting to the same thing in their quest to muzzle their victim (cf. *DT* **15** = Gager **4**).[232] One of the Semitic bowl texts even enlists the same language from Jeremiah 5.21, also utilised by Mark 8.18, to this end ('in the same way as you have eyes but do not see, as you have ears but do not hear', *AMB* **Bowl 6**; cf. Isa. 6.9–10 and Mark 4.10–12).

Several charms draw the comparison with the silence of the corpse (e.g., *DT* **69** Ib (4th c. BC); **25**) and some also introduce the notion of 'chilling' (*DTA* **60** 'chilled and voiceless'), or aim at a corpse's incapacity (*DT* **68, 69** (4th c. BC)). Not only were the curses aiming to make the victim (like) a corpse, but they also utilised corpse-spirits to bring this

[228] Youtie and Bonner, 'Two Curse Tablets', 54, ll. 4–6.
[229] Recall the discussion of silencing texts on Suppliant 1, pp. 65–6.
[230] Cf. MES, 155.
[231] The many curses aiming at muteness can strike at tongues, γλῶσσαι (*DT* **15**; **16** I; **47**; **49**; **50**; **52**; **66**; **69** Ib; **81** a; **87**; *PGM* **05**); or the mouth, στόμα (*DT* **16** I; **15**; **49**; **74**), [στόμ]ιον (*DT* **75** a; **249**); or the voice, ἡ φωνή (*DT* **15**; **16** I; **22**; **24**; **25**; **26**; **29**; **30**; **31**; **32**; **33**; **35**), or even the saliva, [σί]αλον (*DT* **75** b 3; cf. *AMB* **Bowl 9**). See also *PGM* VII.396–404; IX.1–14; XLVI.4–8.
[232] Cf. Jordan, 'Feasts'.

about. Ovid explains that at the Feralia, the festival of the dead (17–21 Feb.), young women would come to an old woman for the preparation and consecration of lead *defixiones* (evidently silencing charms, cf. *PGM* IX.1–14) in connection with the underworld goddess Muta (Ovid *Fasti* 2.571–82 = Gager **144**).[233] Since it seems that these curse tablets were deposited in the cemeteries, it is highly likely that the agency by which Muta worked would involve the dead. Some of the curses make this explicit, by calling upon ghosts to bring about their malicious wishes to deafen and/or silence the victim (e.g., the Cyprus tablets used unknown *nekydaimones*; *AMB* **Bowl 9** was issued 'in the name of Mot and [. . .] the spirit which resides in the cemetery'). There were specialist 'deaf-*daimones*' (Thompson **"X"**; Cyprus tablets *DT* **22–36**[234]) – presumably the *daimones* who caused deafness, rather than being deaf themselves – and mute-*daimones*, against which the fearful needed protection (TSol. 9, 12; *P.Yale* 989.1–7 (3rd/4th c. AD)).[235]

The suppliant and Jesus

The readers may suspect that this deaf man with difficult speech was a victim of magical, and so ghostly, attack. He was certainly one of the living dead, who sat perpetually in the silence of the grave and whose difficult, hoarse speech was only marginally better than a corpse's absolute silence. The suspicion would be that he had been reduced to this state by the dead working against the living.

Nevertheless, Jesus manages to overcome his enormous problem, bringing him back into the land of the living, opening up the opportunity for much further commerce with the living.[236] The crowds from the Gentile Decapolis, with all their sophistication and commitment to Graeco-Roman culture, immediately recognise that something remarkable has occurred in front of their eyes, and their chatter about this man cannot be stopped. In words echoing Israel's prophetic promises, they marvel that Jesus 'has done everything well; he even makes the deaf to hear and the mute to speak' (Isa. 35.5f.).

---

[233] Ovid was suspected of inventing this goddess until her existence was confirmed by the discovery of a *defixio* – Egger, 'Zu einem Fluchtäfelchen' – which reads: 'O Muta Tacita, let Quartus be silent, let him run around disturbed like a scurrying mouse'.

[234] Cf. Jordan, 'Feasts'.

[235] See Daniel, 'Some ΦΥΛΑΚΤΗΡΙΑ', improving on the text offered by O'Callaghan and Proux, 'Papiro'.

[236] Gundry, *Mark*, 492, comments that healing a deaf-mute would be as great a miracle as raising the dead.

The journey's end (Mark 8.1–10)

The second sea journey ends with another feeding miracle (8.1–10), which is so similar to the first that the readers are utterly amazed at the dullness of the disciples, who appear to have forgotten the former feeding so quickly.

Journey 3: how can blind eyes see?

The third sea journey begins with Jesus refusing the Pharisees' demand for a sign (8.11–13). In the boat, through a discussion about bread, Jesus forces the disciples to reflect upon both feeding miracles. Since his language is reminiscent of the parables discourse, the scene causes the readers to review the entire intervening narrative section (4.35 onwards). His warning against the Pharisees and Herod sums up the two poles of Israel's leadership which have received critique (Herod: 6.14–29; Pharisees: 7.1–23). Since Jesus has appeared as the true shepherd of Israel, feeding the leaderless flock of God, this warning forcefully reminds the readers that Mark is presenting Jesus as an alternative leader. Whereas Israel's politico-religious leadership has been exposed as destructive, Jesus has helped those in need. He has not consumed the flock, but has fed it instead.

The first sea journey raised questions about Jesus, faith and mortality. Jesus has been presented as a leader who can deal with death and the shadow it casts across human lives. The forced reflection during the final sea journey reveals that the disciples have a long way to go. Jesus' questions cause the readers to ask whether they yet have faith, or whether their hearts are still hard like the leadership of Israel. Jesus' leadership promises to bring life to the dead, but do they see? Do they hear? Do they understand?

Suppliant 11: a blind man sees (Mark 8.22–26)

The last of the three sea-crossings concludes in this scene (v.22), indicating that the healing of the blind man functions as the climax to this journey and also to Mark's second main section.[237]

---

[237] Identifying the two blind men stories (8.22–26; 10.46–52) as 'frame' often leads to the conclusion that this scene is the beginning of the next section (e.g., Kelber, *Mark's Story*, 43–4). However, this rather formalist division misses the natural movements of the story. Rather than two parts of a frame, or two counterparts of a 'concentric', the blind men stories are both highlighted through the rule of 'end stress', each in their sequence. They are inter-related by way of a linear (not ring) comparison, as the respective conclusions to two linear progressions through the various scenes.

Text to reader: a blind man sees

Apart from their presence in the initial plural verb (v.22; cf. 1.21; 5.1; 6.1), the disciples play no part in this scene. The reader is aligned with the suppliant, who is brought by an undefined group and is characterised as τυφλός (v.22). Since his problem is (non-)visual, this description already has focalising power.

After Jesus leads him out of the village, they are the only two participants in the scene, but the readers are also privileged to take the journey with them and to observe the interaction. They watch Jesus as he performs a series of actions, reminiscent of those performed on the deaf-mute. Spitting into his eyes and laying hands upon him, Jesus asks whether he can see anything (v.23). The direct speech enables the readers to hear the question as if they were the blind man. An inside view of his visual perception (ἀναβλέψας, v.24),[238] ensures that they are aligned with him as he reports his partial sight, as do the inside views reported from his own mouth (βλέπω, ὁρῶ, v.24), and the strangeness of the imagery, since it requires active thought to imagine what he sees. Jesus places his hands upon his eyes again. Three verbs, an adverb and a universal pronoun (διέβλεψεν καὶ ἀπεκατέστη καὶ ἐνέβλεπεν τηλαυγῶς ἅπαντα) stress his success (v.25). These inside views continue to focalise the readers through the man, so that, after being aligned with his partial sight, they now experience its full clarity.[239] The concluding instruction to avoid the village (v.26) confirms the readers' sense of privilege, for, if this command is heeded, the healing they have seen will not become common knowledge.

The healing of this blind man and the one to follow (10.46–52) both gain narrative significance through playing upon sight as a metaphor for understanding. The image first appeared at the climax of the first main section when the parables discourse called upon people to listen (4.3, 9). Drawing a parallel between Isaiah's role and his own, Jesus explained that his parables were given so that Israel may 'be ever seeing but never perceiving; and ever hearing but never understanding' (4.12; cf. Isa. 6.9f. LXX). The importance of hearing the word (vv. 15, 16, 18, 20, 23, 24, 33) was stressed by linking the two senses (v.24). Hearing is the way to 'sight' and this process is the means by which a person enters the coming harvest, i.e., the kingdom of God. Hearing with amazement is not enough (6.2), nor simply hearing the word (6.11, 14, 16, 20), but it must be heard and accepted (4.20) in order to truly 'see'. Positively, the

---

[238] Fowler, *Let the Reader*, 121.

[239] For a discussion of the vocabulary in the light of an extramission theory of vision, see Marcus, 'Optics'.

images are associated with the theme of belief; negatively, the failure to hear and see, and so to understand, is linked with hardness of heart.

The disciples' 'sight' had not proved any better than that of the rest of Israel. Their slowness to believe had reached its climax in the final boat scene, where Jesus asked them: οὔπω νοεῖτε οὐδὲ συνίετε; πεπωρωμένην ἔχετε τὴν καρδίαν ὑμῶν? (8.17; cf. 4.40), before questioning whether they were part of the Israel denounced by the prophets: ὀφθαλμοὺς ἔχοντες οὐ βλέπετε καὶ ὦτα ἔχοντες οὐκ ἀκούετε; (8.18; cf. Jer. 5.21; Ezek. 12.2). Metaphorically speaking, they remain both blind and deaf.

Thus the first blind man is healed as the climax to a long section in which hearing and seeing has been repeatedly on the agenda as a metaphor for believing and gaining insight into Jesus' person. The miracle therefore operates as a concrete illustration of Jesus' ability to open the eyes of the blind. If he can do so for the physically blind, then the hope is erected that he may do so for the metaphorically blind. Granted, his ministry was to have a blinding effect (4.10–11), but he had also promised disclosure (4.22) for those who listen with acceptance. The disciples may be blind, but since Jesus promised to make them into fishers of human beings (1.17), their blindness is an object which he must overcome. The fact that he cured this blind man holds promise that he will cure these other blind men as well.[240] When Jesus sends the man home without entering the village, it is not to contrast the blind man's obedience in remaining silent with the deaf man's disobedience,[241] for no response is reported either way. Instead, this command effectively removes the man from the narrative, and, after the pattern has so often been to provide a response, the lack in this case is intriguing, yielding a sense that the story is somehow incomplete. This open-endedness prepares for the next section in which the disciples' eyes begin to be opened.

Reader to text

Blindness and death

Blindness
Eye-conditions were extremely common in the ancient world, to judge from the abundant material in ancient literature and medical sources;[242]

---

[240] Cf. 'the two-staged healing of the blind man is really paradigmatic of the disciples' future restoration', S.H. Smith, *Lion*, 106.

[241] *Pace* J.F. Williams, *Other Followers*, 130.

[242] This material is surveyed in Sandison, 'Eye'.

from the listings of eye-salves in the literature (Celsus *De med.* 6.2–3, 30ff.; and Scribonius Largus, *Comp.Medic.* 18–37 (both 1st c. AD)) and magical material;[243] from other cures, such as saliva (Pliny *HN* 28.7; Tac. *Hist.* 4.81); from various archaeological findings (ocular cachets; engraved stamps for impressing eye ointments with the manufacturer's name;[244] 'surgical' implements); and from magical spells dealing with eye-conditions.[245] Presumably the frequency of eye disease also increased the incidence of blindness.

Blindness was such an impediment to life that the blind, often coupled with the lame, were proverbial for ineffectual weakness and dependency (cf. 2 Sam. 5.6, 8; Jer. 31.8). They could go nowhere without a guide (Soph. *Ant.* 989; *OC* 1; Apul. *Met.* 8.12) and needed the protection of others (Job 29.15; Soph. *OC* 21).

Metaphorical blindness

For moderns and for ancients (cf. Arr. *Epict.Diss.* 1.20.12), Mark's metaphorical use of blindness would be fairly obvious. This motif finds an ancient parallel, for example, in the *Oedipus*.[246] Initially Oedipus accused (blind) Teiresias of being blind in 'the ears, the mind and the eyes' (τά τ' ὦτα τόν τε νοῦν τά τ' ὄμματα, Soph. *OT* 371, cf. 389), whereas Teiresias and the audience know that Oedipus may have the eyes, but he fails to see what he has done (412).

Blindness and death

Less obvious to the modern, however, is the understanding of blindness as a death-like state. Instead of seeing the light, a blind person dwelt in perpetual darkness. So Polymestor cried out to the sun:

> O couldst thou but heal these eye-pits gory,
> O couldst thou but heal the blind, and restore me,
> O Sun, thy light.   (Eur. *Hec.* 1066–7)

and Oedipus gibed Teiresias:

---

[243] ACBM, 315; ACBM **25**, cf. *SMA* Pl. 5, pp. 112–13, pp. 70–1.

[244] Singer and Wasserstein, 'Medicine', 661; *NewDocs* III.56f.

[245] For example, Babylonian: Farber **2.2**, **4.2**?, **4.3**; Greek (*PGM* VII.197–8, ?XCIV.4–6; XCIV.22–6; XCVII.1–6; *P.Bon* 9 (4th/5th c. AD); *SuppMag* **26** (5th c. AD); **32** (5/6th c. AD); and Coptic (cf. PDM xiv.1097–1103, 1104–9; ?1110–29).

[246] S.H. Smith, 'Divine Tragedy', 211 n. 10.

> Offspring of endless Night, thou hast no power
> O'er me or any man who sees the light.   (Soph. *OT* 374f.)

This meant that they lived in a kind of Hades, since those who are alive 'see the light' (e.g., *Il.* 18.61; *Od.* 4.540; Hes. *Op.* 155, *Theog.* 669; *Hymn to Demeter* 35), whereas the dead are 'those who once looked upon the light' but who now live in the gloom of the underworld (e.g., PGM XXXVI.138; cf. Aesch. *Pers.* 630; Ps-Phoc. 100f.). The loss of sight therefore brings a person to the underworld; even while alive, death invades their body.[247] Charite rejoiced in giving her husband's killer a ghost-like, netherworldly existence by gouging out his eyes:

> You will live, but your eyes will die; You will not see the light and you will need some companion's hand; You will not possess Charite and you will enjoy no marriage; You will neither be refreshed by the sleep of death, nor delighted by the pleasures of life, but you will wander as an uneasy phantom between Orcus and the Sun.   (Apul. *Met.* 8.12)

This cluster of ideas appears in the book of Tobit, in which the overcoming of blindness is central to the plot. Tobit regards his blindness (2.9 ff.) as a living death:

> What joy can I have any more? I, a man without power of eyesight! I cannot see the light of heaven, but I lie in darkness like the dead who do not see the light any more. Living, I am among the dead! I hear the voice of men, yet I cannot see them.   (5.10)[248]

As the book proceeds, Tobit's rescue from blindness is portrayed as a rescue from death.[249]

On some epistemological views, blindness contains a further impediment, for literal sight is necessary to gain understanding. So, for example, on Plato's schema in the *Timaeus* the blind man would not have the ability to see the heavens and be led to contemplate philosophy (Pl. *Ti.*

---

[247] It was a fate worse than death, according to the chorus to Oedipus, 'thou wert better dead than living blind' (Soph. *OT* 1367).

[248] For the last statement, cf. the saying of Heraclitus ὀφθαλμοὶ γὰρ τῶν ὤτων ἀκριβέστεροι μάρτυρες (Diels-Kranz 22B 101a 1, 173, 15f.).

[249] Further, see Bolt, 'Sadducees'.

47A–B).[250] This would mean that his soul could never be expected to rise to the pure regions above. The underworld which has invaded his body now would also be his home in the afterlife. His cure, however, would liberate him to see 'with far-beaming sight' (τηλαυγῶς),[251] and enable him to contemplate the things ensuring a better lot for the soul.

Blindness and the dead

Although by no means common, curses attacking body parts could also attack the eyes. A fragmentary text curses the (finger?)nails, eyes (?), the spine, and the feet (SGD **80** (n.d.)); and a judicial curse (300 BC) wishes the victim's body parts, including the ὀφθαλμοί (*DT* **49** = Gager **44**), to be bound, hidden, buried, and nailed down, perhaps indicating that the curse is seeking the victims' death. The malicious counter-curse from Julius Caesar's day, to which we have already referred several times (Fox = Gager **134**), certainly wishes to kill the person. As a prelude, it hands over the 'brow and eyebrows, eyelids and pupils' as a step towards this end. It even uses blindness to depict this death: 'Mayest thou so irrevocably damn him that his eyes may never see the light of another month', illustrating how close the one was to the other.

As with the other conditions, the dead are also specifically called upon to inflict blindness, as in the series of Carthaginian curses against charioteers and their horses (3rd c. AD) naming the eyes (τὰ ὄμματα *DT* **241** = Gager **12**; **242** = Gager **10** 'pluck out their eyes so that they cannot see'), or the act of sight (ἡ ὅρασις **234**; **235**; **237** = Gager **9**; **238**; **239**; **240**; **242**) which all make use of unknown *nekydaimones* from graves. Presumably a similar vindictive purpose with a similar desired outcome would accompany the use of a waxen doll which has both eyes pricked out (*PGM* CXXIV.1–43; cf. IV.296–466 = Gager **27**). This is used at a tomb and the powers below are invoked. *Sepher ha-Razim* (2.181f.) has a spell 'to bind or rebuke the spirit causing blindness' and a bowl text has a curse based upon Deuteronomy 28 which inflicts blindness 'in the name of Mot and [. . .] the spirit which resides in the cemetery' (*AMB* **Bowl 9**).

---

[250] The schema in the *Phaedo* provides him more opportunity, for the soul's contemplation without the senses of sight and hearing is deemed to be far better than with their utilisation (cf. 65B–C, 66A, 78E–80A). Cf. similar thoughts in Philo, *Ebr.* 88, where sharp sight is needed to gain wisdom.

[251] See Marcus, 'Optics', 254.

This handful of curses and charms shows that blindness could be magically inflicted; it could be associated with death; and it could be caused by the agency of a ghost. Not only did the blind person sit in the darkness of death, but that darkness could be caused by the dead.

Blindness and the healing gods

The gods

The blind were healed by Isis[252] and the inscriptions at Epidaurus indicate that the healing god, Asclepius, apparently dealt frequently with eye complaints.[253] They report several miraculous cures of quite remarkable cases of blindness. In one, the woman concerned had mocked the possibility that the lame and the blind could be healed (Stele A4), which underlines the general perception that to be blind was to be beyond help. Another miraculous cure from Epidaurus provides a remarkable parallel to Mark 8.22–26: 'Alcetas of Halice being blind saw a vision in which the god, he thought, came to him and with his fingers went over his eyes, and the first things which he saw were the trees in the temple precincts' (Stele A8).

The new gods

When Vespasian was in Alexandria, along with the man with a lame hand or leg (see on 2.1–12 and 3.1–6), a blind man came to him for cure. Vespasian's doctors told him it was curable, but, even if it was not, the lack of cure would look bad for the beseecher, not for the future ruler. Vespasian's reputation was enhanced when he moistened the man's eyes with spittle and cured him (Suet. 8 (*Vesp.*).7.2–3; Tac. *Hist* 4.81). He had managed two miracles considered impossible: he had healed the lame and made the blind to see.

This incident, which occurred (AD 69) within a decade or two of when Mark was read, illustrates the increasingly god-like role that Rome's (future) rulers were adopting. The imperial propaganda of a former age had proclaimed Augustus 'son of god', the source of life for the world, the one who healed the nations. This incident suggests that even the older gods, such as Serapis-Asclepius, were now conceding things properly

---

[252] Kee, *Medicine, Miracle & Magic*, 67. Cf. Diod. 1.25.5.
[253] LiDonnici, *Epidauran Miracle Inscriptions*. Cotter, *Miracles*, 17–18, conveniently lists the cures of the blind.

under their own jurisdiction to the new gods who walked upon the earth, the masters of land and sea.

Sight to the blind

Mark's Son of God also opened blind eyes, but he showed no reluctance, nor did he consult the physicians first, or calculate the cost of a failed miracle to his reputation. In fact, Jesus avoided publicity while nevertheless acting on behalf of one in terrible need. This man who already dwelt in the darkness of the underworld was led by the hand to Jesus, and, as a result, could see absolutely clearly. Jesus had brought him from the darkness of death, into the light of life.

5

ENTERING THE COMING KINGDOM (MARK 8.27–10.52)

In Mark's central section, Jesus embarks upon a journey 'on the way' (8.27; 9.33, 34; 10.17, 32, 52), which will eventually take him to his life's end in Jerusalem. Each of its three sub-sections begins with a prediction of Jesus' death and the resurrection to follow. The reader is caught up in the momentum of this journey towards the narrative's goal.

Prediction 1: the Son of Man must die (8.27–9.29)

The first sub-section opens by reissuing the Christological question (cf. 1.27; 4.41; 6.2), as Jesus asks what people were saying about him (8.27–30). After reporting the opinions of others (cf. 6.14–16), Peter confesses Jesus to be the Christ. This finally aligns the disciples with the opinion the narrator shared with the readers at the beginning (1.1), although the following events will show that further progress is required.

Jesus then announces that the Son of Man must die to rise again after three days (v.31). The necessity (cf. δεῖ) no doubt arises from his divine commissioning as the Servant (1.11) and his commitment to continue in the will of God (3.31–35). He announces that his death will come from Israel's leadership. This is no surprise to the readers (3.6), but Peter takes exception (v.32). Peter's rebuke has often been explained in terms of a supposed Christological misunderstanding, i.e., that he could not cope with a Christ who suffered.[1] Cranfield suggests he takes offence at the idea of suffering after being rejected by Israel's religious authorities.[2] This latter view seems to be more consistent with the flow of the discussion, but the likelihood is that Peter's offence springs, not from a Christological misunderstanding, but from a desire for self-preservation.

Peter's rebuke of Jesus should be understood in close relationship with Mark's narrative commentary (8.32a) which it immediately follows, as well as Jesus' counter-reply to Peter, which addresses the experience of

<hr>

[1] Cf. Lane, *Mark*, 304–5; Kelber, *Mark's Story*, 48.   [2] Cranfield, *Mark*, 280.

217

thinking like a human being, rather than God (8.33), as well as that of
being ashamed of Jesus and his words (8.38) – even to the death. In this
context, it seems likely that the problem was not so much a Christological
misunderstanding, but a disagreement over the wisdom of saying such
things about those who are in power. Open speech was easily mistaken
as slander,[3] and, from a human point of view, it is not wise to slander
the authorities who can do you harm. It is better to be silent about such
things. But, according to Jesus, being silent, when seen from God's point
of view, is being ashamed and so this calls forth a counter-rebuke in the
strongest terms,[4] followed by a warning addressed to the crowds.

Jesus calls the crowd and his disciples and talks about what following
him will entail. The repetition of the idea of following him at the beginning
(εἴ τις θέλει ὀπίσω μου ἀκολουθεῖν, cf. 1.20) and end (ἀκολουθείτω μοι)
of his initial statement (v.34) recalls the disciples' call, which is now
generalised. The middle statements indicate what following will entail: let
him deny himself (ἀπαρνησάσθω ἑαυτόν) and take up his cross (ἀράτω
τὸν σταυρὸν αὐτοῦ). Mark's early readers would not immediately resort
to a metaphorical understanding of the denial of self and taking up of one's
cross, for these were very real possibilities in a world ruled by Roman
muscle. Jesus had announced the coming of an alternative kingdom (1.15),
an act which could have placed himself and his followers under threat,
for the assumption of kingship without the permission of Caesar or his
imperium was frowned upon (cf. Tac. *Hist.* 5.1–13). On this occasion,
Jesus announces that he will be killed by the authorities of his own land.
He will eventually reveal (10.33) that they will use the Gentiles to bring
about his end. If anyone wants to follow him, they can do so, but, given
the nature of his cause, they had better reckon with their own death.
Presumably this is what Peter has failed to do.

Jesus reinforces his call with a discussion about where true value is
to be found. The previous section of the Gospel (4.35–8.26) has already
demonstrated salvation to be from death, whether literal, or in the several
forms with which its shadow fell across human life. When Jesus speaks of
his own necessary and impending death at the hands of the authorities, the
act of following him also gains a life and death focus. He urges this choice

[3] Cf. Theophr. Character 28, 'Slander' (κακολογία), who maligns his friends and family
and the dead and calls it free speech, democracy, or openness (παρρησία).

[4] Both rebukes (vv.30, 33) are described using the same vocabulary used for exorcism (ἐπιτιμάω = גער). In addition, Jesus then addresses Peter as 'Satan'. Kotansky,
'Demonology', 272: 'He is in effect performing an exorcism: he is "expelling by rebuke"
(gᵉr) the "Satan" in Peter.' Kotansky draws attention to *AMB* A14, line 9: 'exorcise Satan
from' (gᵉr stn mn).

upon his hearers through a paradoxical use of σῴζω. If a person wishes to save their life (i.e., by not following Jesus), this will mean losing it; but if a person is prepared to lose their life for his sake and the gospel's, this will result in saving it (8.35). Given that he has just announced that his own future will mean death at the hands of Israel's leadership (v.31), and that his potential followers should consider the possibility that they too will be crucified (v.34), then the choice to save life, or to lose it, is clearly a real choice between life and death. Jesus' paradox reverses the normal and logical human viewpoint – which Peter had adopted (cf. 8.33) – in favour of the opinion that life is found by following him to death on a cross. When he talks of being saved, therefore, it is salvation from death.[5] Since his first 'passion prediction' also speaks of resurrection on the third day (v.31, cf. Hos. 6.2), being saved is linked to the long-awaited resurrection from the dead. Jesus is calling people to follow him onwards to death, in the hope of being saved by resurrection.[6]

This call to the crowds acquires urgency by the imminent prospect of the coming of the Son of Man (8.38) and of the kingdom in power (9.1). Both events are integrally related, since, according to Daniel, the Son of Man comes to the throne of God (Dan. 7.13) and receives all authority in God's kingdom (7.14), which is then shared with the saints (7.22). When this cluster of events occurs, the Son of Man will be ashamed of those who have been ashamed of him before the sinful and adulterous generation and the threat of the prevailing power structures (Mark 8.38, cf. 8.12). Since these events will occur before some of the people in the crowd die (9.1), it is time for urgent and wholehearted commitment to him and his cause ('the gospel', v.35; 'my words', v.38), rather than shame. It is time to face up to death in the hope of resurrection.

Suffering before the kingdom (9.2–13)

Text to reader: suffering before the kingdom

Six days later, Jesus takes three of his disciples up a high mountain where he is transfigured (vv.2f.) and speaks with Elijah and Moses (v.3).

---

[5] The question of verse 37 is answered already by Ps. 48 (LXX) 8–9: ἀδελφὸς οὐ λυτροῦ- ται λυτρώσεται ἄνθρωπος; οὐ δώσει τῷ θεῷ ἐξίλασμα αὐτοῦ καὶ τὴν τιμὴν τῆς λυτρώσεως τῆς ψυχῆς αὐτοῦ. The Psalmist pictures Israel as sheep being shepherded by Death, and then holds out the hope that God will ransom his soul from the grave (LXX vv.15–16): πλὴν ὁ θεὸς λυτρώσεται τὴν ψυχήν μου ἐκ χειρὸς ᾅδου.

[6] This preparedness to die in the hope of resurrection is reminiscent of that found during the Maccabees' resistance to Hellenisation under Antiochus IV (cf. 2 Macc. 7).

The disciples are terrified (v.4), a cloud descends, and a voice virtually repeats the words the readers heard at Jesus' baptism, identifying Jesus as God's son, the Beloved (v.7; cf. 1.11), and tells them to listen to him. Finally, they look around to find only Jesus (v.8). After this experience, their journey down the mountain is alive with conversation. Jesus tells them to keep it all secret until after the Son of Man rises from the dead. The disciples eagerly seize[7] on this statement, debating it amongst themselves, discussing 'what rising from the dead will mean', i.e., what it will be like to be a part of the (general) resurrection.

They ask Jesus why the scribes say Elijah must come first, i.e., first before the kingdom (9.1)/resurrection (9.10). Jesus agrees with the scribal exegesis (cf. Mal. 3.23 LXX), but poses his own question about the need for the Son of Man to suffer. This erects a series of expectations: before the resurrection and the coming of the kingdom, the scribes (and Jesus) say that Elijah must come first, but Jesus adds that the Son of Man must suffer many things. When Jesus informs them that Elijah has come – the readers would know that he means John (cf. 1.2–8) – this means that only one of these expectations is left unfulfilled. Before the resurrection and the kingdom arrives, the Son of Man must suffer first. In this way, the scene coming down the mountain reinforces Jesus' first passion-resurrection prediction. He must die, not only because it is according to the divine plan, but because it is the necessary precursor to the coming of the resurrection and the kingdom of God, which has been the object on his horizon from the beginning of his ministry (1.15; 4.26–29, 30–32; 9.1).

Reader to text: a potential apotheosis

Features of translations

The transfiguration scene contains some parallels to stories[8] in which a person either disappeared and/or was translated to heaven. In particular, it has several close parallels to Josephus' account of the disappearance of

---

[7] Interpretations (Swete, *Mark*, 192; Taylor, *Mark*, 394) and translations (RV, RSV, NIV, NRSV) which suggest they 'kept the matter in mind' miss the force of κρατέω, wrongly construe πρὸς ἑαυτούς with the preceding verb rather than the following participle (with Victor; Syr^{sin}) – for which there is no analogous usage, Swete, *Mark*, 192 –, and create a contradiction between the two halves of the verse.

[8] Collins, 'Empty Tomb', 142, claims that 'in the Hellenistic and early Roman periods these traditions of translation and deification were widespread', although, in support, she cites only the retelling of the ancient flood story by the Babylonian historian Berossus, and Josephus. The increasing importance of the apotheosis of the Roman rulers, with its backing in the Romulus story, offers further support to her claim.

Moses.⁹ A small number of stories involved a translation at the point of death, or the disappearance of a body after death, but the transfiguration parallels the larger group of disappearances in which people avoided death altogether.

Translations could take place upon mountains (v.2; Diod. 4.82.6 (Aristaeus); Joseph. *AJ* 4.325 (Moses)), and often under changed weather conditions, be it an eclipse (Cic. *Rep.* 1.25, 2.17, Dio.Hal. 2.56.1–2 (Romulus)), or a storm (Soph. *OC* 1620 (Oedipus); Livy 1.16, Plut. *Rom.* 27.6, Dio.Hal. 2.56.1–2 (Romulus); Diod. 3.57.8 (Basileia)), or, as here, the descent of a cloud (v.7; Livy 1.16 (Romulus); Joseph. *AJ* 4.326 (Moses); Apollod. 2.7.7 (Hercules)). A translation might perhaps even involve white garments (v.3)¹⁰ or a voice from heaven (v.7; Eur. *Bacc.* 1076–9 (Dionysus)).

If this voice from heaven is read as an expression of divine pleasure in Jesus (v.7), it would be reminiscent of the belief that translations took place because of a person's virtue. This feature is highlighted in the LXX account of Enoch (Gen. 5.22–24, εὐηρέστησεν τῷ θεῷ, twice, changing MT's וַיִּתְהַלֵּךְ) which is then transformed by Sirach (44.16) into a paradigm of repentance. Josephus explains (*AJ* 4.326) that Moses wrote that he died, 'for fear lest they should venture to say that by reason of his surpassing virtue he had gone back to the Deity'. The need for this 'correction' evidently arose because of the prevalence in the Graeco-Roman world of the notion of such translations deriving from personal virtue. Cicero had reported that it was the virtue of Romulus which gave rise to the story of his translation (*Rep.* 1.25; 2.17) and the virtue of the rulers was also a presupposition of their apotheosis.¹¹ Plutarch considered the connection between virtue and apotheosis to be not only good sense, but, given his view of the soul, κατὰ φύσιν (Plut. *Rom.* 28.7–8).

⁹ See Tabor, 'Josephus's Portrayal'; Begg, 'Josephus's Portrayal'.

¹⁰ My basis for suggesting this is a detail in Lucian's mockery of the translation tradition in the *Passing of Peregrinus*. When Lucian embellished the story for 'the dullards agog to listen', he added an earthquake, a bellowing of the ground, and a vulture flying out of the flames to heaven with a parting speech (39). The story backfires on him when someone else picks it up, adding the claim that he had seen Peregrinus 'in white raiment a little while ago, and had just now left him walking cheerfully in the Portico of the Seven Voices, wearing a garland of wild olive' (40). Since it is a detail added by one who evidently went along with the tradition, this suggests it was a part of that tradition, at least by the second century.

¹¹ Pease, 'Some Aspects', 17, suggests that it may have been Augustus' attitude to Hercules and Romulus (Hor. *Carm.* 3.3.11–16; *Epist.* 2.1.5–10; Suet. 2 (*Aug.*).95) which encouraged the notion of an immortality *ex virtute*. The lampooning of Claudius' apotheosis in Sen. *Apoc.* proves the point negatively.

Of course, a leading and necessary feature of such stories was the person's sudden disappearance (Soph. *OC* 1647f. (Oedipus); Cic. *Rep.* 2.17, Plut. *Rom.* 27.6 (Romulus); Diod. 2.14.3 (Semiramis); Joseph. *AJ* 4.326 (Moses); 2 Kings 2, *AJ* 9.27–28 (Elijah)),[12] sometimes reinforced by others searching for them. Mark's scene on the mountain concludes with language suggestive of such a search (v.8): looking around (περιβλεψά-μενοι), they saw no-one. However, in a strange twist, Mark adds 'but only Jesus with them' – the person whom the readers would have expected to disappear is the only one still left behind; the heavenly visitors have left without him!

Romulus

When it comes to first-century apotheoses, Romulus, the founder of Rome, 'merits especial attention'.[13] The deification of Romulus appeared as early as Ennius (*Ann.* 65–6, 111–13 (2nd *c.* BC); cf. Cic. *Rep.* 1.25, 2.17). Naturally enough, the events surrounding the moment when he had 'vanished from among men' (ἐξ ἀνθρώπων ἠφανίσθη, Plut. *Cam.* 32.5), so that 'Romulus was no more on earth' (Livy 1.15.6), were debated. Some suspected a senatorial conspiracy (Plut. *Num.* 2, 3), whereas others were convinced he had been 'caught up to the gods' (Plut. *Rom.* 27–8), one person even swearing an oath that he had seen him go (28.1).

The Caesars

As the imperial power took a new turn with Julius Caesar and then Augustus, the mythology surrounding this ancient figure from Rome's past began to be reapplied to her chief man. Although such vanishing figures lay in popular legends, or in literary imitations of popular legends, 'the principle was too suggestive to be overlooked in periods like [. . .] the early Roman Empire, when every occasion for glorifying and legitimising the ruling dynasty was eagerly sought'.[14]

Julius Caesar was the first human to be divinised since Romulus. Although obviously a purely human death (Suet. 1 (*Iul.*).83.2), his demise was nevertheless presented like that of Romulus (App. *B.Civ.* 2.114). The comet which appeared at his death provided the basis for the theory that his soul had become a new star (for his apotheosis, see Ov. *Met.* 15.745).

---

[12] There are many disappearance stories, which are not all translations to heaven; see Pease, 'Some Aspects'.

[13] Ibid., 15.   [14] Ibid., 16.

'Before the emperors could arrogate to themselves the complete trappings of divinity, the story of the ascension of Romulus, a lawgiver and sole ruler, could be made to serve as the model for Julius, the second founder of Rome – thus forming the mythical basis of the emperor's right to rule.'[15]

The poets of the Augustan age utilised the Romulus myth to add weight to the imperial propaganda. 'Livy discusses Romulus's death and the rumours of it in terms reminiscent of the death of Julius Caesar',[16] commenting:

> It is a great marvel what credence was generated by the man's tale, and how the loss of Romulus, for which the common people and the army grieved, was assuaged by the belief in his immortality. (Livy 1.16)

According to Segal, 'Livy's ironic attitude points out the value of the heavenly journey as a proof of immortality and as mythical underpinning of the Imperial system.'[17] Even from the beginning, such notions had their critics, as when Propertius contrasted the Roman love of war with his 'war' of love with his mistress: 'One such night might make any man a god!' (2.15.40–3; cf. 2.5.1f.).

The Romulus myth was pressed into service for the divinisation of Augustus too. Dio Cassius (56.46 1–2), on Augustus, spoke of 'immortalising him' (ἀθανατίσαντες αὐτόν), and of Livia bestowing a million sesterces upon a certain Numerius Atticus, a senator and ex-praetor, because he swore that he had seen 'Augustus ascending to heaven after the manner of which tradition tells concerning Proculus and Romulus'. The pattern was also imitated when, in AD 38, Gaius' sister Panthea was deified and a senator, Livius Geminus, declared on oath he had seen her ascending to heaven and conversing with the gods (59.11.3).[18] Gaius did not succeed in deifying Tiberius, nor did his megalomaniac demands for divine honours in his lifetime succeed, but his endeavours certainly kept the issue of human beings becoming gods on the agenda.

After Augustus, Claudius was the next to be granted an apotheosis. In AD 54, when he was poisoned by his wife Agrippina, 'to the amusement of Rome, Nero had Claudius deified'.[19] When Pliny the Younger reflected on the event he could say that 'Nero deified Claudius only to make him a laughing stock' (Pliny *Pan.* 11.1). Seneca, who was contemporary with the

---

[15] A.F. Segal, 'Heavenly Ascent', 1347, citing Ov. *Met.* 14.805–52, esp. 823–8. Cf. Wedderburn, *Baptism*, 188.
[16] Segal, 'Heavenly Ascent', 1347.   [17] Ibid., 1348.
[18] Jones, 'Christianity', 1026.   [19] Ibid., 1028.

decision, wrote *Apocolocyntosis*, a biting satire of Claudius' deification, in which the gods, climaxing with Augustus himself, express their disgust over Claudius being placed amongst them. Clearly, at the time when Mark was being read, apotheosis was an issue still under debate.

A rejected apotheosis

When Mark's transfiguration is read in the light of the translation stories, it appears that here Jesus was presented with an opportunity for apotheosis which he did not take up. A person who was translated avoided death altogether, as can be seen in the contrast between the translation of Oedipus and the normal manner of dying:

> For without wailing or disease or pain
> He passed away – an end most marvellous.
> (Soph. *OC* 1663–5)

Although the voice from heaven, now for the second time, declared Jesus to be the Son of God, he did not 'disappear from amongst men'. Instead of taking the chance to avoid the death he had predicted (8.31), he came back down the mountain resolved to die, explaining that, before the resurrection could arrive, the Son of Man must suffer (9.9–13). He rejected the opportunity to avoid death through apotheosis and embraced his future suffering for the sake of the divine plan. Thus, in the transfiguration, Jesus continued in his resolve to walk the path of the Suffering Servant (1.11; 3.31–35; 8.31; 9.11–13).[20]

Suppliant 12: a man and boy, torn apart (Mark 9.14–29)

Text to reader: a boy is raised

Mark's final and fullest exorcism story contains a bewildering array of characters, both major (Jesus; disciples; scribes) and minor (crowds; suppliants). The disciples make one of their rare appearances in a healing/exorcism scene, and are portrayed with more sympathy than usual. However, the readers are still aligned most strongly with the suppliants, of which there are two. Although the boy receives dramatic help from Jesus, the father, who is often overlooked,[21] also needs help. While the

---

[20] Cf. Caird, 'Transfiguration', 293.
[21] Contrast J.F. Williams, *Other Followers*, 11, 47, 137–43, 164, for whom the man is the minor character.

boy is torn apart by a spirit, the father is torn apart by his struggle with unbelief.

The scene flows out of a situation of conflict between scribes[22] and disciples (v.14). It is initially focalised through the four who have just descended, using an inside view of perception (εἶδον, v.14).[23] This is the first occasion on which the readers are aligned with (some of) the disciples. This can be explained as a consequence of the disciples having begun to move towards the narrator and readers. Since they have recognised Jesus as the Christ (8.29, cf. 1.1) and heard the voice on the mountain (9.7, cf. 1.11), the text is beginning to 'identify' them with the readers.

If this group is the focaliser, the crowd is the focalised (i.e., what the reader now looks at through their eyes).[24] The presence of the scribes makes the readers suspicious, since the religious leaders have been implicated in the death of John the Baptist (9.13, cf. v.12) and in Jesus' own imminent death (8.31), which the readers recognise as the culmination of a plot hatched long ago (3.6). Since the topic of the debate is not supplied, a gap in the discourse is opened.

On seeing (ἰδόντες, v.15) Jesus, the crowd is 'overwhelmed with wonder' ἐξεθαμβήθησαν – which probably indicates that his appearance was still altered from the experience on the mountain[25] – and they rush towards him. Even if the focalised are viewed 'from within', this does not switch them to being the focaliser,[26] but is simply another example of an external report using visual language (cf. 5.6). The group from the mountain realise the crowd has seen Jesus because it starts rushing towards him and greeting him.

In the face of the onrush of the crowd, Jesus asks his disciples a question,[27] which is given in direct speech, enabling the readers to hear it for themselves (v.16). He inquires into the subject of the debate, showing that he shares the readers' ignorance.[28] Since he voices the readers' question, this promises a closure of the previously opened gap in the discourse. Before the disciples can answer, a man from the crowd speaks up, calling Jesus διδάσκαλε (v.17), which may be respectful,[29] but in itself does not

---

[22] The scribes should not be regarded as a superfluous detail because they so quickly disappear, cf. Taylor, *Mark*, 396f., Hooker, *Mark*, 223. Their importance is stressed by Swete, *Mark*, 195; Lane, *Mark*, 330; Gundry, *Mark*, 487.

[23] Fowler, *Let the Reader*, 121. [24] Rimmon-Kenan, *Narrative Fiction*, 75f.

[25] So Hooker, *Mark*; Gundry, *Mark*.

[26] For these distinctions, see Rimmon-Kenan, *Narrative Fiction*, 74f.

[27] Although not the usual interpretation, I suggest that the two pronouns αὐτούς [. . .] αὐτούς refer to the disciples and the scribes respectively.

[28] Although the question asks 'why' they were disputing with the scribes, it seeks after the subject of the debate.

[29] So Lane, *Mark*, 331, 'respectful'; Gundry, *Mark*, 488, 'honorific'.

tell the readers much about how to evaluate this man as yet.[30] His answer reveals a context of opposition (v.18b), so more needs to be said before it can be perceived which 'side' he is on. Likewise, the statement that he brought his son to Jesus may indicate an 'expectation of deliverance based upon conviction',[31] but the scribal presence throws even this into doubt, since a person in need was possibly 'used' by Jesus' opponents once before (3.1–6).

However, his lengthy description introducing the boy (vv.17b–18) does begin to promote sympathy with him and to focalise the scene through him. That there is a child in need, and that he is described in relation to the man (v.17), further adds to the *pathos*. The father reveals that the boy has a dumb spirit (πνεῦμα ἄλαλον) which causes many problems whenever it seizes him. The seriousness of the boy's condition builds sympathy with him and with his father, whose concern begins to emerge. The revelation that the disciples were not strong enough (οὐκ ἴσχυσαν) to cast the spirit out increases the sense of tragedy and also acts as an indictment of the disciples and a foil for Jesus, who is the stronger one (1.7; cf. 3.27 and 5.1–20).[32]

Jesus answers 'them' (v.19, αὐτοῖς) by bewailing the faithless generation and asking questions about how long he will bear with them. When they bring the boy to Jesus, visual language once again appears (ἰδών, v.20),[33] not as an inside view of the spirit, but as an external report of what apparently happened. On seeing Jesus, the spirit convulses the boy and he falls down foaming.

The boy is left like this on the ground while Jesus asks how long it had been like this for him (v.21). This introduces a delay in the resolution of the boy's problem, which, given Jesus' track record, may enhance the readers' expectation of a happy outcome. In the meantime, it forces the readers to reflect on the problem further, which promotes greater sympathy with the suppliants. The father answers the question ('from childhood'), but also supplies some extra information, which is all the more significant because unsolicited. He explains that the spirit had frequently tried to kill the boy by throwing him into the fire or the water (v.22). Although he has some doubts about Jesus' ability, probably stemming from the disciples' failed first attempt, his final desperate plea indicates that both

---

[30] Cf. 4.38; 5.35; 10.17, 20; 10.35; 12.14, 19.

[31] Lane, *Mark*, 331, who pictures the man as being 'deeply concerned'.

[32] Gundry, *Mark*, 489.

[33] Fowler, *Let the Reader*, 121. The only other case of a visual perception being reported for a spirit appears in 3.11, where it is a case of an 'objective' sighting, rather than an inside view.

suppliants (NB. plurals, ἡμῖν [. . .] ἡμᾶς) need help. When read against the new information (v.22a), his request is not simply for the removal of any spirit, but the removal of *a spirit that is bent upon killing his son*.

Jesus tells him all things are possible for the believer (v.23), which redirects the blame for the disciples' lack of success (cf. v.18) to the man himself. The implicit summons to belief in the face of a death problem is reminiscent of that given to Jairus (5.36). Although unbelief is not a positive textual norm, the readers' sympathy is nevertheless sustained by his awareness of the problem (he is apparently not 'hard-hearted'), his insistence that he does believe, and his emotional cry for help (vv.23f.). At the same time, the paradoxical nature of his statement forces them to consider how both belief and unbelief can co-exist in the one person.[34] Jesus does not give him any extra help for his unbelief, which suggests that what happens with the boy will also be a solution for his father. As for Jairus, the answer to fear/unbelief is trust that Jesus has things in hand, even in the face of death, or in the face of a spirit seeking to kill.

Jesus deals with the spirit when he sees a crowd running together – more visual language describing external observation. He directs the spirit to leave and never return (v.25), revealing that it is dumb and deaf. This recalls the man with a similar problem (7.31–37), which arouses the expectation of a similarly successful cure.

However, what happens next is unexpected. After causing the boy to cry out, and after convulsing him, the spirit goes out of him as expected (v.26a; cf. 1.26; 5.13). But where a report of some response to the exorcism is expected (cf. 1.27), the readers encounter something new: as the spirit left, the boy 'became as though he were a corpse' (v.26b, ἐγένετο ὡσεὶ νεκρός). By adding a piece of intra-narrative commentary, the narrator ensures that the boy's corpse-like state is registered by the readers: many bystanders were saying 'he has died' (ἀπέθανεν, v.26). The references to death are evidently most significant to the proper understanding of Mark's climactic exorcism.

The disciples had failed to cast this spirit out, and, although Jesus succeeds, in the process he has realised the father's fears. The boy appears to have been killed. But that is not the end of the story. Having seized the boy still lying corpse-like, Jesus 'raised him, and he arose' (v.27, ἔγειρεν αὐτόν, καὶ ἀνέστη).[35] The twofold reference to his corpse-like state is answered by a twofold use of 'resurrection' language.[36] Recalling Jairus'

---

[34] For the function of verbal paradoxes, see Fowler, *Let the Reader*, 184f.

[35] 𝔓⁴⁵ᵛⁱᵈ W k l syˢ·ᵖ omit καὶ ἀνέστη, possibly because it was deemed redundant. It is difficult to see why it would be added if it were not original.

[36] Nineham, *Mark*, 243 n.†.

daughter, the readers appreciate this scene, not just as an exorcism, but as an exorcism which brings the dead to life; a corpse to resurrection.[37] Although the disciples were 'not strong enough' (v.18), Jesus was not hampered by this problem.

The scene ends with a private discussion between Jesus and his disciples. The move to the house (v.28) puts some distance from the public events just completed, and privileges the readers to overhear the private reflection upon these events.[38] The disciples ask about their inability and, as one of a number of features ameliorating their failure, Jesus informs them that no-one can cast out this kind of spirit, except by prayer (vv.28f.). The kind of spirit which brings the constant threat of death (v.22, cf. v.26) seems to require special treatment. This ending to the scene underlines how essential it was for Jesus to be there. He alone could help this boy and his father. The disciples' inability is not presented in order to reflect badly upon them, but to highlight Jesus' ability: he was the one strong enough to defeat even this kind of spirit. He is the stronger one who can defeat the Prince of the corpses, the strong man himself (1.7; 3.22–30; 5.1–20).

This exorcism story contains the Gospel in miniature, thus providing a summary which helps to keep the reader on track. Jesus announced that the kingdom was near (1.15) and riddled that it was necessary for the strong man, the prince of the *daimones*, to be bound before he could plunder his domain (3.27). This exorcism pictures this grand scheme in miniature: as with Mark 5.1–20, this story shows that 'the actions of the demons are violent, directed toward injury and death',[39] and yet Jesus restores the dead to life. The reason for the shift from death to resurrection is

> [. . .] identified as due to the victory over the demon, i.e., Satan. Following upon the act of exorcism, the scene is depicted so as to make it evident that violence and death itself have been cast out. Jesus' cure of the epileptic boy is described in terms of resurrection.[40]

On the mountain, the three disciples had seen Jesus clothed in glory. On the way down, they discussed the anticipated resurrection day (9.9–10), and, in response to a question, Jesus told them that only one event had to occur before that day would arrive. Since Elijah had already come, all that remained was for the Son of Man to suffer before the resurrection and the kingdom of God would arrive. Having rejected the opportunity

---

[37] Lane, *Mark*, 334.   [38] Fowler, *Let the Reader*, 211.
[39] Robinson, 'Problem', 87.   [40] Ibid.

of apotheosis, Jesus had descended the mountain to deal decisively with
the spirit of death. On the mountain, the discussion had anticipated the
resurrection; at the base of the mountain, he had performed a resurrection-
like exorcism. When the corpse-like boy was raised from the dead (9.26f.;
ὡσεὶ νεκρός [. . .] ἤγειρεν [. . .], καὶ ἀνέστη), it was a foretaste of the time
when the Son of Man and others would rise from amongst the corpses
(v.9: ὅταν [. . .] ἐκ νεκρῶν ἀναστῇ; v.10: τὸ ἐκ νεκρῶν ἀναστῆναι). If the
dead are being raised, then the kingdom must be very close indeed.

Reader to text

The boy and death

The explicit problem
In this scene, death is the explicit problem (v.22). The father's believing-
yet-unbelieving cry really amounts to another version of the mortality
question: 'Do you not care that we are perishing?' But the boy's condition
is also linked with death in a number of other ways, which all recall
elements of the previous discussion.

Epilepsy and death
The boy's symptoms suggest that his illness was a case of 'epilepsy', as it
is portrayed, for example, in the Hippocratic *On the Sacred Disease*. Mark
does not use any of the words for this condition,[41] but instead presents
the boy as afflicted by a spirit. Nevertheless, given that many of Mark's
readers would recognise his symptoms to be in line with epilepsy, an
understanding of the condition labelled 'the great sickness' (τὸ νοσήμα
τὸ μεγάλον), or the 'sacred disease' (ἱερὰ νόσος, Hipp. *Morb.sacr.*; Pl.
Ti. 85B; cf. *Leg.* 916A; Plut. *Amat.* 755E)[42] could enable a greater appreciation of the depths of his problem.

According to *The Sacred Disease*, the disease arises from the production of phlegm in the brain which then filters down into the body.
This can be brought about in a number of ways. Especially in children
and the elderly, it can be caused when the head is heated in the sun or
near a fire (cf. Mark 9.22) – which melts the phlegm in the brain –, and

---

[41] *Morb.sacr.* itself only uses the term ἐπίληψις once, when referring to a seizure
(ch. 13).
[42] Referring to *comitialis morbus*, Celsus describes a grand mal (*De med.* 3.23.1), although he nowhere uses the term epilepsy, 'probably because it was held to be ill-omened;
the name *comitialis morbus* was given to it because a meeting of the *comitia* was adjourned
if anyone there was attacked by it'; Moss, 'Mental Disorder', 716.

then chilled – which causes the phlegm to separate from the brain and flow down (*Morb.sacr.* 13). The disease is particularly severe in those who have suffered it 'from infancy' (ἐκ παιδίου, *Morb.Sacr.* 13–14; cf. Mark 9.21).

As noted above (Suppliants 4 and 5), it was listed alongside paralysis as one of the 'afflictions concerning the sinews' (πάθη περὶ τὰ νεῦρα, Dsc. 3.78; ?Carlini **32**), although it was associated with their spasm (vv.20, 26) rather than their loosening. Given the arguments already assembled, as a condition of the sinews, epilepsy was a serious illness bringing the presence of death into the body.

This conclusion is reinforced by its association with foaming at the mouth (cf. v.20) and chilling. The Hippocratic author explained the foam as coming from the lungs, 'for when the breath fails to enter them they foam and boil as though death were near' (*Morb.sacr.* 10). The convulsions (cf. vv.20, 22, 26) were linked to phlegm chilling and arresting the blood. The role of 'chilling' in bringing on death has already been noted and this holds true here. If the flow is copious and thick 'it kills automatically' (αὐτίκα ἀποκτείνει), for it overpowers the blood by its coldness.

As well as bringing death into the body of the living, epilepsy was a condition from which people actually died (*Morb.sacr.* 2; cf. *Epid.* 5.22). Although older people were generally not killed, the very old were either killed or paralysed (*Morb.Sacr.* 12), and children were especially prone to die – cf. the bald statement 'little children when attacked by this disease generally die' – and, when they do, it is once again through the chilling of their blood (*Morb.Sacr.* 11). The risks associated with fire have already been mentioned, and the fact that the 'purifiers' who were under attack in the essay refused to give the sufferers medicinal baths, so that they could not be blamed if the patient died (*Morb.Sacr.* 2), may indicate that the risks associated with water (cf. Mark 9.22) were also well known.[43]

When the boy remained on the ground 'as if a corpse', the crowd were quick to conclude that he was dead (v.26). Like them, the readers probably knew quite well that death was one possible outcome of an epileptic fit, and, in the case of a child, it was quite likely to occur.

The deaf and dumb spirit

Apart from the specifically epileptic symptoms, the narrative describes the boy as afflicted with an unclean spirit, which is also identified as

---

[43] It was also believed to cause suicide by hanging, especially in menarchal girls, cf. King, 'Bound', 113f.

τὸ ἄλαλον καὶ κωφόν πνεῦμα (vv.17, 25; cf. 7.31–37).[44] The conclusions from the previous discussion (on Suppliant 10) can be reiterated: his deafness and dumbness also number him amongst those who are dead even though alive.

The boy and the dead

Epilepsy and the dead

The material previously assembled has shown that conditions of the sinews, and deaf/dumbness, could be caused by magical attacks. In particular, τὸ ἄλαλον καὶ κωφόν recalls language from a number of curse tablets,[45] as does the connection with 'chilling'. Although epilepsy itself may not be mentioned in the Greek curses, it is found amongst the Semitic curses,[46] and occasionally found in Greek protective magic (*PGM* XCV.14–18; XCIV.1–14 (3rd/4th *c*. AD)[47]) and its cures were sometimes specifically magical.[48] The principle that if something is magically protected then it was probably also magically caused[49] would suggest that people were just as suspicious of a daemonic origin of this illness, as they were of others. The presence of epileptic symptoms may have been enough to signal that a person was under threat from the dead.

But in this case, Mark explicitly describes the boy's problem as that of being possessed by an unclean spirit, which can be regarded as a spirit of the dead (as argued above, on Suppliant 1). The spirit's many attempts to destroy him in the fire and the water[50] suit the violent and destructive nature of ghosts, as does the crying out (v.26). In this case, it seemed as

---

[44] Gundry, *Mark*, 488, is probably right that the spirit was 'one that prevents him from speaking during seizures' (cf. Lucian *Philops.* 16; Plut. *De defectu* 438A–B), but this tends towards overdiagnosis.

[45] It is also connected with death in the only other extant literary reference to a mute spirit (Plut. *De defectu* 438B), see below.

[46] There is a long history of 'roof demons' (בני אוגרי) causing epilepsy; Geller and Levene, 'Magical Texts', 335–6, referring to Stol, *Epilepsy*.

[47] Daniel, 'Some ΦΥΛΑΚΤΗΡΙΑ', 149, improving on O'Callaghan and Proux, 'Papiro'. See also Barns and Zilliacus, *Antinoopolis Papyri*, no. 140 (5th/6th *c*. AD).

[48] Human blood, smeared on the lips or drunk hot from a gladiator's fresh wounds, could cure epilepsy (Pliny *HN* 28.4), as well as water drunk from a murdered man's skull, the flesh of a beast slain by the same weapon as had killed a man, and goat's meat roasted on a funeral pyre (*HN* 28.8, 34, 226). For more bloody and death-related cures see Temkin, *Falling Sickness*, 22f.

[49] The author of *Sacred Disease* suggests as much: 'he who by purifications and magic can take away such an affection can also by similar means bring it on' (*Morb.sacr.* 3).

[50] Cf. the seventeenth Decan, who causes convulsions in the bath and in the street (TSol. 18.21).

though the ghost had even achieved its destructive aim despite being cast out.

How did the boy become afflicted by such a spirit? Alongside the scenarios already mentioned in discussion of the other suppliants, another possibility arises here.

Boys and magic

In magic, many boys were used as mediums[51] and there may have even been a preference for epileptics.[52] Apuleius was accused of using such boy magic:

> They asserted that I had taken a boy apart to a secret place with a small altar and a lantern [. . .] and there so bewitched him with a magical incantation that he fell in the very spot where I pronounced the charm [. . .] they should have added that the boy uttered many prophecies. (Apul. *Apol.* 42)

The spells show that they were often associated with lamp and water divination, which, for a person familiar with the use of boy mediums, may be evoked by Mark's reference to fire and water (v.22). Would Graeco-Roman readers have suspected that this boy had been used as a medium to contact the spirits of the dead? If so, something had obviously gone wrong.

Being a medium was not without its dangers and could even be life-threatening. Plutarch's prophetess, for example, when forced to receive the oracle's message against her better judgement, suffered from a mute spirit (cf. ἀλάλου καὶ κακοῦ πνεύματος οὖσα πλήρης) as here, and then died (*De defectu* 438A–B). The *daimones* were notoriously untrustworthy and instructions regarding the protection of the user are a constant feature of the magical recipes. Lamp and bowl divination aimed at bringing a *daimon* into the presence of the medium. In order to do so, if the boy sat staring into the water, or into a fire, the opportunity for destroying him was immediately at hand once the *daimon* was conjured. If a session

---

[51] For the use of boys in magic cf. *PGM* V.1–53; 370–446, cf. VII.664–85; 348–58; 540–78; XIII.749–59; LXII.24–46; and frequently in *PDM*. Cf. Plut. *De defectu* 418B and *Vit. Ap.* 3.38. See further, Hopfner, 'Kindermedien', 65–74. For the use of a boy medium in the early nineteenth century, along with methods which are reminiscent of those in the magical papyri, see Hull, *Hellenistic Magic*, 21–3.

[52] Hull, *Hellenistic Magic*, 14. This ancient observation has received some support from modern neuroscientific research. 'Plenty of evidence supports the idea that the limbic system is important in religious experiences. Most famously, people who suffer epileptic seizures restricted to the limbic system, or the temporal lobes in general, sometimes report having profound experiences during their seizures,' Holmes, 'In Search', 27.

involving these boys went wrong, it is not too extraordinary to imagine them being cast into the two 'tools of their trade' in order to damage or to kill them (cf. v.22).

The evidence suggests that some boys did die as part of the magic.[53] This may explain a phrase in an early first-century AD Jewish prohibition against magic: 'Make no potions, keep away from magical books | Do not apply your hand violently to tender children' (Ps-Phoc. 149). Since the untimely dead (ἄωροι) and those dying by violence (βιαιοθάνατοι) were two categories of powerful ghosts specifically used by the spells and curses (e.g., *PGM* CI.1–53), a violently killed youth would be a sought-after commodity.

However, the boys' deaths may have been merely ritual, or perhaps simply some kind of death-like state (cf. *PGM* VII.549). Apuleius was supposed to have bewitched the boy so that 'he fell in the very spot where I pronounced the charm' (*Apol.* 42). In another interesting example, Proclus reports Clearchus of Soli's story of the time when Aristotle met an unnamed magician (between 347 and 345 BC)[54] who, with the help of a magic wand, drew out the soul from the body of a boy, leaving him corpse-like:

> He struck the boy with the wand, drew out his soul [or, life? τὴν ψυχήν], and, so to speak, guided it from the body with the wand, afterwards showing that the body was all the time lying motionless and undamaged, and that it remained insensible to the blows like a corpse (ὅμοιον ἀψύχῳ). The soul had meanwhile departed from the body: after having been led back to the body with the help of the wand, after entering, it told all [what it had seen]. This experiment convinced all the other spectators as well as Aristotle that the soul could separate itself from the body.
> (Proclus 2.122, 22ff.)[55]

Death and resurrection

Jesus commands the spirit to come out and never return (v.25). This latter prohibition is also found in similar contexts (cf. *AJ* 7.2.5; 8.45–9; *Vit. Ap.* 4.20; and, by implication, *PGM* IV.1254; 3015), as is the discussion of

---

[53] For a ritual involving the heart of a boy see *PGM* IV.2646. Simon Magus used a slain boy in *Clem.Rec.* 2.13. See discussion in Henrichs, *Phoinikika*, 31–7, 69–72; Hopfner, 'Kindermedien', 65–74.

[54] Lewy, 'Aristotle', 207.

[55] Text and translation from ibid., 208f. Cf. Hengel, *Judaism*, 258.

'kinds' of *daimon* (v.29; cf. *PGM* IV.3040, 3080; V.165). He apparently knows his spirits, for his exorcism is so successful that he appears to kill the boy (v.26). How would the Graeco-Roman reader familiar with boy magic respond to the news that Jesus had done something to the boy that had made him fall 'as if a corpse' (ὡσεὶ νεκρός)? Had he bewitched him, or ritually killed him, or had he actually put the boy to death in the interests of some further magical purpose?

This comes as quite a shock to the readers. This boy is presented as someone who has a condition which makes him live firmly under the shadow of death. He is possessed by a deathly spirit. He may have suffered years of abuse as a boy medium, constantly forced to engage with the dead and being exposed to their threat. Jesus deals with the spirit and apparently kills the boy. Jesus may have come to destroy the *daimones*, but in the process does he destroy their victims too?

But the initial shock reinforces the ultimate lesson. For when Jesus raises the boy, as if from the dead (v.27), someone who regarded *daimones* as ghosts would see a powerful demonstration that Jesus' dealings with the powers of the dead issued in 'resurrection life' for their victims.

Prediction 2: entering the kingdom (Mark 9.30–10.31)

The disciples do not understand the second passion prediction but they are too afraid to ask for an explanation (9.30–32). They argue about who is the greatest and Jesus resets their priorities by talking about eschatological realities. Using hyperbole, he stresses the importance of entering life (vv.44, 45), which he equates with the kingdom of God (v.47), rather than missing out on this future and ending up in Gehenna (vv.44, 45, 47), the eternal fire (vv.44, 48, cf. Isa. 66.24).

In controversy over divorce, Jesus continues to indict the Pharisees' hardness of heart (10.5). Although the great ones of the land suffer from this problem, some children become the paradigm for entry into the kingdom (10.13–16), given their absolute dependency. When another great one asks how to inherit eternal life (v.17), he goes away disappointed because he chooses his earthly wealth above heavenly treasures (v.21). The disciples are shocked and Jesus tells them that it is difficult for the wealthy (vv.23, 25), in fact for everyone (v.24), to enter the kingdom of God. When, in utter astonishment, they ask 'Who then can be saved?', Jesus answers not in terms of a type of person, or of personal character traits necessary for salvation, but in terms of what God will do. Jesus assures them that although entry to the kingdom is impossible for human beings, God will make it possible (v.27).

He then assures his disciples that they have made the right choice to leave everything in order to follow him (vv.28–31). He promises that they will receive recompense in this age, and, in the age to come, eternal life (v.30). For, in the great eschatological reversal, the 'first' (i.e., the great ones, cf. the rich man) will be the least, and the ones who are now regarded as the least (cf. the disciples), will be the greatest (v.31). In this promise, Jesus' message of the kingdom reaches its climax with a reference to the eternal life of the age to come, which, according to Daniel 12.2, will follow the resurrection.

Prediction 3: the way to the kingdom (Mark 10.32–52)

The third passion prediction introduces the fact that the leadership of Israel will use the Gentiles, i.e., the Romans, as accomplices to put Jesus to death, after they mock him and scourge him (10.32–34). Once again he repeats the promise that this will be followed by resurrection. The coming kingdom is on the agenda for the sons of Zebedee, who ask Jesus if they can share positions of status when he comes in his glory (v.37; cf. 8.38). The ten others are indignant, so Jesus calls them aside to repeat his lessons on service (vv.41ff., cf. 9.33–36), concluding with an explanation of his own death being the death of Isaiah's Servant, as a ransom for many (10.45; cf. Isa. 53.10).[56] Given the argument of this study so far, this saying probably refers to Jesus ransoming others from death (cf. Ps. 49.7–9),[57] although this also encompasses the other options canvassed (i.e., sin, Satan). The death of the Son of Man will be the ransom which brings others from death to life. It will be the great apocalyptic event that will change reality.[58]

The first sub-section (8.31–9.29) stressed the necessity of the death of the Son of Man as the event to precede the kingdom. The second sub-section (9.30–10.31) stressed the need to enter the kingdom and that, although entry was impossible for human beings, God would make it possible. The third sub-section (10.32ff.) has now revealed the means by which God will make it possible. Entry to the 'glory' of the Son of Man, i.e., the kingdom of God, will come about through his death as a ransom for many. At this point, the narrative introduces the final suppliant.

[56] Jeremias, *Theology*, 292f., 299.

[57] Jeremias, *Evangelium*, 144; Collins, 'Suffering', 69.

[58] 'This statement [i.e., 10.45] implies that the death of Jesus has changed reality. The point is not only that Jesus made insight available into the possibilities of human existence in the world, but that his life and death have made new possibilities available. [. . .] Jesus' death is presented as a cosmic event that was prepared and prophesied beforehand,' Collins, *Life?*, 35–6.

Suppliant 13: following in the way (Mark 10.46–52)

Like the previous section (4.35–8.26), Mark's central section (8.27–
10.52) concludes with the cure of a blind man. Bartimaeus is Mark's
last 'suppliant'.

Text to reader: a blind beggar

The report of Jesus' party entering and leaving Jericho (v.46) continues
the sense of movement towards Jerusalem (10.32–33). The suppliant is
introduced by name twice – the Greek translation rather strangely preceding its Semitic original. Since naming encourages a degree of intimacy,[59]
especially given the rarity of the practice with respect to suppliants,[60]
the reader begins to be aligned with him. As with previous suppliants,
he is characterised by his situation of need: he is τυφλὸς προσαίτης. His
status of προσαίτης will be reinforced by his location, his action (vv.47,
48), and his meagre possessions (v.50). Although his name is known, the
remainder of the scene refers to him only in terms of his need, i.e., as
the blind man (vv.46, 49, 51). The description concludes by reference to
his location on the periphery of the movement towards Jerusalem. Bartimaeus was not in motion, but he sat; and he was not on the road, but
he sat παρὰ τὴν ὁδόν (v.46). This description shifts the readers' focus
towards him and his rest-rather-than-motion causes it to linger. The scene
is focalised clearly through him.

This is enhanced by an inside view of aural perception (v.47
ἀκούσας),[61] made all the more powerful by the provision of the actual
words heard, i.e., 'interior speech'.[62] When he begins to cry out (v.47),
the direct speech[63] allows the readers to hear his words for themselves
as he calls out for the Son of David to have mercy on him. Although the
meaning of his chosen title is not clear from the story – since no-one in
the narrative, not even the narrator, has used it before –, its novelty hints
at Bartimaeus' insight. His request for mercy reminds the readers of the
mercy shown to the Gerasene man (5.19f.) and raises the expectation that

---

[59] For naming as a signal of focalisation, see Rimmon-Kenan, *Narrative Fiction*, 82f.

[60] Apart from one other suppliant, Jairus (5.22), naming has been reserved for the disciples and John.

[61] Fowler, *Let the Reader*, 121.

[62] Fowler, ibid., 125f., although he does not list this verse.

[63] Not only does direct speech decrease the distance between the character and the
readers, as normal, but the sheer amount of direct speech in this scene (vv.47a, 47b, 48b,
49a, 49b, 51a, 51b, 52) has the effect of slowing it down to almost a standstill, enabling its
details to be thoroughly heard and absorbed.

this blind beggar, so used to asking for alms, may receive something far greater on this occasion.

Before hearing whether or how Jesus responded to his cry, the readers hear of 'many' who commanded Bartimaeus to be silent (v.48a) rather strongly – ἐπιτιμάω was used previously of Jesus commanding *daimones* (1.25; 3.12; 9.25), or the wind (4.39, with σιωπάω), or recalcitrant disciples (8.30, 33, cf. 32). Although this group is not defined, they are naturally associated with Jesus, which raises the question whether the beggar is being excluded officially from access to him (cf. 7.24). However, the presumption is tipped the other way, since Jesus did not appreciate the disciples' rebuke of the children (10.13–16), other obstacles have been overcome (2.1–12; 5.21–43; 7.24), and it has been almost completely impossible to silence people. This all suggests that this blockage does not come from Jesus and that it will be overcome.

Like others who could not be silenced (1.45; 7.36), the blind man simply calls out all the more (v.48b), the repetition adding urgency to his plea. His persistence and the negative evaluation of his detractors when read against previous textual norms (cf. 10.13–16) ensures that the readers continue to be aligned with Bartimaeus.

Given the determination with which Jesus has been moving towards Jerusalem (10.32; 10.46), it is quite dramatic when he comes to a standstill (v.49, στάς). This is reminiscent of the occasion when he interrupted the journey to heal Jairus' daughter in order to declare that the woman's faith had healed her (5.24–34). The pause in Jesus' movement brings him into Bartimaeus' and the readers' purview, but the readers are not shifted into the role of observers just yet. They hear what Jesus' envoys say to the blind man, see him throw down his cloak, and watch him get up and go to Jesus (vv.49f.). All this shows that the readers are still focalised through the blind man at this stage.

The envoys' direct speech bids the blind man to have courage (θάρσει), which Jesus once used to calm the fearful disciples with his presence, implicitly urging them to have faith (cf. 6.50). They command him to arise (ἔγειρε) and add the encouragement, 'he is calling you' (φωνεῖ σε). When he casts aside his meagre possessions (the garment)[64] to go to Jesus (v.50), Bartimaeus fulfils the requirement for potential followers to leave things behind (1.18; 1.20; 2.14; 8.34ff.; 10.21; 10.28).

Having travelled with the blind man to Jesus, the readers then become observers of the interaction. Jesus' question enables Bartimaeus to assert

---

[64] 'Perhaps the most striking feature in Bartimaeus's response', J.F. Williams, *Other Followers*, 157. He lists usual interpretations before suggesting the one followed here.

his need (v.51). This reminds the readers of the previous miraculous cure of a blind man (cf. 8.24) and so of the wider narrative significance of the blind/sight imagery. Jesus sends him away with a dismissal frequently used with those who have been healed (ὕπαγε, 1.44; 2.11; 5.19; 5.34; 7.29; cf. 10.21) and informs him that his faith has saved him (cf. 5.34). Immediately his sight is restored (v.52, contrast 8.22–26). However, instead of departing, the saved ex-blind beggar follows Jesus (cf. 1.17f.; 2.14f.; 5.24; 6.1; 8.34; 9.38; 10.32)[65] ἐν τῇ ὁδῷ. So the last suppliant is the first of the group to succeed in becoming a follower (cf. 5.18f.).

As Jesus' final miracle,[66] the cure of Bartimaeus plays an important role in Mark's narrative. The scene brings a definite turn in narrative direction. This blind man, as well as his partner at the end of the previous section, are both concrete illustrations of the blindness/sight theme of such importance to Mark. The first cure, by showing that Jesus could make the physically blind see, suggested that if the metaphorically blind were to see, Jesus would be the one to open their eyes. The second cure reinforces this lesson and also shows the cured man entering the mainstream movement of the story.

The role of the two as 'foils for the disciples' is well known. On the metaphorical level, blindness has been equated with the lack of understanding which comes from the lack of faith. This was the state of Israel in general (4.12, cf. Isa. 6.9; 8.17–18, cf. Jer. 5.21) and the disciples have not proved any different, despite their companionship with Jesus. Since the text offered various indications that the unbelief of the disciples would be only temporary (4.40; 8.17), the healing of the blind man at the end of section 2 (8.22–26) held out the hope that Jesus would overcome their metaphorical blindness. By the end of this central section (8.27–10.52), this hope has not been completely realised, although, against the tendency to damn the disciples too quickly, it must be asserted that it has begun. This section has painted a far more positive portrait of the disciples than the previous one (4.35–8.26) and has shown them growing in their understanding. They have correctly recognised that Jesus is the Christ (8.27–30), although further instruction was still required (8.31–9.1). The voice from heaven repeating the commissioning Jesus received at his baptism provided three of the disciples with the same insight given the readers at the beginning (9.7; cf. 1.11). Jesus has continued to teach

---

[65] This time, Williams, ibid., 159, denies it is a case of disobedience since the way was open for anyone to follow Jesus after 8.34.

[66] For different reasons, the curse of the figtree and Jesus' own resurrection can be ignored as not belonging to the series.

them about what lies ahead (the kingdom, his own death and resurrection), and about what it means for them to keep following him in this direction.

However, even as they gain more insight into the future (9.9–13), they show an inadequate grasp of what this entails (10.13–16; 10.35–45, esp. 37, 40, 41) and they still fail (9.18, 28f.;[67] 10.13–16), lack understanding and are afraid (9.32).[68] In contrast, although the readers are unaware of what Bartimaeus knows about the future, they are well aware that, having received mercy through faith, he eagerly heads for it. In this sense it can be said that 'Bartimaeus, who believes, sees and follows, now exemplifies what it means to fulfil the demands of Jesus.'[69]

The hope for the disciples' 'cure' erected at the end of the previous section has been only partially achieved. After the disciples' more sympathetic treatment in this section, Jesus' cure of the second blind man sustains the hope that their 'cure' may be completed. Bartimaeus (and the minor characters after him) cannot be their replacement,[70] for the narrative has not dispensed with them.[71] They will continue to provide some continuity throughout the passion narrative, where they will certainly fail, but will nevertheless be treated sympathetically.[72] Instead of Mark's final suppliant replacing the disciples, he joins them as they journey towards Jerusalem behind the one who has shown him mercy. Whereas the first blind man was removed from the narrative (8.26), the second joins the mainstream narrative movement. Since the readers have been aligned with him,[73] as they have been with all the suppliants so far, they too move from the periphery, to join the central movement towards Jerusalem 'in the way'.

When the beggar receives mercy and Jesus declares him to have been saved, this story links in with another crucial Marcan theme. When Jesus

---

[67] Although, as mentioned above, this scene is not as negative towards the disciples as is often made out.

[68] Nevertheless, the section portrays them with great sympathy. Even the reference to 'fear', for example, is offered as an explanation for their lack of understanding which therefore promotes sympathy, not judgement.

[69] J.F. Williams, *Other Followers*, 166.   [70] *Pace* ibid., 170.

[71] The significance of Bartimaeus as the suppliant with whom the readers *begin* to identify loses a lot of its force when the suppliants' reader-engaging function is properly analysed. He is then not significant as the first with whom the readers 'identify', but as the first who joins the main movement of the story.

[72] On the sympathetic treatment of Peter, for example, see Boomershine, 'Peter's Denial', cf. Boomershine and Bartholomew, 'Narrative Technique'.

[73] This is readily acknowledged, even if the means of 'identification' is usually explained in terms of 'positive traits'; cf. Bassler, 'Parable', 167; J.F. Williams, *Other Followers*, 166, 170.

was about to heal the man with the withered hand on the Sabbath, he had asked whether it was lawful to save a life, or to kill (3.4). Thus, from its first occurrence, σῴζω has overtones of bringing life where there was death, even in a case of 'mere' healing. These overtones were reinforced in the intercalated miracles of Mark 5.21–43, where Jairus asked Jesus to lay his hands on his daughter ἵνα σωθῇ καὶ ζήσῃ (5.23). His request came when she was at the point of death, but she subsequently died and Jairus received even more than anyone could hope for. She was not merely saved and given life from the point of death, but was saved out of death itself and lived again by resurrection. The story of the resurrected girl also affected the story of the haemorrhaging woman intercalated within it. Whereas the woman wanted to be saved from her bleeding problem (5.28), Jesus eventually declared that her faith had saved her (5.34; cf. 10.52). Her affliction had brought her to the end of her life, making her one of the living dead, but Jesus had given her life instead of death. After σῴζω had acquired these overtones of being saved from death, the readers would also hear them echoed in the final summary report of Jesus' Galilean activity (6.54–56), when many came to touch Jesus in a similar manner and found that they too were 'saved' (6.56).

If the first half of the Gospel encouraged σῴζω to be read as a saving from death, this was only reinforced after the turning point (8.27–30). Jesus called people to save their life through following him (8.34), being prepared to lose their life for his sake and the gospel's (8.35) which was a real choice between life and death. Jesus' paradox reversed the normal and logical human viewpoint (cf. 8.33) in favour of the opinion that life is found by following him to death on a cross. Jesus was calling people to follow him onwards to death, in the hope of being saved by resurrection (cf. v.31).

The next sub-section reinforced this by speaking of entering the kingdom (10.13–16, 23–25), inheriting eternal life (10.17) and gaining treasure in heaven (v.21; cf. 8.36f.). When the rich man had left crestfallen, having chosen his earthly treasure, the disciples asked the question: 'then who can be saved?' (v.26). Jesus answered the disciples in terms of God making the impossible possible (v.27) before assuring his disciples that they had made the right choice to follow him, because this was the way to eternal life in the age to come (v.30). Clearly in this context, 'to be saved' is equivalent to inheriting eternal life, having treasure in heaven, entering the kingdom of God, and having eternal life in the age to come. Thus, when Jesus declares Bartimaeus to be saved, the narrative has already erected the framework against which this declaration can be understood.

The blind man has been saved from death and has been given life, even life fit for the kingdom. The disciples' question 'who then can be saved?' has been given a narrative answer: someone like Bartimaeus.[74] But what is it about him that has led to salvation?

In view of the tendency to identify positive character traits, it is necessary at this point to state that he has not contributed anything concrete to his salvation. The faith by which he was saved is not so much a character trait, or a quality. His persistent begging for mercy is an expression of a conviction that Jesus was the one who could help him. This constitutes faith. His status as a beggar is the feature that makes him a paradigm disciple. The story illustrates faith by showing him as the adult counterpart to the child (cf. 10.13–16), namely, as a beggar who has nothing to offer and even leaves what he has in order to plead for mercy. His faith led to this request and, when mercy is extended to him, he is saved and embarks upon a new journey.

The kingdom focus in this section also colours the nature of the journey with which it ends. Although it is true that Bartimaeus 'exemplifies' the characteristics recommended for any follower of Jesus, the concrete details of the story prevent him from becoming simply some abstract character 'type'. His journey is not abstract at all, but has a definite destination. Although the Gerasene had wanted to go with Jesus (5.18f.), but had not been permitted, and anyone who wished to come with Jesus in full cognisance of the direction he was taking had been invited to do so (8.34–9.1), Bartimaeus is the first person who has responded to the invitation. As a representative of the suppliants with whom the readers have been identified, they too, at this point, move from the periphery in order to join the journey alongside the others.

The journey's destination is well known to the readers.[75] At the most basic level, the movement of the characters within the story is towards the story's end in Jerusalem (10.32–34; cf. 8.31; 9.31) and the readers now journey with them to see whether expected events unfold. However, even at the beginning of the story, 'the way' had additional overtones, for the initial citations from Malachi and Isaiah both called for the preparation of the way of the Lord (1.2f.) who was expected to come bringing judgement and salvation. The 'way' became more prominent in this section

[74] So too, Williams, ibid., 166, although he deals with Bartimaeus' faith in isolation from his request for mercy.

[75] On the 'way' motif, see Malbon, *Narrative Space*, 68–71, 104–5; Rhoads and Michie, *Mark*, 64–5.

(?8.27; 9.33f.; 10.17, 32, 46, 52), helping to sustain the movement towards Jerusalem.

In the course of moving towards Jerusalem, the way also acquired a further metaphorical dimension as a journey towards the kingdom. The section is structured around the three predictions raising the expectation of Jesus' death followed by resurrection. When Jesus told his disciples that the one event yet to occur before the arrival of the resurrection day and the kingdom was the suffering of the Son of Man (9.9–13), he associated his coming death with the coming kingdom. The expectation of the imminent kingdom and the urgent need to enter it is particularly prominent in the section: (kingdom: 9.1, 47; 10.14, 15, 23, 24, 25; (eternal) life: 8.35–38; 9.43, 45; 10.17, 30; treasure in heaven: 10.21, cf. 8.35f.; and Jesus' glory: 8.38; 10.37, cf. 40). Thus, as the journey heads towards his death in Jerusalem, the journey also progresses towards the resurrection day and the kingdom of God.

Thus Bartimaeus is not simply a picture of 'discipleship', or 'following', or 'faith', in any abstract sense, but he is an example of a person who has begun following Jesus on 'a path that leads necessarily to suffering'.[76] And, as we have seen, since Jesus' death is linked closely with the resurrection and the coming kingdom, when Bartimaeus steps on to this path, it is not just a path towards suffering, but towards the resurrection by way of whatever suffering or shame may happen to lie ahead. He has taken up his cross to follow Jesus into the kingdom (cf. 8.34–9.1).[77] He is on the way towards eternal life in the age to come (cf. 10.17, 30).

Reader to text

Blindness, death, and the dead

Enough has been said above (on 8.22–26) to establish that the blind were amongst the living dead, and that blindness could be one of the weapons wielded by the dead at the orchestration of magical art. The point flowing out from the Bartimaeus narrative is that the blind beggar asks for mercy, emerges from a living death and joins the path towards a future resurrection.

---

[76] J.F. Williams, *Other Followers*, 162.

[77] When contrasting Bartimaeus with the rich man, Williams, ibid., 166, says of the latter that 'the path to the kingdom of God is too hard, the cost of eternal life too high' and yet fails to draw the parallel with Bartimaeus' destination.

The Son of David

Solomon was widely recognised as having magical powers.[78] If the Graeco-Roman readers knew of his reputation and recognised him in the title used here, then this would reinforce Jesus' reputation as a worker of 'magic'. In addition to being a reminder that his 'magical' abilities were powerful enough to cure the blind (cf. 8.22–26), this story would then also provide a reason for his magical ability, by virtue of his family connection with David/Solomon.

The imperial comparison

We have also seen that, at least in some quarters of the Roman world, her rulers were increasingly accorded god-like status. So, for example, in AD 69 some Alexandrians would ask Vespasian to heal the blind. Jesus' abilities in this area certainly make him compare favourably with the imperial power.

---

[78] Cf. 11QPsAp^a; *AJ* 8.45–9; Kotansky and Spier, 'Horned Hunter', 323 n.35; *DT* **24** 2.15 = Gager **10**; TSol. Greek Title.

6

THE CLASH OF KINGDOMS
(MARK 11.1–13.37)

The fourth main section presents the story's 'rising action',[1] as events begin to head inevitably towards the promised death of the Son of Man which will be followed by the promised resurrection. The section begins with a clear temporal and geographical patterning which builds momentum towards the events in Jerusalem.[2] It spans three days. The first two days establish the geographical pattern: a journey from Bethany to Jerusalem and back (Day 1: 11.1–11; Day 2: 11.12–19). On the third day, the same pattern commences: the morning journey to Jerusalem (11.20) ends in the temple (11.27). Although the journey home begins as they move away from the temple (13.1) across the Mount of Olives (13.3), its conclusion is never reported, even though it is assumed to have occurred (14.3). The journey home is delayed on the Mount of Olives while Jesus delivers his longest speech which functions as a narrative aside, i.e., it creates a pause in the movement in order to force reflection on the narrative. Because of the open-ended third day, the entire section (11.27–13.37) reads as a connected sequence, with the three days functioning together to bring the narrative to its crisis.[3]

Day 1: the coming kingdom of David (11.1–11)

The first day is filled with expectation, but nothing happens. Jesus enters Jerusalem in a manner which appears to make a deliberate messianic claim.[4] Whether or not the crowd realise what is going on, their words have great significance, sustaining the readers' expectation of the coming kingdom (vv.10f.).

---

[1] 'That part of a play which precedes the climax'; Cuddon, *Dictionary*, 575.

[2] S.H. Smith, 'Literary Structure', 105–6.

[3] 'That point in a story [. . .] at which the tempo reaches a maximum and resolution is imminent', Cuddon, *Dictionary*, 166.

[4] Smith, *Literary Structure*, 121; Hooker, *Mark*, 257–9.

His arrival in the temple creates an expectation of action (11.11), and, since nothing occurs, suspense: what had he seen? and what will he do?

Day 2: the harvest is not ready (11.12–19)

On the second day, two events occur, but nothing is explained. First, Jesus seeks some fruit from the tree, but it is not the season for it so he curses the tree with barrenness. Mark's unexplained comment that the disciples heard him adds to the suspense. Secondly, Jesus upsets the traffic in the temple. Despite the debate over whether this action is a cleansing or a prophecy of destruction, within the narrative it is directed at the leadership of Israel. Jesus cites Isaiah 56.7 and then adds Jeremiah 7.11, saying, 'but you (ὑμεῖς δέ) have made it "a den of robbers" ' (v.17). The text immediately reveals the referent for the emphatic pronoun by showing that the chief priests and scribes hear what he said and begin seeking a way to destroy him (v.18). The action in the temple is not against the structure as such, but against Israel's power-brokers who had allowed it to become a commercial venture.

Day 3: the clash of the kingdoms (11.20–13.37)

The explanation: the figtree (11.20–26)

The next day provides a series of reflections upon the events of Day 2. When the disciples see that the figtree is now withered, Peter remembers that they had heard Jesus' curse, and draws Jesus' attention to the fact (vv.20f.). Jesus' reply, although difficult to interpret, need not be understood as peripheral or opportunistic, but can be explained in terms of the ongoing story-line. If ἔχετε (v.22) is taken as indicative not imperative,[5] it indicates that the substance of Jesus' answer is grounded on the faithfulness of God. Since 'this mountain' (v.23) was the Mount of Olives, which they crossed twice each day, his statement can be taken as a dramatic restatement of the prophecy of Zechariah (14.10, 14) which promised that Palestine would be a plain from Jerusalem to the sea, the Mount of Olives being split in two and levelled.[6] Thus the mountain moving is a call upon God to be faithful to his promises. The one who does not doubt that this prophecy is becoming a reality will have the pleasure of seeing it come

[5] Lane, *Mark*, 410.
[6] Ibid. Plut. *De I et O* 370C mentions a similar belief amongst the Chaldeans, in association with the future resurrection.

true. Against this background, the prayer (v.24) would be specifically concerned with the coming of the kingdom; πάντα ὅσα referring to actual requests, and the present tenses προσεύχεσθε καὶ αἰτεῖσθε, – taken together 'asking in prayer' – suggesting that Jesus is addressing current hopes and prayers in which the disciples share, i.e., 'the things you are actually asking in prayer'. ἐλάβετε therefore points to the fact that their hopes are fulfilled (namely, in Jesus), urging the disciples to continue to believe (present imperative πιστεύετε) that the prophetic expectations are fulfilled in him. It is as they believe this that they will find it to be true (cf. 4.25) and they will enter the kingdom. As they pray for the kingdom, they need to live out its characteristic forgiveness (v.25).

Because this discussion was in response to Jesus' curse on the figtree, it must also have something to do with his acting upon a scriptural promise which indicated that the end was near. Although other options have been proposed, Micah 7.1ff. provides the best scriptural backing. There the prophet's misery is likened to one who cannot find an early fig to eat. This is an image of Israel being so badly in ruins due to the corruption of the leadership (vv.3f.) that there is not one godly man to be found (v.2), but the day of God's visitation has come when he will shepherd his flock as he did in days long gone (vv.14ff.).

Jesus' action shows that the same situation prevails in the Israel of his day. The land has been devastated through the corruption of the leadership, the end is nigh, the kingdom of God has drawn near. The Son of Man must yet suffer, but that is the last thing that must occur before the resurrection from the dead and the arrival of the age to come. Jesus therefore encourages his disciples to keep on believing that their eschatological hopes are fulfilled in him (11.20–26).

The explanation: the temple (11.27–12.12)

In the next unit (11.27–33), the religious leaders once again question his authority, this time reflecting on his action in the temple ('these things'). The riddle about John enables him to avoid a direct answer and also reminds the readers of the importance of John in the story so far. He was Jesus' forerunner, in accordance with Isaianic prophecies (1.3–8), whose fate contained a foreshadowing of Jesus' own suffering (1.14; 6.14–29); but, most importantly, Jesus has hinted that his suffering was that of Elijah, which means that that awaited eschatological event has occurred and there is only the suffering of the Son of Man to occur before the resurrection from the dead and the kingdom of God will arrive (9.11–13). Although Jesus' opponents decline to answer Jesus' riddle, Mark's readers know by what authority Jesus has acted. He was divinely commissioned as the servant-Son (1.11) and has offered an alternative leadership which has brought him into conflict with those who are currently pretending to act in that capacity.

Although he refuses to answer their question directly, once Jesus has regained the initiative, he answers it in a parable (12.1–12). It reissues Isaiah's parable (Isa. 5.1–7), in which the ruin of Israel was caused by the nation's leaders (Isa. 3.13–15, cf. 1.23; 3.1–7), for it was they who, through political alliances, idolatry and magic (Isa. 1.29–31; 2.6–9, 12–18, 22), led the decline which resulted in the death of the nation in the exile (cf. Isa. 5.13f.).

In Jesus' elaboration of Isaiah's parable the expectation of a harvest, the tenants' resistance to the landlord, and the son who is abused and killed can all find counterparts in Mark's preceding story. The parable suggests that the tenants resist the landlord in an endeavour to maintain their position in the vineyard, so that they can reap its harvest for themselves (cf. Ezek. 34–36). The clear allusion to the voice from heaven in the baptismal scene (12.6, cf. 9.7 and 1.11), ensures that the reader recognises Jesus in the parabolic son and so his opponents as the tenants who end up killing him. When Jesus finishes, his opponents also make the same equation, with the result that they continue to search for a way to arrest him (12.12; cf. 3.6, 11.18).

The confrontation (12.13–44)

Their attempt to arrest him issues in a series of controversies. Because these seek to trap him in his words (12.13), the readers recognise each question as laden with the intent to arrest Jesus and to kill him (3.6; 11.18; 12.12). He is questioned about paying tribute (12.13–17), about the resurrection from the dead (12.18–27), and about the greatest commandment (12.28–34).

Rendering to God (12.13–17)

Wherever Rome went, taxation inevitably followed. The use of κῆνσος here (12.14b) implies the poll tax, the notorious *tributum capitis* (φόρος σωμάτων) – the one denarius per head provincial subjects were required to pay using imperial coinage.[7] Of course, in any patronage system there would always be questions of the rightness of the exacted amounts

---

[7] Finney, 'Rabbi', 632.

(cf. Aristotle's poor man saying: 'This is sport to you, but death to me'; *EE* 1243ᵃ20), but there were also larger issues at stake. As Tacitus has the Roman general Cerialis say, after he suppressed a revolt in Trier: 'You cannot secure tranquillity without armies, nor maintain armies without pay, nor provide pay without taxes; [. . .]' (Tac. *Hist.* 4.74). The payment of taxes secured the *Pax Romana*, and, since this was a military peace, through taxes the provinces were buying their own subjugation.[8] It is little wonder that the question whether to pay or not was a live issue.

The coins themselves were not only legal tender, but provided a value judgement on the character and role of the individual portrayed. This could be used to advantage from both directions: the subject nations could use them to represent their recognition and respect of the emperor, but, alternatively, they could also be used as an instrument of the imperial propaganda.[9] In the tradition of the Hellenistic kings, Julius Caesar was the first Roman to put himself on coins as a claim to divinity, but he was not the last. Augustus 'made an unprecedented use of coins, with special captions and symbols'.[10] Pontius Pilate had introduced into Judea the coin of Tiberius which stated he was 'son of the deified Augustus',[11] and, on the reverse, showed Pax seated in the guise of a priestess, with the superscription PONTIF MAXIM, which meant that both sides were 'equally impregnated with religious propaganda offensive to Jews'.[12] The coins were a constant presence reminding the provinces that 'God has settled in Italy' (*BJ* 5.366f., cf. 2.362).

So should they pay or not pay? The cleverness of the trap is well known. At least one former Roman collaborator had left his occupation to throw in his lot with Jesus, maybe more (2.14f.), so what will their Master say? Jesus' answer is equally masterful. He requests a coin which apparently has to be fetched,[13] which causes a pause in the flow of the dialogue while the antagonists 'rummage through their pockets'.[14] By this means the dialogue is shifted to another level of discourse, from his

---

[8] When urging her people to fight for their freedom (AD 61), Boadicea spoke of the annual tribute 'for our very bodies' paid to Rome: 'How much better it would be to have been sold to masters once for all than, possessing empty titles of freedom, to have to ransom ourselves every year (κατ᾽ ἔτος λυτροῦσθαι)' (Dio 62.3).

[9] Huzar, 'Emperor Worship', 3095.

[10] Barnett, *Servant King*, 6.   [11] Ibid., 7; Finney, 'Rabbi', 632.

[12] Finney, 'Rabbi', 633. It was also propaganda 'with teeth', cf. Philostr. *Vit. Ap.* 1.15 in which a master who strikes his slave who was carrying a coin bearing the image of Tiberius is found guilty of *asebeia*.

[13] 'This detail may confirm what is known from other provincial contexts – namely, that the imperial denarius was not a denomination used in common, everyday market exchange', Finney, 'Rabbi', 632.

[14] Finney, ibid., 631, upon whom I rely for this section.

person to a thing. It may be that this shift would divide his questioners, since the aniconism of Palestine was dealt with differently by different groups. Apparently the Essenes refused to touch a coin because Jews were forbidden to carry or look at or make images (Hippol. *Ref.* 9.21), and here it may be that the Pharisees would have taken umbrage at the suggestion to look at it, whereas the Herodians would not.[15]

Jesus' response sets the question in terms of legitimate spheres of authority. If the coin is Caesar's, then what is the problem in giving back his property? But the duty with respect to God is a separate issue, and what expresses the image of God, i.e., human life, must be given back to him. His answer to the first trap produces utter amazement (v.17).

The resurrection of the dead (12.18–27)

The Sadducees ask the second question which begins as an inquiry about levirate marriage, but its real concern is the resurrection of the dead, as Mark indicates (v.18). They attempt to bring the belief in resurrection (which they do not hold) into conflict with the Law by means of a case study. The case study most probably draws upon the book of Tobit, which, as I have argued elsewhere, sustains the resurrection hope by narrative means.[16] Because Israel's exile still continues and the nation is under God's judgement, Tobit pictures Israel as blind, barren and subject to the *daimon* of death, and in great need of rescue by their kinsman-redeemer. Since Tobit's solution to these problems is a series of movements from 'death to life', I have suggested that the book can be understood as an attempt to keep the hope of resurrection alive. If so, the Sadducees' use of the story as a critique of this hope is a shrewd move.

Their question is not an attack on a random feature of what Jesus stands for, but an attack on the central aspect of Jesus' teaching and ministry. By attempting to ridicule the resurrection hope, they have attacked the notion of a coming kingdom which the resurrection will inaugurate. The implication of their attempted argument *ad absurdum* is that life is all about 'now', for there is no 'then'. Jesus argues from the Law that God is the God of the living, not the dead. Although the contracting of marriages is a thing for this age, in the age to come God will certainly make his people 'like the angels', i.e., they will live eternally (cf. Luke 20.36; Philo *Sacr.* 5, cf. *QG* 3.11).

But why these questions? In the context of Mark's narrative, both controversies gain greater significance. The use of the image underlines

---

[15] Ibid., 640.   [16] See Bolt, 'Sadducees'.

that Mark is making counter-claims for Jesus to those of the emperor. The king's image is the presence of the king. Similarly, the Sadducean question is not just an interesting point of theological debate, but, since it attacks the resurrection from the dead, it has gone to the heart of Jesus' message about the kingdom of God, for the preaching of the kingdom is, at one and the same time, the preaching of the resurrection of the dead. Thus both these controversies are kingdom controversies: who is the real king, Caesar or God? What is the nature of these kingdoms? Are the Sadducees right to reject a future resurrection and to curry favour with the kingdoms of this world? Or is Jesus right to proclaim a kingdom of the age to come, in which people will live for ever, just like the angels? The God to whom human lives must be rendered is also the God of the living, whose promises to his people endure even when their earthly life comes to an end.

Close to the kingdom (12.28–34)

The final question comes from a scribe. In terms of previous narrative norms, by being labelled 'one of the scribes' (v.28) he is automatically identified as one of Jesus' opponents. Given the immediate context of opposition, his question about the greatest commandment is also most naturally read as an attempt to trap Jesus. However, by the end of the incident he has recognised Jesus' wisdom (vv.32f.) and has apparently moved close to the kingdom of God (v.34a). This brings the hostile questioning to an end (v.34b). This story represents the defeat of the scribes. Their plot to trap Jesus in his words has failed: one of their own number has been forced to 'change sides' and it is no longer possible to ask any more questions. They have been silenced.[17] If they are to succeed in their plans to destroy Jesus, they will require a new strategy (cf. 14.1, 10f.).

Jesus now begins openly to question the scribal teaching on the Messiah (12.35–37) and to warn the crowds against them (12.38–40), before commenting upon a tragic example of the human misery they have caused (12.41–44).

A messianic puzzle (12.35–37)

Once his opponents' plot has failed, Jesus goes on the attack. He questions the adequacy of the scribal teaching on the Christ being David's son, by introducing a puzzle based upon Psalm 110.1. Although the puzzle

---

[17] Cf. S.H. Smith, *Literary Structure*, 118; 'Opponents', 177f.

receives no answer here, the readers have some hints at a partial answer, for, if Jesus is God's son, and Christ, then it would be appropriate for David to call the Christ his 'Lord'. This puzzle therefore indirectly continues the narrative's interest in the identity of Jesus.

The warning against the scribes (12.38–40)

Jesus warns the crowds against siding with the scribes, whose behaviour shows them to be self-interested and exploitative. These outwardly religious men devour those whom they are supposed most to protect (cf. Isa. 1.23). Jesus warns the crowds against them, for their judgement will be most severe and it will presumably also fall upon those under their influence. In this way, this warning indirectly continues the narrative's portrayal of Jesus as an alternative leader for Israel.

The plunder of Israel (12.41–44)

The widow provides a tragic illustration of Israel's ruin. No matter what godly motives she may have had for contributing her coins to the temple tax, the narrative point of the story is to provide a case study of the failure of Israel's leadership to care for God's people.[18] She is one who should have been protected, and yet they have devoured her house (cf. v.40). Since her gift is from her utter poverty, 'the devourers' have taken away 'her whole life' (ὅλον τὸν βίον αὐτῆς, v.44). By bringing her to economic ruin, they have, in effect, killed her. This scene indirectly reveals the ruin into which the failed leadership has plunged the nation.

The widow's tragic story would strike chords for Graeco-Roman readers who were aware of one of the great changes brought to Graeco-Roman societies by the imperial cult. When Tacitus reports on the worship of Claudius in Britain (*Ann.* 14.31), he remarks that the men who had been picked for priestly office 'were bound under the pretext of religion to pour out their fortunes like water'. This is illustrated from the many inscriptions recording the gifts of various people to the cult.[19] It is of little consequence that Israel may have avoided the imperial cult as such, for the Graeco-Roman readers would recognise in this story a practice analogous to that of their own society. The cult officials were selected from the aristocratic families of the conquered territories, as the Jewish

---

[18] See Wright, 'Widow's Mites', whose arguments are not overturned by Malbon, 'Poor Widow'.

[19] Cf. discussion of the Galatian examples in Mitchell, *Anatolia*, 108–11.

leaders had been.[20] The local temple worship was one of the ways the *imperium* continued to plunder the provinces, managing to keep control of the aristocracy, whilst at one and the same time increasing their local power and prestige.[21] Thus, although some might complain about the poll tax, this money to the temple was indirectly, and so perhaps even more powerfully, supporting the same imperial subjugation of the nation. The shepherds have not only plundered the flock, but, as was the practice of the provincial aristocracy throughout the Roman world, they have even fed them to the wolves.

The widow epitomises Israel's ruin. The nation has been robbed and it now lives in a state of death, for the 'devourers' have taken the last two pence.

The explanation: the Son of Man (13.1–37)

The climax of this section is the 'apocalyptic discourse', a section which has exercised interpreters greatly. Following the lead of R.H. Lightfoot, I have previously argued for an intra-narrative understanding of this chapter, in which Jesus' Olivet discourse is read as an apocalyptic preparation for the events about to unfold in the passion narrative.[22]

The speech warns the disciples of the special problems associated with being a part of Jesus' cause in a world where 'kingdom rises against kingdom', before telling them of two key events for which the disciples are to watch, both of which draw upon Daniel. There will be a time of distress, such as the world has never known (v.19; cf. Dan. 12.1) – nor, adds Jesus, will such a time ever be seen again. This will be followed by the coming of the Son of Man and the subsequent gathering of the elect (vv.24–27). Both events signal the arrival of the kingdom (v.29, translating 'it' rather than 'he'; cf. 1.15). In Daniel, the great distress preceded the resurrection from the dead (Dan. 12.1–2), and the coming of the Son of Man represented his ascent to the throne of the Ancient of Days to receive the kingdom of God which would never pass away (Dan. 7.13–14, cf. 2.44); a kingdom which was then shared with the saints (7.22), presumably also through resurrection (Dan. 12.2f.).

---

[20] 'Caesar appeared in Palestine as the one who settled quarrels within Judaism over the leadership,' Wengst, *Pax Romana*, 20, citing Joseph. *BJ* 1.199f.

[21] Rivalry in public benefactions could be taken for granted amongst the successive holders of office, and 'the liberality and public generosity of the wealthy [was] designed in the first place to confirm the prestige of the donor and to secure in the widest sense his political authority,' Mitchell, *Anatolia*, 112.

[22] Bolt, 'Narrative Integrity', now summarised in Bolt, 'Apocalyptic Precursor'. Cf. Lightfoot, 'Connexion'.

This sequence is placed before the disciples and they are told to watch for it. Lightfoot argued that the passion narrative was structured around the expectations erected by Mark 13, especially signalled by the time references in the final parable (vv.32–37). This suggestion can be extended to say that the expectations find their fulfilment respectively in the crucifixion of Jesus (= the great distress, the desolating sacrilege) and in his vindication in the resurrection (= the coming of the Son of Man). Such an understanding will be assumed in the comments to follow.

Preparation for the passion narrative

In this section the clash between Jesus and his opponents has reached a crisis. Throughout the section Jesus appears to be firmly in charge,[23] which gives the impression that he provokes his own passion. He enters Jerusalem as a king, surrounded by acclamations that suggest the hoped-for kingdom is near; but Israel is in ruins because of the nation's leadership; he encourages his disciples to keep seeing him as the fulfilment of their nation's hopes; but the leadership continue to resist his divine appointment, in their own self-interest; they attempt to destroy him by trapping him with questions, but they fail; he, in turn, indicts them for their misguided Christological understanding and their exploitative behaviour, which has led to Israel's death; he then sets the disciples' sights on to the prospect of a terrible distress followed by the coming of the Son of Man and the kingdom of God. He lifts their eyes from the ruin all around them, and asks them to watch, instead, for these things which will most certainly be coming (13.32), and coming very soon indeed (13.30).

---

[23] 'Jesus appears to be beyond the opponents' power', Tannehill, 'Narrative Christology', 77.

7

THE COMING OF THE KINGDOM (MARK 14–16)

Since the story has already erected the interpretative framework for the events of the passion narrative, they now simply need to unfold.

Preparation for Jesus' death (14.1–31)

The plot and the anointing (14.1–11)

Each of the three scenes in the initial 'sandwich' (14.1–11) prepares for Jesus' death: the first negatively, when the leaders reissue the plot to kill Jesus (vv.1f.; cf. 3.6; 8.31; 9.13; 9.31; 10.31; 12.13) after it had come to a standstill with the 'defeat' of the scribe (12.28–34); the second positively, as the woman anoints Jesus in preparation for his burial (vv.3–9); and the third negatively, as Judas provides the high priests with the vehicle by which their plot can become a reality (vv.10f.; cf. 3.19).

It is now clear that Jesus' predictions of his death will be fulfilled. This therefore heightens the expectation that his predictions about the coming resurrection and the kingdom will also be fulfilled, since his death was all that had to occur before the arrival of these major events.

Passover predictions (14.12–31)

During the celebration of the Passover Jesus continues to prepare the disciples for his death and the narrative reinforces the readers' expectations by providing predictions and fulfilments. The preparations unfold as announced (vv.12–16). Jesus tells the disciples of the betrayal of which the readers had learned in the initial scenes (vv.17–21). Their reaction underlines the horrific nature of Jesus' betrayal by one of them. Jesus further prepares for his death by explaining that it will be the blood of the covenant which is poured out for many (v.24; cf. 10.45) as a Passover sacrifice (cf. Isa. 53.10).[1] Since the death of the Son of Man was previously

[1] Jeremias, *Theology*, 292f.

254

presented as the ransom by which God made the impossible possible, enabling people to enter the kingdom (10.45), it is no surprise that the expectation of the coming kingdom makes yet another appearance at this point (v.25). Having spoken of his death as a covenant sacrifice, Jesus looks ahead to the kingdom feast. His prediction that this will be his last meal until the kingdom reinforces the expectation of its imminent arrival.

As the hour heads towards midnight, they go to the Mount of Olives where Jesus predicts that they will all fall, in accordance with Zechariah's prophecy (v.27; Zech. 13.7). Peter's protest of loyalty is met with the prediction that he too will deny Jesus before cock-crow (vv.29f.). The disciples' denial that they will fall when their shepherd is struck down displays commendable loyalty, which, in turn, arouses sympathy in the reader (v.31).

The hour is come! (14.32–52)

Alone in the will of God (14.32–42)

The scene in Gethsemane is filled with emotion as Jesus faces his imminent death (vv.32–42). He is afraid, distressed, agitated; he feels alone; he wants to avoid this hour, in so far as it is possible, and yet he wants to continue to do God's will. All these devices draw the readers towards Jesus.

At the same time, they are drawn towards the failing disciples. Although the disciples fail to stay awake, their failure is explained – in terms of their tiredness (vv.37, 40, 41), their regret (v.41b) and, above all, their human weakness (v.38). Because the explanation of weaknesses promotes sympathy, the readers are drawn towards them, recognising how very human all of this is. At one end of the garden a great cosmic drama is occurring, as Jesus struggles in the depths of emotion to face a death that will be the ransom for many, the Passover sacrifice of the new covenant, a death which is a necessity according to God's great unfolding plan and which must happen before the kingdom comes. At the disciples' end of the garden they struggle to stay awake.

Gradually it is becoming clear that only Jesus can face this death, so their failure can be excused. Although the readers are in sympathy with Jesus and feel for him, they would also recognise their own humanity in that of the disciples. They, too, although longing to be with Jesus, find themselves at the disciples' end of the garden, knowing that their flesh is just as weak.

'The hour', previously expected, now arrives as the betrayer walks into the garden (vv.41f., cf. 13.32). At this point the two plots come together: the opponents are about to get their man; and, as they do so, God's purposes surrounding that man are about to reach resolution.

Deserted in his distress (14.43–52)

In the arrest scene (vv.43–52), the tragedy of the betrayal is underlined by Judas being described as 'one of the twelve' and 'the betrayer', and through his use of a token of affection to identify the victim. When the arrest occurs, after an ineffectual show of resistance (v.47), everyone deserts Jesus (v.50). Despite their great resolve to remain loyal, the disciples have failed. But through a subtle allusion to Amos 2.16, Mark ameliorates their failure: even the young man has fled away naked, such is the nature of this great day of distress.

Trials within and without (14.53–72)

The narrative then provides a moment of pleasant surprise. As the Sanhedrin assembles, Peter appears, still following, albeit at a distance (vv.53f.). For the moment, it looks as if his commitment to be there when all others have failed has been realised, although the readers recall Jesus' counter-prediction of what will occur before the night is out. By way of another intercalation, the narrative enables the readers to simultaneously watch the trial of Jesus within and the 'trial' of Peter without. Outside, Jesus' prediction of Peter's fall comes true, but his failure is ameliorated by that prediction, by the natural way that he was led into the denial, and by his own bitter sorrow when he realises what has occurred, so that the readers remain sympathetic. Inside, Jesus' death is almost taken for granted and the hearing ends in the climactic scene in which Jesus predicts yet again the coming of the Son of Man who is to be installed at the right hand of power (v.62, cf. Dan. 7.13 and Ps. 110.1). He had once warned his opponents against blaspheming by failing to recognise the true source of his authority (3.28f.) and now, as his true identity is climactically revealed, they charge him with blasphemy and his death is assured.

Since Jesus' predictions continue to be fulfilled before the readers' eyes, the expectation is heightened that the outstanding predictions will also be fulfilled. This is reinforced by the repetition of the prediction of the coming of the Son of Man to be installed at the right hand of God (v.62, cf. 8.38–9.1, 13.24–27). The narrative is expecting resurrection to follow his death and the coming of the kingdom of God, in which the Son of Man plays a key role. Here, at the moment of Jesus' greatest vulnerability, he proclaims the Son of Man's ultimate vindication. As they seek to put him to death (vv.55, 64), Jesus is already looking beyond that death to the resurrection and the kingdom of God. As the readers watch the scene outside come to its tragic conclusion in Peter's denial – exactly as Jesus predicted –, their expectation is increased that his other predictions too will no doubt occur. The Son of Man will be vindicated and the kingdom of God will arrive in power.

The death of the king (Mark 15.1–39)

The readers know the sequence of expectation and the significance with which Jesus' death has been invested. They must simply wait for the events to play out according to plan. As they watch, the sense of tragedy deepens as Jesus gradually becomes more and more alone: deserted by friends, he is now deserted by his nation's leaders, by the Roman officials, and eventually by God himself. The readers too, occupying the role of observers, sit at some distance from the events, which gives the impression that, they too, in a sense, have deserted him. They are like the women at the end of the account who watch the crucifixion from a distance (v.40).[2]

The hint that there would be a clash with Rome (10.33) now becomes a reality as Pilate and his soldiers enter in force. The Romans showed no sympathy for kingly pretenders, or even for rival kings who had not been appointed by imperial decree.[3] Pilate's 'trial' condemns him to crucifixion as 'the king of the Jews' – no doubt in great contempt of the nation under his charge.[4] His soldiers mock Jesus as soldiers were prone to do with

---

[2] I have attempted to show the readers' engagement with the crucifixion account and its subsequent impact upon them in Bolt, 'Feeling the Cross'.

[3] Cf. the characterisation of the Jewish kings in Tac. *Hist*. 5.8. Only the Romans had the right to appoint and depose kings in the Roman world: Mark Antony made Herod King (*BJ* 1.282), whereas the Hasmonean Antigonus forfeited his kingdom because he had been appointed by the Parthians (*AJ* 14.384). He was executed as a rebel with an axe, after being bound to a stake and flogged, something no Roman-appointed king suffered (Dio Cass. 49.22.6; cf. Strabo acc. to Joseph. *AJ* 15.9). Evidently some had short memories. After the death of Herod, without waiting for the imperial decision, a certain Simo usurped the title of king. He was punished by Quintilius Varus, the people reduced to obedience, and the kingdom divided among the three sons of Herod (Tac. *Hist*. 5.9).

[4] Hengel, *Son of God* , 61 n. 113: 'we cannot overestimate the scandal of a crucified *Jewish* Messiah king who was to be proclaimed "Lord" and "Son of God". Pilate's question (Mark 15.9, 12), and still more the *titulus* on the cross, are expressions of hostility to Judaism.'

imperial pretenders.[5] But, in the whole process, and although dripping with tragic irony, it is clear that Mark insists that when Jesus died, he died as a king. The only 'king' in Mark's narrative so far was Herod, whose kingdom led to the death of God's prophet. Now Jesus is put to death by those who had given Herod his power, and when they did so, Mark insists, they killed him as a rival king. Such was the testimony of their own officials (vv.2, 9, 12, 17–20, 26), as well as that of the local elite who retained their privilege by the grace of Rome (v.32) and who here affirm their links with Rome, rather than with Jesus, through assisting in the execution of a rival king.[6]

Given the foregoing narrative, as the local leadership add their mockery to that of the soldiers (vv.29–32), their words contain great irony. They cause the readers to recall the great events that have occurred as Jesus 'saved others'. Since the mockers wish Jesus to save himself from death, their words endorse the point of this study that these other 'salvations' were regarded as salvations from death as well. What Jesus has done for them, his mockers now demand that he does for himself.

But the readers are also aware that Jesus has been heading relentlessly for this moment. He had to die, in order to do God's will (cf. 3.35). He was the Servant who had to suffer (8.31; 9.31; 10.42–45), the Son of Man whose death would be a ransom for many and was the necessary preliminary to the arrival of the great resurrection harvest and the kingdom of God. In order to 'save others' he had to die, so he cannot save himself.[7]

Their demand for a final miracle is also ironic. He had given life where there was death. He had brought others 'down from the cross' and now they say that the hard-hearted unbelief they have displayed throughout the story will dissolve if he comes down from the cross right now. They demand the impossible: if he can defeat death, then they will believe. But they clearly believe the opposite: death has defeated him, and their problems are over.

But events around the time of his death could be read as if he had right on his side. As Jesus was dying there was an eclipse for three hours (v.33), which could purportedly be achieved through magic,[8] but was also the kind of sign which accompanied important moments in a ruler's

---

[5] Cf. the mockery of Vitellius (AD 69) by troops loyal to Vespasian (Dio Cass. 64.20–1); and the Carabas episode in Alexandria, Philo *Flacc.* 36ff.

[6] Mitchell, *Anatolia*, 113: 'Roman provincial officials and the local populations were bound together by their relations with the emperor.'

[7] Tannehill, 'Narrative Christology', 80.

[8] Hipp. *Morb.Sacr.* 4: 'For if they profess to know how [. . .] to eclipse the sun (ἥλιον ἀφανίζειν) [. . .]'

life.[9] Another portent occurred as he cried out and breathed his last: the temple curtain was torn (v.38). Portents were also associated with the death of Rome's former rulers (Caesar: Pliny *HN* 2.25.93; Augustus: Suet. 2 (*Aug.*).97; ghosts had appeared after the death of Caligula, Suet. 4 (*Gaius*).59). When the Roman centurion saw how Jesus died, he recognised that this man was 'son of God'. Although possibly another Marcan irony, in this title he agrees with the narrator (cf. 1.1) that Jesus had a right to the imperial title given to Augustus and Tiberius. To this man, his death showed that he was a ruler in the same class as they were.

If he was a son of God, then the next item on the agenda could be some kind of apotheosis. However, his manner of death would probably debar him from any such hope.[10] Far from receiving apotheosis, those who died violently, such as the crucified, were not even guaranteed a restful death. In the underworld, these people would remain at the edge of the Acheron,[11] and they would be the ghosts so eagerly sought after by the magicians. Nevertheless, despite the kind of death Jesus died, this representative of Rome declared him to be 'Son of God' – in fact, because of it.

The end of the passion (15.40–16.8)

The final 'sandwich' in Mark's story consists of the introduction of some women, who watch the crucifixion at a distance (vv.40f.); Jesus' burial (vv.42–47); and the discovery of the empty tomb (16.1–8).

The women from Galilee (15.40f.)

Once introduced, this group of named women provide continuity between the three final scenes. They are sympathetic characters, for they have been with Jesus from the beginning in Galilee, and, rather than deserting him at the crucifixion, they watch from a distance.

[9] Wengst, *Pax Romana*, 2. Signs accompany the course of his life: birth, comet at accession and signs at his death 'declare his assumption into the ranks of the gods' (cf. P.Giss I, 3 the ruler is borne aloft in a chariot with white horses). For cosmic signs, see Friedrich, 'εὐαγγελίζομαι', 724.

[10] Cf. the Stoic prefect overseeing the martyrdom of Justin (AD 165) who seemed to doubt that one who was scourged and beheaded would ascend to heaven; Whittaker, *Jews*, 164.

[11] Cf. the underworld journey in which a man sits at the shores of ugliness and 'stretched around there lay a vast plain, full of corpses of dreadful doom, beheaded or crucified. Above the ground stood pitiable bodies, their throats but lately cut. Others, again, impaled, hung like the trophies of a cruel destiny. The Furies, crowned with wreaths, were laughing at the miserable manner of the corpses' death' (Page **94**.12ff. (2nd c. AD)).

The burial (15.40–47)

Joseph, a member of the group who put Jesus to death, arranged for Jesus to be buried, which he did under the watchful eye of the women. Whether Joseph was a secret follower of Jesus, or simply a pious Jew fulfilling custom by burying fellow Israelites, he 'too' (καί) was awaiting the kingdom of God – as Jesus had been, and as the readers are still. The king has been declared (ch. 15), but the long-awaited kingdom is yet to appear.

According to the timetable which has been clearly established, Jesus would die and then rise (8.31; 9.31; 10.33f.; 14.27f.); or, in other words, the suffering of the Son of Man would precede his coming/the kingdom (8.31, 38, 9.1; 9.9–13; 13.24–27, 29; 14.24f.; 14.62). By carefully indicating intra-narrative predictions and fulfilments, the passion narrative has reinforced the expectation that Jesus' major predictions will also come true. In the death of the 'king', the suffering of the Son of Man has occurred. The next item on the agenda is his resurrection/vindication, when he will come to the throne of God and receive the kingdom. So where is the kingdom?

The empty tomb (16.1–8)

The discovery

In the early morning, the women discovered an empty tomb (vv.1–4, 6). The messenger who alarmed them with his presence (v.5) informed them that the crucified one had risen, as predicted. He stressed that the tomb was now empty (v.6) and instructed them to inform the disciples that Jesus would meet them in Galilee, as he had promised (14.28). Instead of doing so, the women did the opposite: they went out and fled, saying nothing to anyone. Mark explains this as being due to their fear (v.8).[12] Thus the closing sentence of the Gospel leaves the readers with women who are silent about Jesus' resurrection, because they are afraid.

The impact

Time for a proper burial
The women went to the tomb to provide Jesus with a proper burial, doing so at exactly the day and time specified by ancient Greek law (cf. Solon's law, in Dem. 43.62; cf. Thuc. 2.34). Unlike John's disciples (6.29), Jesus'

---

[12] I assume that 16.8 was the original and intended ending which provides a complete and fitting conclusion to Mark's narrative enterprise.

disciples had deserted him, which meant that he was buried by a stranger from the council that condemned him. The women sought to rectify this situation.

The readers, however, are also aware that Jesus had predicted that on the same day the ἐκφορά should take place, the Son of Man would rise from the dead (8.31; 9.31; 10.34). Since it is now the third day, the discovery of the empty tomb speaks loudly of yet another prediction being fulfilled, even before the young man confirms that this is what has happened (v.6).

A lost body

Some have suggested that the disappearance of the body should be read as a signal that Jesus had either become a hero, or had been translated.[13] Although at this point it is only possible to summarise the evidence, I have argued elsewhere that Mark's account fits neither of these options.[14]

A hero?

The 'empty tomb' does not signal that this is the story of a hero. The hero cult required the body of the hero to be in the grave, for his power was localised around that site. Occasionally 'empty graves' were used, but this was in cases where the hero was known to have died elsewhere, making his body inaccessible. Since the body was necessary for the hero cult, the empty tombs were erected to do service for the cult as if the body were there.[15] Whereas these 'empty tombs' were genuine cenotaphs (κενοὶ τάφοι), Mark's narrative stresses that Jesus' body used to be there, but it has now gone from the tomb; i.e., it is an empt-*ied* tomb. Far from his post-death presence being localised at the grave-site, as was the case for a hero, Jesus had promised that he would meet his disciples in Galilee.

This is not a story of Jesus' inauguration as a hero.[16]

---

[13] Bickermann, 'Grab'; Hamilton, 'Resurrection Tradition'; Collins, 'Empty Tomb' and 'Apotheosis'.

[14] Bolt, 'Mk 16:1–8'.

[15] Thucydides (2.34.3) reports a similar practice: during the ἐκφορά for those who had fallen in war, the Athenians 'carried one empty bier for the missing whose bodies could not be found for burial'.

[16] It seems odd to argue that 'the focus on the tomb in Mark may have been inspired by the importance of the graves of the heroes in the Graeco-Roman world. Even if the location of the tomb of Jesus was unknown to the author of Mark, and even if there were no cultic observances at the site of the tomb, it would still be important as a *literary* motif in characterising Jesus as hero-like,' Collins, 'Apotheosis', 93. If it is a *literary* motif, then why is there nothing in Mark's account to suggest a hero cult, and, in fact, features which deny it? In terms of actuality, if the tomb was unknown, and if there was no cult, then there is nothing to indicate Jesus was a hero here either. It was the cult given at a tomb that made a hero a hero!

A translation?

Is it instead a translation story?[17] The stories of people who disappeared, translated to another location, be it to some place on or under the earth, or to heaven, did not usually give them a tomb – let alone an empty one –, because a translation avoided death altogether.[18] The occasional exceptions which seem to be translations from out of a 'tomb', are, on closer examination, simply variants on the same theme.[19] To be translated was to avoid death altogether, or, in the case of Alcmene, at least to avoid being buried and going into the underworld (Plut. *Rom.* 28.6–8).

Once again, these stories do not compare favourably with Mark: Jesus very definitely dies, in fact, he is crucified; he is buried; and the supposed 'translation' occurs far too late, after he has presumably been in the underworld for three days.

The other problem with the proposal that Mark was using translation as a literary motif is that, by the first century, these translation stories were a thing of the mythological past based upon a psychology that had been largely superseded. Where they were utilised, as in the rhetoric surrounding the apotheosis of the rulers, it was in a modified form which no longer required a bodily translation.

A risen body

The young man did not announce Jesus had become a hero; nor that he had been translated; still less an aberrant mixture of the two;[20] but that 'he is risen' (ἠγέρθη).[21] What would this mean for Mark's Graeco-Roman readers?

Real bodies; insubstantial shades

The translation stories assumed an older view of the nature of human life. In Homeric tradition, real life was bodily life, and the afterlife could not properly be called 'life'.[22] Normally, at death the 'soul' flitted away from the body as its sinews were no longer able to hold the flesh and bones together (*Od.* 11.218ff.; cf. *Il.* 23.97ff.), and went to the afterlife as a shadow, not a body (cf. *Il.* 1.3–5; *Od.* 11).[23] When the privileged few

---

[17] Collins, 'Apotheosis', 88.   [18] Bolt, 'Mk 16:1–8', 34.   [19] Ibid., 35–7.

[20] The hero was distinguished from those who have been translated; see Rohde, *Psyche*, 121; Bolt, 'Mk 16:1–8', 34–6.

[21] This is not the language of translation, as even Bickermann, 'Grab', 286, admitted. Narratives used a range of language to refer to translations, e.g. the notion of disappearing, or becoming invisible (ἀφανιζ-), is frequent; if divinisation was involved, the ἀποθεωσ- or ἐκθειωσ- groups can be used; phrases expressing the changed location also occur ('from amongst men'/'to amongst the gods'). Cf. Pease, 'Some Aspects'.

[22] Rohde, *Psyche*, 4, 9.   [23] Riley, *Resurrection*, 29.

were granted immortality in the myths – being translated to immortality,[24] or to a special region on the edge of the world (the Elysian fields,[25] or Oceanus,[26] or the Isles of the Blessed[27]), or even to subterranean regions, separate from Hades[28] –, because they had avoided death altogether, their immortality was in the body.[29]

Soul to heaven; body to the earth

Between Homer and Plato this conception changed: the soul was derived from the upper world, and it was set in opposition to the body.[30] Orphism linked the soul and the air, for it came from τὸ ὅλον and was borne by the winds and entered the body through breathing (Arist. *De anima* 410^{b}28). At death, the soul abides in the air, but the bodies return to the earth, an idea which reverberates through literature and inscription (e.g. Eur. *Supp.* 531–6; *IG* I.2 945.6; *CIL* 3.6384; Peek, *GG* **353**, 2ff. (1st/2nd c. AD); Jub. 23.22; Sen. *ad Helv.*11.7; Philostr. *Vit. Ap.* 8.31).

With such ideas on the fate of the body at death, how would Graeco-Roman readers have heard the story of the empty tomb?

Apotheosis of virtuous souls

It had long been believed that the virtuous person's death was somehow different from that of others. 'By the quality of their lives, such outstanding individuals have overcome death itself.'[31] We have already seen the Pythagorean notion that the soul is released from the body on death, and, depending on its state of purgation, it is either reincarnated, or, if pure, it

---

[24] Calypso wishes to do so for Odysseus (*Od.* 5.135f.; 209f.; 23.335f.). Odysseus is rescued from the sea by Ino Leucothea who used to be mortal (*Od.* 5.333ff.) – had she been carried away by a god (cf. *Od.* 6.280f.)? Ganymede was similarly carried off (*Il.* 20.232ff.). Eos bore off the beautiful Orion (*Od.* 5.122ff.; cf. the story of Cleitos, 15.249f.).

[25] Menelaus is informed of the Elysian plain, where Rhadamanthys already dwells (*Od.* 4.560ff.).

[26] To where Penelope wishes to be transported, *Od.* 20.61–5; 79ff.

[27] The realm of Hesiod's fourth race, the heroes (*Op.* 170ff.).

[28] Rohde, *Psyche*, ch. III, mentions Amphiaraus; Trophonius; Caineus; Althaimenes; Amphilochus; Laodice; and Aristaius. Erechtheus, Hyacinthus, and Asclepius are examples of ancient gods living beneath the earth, whose subterranean dwelling becomes the 'grave' of their later hero worship.

[29] The post-Homeric poems increased the number of translations: in the *Cypria* Artemis immortalises Iphigeneia in the land of the Taurians; the *Aithiopis* has Eos giving immortality to Memnon, who had been killed by Achilles (rather than the *Iliad* story which had Sleep and Death bear off the body of Sarpedon to his own country for burial) and Thetis carrying the body of Achilles from the funeral pyre and bringing him to Leuke (contrast *Od.* 24.47ff.); in the *Telegoneia*, Odysseus is made immortal after being slain by Circe, and they dwell over the sea.

[30] Riley, *Resurrection*, 29.   [31] Parker, *Miasma*, 43, citing literature.

soars aloft, back to the divine (chapter 3, Suppliant 1). It is a small step to the idea that a man of great virtue would join the gods in some special kind of sense (cf. Cic. *Rep.* 2.17; Sir. 45.4–5 (Moses)).[32]

Unlike the older translations, apotheosis involved not the body, but only the soul. The funeral pyre was said to burn away the body so that the immortal part could ascend to the gods (Apollod. 2.7.7; Lucian *Herm.* 7; cf. *Pereg.* 4, 6, 30, cf. 33; *AG* 16.185). Heaven was the domain of souls, not bodies – which the virtuous man had spent his lifetime seeking to overcome.

This view of apotheosis rewarding virtue lay behind the imperial *apotheoseis*.

Apotheosis of the Roman rulers

As we have seen, Mark was launched upon the Roman world when it was still in transition with regard to the apotheosis of its rulers. The Romulus mythology had been pressed into its service, but the prevailing psychology meant that this was not bodily. When apotheosis became standard, the funeral ritual symbolised the heavenly ascent of the soul by releasing an eagle from a cage on top of the pyre (Dio 35.4; Hdn. 4.2; cf. Lucian *Pereg.* 39). But down below, the body (or an effigy) was still burning.

Bodily?

As we have seen, the idea of a temporary restoration to bodily life was not completely foreign to the Graeco-Roman. Some, such as Plutarch, had even heard of certain Oriental views on a more lasting future resurrection (Plut. *De I et O* 370C). But, given his Platonic views of soul and body, such views had to be labelled fabulous, for it was simply 'against nature' to insist that the body had a role in the afterlife. Even the mythological bodily translations were abhorrent (*Rom.* 28.4), 'improbably ascrib[ing] divinity to the mortal features in human nature, as well as to the divine' (6). Although he does not want to reject divinity arising from virtue, he is nonetheless adamant that 'to mix heaven with earth is foolish' (οὐρανῷ μιγνύειν γῆν ἀβέλτερον). The soul separates from the body, so that it 'becomes altogether pure, fleshless (ἄσαρκον)'.

> We must, therefore, definitely not against nature send the bodies of good people up together into heaven (οὐδὲν οὖν δεῖ τὰ σώματα τῶν ἀγαθῶν συναναπέμπειν παρὰ φύσιν εἰς οὐρανόν), but implicitly believe that in accordance with nature their virtues

---

[32] Cf. Hengel, *Son of God*, 25 n. 54, on Hercules' apotheosis.

and their souls, and divine justice, ascend from men to heroes, from heroes to demi-gods, and from demi-gods, after they have been made pure and holy, as in the final rites of initiation and have freed themselves from mortality and sense, to gods, not by civic law, but in very truth and according to right reason, thus achieving the fairest and most blessed consummation.

(Plut. *Rom.* 28.7–8)

The phrase 'by civic law' (νόμῳ πόλεως) may be directed at the Roman practice of divinising rulers by Senatorial decision. Plutarch's Pythagoreanism taught that all good souls will achieve this end, not by public law but by the practice of virtue. But, even with that quibble aside, he clearly considers a bodily apotheosis to be completely misguided, for 'to send bodies to heaven' is completely 'against nature'.[33]

Despite these views, Mark's concluding chapter presents an emptied tomb and an announcement that the 'body' which once lay in it 'is risen'.

The crucified one is risen
In what would be seen as a great paradox, the young man closely connects the risen one with the crucified one (v.6). To be crucified was such a horrendous death that it generally signalled that the person was under a curse. Such people did not gain rest in the underworld, and they were therefore the kind of ghosts that the magicians loved to use (βιαιοθάνατοι). On the other hand, any kind of removal from death was connected with a person's great virtue. If the apotheosis of Claudius was questioned partly because his lame foot showed him to be under the wrath of heaven (Sen. *Apoc.* 11, cf. 1), how would a crucified man ever be amongst the likely candidates for an apotheosis? He would be departing to dwell restlessly on the shores of Acheron, not amongst the gods.

But Mark's story has already insisted upon the fact that Jesus had to die and to die in this horrendous way. The portrayal of the scene on the mount of transfiguration suggested that Jesus refused the opportunity for an apotheosis. That was the moment when it should have occurred and yet he did not disappear, but came back down the mountain, for 'the Son of Man must suffer'. There would be no resurrection and no glorious kingdom of God without his prior suffering. From then on the narrative

---

[33] Cf. Celsus' vehement attacks against the doctrine of *bodily* resurrection, *c.Cels.* 5.14–15, e.g.: 'The soul may have everlasting life, but corpses, as Heraclitus said "ought to be thrown away as worse than dung"'; 2.55, 'But we must examine the question whether anyone who really died ever rose again with the same body.'

pressed relentlessly forward to his inevitable death. But now that he has suffered and died, resurrection has occurred: he is risen.

He was not a hero who died and from the underworld managed to make his presence still felt in the upper world. Nor was he translated, as one of the privileged few who avoided death altogether. Nor did he receive an apotheosis of soul, as some kind of reward above and beyond the rest of humanity, because of his own great virtue. Jesus' body was in the tomb, then it was no longer there, for 'he is risen'. This is clearly a resurrection, where a body – in fact, a crucified body – returns to life from the grave.

The resurrection of the Son of Man
Crucified

Jesus rose as the one who had been crucified. He had died a political death, crushed by those in power who refused to recognise his identity as Christ, Son of God. Ultimately, his death was because his leadership claims set him up as a king rivalling the Caesars. Unlike them, his leadership really did bring life where there was death, and this desire to bring life was a precipitating cause of his own death (3.5f.). But from Mark's point of view, he was crucified as part of the divine plan. He had saved others from the shadow of death, but, if he was to save others from death itself and bring them into the life of the kingdom, then he could not save himself. His death was the means by which others were ransomed from the grave.

Risen

His resurrection was therefore more than his own personal vindication. It was not a reward for his own moral virtues, which is then held out as a model to which Mark's readers can aspire. This would be to treat his resurrection as if it were an apotheosis on the imperial model. He had become so immersed in the pain and suffering of humanity that he was crushed by it himself. When he rose, his resurrected crucified body speaks of a hope for those similarly crushed by the various forces of death in the world. But it would be a misunderstanding of the event to interpret it in some kind of moralistic framework, as a hope held out to people in similar circumstances to those of Jesus, if they appropriately follow in his steps. Mark's suppliant stories have depicted a world filled with people in great need, who are all, in one way or another, victims of death and under its dark shadow. Not one of them had the resources simply to follow a perfect exemplar. They did not need an example, they needed to be rescued, which is exactly what Jesus did for them. To be saved, they needed to take what he had to give.

His actions on their behalf provide a picture of the larger theme of entering the kingdom. The narrative has stressed the impossibility of entering the kingdom through human means, but that it is achieved by God making the impossible possible. In the flow of the story, he does this by providing the ransoming death of the Son of Man. Entering the kingdom is not a matter of following an example, but of receiving what Jesus has to give.

When he rises from the dead, he does so as the Son of Man, who does not act on his own behalf, but on behalf of others. Jesus' resurrection is not only the defeat of death for himself, but it is also the defeat of death for others.

The kingdom in power
In Jesus' victory over death the kingdom of God comes with power – at least in his case. But according to Daniel 7, when the Son of Man received the kingdom, it would flow over to the rest of the saints. If Jesus has now risen and received the promised kingdom, then this holds hope for others. As the one who acted on behalf of the many, his victory was also victory for the many and he will share the kingdom with them.

But what kind of people were these 'many'? Mark's Gospel has already shown the kind of people these are: they are people like the suppliants, the crowds, the children, yes, and even the lapsed disciples. People in all kinds of very real, and very tragic, situations so much a part of the first-century world. Apotheosis of the soul held promise only for an elite. Those who were not amongst the great ones in terms of their achievements or their morality would have little hope. If they had some bodily disability, their chances were perhaps even more remote – see, for example, as one of the items mocking the apotheosis of Claudius, who suffered various defects,[34] in Seneca's satire: 'Look at his body, born under the wrath of heaven' (*Apoc.* 11, cf. 1). But, on the other hand, 'resurrection' was filled with promise to all those in a broken world who could not raise themselves from the dust and whose virtue could not save them. They had a champion who had gone ahead of them and, in going ahead of them, he had provided a ransom which guaranteed their future.

---

[34] Disturbed speech (Suet. 5 (*Claud.*).30; Dio Cass. 60.2); weak legs and ungainly gait (Suet. 5 (*Claud.*).30); inappropriate laughing fits and slobbering (Suet. 5 (*Claud.*).30; Juvenal 6.623); tremor (Suet. 5 (*Claud*).30; Dio Cass. 60.2; Juvenal 6.622). For brief discussion, see Moss, 'Mentality', 166–7, who suggests that he suffered from congenital cerebral palsy. His mother apparently often said that he was 'a monster: a man whom mother nature had begun to work upon but then flung aside' (Suet. 5 (*Claud.*).3).

For Mark's readers, the 'kingdoms of the beasts' (Dan. 7.1–12) were harsh reality, for the ability of human power to wreak havoc and to kill was painfully obvious. They also knew what it was like when unseen forces caused so much pain and suffering, before suddenly taking life away. Human mortality was a painful reality and the shadow of death hung heavily across the nations. Mark's Gospel spoke of a coming kingdom, which was life, not death; salvation, not corruption; and for those who continued to live under the shadow of death, Mark presented the assurance that something had been done about human mortality: a crucified man had defeated death.

8

CONCLUSIONS: MARK'S IMPACT ON EARLY READERS

Conclusions on method

This study has adopted a reader-oriented method, but has attempted to move beyond the textual construct known as the implied reader to examine the potential impact of the Gospel on real flesh-and-blood readers. The examination of the interface between the ancient text and the ancient reader utilised the combination of a reader-oriented literary analysis and a type of social description closely linked to Mark's vocabulary. The analysis of the text from two directions (text to implied reader; flesh-and-blood reader to text) has proved to be a useful way of approaching the ancient reading experience in order to examine the potential impact of Mark upon its early readers.

In particular, the study has focused upon the role of the thirteen suppliants in the creation of Mark's narrative impact. The analysis of the axis 'text to implied reader', paying close attention to focalisation and the dynamics of distance, showed that the narrative creates strong identification, aligning these characters with the implied readers. In addition, it was noted that the suppliants are not presented merely as types, subordinated to a plot deemed more important. Instead, through the often quite detailed presentation of their situations of need, i.e., their physical and social circumstances, the narrative presents them as person-like characters whom real readers could recognise as examples of people known to them from their real world. If the arguments of this study are accepted, future discussions of Mark's narrative dynamics will have to give greater attention to these characters, and the previous functionalist framework within which the discussion has been conducted will have to be rejected in favour of one allowing greater complexity. Since the text presents these characters as person-like and creates strong identification with them, the suppliants form a natural contact-point between the text and the real world. The early flesh-and-blood readers would see the suppliants not as role models whom they ought to emulate, but as people like themselves

living in a world with great problems, and so they would be drawn into
the story. As a slice-of-life drawn from the first-century Graeco-Roman
world, their presence in the narrative reveals that Mark is concerned less
with morality, than mortality.

The analysis of the axis '(flesh-and-blood) reader to text' attempted
to recover the assumptions which early Graeco-Roman readers would
have in regard to the suppliants' various problems. The starting point for
the recovery of their 'mental register' or 'repertoire' was the vocabulary
used by Mark to describe the suppliants' problems, or closely related
vocabulary and concepts, although the direction in which the discussion
moved varied with the particular condition. A special feature of the study
is the discussion of material of relevance to the various conditions in Mark
drawn from the magical sources. By this means, it was discovered that
the various conditions would have all been regarded far more seriously
by first-century readers than by those of the present day.

Without a doubt more research could be done along these lines. This
study has by no means exhausted the relevant material in the ancient
sources. More could still be done to provide an 'emic' explanation through
the recovery of ancient understandings of these illnesses and their social
effects, and the understanding(s) of the body and disease as taught by
the philosophers and as assumed by medical practice. Although the discussion of Mark's illnesses has not been exhaustive, it has vindicated the
method. The recovery of ancient perceptions of the illnesses represented
in Mark's suppliant stories has enhanced the understanding of the potential impact of these stories on early readers. The study has argued that
each illness was a serious condition closely linked to death.

Similar points could be made concerning the comparative use of the
magical material. As the renaissance of the study of magic continues
and more information comes to light, further research into magical view-
points and practices could be profitably done in the attempt to enhance
the understanding of the early impact of Mark's suppliant stories. Further
attention to questions of the development (or otherwise) of magical thinking and practice, and of the use for first-century comparative purposes of
material from other time periods, is bound to offer fruitful insights into
Mark's potential impact on early readers. Closer attention to geographical distinctives in the magical material may also prove useful, despite
the fact that Mark's geographical provenance will probably continue to
be a matter of some debate. But once again, even though more could be
done, the comparative work in this study has achieved at least two key
results. It has been argued that in Mark's world *daimones* were linked
with the dead, and that each of the conditions suffered by the suppliants

could have drawn the suspicion that it had a magical cause. The stronger the suspicion, the more the suppliant would be seen to be under the sway of the dead.

Jesus' defeat of death

The result of the inquiry for understanding Mark's narrative has been to suggest that each of the suppliants in Mark lived under the shadow of death. Albeit with varying degrees of certainty, it has been argued that each condition depicted in the healing and exorcism scenes brought the sufferer close to death itself and/or under the sway of the dead. As such, each of the thirteen suppliant stories relates to Jesus' defeat of death. Jesus dealt with the spirits of the dead (Suppliants 1, 6, 9, 12). He cured people from death-dealing disease (Suppliants 2,?9, 12) and from illnesses which made a person almost dead – since they attacked crucial bodily structures (Suppliants 4, 5, 12). He rescued others from being numbered amongst the living dead (Suppliants 3, 6, 8, 9, 10, 11, 12, 13), from being 'metaphorically dead' (Suppliant 5), from the point of death (Suppliant 7a), and, even better, from death itself (Suppliant 7b). Thus, when read from this reconstructed perspective, the healing/exorcism scenes show Jesus dealing with death on two fronts: he rescued people from the power of death and from the power of the dead. This study has therefore endorsed the conclusion that, in Mark, Jesus' 'overarching opponent is death itself'.[1]

It also endorses the opinion that the scenes involving the suppliants contain the message of the Gospel in microcosm.[2] By showing Jesus defeating death in some form, the suppliants provide entry-points to Mark's larger narrative which presents the same message: Jesus died in order to bring in the (general) resurrection of the dead and the kingdom of God. The 'salvation' and 'life' which the suppliants received from Jesus, i.e., removal of their physical, bodily ailments, with all the associated encumbrances which went with the illness, were, for them, a foretaste of the 'salvation' and 'life' that will be eternal, i.e., beyond the resurrection from the dead in the kingdom of God. For the reader, this foretaste becomes a demonstration within human history that there is a 'living hope' (cf. 1 Peter 1.3) secured by Jesus Christ's resurrection.

[1] Wegener, *Cruciformed*, 78.

[2] Robinson, *Problem*, 87–8, on 5.1–20 and 9.14–29, compared the victory over death and violence in the exorcisms to the victory over death in Jesus' resurrection (cf. Nineham, *Mark*, 243 n.†). 'In the exorcisms, Jesus is struggling for life and communion on behalf of the possessed person. Both of these characteristics of a true historical existence had been opposed by the demon' (p. 90). Wilder, *Rhetoric*, 37, also spoke of the healing and exorcism stories as the dramatisation of the Gospel story.

Jesus' defeat of death and Mark's early readers

From the beginning of the Gospel, Jesus' story is set within the framework of the expectation of the coming of the kingdom of God. The narrative presents him as an alternative leader to those in power in the first-century world, and it heads relentlessly towards his crucifixion when he is loudly proclaimed to be king. The narrative presents his death as a divine necessity, for he had to die before the resurrection and the kingdom of God would arrive. Refusing to avoid death through apotheosis, Jesus willingly embraced this difficult necessity. When he died, he was recognised as Son of God, but even then he did not undergo an apotheosis of soul as the great Caesars had done. Instead, Mark's final chapter shows that he was raised bodily from the dead.

Jesus, despite being crucified, had defeated death. This was not simply an act of virtue on his own behalf, but, according to the expectations erected by the narrative, his death was the ransom which was God's means of guaranteeing entry to the kingdom of God for the many, for whom it would be impossible to enter any other way. Through delivering the suppliants out from the shadow of death, Jesus was demonstrating in individual cases what he had come to do on the grand scale. Their liberation from death was part of a programme aiming at the liberation of many others from death itself.

Jesus' resurrection holds hope for others. This hope was not just for the virtuous, or for the bodily whole, but for all who cared to take up his invitation to follow him. It was more difficult for the great ones of the world to respond than it was for those regarded as least. The suppliants were concrete historical recipients of the mercy of God through Jesus. They represent a moment in time when Jesus' salvation was felt in an embodied form. They came to him in all the brokenness of their particular expression of human mortality and Jesus brought them from the shadow of death into life. They were paradigmatic for any who recognised their own mortality and their need to plead for mercy to someone who could do something about this problem. Any who knew what it was like to live under the shadow of death could draw hope from Jesus' action on their behalf. With Bartimaeus, they could hear Jesus' call to follow, being prepared to die for his sake and the gospel's in order to rise again in the resurrection.

For Mark presents Jesus as more than simply a role model, whose example is relevant even when facing death. Jesus is presented as the one who defeated death, both in his ministry to the suppliants and ultimately through his own death and resurrection. Living in a world so keenly aware of human mortality, Mark's readers would know what it meant to cry, 'Do you not care that we are perishing?' Once they had been engaged by Mark's Gospel, they would also know the answer to this question: Jesus cared enough to die, so that others might live. To save others, he did not even save himself. He cared for those who are perishing and opened the way into the kingdom of God.

Jesus' defeat of death as 'gospel' for the early readers

Mark's Gospel claims to provide the foundation of the gospel message (cf. 1.1) that was already being proclaimed to the first-century world by the movement which arose in the wake of the events surrounding Jesus of Nazareth. It proclaimed Jesus in terms familiar to that world from the imperial rhetoric. The imperial cult was an instrument which structured the reality of the Roman world and which imposed a definition of the world and its relationship to the Caesars. Mark's narrative also attempted to structure reality, but through an alternative definition of the world and in relationship to God, not Caesar. The ultimate future concerned the coming kingdom of God, not the future of Rome. The ruler who held the hope of the healing of the nations did not arise from Caesar's household, but from an obscure family in Galilee. The Son of God who was the source of life for a world on the brink of destruction was not Caesar, but Jesus of Nazareth. His coronation was not by way of a grand public triumph, but by way of the public humiliation of a cross.

His leadership was not established through military muscle and it left no trail of blood, but, instead, it brought life where there was already death. To those who experienced the *imperium* 'from below', his leadership offered an alternative 'beginning of good news' by bringing the hope of resurrection. Daily life was lived under the shadow of death, but, by dying, this Son of God had cared for those who were perishing. He had defeated death.

This was good news for the Graeco-Roman world. The sociologist Rodney Stark suggests that the 'immense popular appeal of the early church' needs to be explained by reference to 'how the message of the New Testament and the social relations it sustained solved acute problems afflicting Greco-Roman cities'.[3] He reconstructs a portrait of these cities, as being places filled with 'urban disorder, social dislocation, filth, disease, misery, fear, and cultural chaos', and he argues that these circumstances 'gave Christianity the opportunity to exploit fully its immense competitive

---

[3] Stark, *Rise*, 147.

advantages vis-à-vis paganism and other religious movements of the day as a *solution* to these problems'.[4] Christianity acted as a 'revitalisation movement that arose in response to the misery, chaos, fear, and brutality of life in the urban Greco-Roman world'.[5]

Despite the long-standing approach to sociology which downplays the importance of belief,[6] Stark has demonstrated that belief – and so doctrine – was an 'essential factor'[7] in the rise of early Christianity. Ideas cannot be reduced to mere epiphenomena, but are often 'critical factors in determining not only individual behavior but, indeed, the path of history'.[8] Early Christianity's focus on the centrality of belief was a radical departure in the ancient world,[9] where 'religion' was about practice and ritual, not belief and behaviour. The corresponding focus upon words, with preaching, teaching and discussion, on the one hand, and hearing, teaching and persuasion, on the other, which was such a trademark of the early churches, aligned them more with a philosophical movement than with traditional religion.[10] Perhaps this is one reason why Christianity made such a great impact upon the intellectual classes from the beginning.[11]

But it was also the radical difference between the *content* of paganism and Christian belief that was a crucial factor in the success of this new movement.[12] One doctrine is particularly singled out by Stark, namely, the belief in the future resurrection from the dead (Stark: 'future heavenly existence'). In sociological terms, the attractiveness of a religion can be explained in terms of its ability to compensate people for desired rewards

[4] Ibid., 149.   [5] Ibid., 161.

[6] Ibid., 14–15. Some historians are 'allergic' to discussions about how doctrines shape social factors, because they are 'too much influenced by out-of-date, and always absurd, Marxist claims that ideas are mere epiphenomena'; others, because they wish to avoid a 'triumphalism', in which Christianity succeeds due to having 'better' doctrines; ibid., 209. Stark mentions A. von Harnack, L. Michael White and Jaroslav Pelikan as being disparaged for this latter 'crime'.

[7] Ibid., 4. To give one example, Stark shows how the well-known initial influx of women into the early Christian movement 'resulted from Christian doctrines prohibiting infanticide and abortion' (p. 95).

[8] Ibid., 79.   [9] Brooten, 'Belief?', 472, 475, 479.

[10] Cf. '[T]he meetings which had first assembled in the wake of Paul's preaching would hardly have been recognised by their contemporaries as religious societies', Judge, *Conversion*, 6. Cf. 'Social Identity', 209, 212–17; 'Early Christians'.

[11] Ramsay, *Church*, 57; cf. 133–4, 146–7. Cf. Judge, 'Social Identity', 209, 212–17; *Conversion*. As a cult movement, sociologically speaking, it is to be expected that the greatest success would be amongst the middle and upper classes. Stark, *Rise*, 45 (summing up the arguments of ch. 2).

[12] 'The *contents* of Christian and pagan beliefs were *different* in ways that greatly determined not only their explanatory capacities but also their relative capacities to mobilize human resources', ibid., 79.

which are either scarce, or which seem to be unavailable to anyone, at least in this world.[13] 'The most obvious of these [i.e., the latter], and perhaps the one most intensely sought by humans, is victory over death. No one, rich or poor, can gain eternal life by direct methods in the here and now.'[14] This helps to explain what Stark calls 'the *universal* aspect of religious commitment', since it accounts for the fact that

> in certain respects everyone is potentially deprived and in need of the comforts of faith. It is this proposition that explains why the upper classes are religious at all, why they too are susceptible to faith (something Marxist theories can only dismiss as aberration or as a phoney pose meant to lull the proletariat into false consciousness). Moreover, [it] explains why the more privileged are drawn to cult movements.[15]

This belief contrasted with the pagan gods, who 'offered no salvation [. . . and neither did they] provide an escape from mortality'.[16] Galen, with no belief in an afterlife, deserted the sick in the great plague of AD 180, but the Christians, finding comfort in their belief in a future heavenly existence, were enabled to care for the sick, despite the personal risk to themselves.[17] Galen himself recognised the action springing from this doctrine, 'their contempt of death (and of its sequel) is patent to us every day'.[18] Lucian had also noticed the importance of this doctrine to the Christians subject to his ridicule: 'The poor wretches have convinced themselves [. . .] that they are going to be immortal and live for all time' (*Pereg.* 13). Noting its centrality to the Christian movement, Celsus spent a great deal of time refuting the resurrection of the flesh.[19] What the second-century pagan critics of Christianity noticed, the apostle Paul had already proclaimed. If this new movement was to be distilled to the level of a slogan, then he would say that, like him, it 'was on trial for the resurrection of the dead' (Acts 23.6; 24.14–21; 26.4–8; cf. 1 Cor. 15). It was this central belief that met people in their mortality, and gave them back their humanity.[20]

---

[13] Ibid., 35–6.   [14] Ibid., 36.
[15] Ibid., 36–7. 'Cult' is a technical, descriptive term in sociology, for which early Christianity qualifies.
[16] Ibid., 88.
[17] Ibid., 80, 36. See the evidence and argument of ibid., ch. 4, and also 'Epidemics, Rise'.
[18] Quoted from Benko, *Pagan Rome*, 142.
[19] According to Origen, Celsus 'often reproached us about the resurrection' (*c.Cels.* 8.4.9).
[20] Stark, *Rise*, 215, concludes his book with: 'What Christianity gave to its converts was nothing less than their humanity.'

If the arguments in this book are correct, Mark's Gospel could have played an important role in the early Christian mission, persuading people to this central belief.

Mark's narrative impact on early Graeco-Roman readers

Mark certainly aims to promote belief, or faith – which are, of course, two English renderings of the same Greek word (πίστις). Faith, however, is not a trait or attribute to be adopted and imitated, but a stance towards Jesus produced by the narrative as it works on the reader during the reading experience. During the reading, Mark is working to produce an impact upon the implied readers such that their beliefs conform to those of the implied author.

> It is only as I read that I become the self whose beliefs must coincide with the author's. Regardless of my real beliefs and practices, I must subordinate my mind and heart to the book if I am to enjoy it to the full. The author creates, in short, an image of himself and another image of his reader; he makes his reader, as he makes his second self, and the most successful reading is one in which the created selves, author and reader, can find complete agreement.[21]

Given the ideal reading experience, the narrative itself moves the reader towards this position of 'faith'. The ideal reader (unlike the 'critic') does not have a detachment, an 'aesthetic distance', from the story, but is thoroughly engaged in it and is moved by it. From the beginning, the implied author guides the readers, moving them to adopt a stance towards the events and characters of the story which they are expected to believe. In this way, 'the narrative obliges the reader to adopt the position of believer for the duration of the story'.[22]

In several of the suppliant stories, the people concerned were commended by Jesus for having faith, and they were told that it was by faith they were saved. For the suppliants, faith was the attitude which turned to Jesus in their need as the one who could deal with the sufferings of their mortality. The reader is being educated by all these scenes to give his/her assent: this is exactly the right thing for the suppliants to have done! As the suppliant stories are read within the complexity of the narrative, the reader is also led to know who Jesus really is, to see him reacting in all kinds of circumstances, and eventually to see him crucified as king and

[21] Booth, *Fiction*, 138.   [22] Sankey, 'Promise', 17.

then rise from the grave. All of this is transmitted to the ideal reader in such a way as to command his/her assent implicitly. In other words, the narrative has so worked on the reader that the correct stance towards Jesus (i.e., 'faith') is already created in the process of reading.

If a flesh-and-blood reader is willing to 'suspend disbelief' and enter into Mark's story, then he/she has already become a believer, at least for the duration of the story. If the reader is persuaded that Mark's message is true, then they remain a believer, even beyond the reading experience. On this understanding, Mark's Gospel would be creating a believing community as it is being read. We have already noted, in regard to irony, that the relationship between reader and narrator creates community. What is true on the micro level of the various scenes is also true on the macro level of the whole Gospel.

> All persons reading the [G]ospel, to the extent that they see through the author's use of irony, become a community, a community not produced by ties of race, culture, or politics, but produced by the common experience of reading and understanding Mark's irony. In short, Booth has given us what I think is the clearest insight into the rhetorical strategy of the Gospel writer that has hitherto existed.[23]

The whole narrative has worked towards the one goal, i.e., to persuade the reader to adopt a certain stance towards Jesus. This stance is 'faith', and this 'faith' creates community.

Mark achieves this through his total narrative presentation. Within this portrayal the characters have an important role, as they interact in the web of relationships between other characters, and with the other features and events of the narrative.[24] This study has argued that the suppliants contribute to the narrative complexity through 'making contact' with real readers, in order to deliver them up to the main story. The disciples provide continuity, so that by the end of the narrative the readers are following along with them towards Jesus' death and resurrection, which must occur before the kingdom of God arrives. All the time, the focus is upon Jesus at the centre of all viewing angles, for his identity and his action on behalf of real people suffering in this mortal world are a key issue in Mark. Understanding him correctly is what promotes faith. He is the Christ, the divine Son of God. He is the one who cares for the perishing. He is the

---

[23] Fowler, 'Reader – Mark?', 53, referring to Booth, *Irony*.

[24] Cf. Pelling, 'Conclusion', 261–2, warns of the need to do character study as an aspect of the whole narrative.

one who did not shrink from going to the cross as a ransom for many. He is the crucified man who rose from the grave to give mortal human beings the solid hope of resurrection.

Mark's Gospel: Jesus' defeat of death

Although the suppliants are presented to the reader with a variety of conditions, these are all variants of the one problem, namely, mortality. Thus the suppliants, both individually and collectively, combine to show that the real concern of the narrative is with Jesus caring for the perishing (cf. 4.38). These 'case studies', drawn from amongst those who experienced the embodiment of Jesus' salvation while he was bodily present in human history, point to his greater victory when 'death shall be no more' (Rev. 21.4; cf. 1 Cor. 15.26, 54–55). The 'salvation' and 'life' they received point to the eternal 'salvation' and 'life' that will be found in the kingdom of God.

The narrative dynamics do not lead flesh-and-blood readers to expect healing from their own particular suffering. The historical nature of Mark's narrative (albeit in 'apocalyptic mode') clearly associates such healing with the physical presence of Jesus and his disciples. But the stories of these real-world people point to the abiding significance of Jesus for generations to come. Illness in the first century was no mere inconvenience, but almost every illness was a potential manifestation of death itself. It was not the fear of illness that had to be addressed by all the philosophers, but the fear of death. According to Seneca, 'most men ebb and flow in wretchedness between the fear of death and the hardships of life' (*Ep.* 4.6). As Jung would say of many modern anxieties,[25] Lucretius evaluated the worries of Roman aristocrats as 'the symptoms of a "sickness" whose primary cause is an unrecognized fear of death'.[26] The world reading Mark's Gospel was well aware of living under the shadow of death. This is the problem that was dealt the decisive blow by Jesus.[27]

As the alternative to other proposed solutions to this problem, Mark proclaims the gospel of Jesus Christ, the Son of God. There is a world

[25] 'Jung suggests that a good many of the people who go to psychotherapists in the twentieth century are really suffering from the lack of any strong moral or spiritual conviction; and that older people, especially, are troubled essentially by the fear of death. If people were troubled for similar reasons in the Ancient World, they had no shortage of would-be therapists, especially for the treatment of the fear of death,' Gill, 'Ancient Psychotherapy', 325. Here he draws upon Jung, *Modern Man*, 120ff.

[26] Gill, 'Ancient Psychotherapy', 322, referring to Lucretius 3.105ff. (see 31–116).

[27] Several interpreters have noticed that the narrative impact of Mark strikes at the fear of death: e.g., Wegener, 'Reading Mark's Gospel', 468–70.

ruler other than Caesar. Death is no longer the only thing hovering on the horizon of human life. Jesus brought the promise of the kingdom of God, entered through the resurrection from the dead. After dealing with so many manifestations of death in our world while he was alive, Jesus himself rose from the dead. Jesus is the champion who has clearly shown to a suffering world that he cares that we are perishing. He cared enough to die, on behalf of the many, and then this crucified man rose again from the grave, bringing hope for all. In the midst of a world crying out in its suffering and mortality, 'Don't you care that we are perishing?', Jesus has defeated death.

BIBLIOGRAPHY

Primary Sources

Computer Resources

CD Rom & software

In order to do the vocabulary research necessary for this book, I had frequent recourse to the TLG and PHI data bases on CD Rom. I used the IBYCUS computer at Tyndale House Centre for Biblical Research, Cambridge, as well as the Silver Mountain TLG Workplace software both at Tyndale and at Moore Theological College library, Sydney. The TLG/PHI CD Roms gave me access to all the critical editions of the relevant texts, but, for convenience, I have also made extensive use of Loeb series, and so I have included this series in the bibliography below. The computerised texts enabled me to check the Loeb texts against the critical editions. Where a source has been accessed solely through the CD Rom, this is indicated in the bibliography by the annotation: [TLG].

In conjunction with the use of the CD Rom databases, reference was made to

Bercowitz, L., Squitier, K.A. & Johnson, W.A. *Thesaurus Linguae Graecae. Canon of Greek Authors and Works* (New York & Oxford: Oxford University Press, ^{3}1990).

Websites referred to in text

http://www.geographic.org

http://www.lib.umich.edu/pap/magic/agg.display.html

Literary sources

Aelianus

A.F. Scholfield, *Aelian On the Characteristics of Animals* II *Bks VI–XI* (LCL; Cambridge, Mass. & London: Harvard University Press & W. Heinemann, 1959, repr. 1971).

Aelius Aristides

C.A. Behr, *P. Aelius Aristides. The Complete Works* II *Orations XVII–LIII* (Leiden: E.J. Brill, 1981).

Aeschines
M.R. Dilts, *Scholia in Aeschinem* (Leipzig: Teubner, 1992).

Aeschylus
H.W. Smyth, *Aeschylus* I (LCL; Cambridge, Mass. & London: Harvard University Press & W. Heinemann, 1922, repr. 1973).
H.W. Smyth, *Aeschylus* II (LCL; Cambridge, Mass. & London: Harvard University Press & W. Heinemann, 1926, repr. 1983).

Alexander
F. Jacoby, *Die Fragmente der griechischen Historiker* (Leiden: E.J. Brill, 1962), II.B.650.
L. Pearson, *The Lost Histories of Alexander* (London: Blackwell, 1960).

Anonymi Medici
TLG 021 = Περὶ τροφῶν δυνάμεως, in A. Delatte, *Anecdota Atheniensa et alia* (Paris: Droz, 1939), II: 467–79. [TLG]

Anthologia Graeca
W.R. Paton, *The Greek Anthology* II (LCL; London & Cambridge, Mass.: W. Heinemann & Harvard University Press, 1917, repr. 1970).
W.R. Paton, *The Greek Anthology* V (LCL; Cambridge, Mass. & London: Harvard University Press & W. Heinemann, 1918, repr. 1979).

Antiphanes
Aphrodisius fr. 53, in T. Kock, *Comicorum Atticorum fragmenta* II *Novae Comoediae fragmenta pars I* (Leipzig: Teubner, 1884).

Apocryphal New Testament
J.K. Elliott, *The Apocryphal New Testament. A Collection of Apocryphal Christian Literature in an English Translation* (Oxford: Clarendon, 1993).

Apollodorus
J.G. Frazer, *Apollodorus. The Library* I (LCL; Cambridge, Mass. & London: Harvard University Press & W. Heinemann, 1921, repr. 1967).
J.G. Frazer, *Apollodorus. The Library* II (LCL; London & New York: W. Heinemann & W.H. Putnam, 1921, repr. 1963).

Apollonius Rhodius
R.C. Seaton, *Apollonius Rhodius. The Argonautica* (LCL; Cambridge, Mass. & London: Harvard University Press & W. Heinemann, 1912, repr. 1988).

Appian
H. White, *Appian's Roman History* III (London & New York: W. Heinemann & W.H. Putnam, 1913, repr. 1933).

Apuleius
H.E. Butler & A.S. Owen, *Apulei Apologia sive pro se de magia liber* (Oxford: Clarendon, 1914).
H.E. Butler, *The Apologia and Florida of Apuleius of Madaura* (Oxford: Clarendon, 1909).
J.A. Hanson, *Apuleius Metamorphoses* I *Bks 1–6* (LCL; Cambridge, Mass. & London: Harvard University Press, 1989).
J.A. Hanson, *Apuleius Metamorphoses* II *Bks 7–11* (LCL; Cambridge, Mass. & London: Harvard University Press, 1989).

Aretaeus [TLG]
K. Hude, *Aretaeus. De causis et signis acutorum morborum*, in *Corpus medicorum Graecorum* II (Berlin: Akademie-Verlag, ²1958), 3–143.

Aristophanes
B.B. Rogers, *Aristophanes* I (LCL; London & Cambridge, Mass.: W. Heinemann & Harvard University Press, 1924, repr. 1982).
B.B. Rogers, *Aristophanes* II (LCL; London & Cambridge, Mass.: W. Heinemann & Harvard University Press, 1924, repr. 1979).
B.B. Rogers, *Aristophanes* III (LCL; Cambridge, Mass. & London: Harvard University Press & W. Heinemann, 1924, repr. 1991).
Tagēnistai, fr. = Stob. 121.18, in J.M. Edmonds, *The Fragments of Attic Comedy After Meineke, Bergk, and Kock* I (Leiden, E.J. Brill, 1957).

Aristor of Keos
F. Wehrli, *Lykon und Ariston von Keos* (Die Schule des Aristoteles, vol. XVI; Basel: Schwabe, ²1968).

Aristotle
W.S. Hett, *Aristotle* VIII *On the Soul. Parva Naturalia. On Breath* (LCL; Cambridge, Mass. & London: Harvard University Press & W. Heinemann, 1936, rev. 1957, repr. 1986).
W.S. Hett, *Aristotle* XIV *Minor Works* (LCL; London & Cambridge, Mass.: W. Heinemann & Harvard University Press, 1936, repr. 1980).
W.S. Hett, *Aristotle* XV *Problems I* (LCL; London & Cambridge, Mass.: W. Heinemann & Harvard University Press, 1926, repr. 1970).
H. Rackham, *Aristotle* XX *The Athenian Constitution. The Eudemian Ethics. On Virtues and Vices* (LCL; Cambridge, Mass. & London: Harvard University Press & W. Heinemann, 1935, rev. 1952, repr. 1981).

Arnobius
A. Reifferscheid, *Corpus Scriptorum Ecclesiasticorum Latinorum (1866–)*.

Arrian

W.A. Oldfather, *Epictetus. The Discourses as Reported by Arrian, the Manual, and Fragments* I (LCL; Cambridge, Mass. & London: Harvard University Press & W. Heinemann, 1925, repr. 1967).

W.A. Oldfather, *Epictetus. The Discourses as Reported by Arrian, the Manual, and Fragments* II (LCL; Cambridge, Mass. & London: Harvard University Press & W. Heinemann, 1928, repr. 1966).

Artemidorus

R. A. Pack, *Artemidori Daldiani onirocriticon libri v* (Leipzig: Teubner, 1963).

Athenaeus

C.B. Gulick, *Athenaeus. The Deipnosophists* V *Bks. XI–XII* (LCL; London & Cambridge, Mass.: W. Heinemann & Harvard University Press, 1933, repr. 1963).

Ausonius

H.G. Evelyn White, *Ausonius* (LCL; Cambridge, Mass. and London: Harvard University Press and W. Heinemann, 1919–21).

Caelius Aurelianus

I.E. Drabkin, *On Acute Diseases & On Chronic Diseases. Caelii Aureliani Methodici Siccensis celerum vel acutarum passionum* (Chicago: University of Chicago Press, 1950).

Calpurnius Siculus

J.W. Duff & A.M. Duff, *Minor Latin Poets* I (LCL; Cambridge, Mass. & London: Harvard University Press & W. Heinemann, 1934, rev. 1935, repr. 1982).

Cat. Cod. Astr.

F. Cumont, *Catalogus Codicum Astrologorum* (Brussels, 1898–).

Celsus

H. Chadwick, *Origen: Contra Celsum* (Cambridge: Cambridge University Press, 1953).

Celsus Med.

W.G. Spencer, *Celsus. De medicina* I *Bks. I–IV* (LCL; London & Cambridge, Mass.: W. Heinemann & Harvard University Press, 1935).

W.G. Spencer, *Celsus. De medicina* II *Bks. V–VI* (LCL; London & Cambridge, Mass.: W. Heinemann & Harvard University Press, 1938, repr. 1961).

W.G. Spencer, *Celsus. De medicina* III *Bks. VII–VIII* (LCL; London & Cambridge, Mass.: W. Heinemann & Harvard University Press, 1938, repr. 1961).

Christ's Descent into Hell = Gospel of Nicodemus 17–27
E. Hennecke, *New Testament Apocrypha* I *Gospels and Related Writings* (trans. and ed. R.McL. Wilson; London: Lutterworth, 1963 (German: 1959)).

John Chrysostom
A Library of Fathers of the Holy Catholic Church Anterior to the Division of the East and the West. Homilies on Matthew II (Oxford: J.H. Parker, 1843).

Cicero
R. Gardner, *Cicero. The Speeches. Pro Sestio and In Vatinum* (LCL; London & Cambridge, Mass.: W. Heinemann & Harvard University Press, 1958).
H.G. Hodge, *Cicero. The Speeches. Pro lege Manilia. Pro Caecina. Pro Cluentio. Pro Rabirio. Perduellionis* (LCL: Cambridge, Mass. & London: Harvard University Press & W. Heinemann, 1927, repr. 1966).
C.W. Keyes, *Cicero. De re republica. De legibus* (LCL; London & New York: W. Heinemann & W.H. Putnam, 1928).
W. Miller, *Cicero* XXI *De officiis* (LCL; Cambridge, Mass. & London: Harvard University Press, 1913, repr. 1990).
D.R. Shackleton Bailey, *Cicero* XXIX. *Cicero Letters to Atticus IV* (LCL: Cambridge, Mass. & London: Harvard University Press, 1999).

Clement of Alexandria
A. Roberts & J. Donaldson, *The Ante-Nicene Fathers* II *Fathers of the Second Century* (Edinburgh & Grand Rapids: T. & T. Clark & Eerdmans, repr. 1989).

Clementine Recognitions
A. Roberts & J. Donaldson, *The Ante-Nicene Fathers* VIII *The Twelve Patriarchs, Excerpts and Epistles, The Clementina, Apocrypha, Decretals, Memoirs of Edessa and Syriac Documents, Remains of the First Ages* (Edinburgh & Grand Rapids: T. & T. Clark & Eerdmans, repr. 1989).

Cyranides
D. Kaimakis, *Die Kyraniden* (Meisenheim am Glan: Hain, 1976) [TLG]

Demosthenes
J.H. Vince, *Demosthenes* III *Against Meidias, Androtion, Aristocrates. Timocrates, Aristogeiton XXI–XXVI* (LCL: Cambridge, Mass. & London: Harvard University Press & W. Heinemann, 1935, repr. 1986).
A.T. Murray, *Demosthenes* V *Private Orations XLI–XLIX* (LCL; London & Cambridge, Mass.: W. Heinemann & Harvard University Press, 1939, repr. 1964).
N.W. & N.J. De Witt, *Demosthenes* VII *Funeral Speech, Erotic Essay (Or. LX, LXI). Exordia and Letters* (LCL; London & Cambridge, Mass.: W. Heinemann & Harvard University Press, 1949, repr. 1986).
M.R. Dilts, *Scholia Demosthenica* I (Leipzig: Teubner, 1983).

Dio Cassius

E. Cary, *Dio's Roman History* VI (LCL; London & Cambridge, Mass.: W. Heinemann & Harvard University Press, 1917, repr. 1968).

E. Cary & H.B. Foster, *Dio's Roman History* VII (LCL; London & Cambridge, Mass.: W. Heinemann & Harvard University Press, 1924, repr. 1968).

E. Cary & H.B. Foster, *Dio's Roman History* VIII (LCL; London & Cambridge, Mass.: W. Heinemann & Harvard University Press, 1925, repr. 1968).

Dio Chrysostom

J. W. Cohoon, *Dio Chrysostom* II (LCL; Cambridge, Mass. & London: Harvard University Press & W. Heinemann, 1939, repr. 1977).

J.W. Cohoon & H.L. Crosby, *Dio Chrysostom* III *Discourses XXI–XXXVI* (LCL; London & Cambridge, Mass.: W. Heinemann & Harvard University Press, 1940, repr. 1979).

H.L. Crosby, *Dio Chrysostom* IV *Discourses XXXVII–LX* (LCL; London & Cambridge, Mass.: W. Heinemann & Harvard University Press, 1946, repr. 1962).

H.L. Crosby, *Dio Chrysostom* V *Discourses LXI–LXXX* (LCL; London & Cambridge, Mass.: W. Heinemann & Harvard University Press, 1951, repr. 1964).

Diodorus Siculus

C.H. Oldfather, *Diodorus of Sicily* I (LCL; London & Cambridge, Mass.: W. Heinemann & Harvard University Press, 1933, repr. 1968).

C.H. Oldfather, *Diodorus of Sicily* III (LCL; London & Cambridge, Mass.: W. Heinemann & Harvard University Press, 1939, repr. 1970).

C.H. Oldfather, *Diodorus of Sicily* IV (LCL; London & Cambridge, Mass.: W. Heinemann & Harvard University Press, 1946, repr. 1970).

C.H. Oldfather, *Diodorus of Sicily* V (LCL; London & Cambridge, Mass.: W. Heinemann & Harvard University Press, 1950, repr. 1976).

F.R. Walton & R.M. Geer, *Diodorus of Sicily* XII (LCL; London & Cambridge, Mass.: W. Heinemann & Harvard University Press, 1967).

Diogenes Laertius

R.D. Hicks, *Diogenes Laertius. Lives of Eminent Philosophers* I (LCL; Cambridge, Mass. & London: Harvard University Press & W. Heinemann, 1925, repr. 1980).

R.D. Hicks, *Diogenes Laertius. Lives of Eminent Philosophers* II (LCL; Cambridge, Mass. & London: Harvard University Press & W. Heinemann, 1925, repr. 1979).

Dionysius of Halicarnassus

E. Cary & E. Spelman, *The Roman Antiquities of Dionysius of Halicarnassus* I *Bks. I–II* (LCL; Cambridge, Mass. & London: Harvard University Press & W. Heinemann, 1937, repr. 1968).

E. Cary & E. Spelman, *The Roman Antiquities of Dionysius of Halicarnassus* II *Bks. III–IV* (LCL; Cambridge, Mass. & London: Harvard University Press & W. Heinemann, 1939, repr. 1978).

Dioscorides
M. Wellmann, *Pedanii Dioscuridis Anazarbei de materia medica libri quinque* (3 vols.; Berlin: Weidmann, I: 1907; II: 1906; III: 1914). [TLG]

Egyptian Book of the Dead
E.A.W. Budge, *The Book of the Dead: An English Translation of the Chapters, Hymns, etc; of the Theban Recension, with introduction, notes, etc* (London: Routledge and Kegan Paul, ²1951).

Ennius
O. Skutsch, *The Annals of Q. Ennius* (Oxford: Clarendon, 1985).

Epicharmus
Fr. 22 = ClemA *Strom.* 4.170, in H. Diels and W. Kranz, *Die Fragmente der Vorsokratiker* I (Zurich & Berlin: Weidmann, ⁶1964).

Epictetus
W.A. Oldfather, *Epictetus. The Discourses as Reported by Arrian, the Manual, and Fragments* I (LCL; Cambridge, Mass. & London: Harvard University Press & W. Heinemann, 1925, repr. 1967).
W.A. Oldfather, *Epictetus. The Discourses as Reported by Arrian, the Manual, and Fragments* II (LCL; Cambridge, Mass. & London: Harvard University Press & W. Heinemann, 1928, repr. 1966).

Epidaurus Miracles
L.R. LiDonnici, *The Epidaurian Miracle Inscriptions. Text, Translation and Commentary* (Atlanta: Scholars, 1995).

Pseudo-Eratosthenes, *Catast.* fr. 32
H.G. Evelyn-White, *Hesiod. The Homeric Hymns and Homerica* (LCL; Cambridge, Mass. and London: Harvard University Press and W. Heinemann, 1914, repr. 1982), 70–4.

Euphranor, Med. [TLG]
Fragments in Galen, Kuhn vol. XIII: 525.

Euripides
A.S. Way, *Euripides* I *Iphigineia at Aulis. Rhesus. Hecuba. The Daughters of Troy. Helen* (LCL; Cambridge, Mass. & London: Harvard University Press & W. Heinemann, 1912, repr. 1988).
A.S. Way, *Euripides* II *Electra. Orestes. Iphigeneia in Taurica. Andromache. Cyclops* (LCL; Cambridge, Mass. & London: Harvard University Press & W. Heinemann, 1912, repr. 1988).

A.S. Way, *Euripides* III *Bacchanals. Madness of Hercules. Children of Hercules. Phoenician Maidens. Suppliants* (LCL; Cambridge, Mass. & London: Harvard University Press & W. Heinemann, 1912, repr. 1988).

D. Kovacs, *Euripides* III. *Suppliant Women. Electra. Heracles* (LCL; Cambridge, Mass. & London: Harvard University Press, 1998).

A.S. Way, *Euripides* IV *Ion. Hippolytus. Medea. Alcestis* (LCL; Cambridge, Mass. & London: Harvard University Press & W. Heinemann, 1912, repr. 1980).

Eusebius

G. Dindorf, *Eusebii Caesariensis opera* (2 vols; Leipzig: Teubner, 1867).

Hierocl.

F.C. Conybeare, *Philostratus* II (LCL; London & Cambridge, Mass.: W. Heinemann & Harvard University Press, 1912, rev. 1950, repr. 1969).

H.E.

K. Lake, *Eusebius. Ecclesiastical History* I (LCL; Cambridge, Mass. & London: Harvard University Press & W. Heinemann, 1926, repr. 1965).

Eustathius

M. van der Valk, *Eustathii archiepiscopi Thessalonicensis commentarii ad Homeri Iliadem pertinentes*, vol. IV (4 vols; Leiden: Brill, 1987 (4 vols: 1971–87)).

Fronto

C.R. Haines, *The Correspondence of Marcus Cornelius Fronto* I (LCL; Cambridge, Mass. & London: Harvard University Press & W. Heinemann, 1919, repr. 1962).

C.R. Haines, *The Correspondence of Marcus Cornelius Fronto* II (LCL; Cambridge, Mass. & London: Harvard University Press & W. Heinemann, 1920, repr. 1963).

Galen [TLG]

C.G. Kuhn, *Claudii Galeni opera omnia* (19 vols; Hildesheim: Georg Olms, repr. 1964 (original 1821)).

Heraclitus

W.H.S. Jones, *Hippocrates* IV *Heracleitus on the Universe* (LCL; Cambridge, Mass. & London: Harvard University Press & W. Heinemann, 1931, repr. 1979).

Herodianus

C.R. Whittaker, *Herodian* I (LCL; Cambridge, Mass. & London: Harvard University Press & W. Heinemann, 1969).

Herodotus

A.D. Godley, *Herodotus* I (LCL; London & Cambridge, Mass.: W. Heinemann & Harvard University Press, 1920, rev. 1926, repr. 1981).
A.D. Godley, *Herodotus* II (LCL; Cambridge, Mass. & London: Harvard University Press & W. Heinemann, 1921, rev. 1938, repr. 1971).
A.D. Godley, *Herodotus* III (LCL; Cambridge, Mass. & London: Harvard University Press & W. Heinemann, 1922, repr. 1971).

Hesiod

H.G. Evelyn-White, *Hesiod. The Homeric Hymns and Homerica* (LCL; Cambridge, Mass. & London: Harvard University Press & W. Heinemann, 1914, repr. 1982).
R. Merkelbach and M.L. West, *Fragmenta Hesiodea* (Oxford: Clarendon, 1967).

Hippocrates

É. Littré, *Oeuvres complètes d' Hippocrate* (9 vols; Paris: Baillière, 1839–53). [TLG]
W.H.S. Jones, *Hippocrates* I (LCL; Cambridge, Mass. & London: Harvard University Press & W. Heinemann, 1923, repr. 1984).
W.H.S. Jones, *Hippocrates* II (LCL; Cambridge, Mass. & London: Harvard University Press, 1923, repr. 1992).
W.H.S. Jones, *Hippocrates* IV *Heracleitus on the Universe* (LCL; Cambridge, Mass. & London: Harvard University Press & W. Heinemann, 1931, repr. 1979).
P. Potter, *Hippocrates* V (LCL; Cambridge, Mass. & London: Harvard University Press & W. Heinemann, 1988).
P. Potter, *Hippocrates* VI (LCL; Cambridge, Mass. & London: Harvard University Press & W. Heinemann, 1988).
W.D. Smith, *Hippocrates* VII (LCL; Cambridge, Mass. & London: Harvard University Press, 1994).

Hippolytus

A. Roberts & J. Donaldson, *The Ante-Nicene Fathers* V *Hippolytus Cyprian Caius Novatian Appendix* (Edinburgh & Grand Rapids: T. & T. Clark & Eerdmans, repr. 1989).

Homer

Iliad

A.T. Murray, *The Iliad* I (LCL; London & Cambridge, Mass.: W. Heinemann & Harvard University Press, 1924, repr. 1988).
A.T. Murray, *The Iliad* II (LCL; London & Cambridge, Mass.: W. Heinemann & Harvard University Press, 1925, repr. 1985).

Odyssey

A.T. Murray, *The Odyssey* I (LCL; Cambridge, Mass. & London: Harvard University Press & W. Heinemann, 1919, repr. 1984).

A.T. Murray, *The Odyssey* II (LCL; London & Cambridge, Mass.: W. Heinemann & Harvard University Press, 1919, repr. 1980).

Homerica
H.G. Evelyn-White, *Hesiod. The Homeric Hymns and Homerica* (LCL; Cambridge, Mass. & London: Harvard University Press & W. Heinemann, 1914, repr. 1982).

Horace
C.E. Bennet, *The Odes and Epodes* (LCL; Cambridge, Mass. & London: Harvard University Press & W. Heinemann, 1914, rev. & repr. 1978).
C.O. Brink, *Horace on Poetry. Epistles Book II: The Letters to Augustus and Florus* (Cambridge: Cambridge University Press, 1982).

Iamblichus
J. Dillon & J. Hershbell, *Iamblichus: On the Pythagorean Way of Life. Text, Translation, and Notes* (SBL Texts & Translations 29; Atlanta: Scholars, 1991).

Ignatius
K. Lake, *The Apostolic Fathers* (LCL; Cambridge, Mass. & London: Harvard University Press & W. Heinemann, 1912, repr. 1977).

Josephus
AJ
H.St.J. Thackeray, *Josephus* IV *Jewish Antiquities Bks I–IV* (LCL; Cambridge, Mass. & London: Harvard University Press & W. Heinemann, 1930, repr. 1978).
H.St.J. Thackeray & R. Marcus, *Josephus* V *Jewish Antiquities Bks V–VIII* (LCL; London & Cambridge, Mass.: W. Heinemann & Harvard University Press, 1934, repr. 1988).
R. Marcus, *Josephus* VI *Jewish Antiquities Bks IX–XI* (LCL; London & Cambridge, Mass.: W. Heinemann & Harvard University Press, 1937, repr. 1987).
R. Marcus, *Josephus* VII *Jewish Antiquities Bks XII–XIV* (LCL; London & Cambridge, Mass.: W. Heinemann & Harvard University Press, 1933, repr. 1976).
R. Marcus, *Josephus* VIII *Jewish Antiquities Bks XV–XVII* (LCL; London & Cambridge, Mass.: W. Heinemann & Harvard University Press, 1963, repr. 1980).

Ap
H.St.J. Thackeray, *Josephus* I *The Life. Against Apion* (LCL; London & Cambridge, Mass.: W. Heinemann & Harvard University Press, 1926, repr. 1961).

BJ

H.St.J. Thackeray, *Josephus* II *The Jewish War Bks I–III* (LCL; Cambridge, Mass.
& London: Harvard University Press, 1927, repr. 1989).
H.St.J. Thackeray, *Josephus* III *The Jewish War Bks IV–VII* (LCL; Cambridge,
Mass. & London: Harvard University Press & W. Heinemann, 1928, repr.
1979).

Julian

W.C. Wright, *The Works of the Emperor Julian* I (LCL; Cambridge, Mass. &
London: Harvard University Press & W. Heinemann, 1913, repr. 1980).
W.C. Wright, *The Works of the Emperor Julian* II (LCL; London & Cambridge,
Mass.: W. Heinemann & Harvard University Press, 1913, repr. 1969).

Justin

G.J. Davie, *The Works now extant of S. Justin the Martyr* (Oxford: Parker, 1861).
M. Dods, G. Reith & B.P. Pratten, *The Writings of Justin Martyr and Athenagoras*
(Edinburgh: T. & T. Clark, 1867).

Justinus

J.C. Yardley, *Justin. Epitome of the Philippic History of Pompeius Trogus* (Atlanta:
Scholars, 1994).

Juvenal

G.G. Ramsay, *Juvenal and Persius* (LCL; Cambridge, Mass. and London: Harvard
University Press, 1918, rev. and repr. 1990).

Lactantius

M.F. McDonald, *The Divine Institutes Bk. I–VII* (Washington: Catholic University
of America Press, 1964).

Libanius

A.F. Norman, *Libanius. Selected Works* II (LCL; London & Cambridge, Mass.:
W. Heinemann & Harvard University Press, 1977).

Livy

B.O. Foster, *Livy* I *Bks. I–II* (LCL; London & Cambridge, Mass.: W. Heinemann
& Harvard University Press, 1919, 1957).
E.T. Sage, *Livy* XI *Bks. XXXVIII–XXXIX* (LCL; Cambridge, Mass. & London:
Harvard University Press & W. Heinemann, 1936, repr. 1949).

Lucian

A.M. Harmon, *Lucian* I (LCL; London & Cambridge, Mass.: W. Heinemann &
Harvard University Press, 1913, repr. 1979).
A.M. Harmon, *Lucian* II (LCL; London & Cambridge, Mass.: W. Heinemann &
Harvard University Press, 1915, repr. 1968).

A.M. Harmon, *Lucian* III (LCL; London & Cambridge, Mass.: W. Heinemann & Harvard University Press, 1921, repr. 1969).

A.M. Harmon, *Lucian* IV (LCL; London & Cambridge, Mass.: W. Heinemann & Harvard University Press, 1925, repr. 1969).

A.M. Harmon, *Lucian* V (LCL; London & Cambridge, Mass.: W. Heinemann & Harvard University Press, 1936, repr. 1972).

K. Kilburn, *Lucian* VI (LCL; London & Cambridge, Mass.: W. Heinemann & Harvard University Press, 1959, repr. 1968).

M.D. Macleod, *Lucian* VII (LCL; London & Cambridge, Mass.: W. Heinemann & Harvard University Press, 1961, repr. 1969).

M.D. Macleod, *Lucian* VIII (LCL; London & Cambridge, Mass.: W. Heinemann & Harvard University Press, 1967).

Lucretius

W.H.D. Rouse & M.F. Smith, *Lucretius. De rerum natura* (LCL; Cambridge, Mass. & London: Harvard University Press & W. Heinemann, [2]1975 (1924), rev. 1982).

Lycon

F. Wehrli, *Lykon und Ariston von Keos* (Die Schule des Aristoteles, vol. XVI; Basel: Schwabe, [2]1968).

Lycophron

E. Scheer, *Lycophronis Alexandra* II *Scholia continens* (Berlin: Weidmann, 1908).

Macarius Magnes

T.W. Crafer, *The Apocriticus of Macarius Magnes* (London: SPCK, 1919).

Marcus Aurelius Antoninus

C.R. Haines, *Marcus Aurelius Antoninus* (London & Cambridge, Mass.: W. Heinemann & Harvard University Press, 1916, rev. 1930, repr. 1970).

Martial

D.R. Shackleton Bailey, *Martial Epigrams* III (LCL; Cambridge, Mass. & London: Harvard University Press, 1993).

Menander

F.G. Allinson, *Menander. The Principal Fragments* (LCL; Cambridge, Mass. & London: Harvard University Press & W. Heinemann, 1921, rev. 1930, repr. 1964).

Nicander

A.S.F. Gow and A.F. Schofield, *Nicander. The Poems and Poetical Fragments* (Cambridge: Cambridge University Press, 1953).

Old Testament Pseudepigrapha
J.H. Charlesworth, *The Old Testament Pseudepigrapha* (2 vols; New York: Doubleday, 1983 and 1985).

Oribasius Med. [TLG]
J. Raeder, *Oribasii collectionum medicarum reliquiae* (4 vols; Corpus medicorum Graecorum, vols. 6.1.1–6.2.2; Leipzig: Teubner, 1928–33).

Origen
G.W. Butterworth, *Origen on First Principles* (London: SPCK, 1936).
H. Chadwick, *Origen: Contra Celsum* (Cambridge: Cambridge University Press, 1953).

Orphic Hymns [TLG]
W. Quandt, *Orphei hymni* (Berlin: Weidmann, ³1962, repr. 1973).

Ostanes Magus
J. Bidez & F. Cumont, *Les mages hellénisés* (Paris: Les Belles Lettres, 1938).

Ovid
J.G. Frazer, *Ovid's Fasti* (LCL; London & New York: W. Heinemann & W.H. Putnam, 1931).
J.H. Mozley & G.P. Goold, *The Art of Love, and Other Poems* (LCL; Cambridge, Mass. & London: Harvard University Press & W. Heinemann, 1929, rev. 1939, ²1979).
F.J. Miller & G.P. Goold, *Ovid. Metamorphoses* (LCL; Cambridge, Mass. & London: Harvard University Press & W. Heinemann, 1916, ²1984).
G. Showerman & G.P. Goold, *Ovid. Heroides and Amores* (LCL; Cambridge, Mass. & London: Harvard University Press & W. Heinemann, 1914, ²1977).

Paulus Aegineta [TLG]
J.L. Heiberg, *Epitomae medicae libri septem: Paulus Aegineta* (2 vols; Corpus medicorum Graecorum, vols 9.1–2; Leipzig: Teubner, 1921 & 1924).

Pausanius
W.H.S. Jones & H.A. Ormerod, *Pausanias Description of Greece* II (LCL; London Cambridge, Mass.: W. Heinemann & Harvard University Press, 1926, repr. 1977).
W.H.S. Jones, *Pausanias Description of Greece* III (LCL; Cambridge, Mass. & London: Harvard University Press & W. Heinemann, 1933, repr. 1988).
W.H.S. Jones, *Pausanias Description of Greece* IV (LCL; London & Cambridge, Mass.: W. Heinemann & Harvard University Press, 1935, repr. 1979).

Petronius

M. Heseltine & E.H. Warmington, *Petronius*; W.H.D. Rouse, *Apocolocyntosis* (LCL; Cambridge, Mass. & London: Harvard University Press & W. Heinemann, 1913, rev. 1969, repr. 1975).

Philo

F.H. Colson, *Philo* I (LCL; London & Cambridge, Mass.: W. Heinemann & Harvard University Press, 1929, repr. 1981).

F.H. Colson, *Philo* II (LCL; London & Cambridge, Mass.: W. Heinemann & Harvard University Press, 1927, repr. 1979).

F.H. Colson & G.H. Whitaker, *Philo* III (LCL; London & Cambridge, Mass.: W. Heinemann & Harvard University Press, 1930, repr. 1960).

F.H. Colson & G.H. Whitaker, *Philo* IV (LCL; London & Cambridge, Mass.: W. Heinemann & Harvard University Press, 1932, repr. 1985).

F.H. Colson & G.H. Whitaker, *Philo* V (LCL; London & Cambridge, Mass.: W. Heinemann & Harvard University Press, 1934, repr. 1988).

F.H. Colson, *Philo* VI (LCL; London & Cambridge, Mass.: W. Heinemann & Harvard University Press, 1935, repr. 1984).

F.H. Colson, *Philo* VII (LCL; London & Cambridge, Mass.: W. Heinemann & Harvard University Press, 1937, repr. 1984).

F.H. Colson, *Philo* VIII (LCL; Cambridge, Mass.: Harvard University Press, 1939, repr. 1989).

F.H. Colson, *Philo* IX (LCL; London & Cambridge, Mass.: W. Heinemann & Harvard University Press, 1941, repr. 1967).

F.H. Colson, *Philo* X *The Embassy to Gaius* (LCL; Cambridge, Mass. & London: Harvard University Press & W. Heinemann, 1962, repr. 1971).

R. Marcus, *Philo. Questions and Answers on Genesis* (LCL; London & Cambridge, Mass.: W. Heinemann & Harvard University Press, 1953, repr. 1961).

Philodemus

W. Crönert, *Kolotes und Menedemus* (Leipzig: Avenarius, 1906; repr. Amsterdam: Hakkert, 1965), 127 n. 534.

Philostratus

F.C. Conybeare, *Philostratus The Life of Apollonius of Tyana. The Epistles of Apollonius and the Treatise of Eusebius* I (Cambridge, Mass.: Harvard University Press, 1912, repr. 1989).

F.C. Conybeare, *Philostratus The Life of Apollonius of Tyana. The Epistles of Apollonius and the Treatise of Eusebius* II (Cambridge, Mass.: Harvard University Press, 1912, rev. 1950, repr. 1989).

Pseudo-Phocylides

P.W. van der Horst, *The Sentences of Pseudo-Phocylides With Introduction and Commentary* (Leiden: E.J. Brill, 1978).

294   *Bibliography*

Pindar

H. Maehler, *Pindari carmina cum fragmentis* (Leipzig: Teubner, 1989).
A.B. Drachmann, *Scholia Vetera in Pindari Carmina* II *Scholia in Pythionicas* (Leipzig: Teubner, 1910; repr. Amsterdam: Hakkert, 1967).

Plato

H.N. Fowler & W.R.M. Lamb, *Plato* I *Euthyphro. Apology. Crito. Phaedo. Phaedrus* (LCL; Cambridge, Mass. & London: Harvard University Press & W. Heinemann, 1914, repr. 1982).
W.R.M. Lamb, *Plato* III *Lysis. Symposium. Gorgias* (LCL; Cambridge, Mass. & London: Harvard University Press & W. Heinemann, 1925, repr. 1983).
H.N. Fowler, *Plato* IV *Cratylus. Parmenides. Greater Hippias. Lesser Hippias* (LCL; Cambridge, Mass. & London: Harvard University Press & W. Heinemann, 1926, repr. 1977).
P. Shorey, *Plato* V *The Republic I (I–V)* (LCL; Cambridge, Mass. & London: Harvard University Press & W. Heinemann, 1930, rev. 1937, repr. 1982).
P. Shorey, *Plato* VI *The Republic II (VI–X)* (LCL; Cambridge, Mass. & London: Harvard University Press & W. Heinemann, 1935, repr. 1987).
H.N. Fowler & W.R.M. Lamb, *Plato* VIII *Statesman. Philebus. Ion* (LCL; Cambridge, Mass. & London: Harvard University Press & W. Heinemann, 1925, repr. 1975).
R.G. Bury, *Plato* IX *Timaeus. Critias. Cleitophon. Menexenus. Epistles* (LCL; Cambridge, Mass. & London: Harvard University Press, 1929, repr. 1989).
R.G. Bury, *Plato* X *Laws I* (LCL; Cambridge, Mass. & London: Harvard University Press & W. Heinemann, 1926, repr. 1984).
R.G. Bury, *Plato* XI *Laws II* (LCL; Cambridge, Mass. & London: Harvard University Press & W. Heinemann, 1926, repr. 1984).

Pseudo-Plato

E.H. Blakeney, *The Axiochus. On Death and Immortality. A Platonic Dialogue* (London: Muller, 1937).

Plautus

P. Nixon, *Plautus* III (LCL; London & Cambridge, Mass.: W. Heinemann & Harvard University Press, 1924, repr. 1957).
P. Nixon, *Plautus* V (LCL; London & Cambridge, Mass.: W. Heinemann & Harvard University Press, 1938, repr. 1952).

Pliny

H. Rackham, *Pliny Natural History* I *Bks I–II* (LCL; Cambridge, Mass. & London: Harvard University Press & W. Heinemann, 1938, rev. 1949, repr. 1958).
H. Rackham, *Pliny Natural History* II *Bks III–VII* (LCL; London & Cambridge, Mass.: W. Heinemann & Harvard University Press, 1942, repr. 1961).
H. Rackham, *Pliny Natural History* III *Bks VIII–XI* (LCL; Cambridge, Mass. & London: Harvard University Press & W. Heinemann, 1940, repr. 1956).
H. Rackham, *Pliny Natural History* V *Bks XVII–XIX* (LCL; London & Cambridge, Mass.: W. Heinemann & Harvard University Press, 1950, repr. 1961).

W.H.S. Jones, *Pliny Natural History* VI *Bks XX–XXIII* (LCL; Cambridge, Mass. & London: Harvard University Press & W. Heinemann, 1951, repr. 1961).
W.H.S. Jones, *Pliny Natural History* VII *Bks XXIV–XXVII* (LCL; London & Cambridge, Mass.: W. Heinemann & Harvard University Press, 1956, repr. 1966).
W.H.S. Jones, *Pliny Natural History* VIII *Bks XXVIII–XXXII* (LCL; London & Cambridge, Mass.: W. Heinemann & Harvard University Press, 1963).

Pliny Younger

B. Radice, *Pliny. Letters and Panegyricus* II (LCL; Cambridge, Mass. & London: Harvard University Press & W. Heinemann, 1969, repr. 1976).

Plutarch

Lives
B. Perrin, *Plutarch's Lives* I *Theseus and Romulus. Lycurgus and Numa. Solon and Publicola* (LCL; Cambridge, Mass. & London: Harvard University Press & W. Heinemann, 1914, repr. 1982).
B. Perrin, *Plutarch's Lives* II *Themistocles and Camillus. Aristides and Cato Major. Cimon and Lucullus* (LCL; Cambridge, Mass. & London: Harvard University Press & W. Heinemann, 1914, repr. 1968).
B. Perrin, *Plutarch's Lives* III *Pericles and Fabius Maximus. Nicias and Crassus* (LCL; Cambridge, Mass. & London: Harvard University Press & W. Heinemann, 1916, repr. 1984).
B. Perrin, *Plutarch's Lives* V *Agesilaus and Pompey. Pelopidas and Marcellus* (LCL; Cambridge, Mass. & London: Harvard University Press & W. Heinemann, 1917, repr. 1968).
B. Perrin, *Plutarch's Lives* VI *Dion and Brutus. Timoleon and Aemilius Paulus* (LCL; Cambridge, Mass. & London: Harvard University Press & W. Heinemann, 1918, repr. 1970).
B. Perrin, *Plutarch's Lives* VII *Demosthenes and Cicero. Alexander and Caesar* (LCL; Cambridge, Mass. & London: Harvard University Press & W. Heinemann, 1919, repr. 1971).
B. Perrin, *Plutarch's Lives* IX *Demetrius and Antony. Pyrrhus and Caius Marius* (LCL; Cambridge, Mass. & London: Harvard University Press & W. Heinemann, 1920, repr. 1968).
B. Perrin, *Plutarch's Lives* X *Agis and Cleomenes. Tiberius and Caius Gracchus. Philopoemen and Flamininus* (LCL; London & Cambridge, Mass.: W. Heinemann & Harvard University Press, 1921, repr. 1968).

Moralia
F.C. Babbitt, *Plutarch's Moralia* I (LCL; London & Cambridge, Mass.: W. Heinemann & Harvard University Press, 1927, repr. 1969).
F.C. Babbitt, *Plutarch's Moralia* II (LCL; Cambridge, Mass. & London: Harvard University Press & W. Heinemann, 1928, repr. 1971).
F.C. Babbitt, *Plutarch's Moralia* III (LCL; Cambridge, Mass. & London: Harvard University Press & W. Heinemann, 1931, repr. 1968).
F.C. Babbitt, *Plutarch's Moralia* IV (LCL; Cambridge, Mass. & London: Harvard University Press & W. Heinemann, 1936, repr. 1972).

F.C. Babbitt, *Plutarch's Moralia* V (LCL; Cambridge, Mass. & London: Harvard University Press & W. Heinemann, 1936, repr. 1984).

W.C. Helmbold, *Plutarch's Moralia* VI (LCL; Cambridge, Mass. & London: Harvard University Press & W. Heinemann, 1939, repr. 1970).

P.H. De Lacy & B. Einarson, *Plutarch's Moralia* VII (LCL; Cambridge, Mass. & London: Harvard University Press & W. Heinemann, 1959, repr. 1968).

P.A. Clement & H.B. Hoffleit, *Plutarch's Moralia* VIII (LCL; Cambridge, Mass. & London: Harvard University Press & W. Heinemann, 1969).

E.K. Minar, F.H. Sandbach and W. C. Helmbold, *Plutarch's Moralia* IX (LCL; Cambridge, Mass. & London: Harvard University Press & W. Heinemann, 1961, repr. 1969).

H. Cherniss & W.C. Helmbold, *Plutarch's Moralia* XII (LCL; Cambridge, Mass. & London: Harvard University Press & W. Heinemann, 1957, repr. 1984).

F.H. Sandbach, *Plutarch's Moralia* XV *Fragments* (LCL; London & Cambridge, Mass.: W. Heinemann & Harvard University Press, 1969).

Pseudo-Plutarch, *De Fluv.*

G.N. Bernardakis, *Plutarchi Chaeronensis Moralia* VII (Leipzig: Teubner, 1896).

Polybius

W.R. Paton, *Polybius. The Histories* VI (LCL; Cambridge, Mass. & London: Harvard University Press & W. Heinemann, 1927, repr. 1980).

Porphyry

H. Armstrong, *Plotinus* I (LCL; London & Cambridge, Mass.: W. Heinemann & Harvard University Press, 1966).

É. des Places, *Vie de Pythagore, Lettre à Marcella* (Collection des Universités de France; Paris: Les Belles Lettres, 1982).

M. Hadas & M. Smith, *Heroes and Gods: Spiritual Biographies in Antiquity* (Freeport, NY: Books for Libraries Press, 1970).

Posidonius

L.G. Edelstein and I.G. Kidd, *Posidonius* I *The Fragments* (Cambridge: Cambridge University Press, 1972).

Propertius

G.P. Goold, *Propertius. Elegies* (LCL; Cambridge, Mass. & London: Harvard University Press, 1990).

Quintilian

H.E. Butler, *Quintilian* II. *Books IV–VI* (LCL; Cambridge, Mass. & London: Harvard University Press & W. Heinemann, 1926, repr. 1985).

Qumran

F. García Martínez, *The Dead Sea Scrolls Translated* (Leiden: E.J. Brill, 1994).

R.H. Eisenman and M. Wise, *The Dead Sea Scrolls Uncovered* (Shaftesbury, Dorset: Element, 1992).

Rufus of Ephesus, *De satyriasmo et gonorrhoea* [TLG]
C. Daremberg and C.É. Ruelle, *Oeuvres de Rufus d'Éphèse* (Paris: Imprimerie Nationale, 1879; repr. Amsterdam: Hakkert, 1963), 64–84.

Rutilius Lupus
E. Brooks, *Rutilius Lupus, Publius. De figuris sententiarum et elocutionis* (Leiden: E.J. Brill, 1970).

Satyrus
fr. in Athenaeus 4.168e.
C.B. Gulick, *Athenaeus* II (LCL; Cambridge, Mass. and London: Harvard University Press and W. Heinemann, 1928, repr. 1987).

Scholia Aeschylus
O.L. Smith, *Scholia Graeca in Aeschylum quae exstant omnia*, vols 1 and 2.2 (Leipzig: Teubner, 1: 1976; 2.2:1982).

Scholia Demosthenes
M.R. Dilts, *Scholia Demosthenica* (2 vols; Leipzig: Teubner, I: 1983, II: 1986).

Scribonius Largus
S. Sconocchia, *Scribonii Largi compositiones* (Leipzig: Teubner, 1983).

Seneca
M. Heseltine & E.H. Warmington, *Petronius*; W.H.D. Rouse, *Apocolocyntosis* (LCL; Cambridge, Mass. & London: Harvard University Press & W. Heinemann, 1913, rev. 1969, repr. 1975).
R.M. Gummere, *Seneca* IV *Ad Lucilium. Epistulae morales I* (LCL; Cambridge, Mass. & London: Harvard University Press & W. Heinemann, 1917, repr. 1979).
R.M. Gummere, *Seneca* V *Ad Lucilium. Epistulae morales II* (LCL; London & Cambridge, Mass.: W. Heinemann & Harvard University Press, 1920, repr. 1970).
J.W. Basore, *Seneca Moral Essays* I (LCL; Cambridge, Mass. & London: Harvard University Press & W. Heinemann, 1928, repr. 1985).
J.W. Basore, *Seneca Moral Essays* II (LCL; Cambridge, Mass. & London: Harvard University Press, 1932, repr. 1990).

Pseudo-Seneca
F.J. Miller, *Seneca* VIII *Tragedies I Hercules Furens. Troades. Medea. Hippolytus. Oedipus* (LCL; Cambridge, Mass. & London: Harvard University Press & W. Heinemann, 1917, repr. 1979).

F.J. Miller, *Seneca* IX *Tragedies II Agamemnon. Thyestes. Hercules Oetaeus. Phoenissae. Octavia* (LCL; London & Cambridge, Mass.: W. Heinemann & Harvard University Press, 1917, rev. 1929, repr. 1968).

Sepher Ha-razim

M.A. Morgan, *Sepher Ha-razim. The Book of the Mysteries* (Chico: Scholars, 1983).

Sextus Empiricus

R.G. Bury, *Sextus Empiricus* I (LCL; Cambridge, Mass. & London: Harvard University Press & W. Heinemann, 1933, repr. 1976).

R.G. Bury, *Sextus Empiricus* III (LCL; Cambridge, Mass. & London: Harvard University Press & W. Heinemann, 1936, repr. 1987).

Sophocles

F. Storr, *Sophocles* I (LCL; Cambridge, Mass. & London: Harvard University Press & W. Heinemann, 1912, repr. 1977).

F. Storr, *Sophocles* II (LCL; Cambridge, Mass. & London: Harvard University Press & W. Heinemann, 1913, repr. 1967).

Sophronius

Narratio miraculorum sanctorum Cyri et Joannis, in J.-P. Migne, *Patrologiae cursus completus, series Graeca* (Paris: J.-P. Migne, 1857–87), 87.3: 3424–676.

Soranus

J. Ilberg, *Sorani Gynaeciorum libri iv, de signis fracturarum, de fasciis, vita Hippocratis, secundum Soranum* (Corpus medicorum, vol. IV; Leipzig: Teubner, 1927), 3–152. [TLG]

O. Temkin, *Soranus' Gynaecology* (Baltimore & London: Johns Hopkins University Press, 1956).

Stobaeus

O. Hense, *Ioannis Stobaei. Anthologii libri duo posteriores* (2 vols; Berlin: Weidmann, 1894).

Strabo

H.L. Jones, *The Geography of Strabo* IV (LCL; London & Cambridge, Mass.: W. Heinemann & Harvard University Press, 1927, repr. 1961).

H.L. Jones, *The Geography of Strabo* V (LCL; London & Cambridge, Mass.: W. Heinemann & Harvard University Press, 1928, repr. 1961).

H.L. Jones, *The Geography of Strabo* VII (LCL; Cambridge, Mass. & London: Harvard University Press & W. Heinemann, 1930, repr. 1961).

Suda [TLG]
A. Adler, *Suidae lexicon* (4 vols; Leipzig: Teubner, 1928–34; repr. 1967–71).

Suetonius
J.C. Rolfe, *Suetonius* I (LCL; London & Cambridge, Mass.: W. Heinemann & Harvard University Press, 1913, rev. 1951, repr. 1964).
J.C. Rolfe, *Suetonius* II (LCL; London & Cambridge, Mass.: W. Heinemann & Harvard University Press, 1914, repr. 1965).

Sword of Moses
M. Gaster, *Studies and Texts in Folklore, Magic, Mediaeval Romance, Hebrew Apocrypha and Samaritan Archaeology* (3 vols; New York: Ktav, 1971).

Tacitus
M. Hutton & R.M. Ogilvie, *Agricola*; M. Hutton & E.H. Warmington, *Germania*; W. Peterson & M. Winterbottom, *Dialogus*; *Tacitus* I (LCL; London & Cambridge, Mass.: W. Heinemann & Harvard University Press, 1914, rev. 1970, repr. 1980).
C.H. Moore, *Tacitus* II *Histories (Books I–III)* (LCL; Cambridge, Mass. & London: Harvard University Press & W. Heinemann, 1925, repr. 1962).
C.H. Moore & J. Jackson, *Tacitus* III *Histories (Books IV–V) Annals (Books I–III)* (LCL; London & Cambridge, Mass.: W. Heinemann & Harvard University Press, 1931, repr. 1962).
J. Jackson, *Tacitus* V *Annals (Books XIII–XVI)* (LCL; London & Cambridge, Mass.: W. Heinemann & Harvard University Press, 1937, repr. 1962).

Tatian
M. Whittaker, *Tatian. Oratio ad Graecos and Fragments* (OECT; Oxford: Clarendon, 1982).

Theocritus
J.M. Edmonds, *The Greek Bucolic Poets* (LCL; Cambridge, Mass. & London: Harvard University Press & W. Heinemann, 1912, rev. 1928, repr. 1977).

Theophrastus
F. Wimmer, *Theophrasti Eresii opera, quae supersunt, omnia* III *Fragmenta* (Leipzig: Teubner, 1862).
[*De nervorum resolutione*] F. Wimmer, *Theophrasti Eresii opera, quae supersunt, omnia* (Paris: Didot, 1866, repr. Frankfurt am Main: Minerva, 1964), 409–410. [TLG]
J. Rusten, I.C. Cunningham & A.D. Knox (trans. & eds), *Theophrastus, Characters. Herodas, Mimes. Cereidas & the Choliambic Poets* (LCL; Cambridge, Mass. & London: Harvard University Press, [2]1993 [1929]).

Thucydides
C.F. Smith, *Thucydides* I (LCL; Cambridge, Mass. & London: Harvard University
Press & W. Heinemann, 1919, rev. 1928, repr. 1980).

Ulpian
O. Lenel, *Palingenesia Iuris Civilis* (2 vols, 1889), II.379–1200.

Vettius Valens
W. Kroll, *Vettii Valentis anthologiarum libri* (Berlin: Weidmann, 1908, repr.
1973).

Virgil
H.R. Fairclough, *Virgil* I (LCL; London & Cambridge, Mass.: W. Heinemann &
Harvard University Press, 1918, repr. 1934, rev. 1950).
H.R. Fairclough, *Virgil* II (LCL; London & Cambridge, Mass.: W. Heinemann &
Harvard University Press, 1918, repr. 1934, rev. 1953).
C.D. Lewis, *Virgil. The Eclogues, Georgics, and Aeneid* (London: Oxford
University Press, 1966).

Xenophon
E.R. Marchant, *Xenophon* IV *Memorabilia Oeconomicus Symposium Apology*
(LCL; Cambridge, Mass. & London: Harvard University Press & W. Heine-
mann, 1923, repr. 1979).

Other Primary Sources & Translations

Audollent, A. *Defixionum Tabellae* (Paris: A. Fontemoing, 1904).
Barns, J.W.B. and H. Zilliacus. *The Antinoopolis Papyri* III (London: Egypt
Exploration Society, 1967).
Barrett, C.K. *The New Testament Background. Selected Documents* (London:
SPCK, 1956).
Benoit, P. 'Fragment d'une prière contre les esprits impurs?', *RB* 58 (1951), 549–
65.
Betz, H.D. *The Greek Magical Papyri in Translation Including the Demotic Spells*
(Chicago: University of Chicago Press, ²1986).
Bonner, C. *Studies in Magical Amulets Chiefly Graeco-Egyptian* (Ann Arbor &
London: University of Michigan Press & Oxford University Press, 1950).
'Amulets Chiefly in the British Museum', *Hesperia* 20 (1951), 301–45.
'A Miscellany of Engraved Stones', *Hesperia* 23 (1954), 138–57.
Brashear, W.M. 'Ein Berliner Zauberpapyrus', *ZPE* 33 (1979), 261–78.
'New Greek Magical and Divinatory Texts in Berlin', in M.W. Meyer and P.A.
Mirecki (eds), *Ancient Magic and Ritual Power* (Leiden: E.J. Brill, 1995),
209–42.
Braund, D.C. *Augustus to Nero. A Sourcebook on Roman History 31 BC–AD 68*
(London: Croom Helm, 1985).
Bruneau, P. *Recherches sur les cultes de Délos à l'époque impériale* (Paris:
Boccard, 1970).

Bücheler, F. *Carmina latina epigraphica* (Leipzig: Teubner, 1897, repr. 1921).

Carlini, A. et al. *Papiri letterari greci* (Pisa: Giardini editori e stampatori, 1978).

Cartlidge, D.R. and D.L. Dungan (eds). *Documents for the Study of the Gospels* (Minneapolis: Fortress, 1980, rev. 1994).

Charlesworth, J.H. *The Old Testament Pseudepigrapha* (2 vols; New York: Doubleday, 1983 and 1985).

Corell, J. 'Defixionis tabella aus Carmona (Sevilla)', *ZPE* 95 (1993), 261–8.

Daniel, R.W. 'Two Love-Charms', *ZPE* 19 (1975), 249–64.

'Some ΦΥΛΑΚΤΗΡΙΑ', *ZPE* 25 (1977), 145–54.

Daniel, R.W. and F. Maltomini. 'Una gemma magica contro l'infiammazione dell'ugola', *ZPE* 78 (1989), 93–4.

Supplementum magicum (Papyrologica Coloniensia 16; Opladen, Westdeutscher Verlag, 1990–2).

Defixionum Tabellae Atticae (Paris: A. Fontemoing, 1904).

Dickie, M.W. 'The Dionysiac Mysteries in Pella', *ZPE* 109 (1995), 81–6.

Diels, H. (ed.). *Anonymi Londinensis ex Aristotelis Iatricis Menoniis et aliis medicis eclogae* (Supplementum Aristotelicum iii pars i; Berlin: Reimer, 1893). [TLG]

Diels, H. and W. Kranz. *Die Fragmente der Vorsokratiker* (Zurich & Berlin: Weidmann, ⁶1964).

Dittenberger, W. *Orientis Graeci Inscriptiones Selectae* (Leipzig: Hirzel, 1903–5).

Dunst, G. 'Ein samischer Fiebergott', *ZPE* 3 (1968), 150–3.

Ebeling, E. *Literarische Keilschrifttexte aus Assur* (Berlin, 1953).

Eger, O., E. Kornemann and P.M. Meyer. *Griechische Papyri im Museum des oberhessischen Geschichtsvereins zu Giessen* (Leipzig & Berlin: Teubner, 1910–12).

Egger, R. 'Zu einem Fluchtäfelchen aus Blei', *Römische Antike und frühes Christentum* 2 (1963), 247–53.

Ehrenberg, V. and A.H.M. Jones. *Documents Illustrating the Reigns of Augustus and Tiberius* (Oxford: Clarendon, 1949).

Eisenman, R.H. and M. Wise. *The Dead Sea Scrolls Uncovered* (Shaftesbury, Dorset: Element, 1992).

Engelmann, H. *Die Inschriften von Kyme* (Bonn: Habelt, 1976).

Faraone, C.A. 'Binding and Burying the Forces of Evil: The Defensive Use of "Voodoo Dolls" in Ancient Greece', *ClAnt* 10 (1991), 165–220.

Farber, W. '*MANNAM LUŠPUR ANA ENKIDU*: Some New Thoughts about an Old Motif', *JNES* 49 (1990), 299–321.

Fox, W.S. 'An Infernal Postal Service', *Art and Archeology* 1 (1914), 205–7.

Gager, J. *Curse Tablets and Binding Spells from the Ancient World* (Oxford: Oxford University Press, 1992).

García Martínez, F. *The Dead Sea Scrolls Translated* (Leiden: Brill, 1994).

Geissen, A. 'Ein Amulett gegen Fieber', *ZPE* 55 (1984), 223–7.

Gibson, J.C.L. *Canaanite Myths and Legends* (Edinburgh: T. & T. Clark, 1978).

Grant, F.C. *Ancient Roman Religion* (New York: Liberal Arts Press, 1957).

Grenfell, B.P. and A.S. Hunt. *Oxyrhynchus Papyri* Part I (London: Egypt Exploration Society, 1898).

Oxyrhynchus Papyri Part XI (London: Egypt Exploration Society, 1915).

Oxyrhynchus Papyri Part XII (London: Egypt Exploration Society, 1916).

Heinze, R. *Xenocrates. Darstellung der Lehre und Sammlung der Fragmente* (Hildesheim: Olms, 1892, repr. 1965).

Henrichs, A. *Die Phoinikika des Lollianos. Fragmente eines neuen griechischen Romans* (Papyrologische Texte und Abhandlungen 14; Bonn: Habelt, 1972).

Hondius, J.J. et al. *Supplementum Epigraphicum Graecum* (Leyden: Sijthoff, 1923→).

Horsley, G.H.R. *New Documents Illustrating Early Christianity 2* (Sydney: Macquarie University AHDR Centre, 1982).

New Documents Illustrating Early Christianity 3 (Sydney: Macquarie University AHDR Centre, 1983).

Hunt, A.S. *Oxyrhynchus Papyri* Part VII (London: Egypt Exploration Society, 1910).

Isbell, C.D. *Corpus of the Aramaic Incantation Bowls* (SBLDS 17; Missoula: Scholars, 1975).

Jacoby, F. *Die Fragmente der griechischen Historiker* (Berlin: Weidmann, 1923– 58).

Jameson, M.H., D.R. Jordan et al. *A Lex sacra from Selinous* (GRBM 11; Durham, N.C.: Duke University, 1993).

Jordan, D.R. 'A Curse Tablet from a Well in the Athenian Agora', *ZPE* 19 (1975), 245–8.

'Two Inscribed Lead Tablets from a Well in the Athenian Kerameikos', *AM* 95 (1980), 225–39.

'Defixiones from a Well Near the Southwest Corner of the Athenian Agora', *Hesperia* 54 (1985), 205–55.

'A Survey of Greek Defixiones not included in the Special Corpora', *GRBS* 26 (1985), 151–97.

'A Love Charm with Verses', *ZPE* 72 (1988), 245–59.

'New Defixiones from Carthage', in J.H. Humphrey (ed.), *The Circus and a Byzantine Cemetery at Carthage* (Ann Arbor: University of Michigan Press, 1988), 117–34.

'A New Reading of a Papyrus Love Charm in the Louvre', *ZPE* 74 (1988), 231–43.

'A New Reading of a Phylactery from Beirut', *ZPE* 88 (1991), 61–9.

'The Inscribed Lead Tablet from Phalasarna', *ZPE* 4 (1992), 191–4.

'Inscribed Lead Tablets from the Games in the Sanctuary of Poseidon', *Hesperia* 63 (1994), 111–26.

'Late Feasts for Ghosts', in R. Hägg (ed.), *Ancient Greek Cult Practice from the Epigraphical Evidence. Proceedings of the Second International Seminar on Ancient Greek Cult. Athens, 22–24 November 1991* (Stockholm: Swedish Institute Athens, 1994), 131–43.

'Magica Graeca Parvula', *ZPE* 100 (1994), 321–35.

'Notes from Carthage', *ZPE* 111 (1996), 115–23.

Jordan, D.R. & R. Kotansky. 'Two Phylacteries from Xanthos', *RevArch* 1 (1996), 161–71.

Kaibel, G. *Epigrammata Graeca ex lapidibus conlecta* (Berlin: Reimer, 1878).

Kambitsis, S. 'Une nouvelle tablette magique d'Égypte, Musée du Louvre, Inv. E ^{2}7145, 3e/4e siècle', *BIFAO* 76 (1976), 213–30.

Kirchhoff, A. et al. *Inscriptiones Graecae* I–XV (Berlin: Reimer, 1923→).

Kock, T. *Comicorum Atticorum Fragmenta* II *Novae Comoediae Fragmenta pars I* (Leipzig: Teubner, 1884).

Kotansky, R. *Greek Magical Amulets. The Inscribed Gold, Silver, Copper, and Bronze Lamellae* (Opladen: Westdeutscher Verlag, 1994).

Kotansky, R. and J. Spier. 'The "Horned Hunter" on a Lost Gnostic Gem', *HTR* 88:3 (1995), 315–37.

Lattimore, R. *Themes in Greek and Latin Epitaphs* (Urbana, Ill.: University of Illinois Press, 1942).

Lewis, N. and M. Reinhold. *Roman Civilization.* I: *The Republic* (New York: Columbia University Press, 1951).

Roman Civilization. Sourcebook II: *The Empire* (New York: Harper, 1966).

Llewelyn, S.R. *New Documents Illustrating Early Christianity 6* (Sydney: Macquarie University AHDR Centre, 1992).

Llewelyn, S.R. *New Documents Illustrating Early Christianity 7* (Sydney: Macquarie University AHDR Centre, 1994).

Lobel, E. *Oxyrhynchus Papyri* Part XXVIII (London: Egypt Exploration Society, 1962).

McCullough, W.S. *Jewish and Mandaean Incantation Bowls in the Royal Ontario Museum* (Toronto: University of Toronto Press, 1967).

Martinez, D.G. *P.Michigan XVI. A Greek Love Charm from Egypt (P.Mich. 757)* (ASP 30; Atlanta: Scholars, 1991).

Merkelbach, R. 'Bakchisches Goldtäfelchen aus Hipponion', *ZPE* 17 (1975), 8–9.

'Zwei neue orphisch-dionysische Totenpässe', *ZPE* 76 (1989), 15–16.

Meyer, M.W. (ed.). *The Ancient Mysteries. A Sourcebook. Sacred Texts of the Mystery Religions of the Ancient Mediterranean World* (San Francisco: Harper & Row, 1987).

Mirecki, P.A. 'The Coptic Wizard's Hoard', *HTR* 87:4 (1994), 435–60.

Mommsen, T. et al. *Corpus Inscriptionum Latinarum* (Berlin: Reimer, 1862–1963).

Montgomery, J.A. *Aramaic Incantation Texts from Nippur* (Philadelphia: University of Pennsylvania Museum, 1913).

Nauck A. *Tragicorum graecorum fragmenta* (Hildesheim: Georg Olms, 1964 (²1889)), Supp. B.Snell (1964).

Naveh, J. and S. Shaked. *Amulets and Magic Bowls. Aramaic Incantations of Late Antiquity* (Jerusalem: Magnes, 1985).

'Fragments of an Aramaic Magic Book from Qumran', *IEJ* 48:3–4 (1998), 252–61.

O'Callaghan, J. and P. Proux. 'Papiro mágico cristiano (P.Yale inv. 989)', *SPap* 13:2 (1974), 83–8.

Oikonomides, A.N. *Inscriptiones Atticae: supplementum inscriptionum Atticarum* I (Chicago: Ares, 1976).

Page, D.L. *Select Papyri* III *Literary Papyri, Poetry* (LCL; London & Cambridge, Mass.: W. Heinemann & Harvard University Press, 1941, repr. 1970).

Peek, W. 1955: *Griechische Vers-Inschriften* I (Berlin: Akademie-Verlag, 1955). *Griechische Grabgedichte* (Berlin: Akademie-Verlag, 1960).

Penney, D.L. and M.O. Wise. 'By the Power of Beelzebub. An Aramaic Incantation Formula From Qumran (4Q560)', *JBL* 113 (1994), 627–50.

304   Bibliography

Powell, J. Enoch. *The Rendel Harris Papyri of Woodbroke College, Birmingham* (Cambridge: Cambridge University Press, 1936).
Preisendanz, K. and A. Henrichs. *Papyri Graecae Magicae: Die griechischen Zauberpapyri* (2 vols; Stuttgart: Teubner, 1973–4).
Pritchard, J.B. *Ancient Near Eastern Texts Relating to the Old Testament* (Princeton: Princeton University Press, ³1969).
Ramsay, W. *Cities and Bishoprics of Phrygia* Vol. I, Part II: *West and West-Central Phrygia* (Oxford: Clarendon, 1897).
Sammelbuch griechischer Urkunden aus Ägypten (successively published by F. Preisigke, F. Bilabel, E. Kiessling and H.-A. Rupprecht; 1915→).
Scurlock, J.A. 'Magical Means of Dealing With Ghosts in Ancient Mesopotamia' (unpublished PhD dissertation; University of Chicago, 1988).
Segal, C. 'Dionysus and the Gold Tablets from Pelinna', *GRBS* 31 (1990), 411–19.
Shelton, Jo-Ann (ed.). *As the Romans Did. A Sourcebook in Roman Social History* (Oxford: Oxford University Press, ²1998 (1988))
Sherk, R.K. *The Roman Empire: Augustus to Hadrian* (Cambridge: Cambridge University Press, 1988).
Sijpesteijn, P.J. *The Wisconsin Papyri* I (Leiden: Brill, 1967).
Smallwood, E. M. *Documents Illustrating the Principates of Gaius, Claudius and Nero* (Cambridge: Cambridge University Press, 1967).
Sokolowski, F. *Lois sacrées des cités grecques* (Paris: De Boccard, 1969).
Lois sacrées des cités grecques, Supplément (Paris: De Boccard, 1969).
Thompson, R.C. *The Devils and Evil Spirits of Babylonia. Being Babylonian and Assyrian Incantations against the Demons, Ghouls, Vampires, Hobgoblins, Ghosts, and Kindred Evil Spirits, which attack Mankind.* Vol. I: *Evil Spirits.* Vol. II: *"Fever Sickness" and "Headache", etc.* (London: Luzac, 1903 & 1904).
Whittaker, M. *Jews & Christians: Graeco-Roman Views* (Cambridge: Cambridge University Press, 1984).
Wortmann, D. 'Neue magische Texte', *Bonner Jahrbücher* 168 (1968), 56–111.
Wünsch, R. *Defixionum Tabellae Atticae* (IG III³; Berlin: Reimer, 1897). Reprinted in A.N. Oikonomides, *Inscriptiones Atticae: supplementum inscriptionum Atticarum* I (Chicago: Ares, 1976).
Youtie, H.C. and C. Bonner. 'Two Curse Tablets from Beisan', *TAPA* 68 (1937), 43–72.

Rabbinic Sources

Schachter, J. & H. Freedman. *Hebrew-English Edition of the Babylonian Talmud. Seder Nezikin. Sanhedrin* (London: Soncino, 1969).

Secondary Sources

Alexander, P.S. 'Incantations and Books of Magic', in E. Schürer et al. (eds), *The History of the Jewish People in the Age of Jesus Christ*, vol. 3.1 (Edinburgh: T. & T. Clark, 1986), nos 32.7, 342–79.

Anderson, J.C. & S.D. Moore (eds). *Mark & Method: New Approaches in Biblical Studies* (Minneapolis: Fortress, 1992).

Arnold, C.E. *Ephesians: Power and Magic. The Concept of Power in Ephesians in Light of Its Historical Setting* (SNTSMS 63; Cambridge: Cambridge University Press, 1989).

Aubert, J.-J. 'Threatened Wombs: Aspects of Ancient Uterine Magic', *GRBS* 30 (1989), 421–49.

Auguet, R. *Cruelty and Civilization. The Roman Games* (London: Routledge, 1994 (1972)).

Aune, D. 'Magic in Early Christianity', in W. Haase (ed.), *ANRW* II.23.2 (Berlin: De Gruyter, 1980), 1507–57.

Avalos, H. *Health Care and the Rise of Christianity* (Peabody, Mass.: Hendrickson, 1999).

Bal, M. 'The Narrating and the Focalizing: A Theory of Agents in the Narrative', *Style* 17.2 (1983), 234–69. Originally published in French, in *Narratologie. Essais sur la signification narrative dans quatre romans modernes* (Paris: Klinksieck, 1977), 21–55.

Barnett, P.W. *The Servant King. Reading Mark Today* (Sydney: AIO, 1991).

Baroja, J.C. 'Magic and Religion in the Classical World (1964)', in M. Marwick (ed.), *Witchcraft and Sorcery* (Harmondsworth: Penguin, 1970), 73–80.

Bassler, J.M. 'The Parable of the Loaves', *JR* 66:2 (1986), 157–72.

Bauckham, R. 'Resurrection as Giving Back the Dead: A Traditional Image of Resurrection in the Pseudepigrapha and the Apocalypse of John', in J.H. Charlesworth & C.A. Evans (eds), *The Pseudepigrapha and Early Biblical Interpretation* (Sheffield: JSOT, 1993), 269–91.

'Jesus and the Wild Animals (Mark 1:13): A Christological Image for an Ecological Age', in J.B. Green & M. Turner, *Jesus of Nazareth, Lord and Christ. Essays on the Historical Jesus and New Testament Christology* (Grand Rapids & Carlisle: Eerdmans & Paternoster, 1994), 3–21.

'For Whom Were Gospels Written?', in R. Bauckham (ed.), *The Gospels for All Christians. Rethinking the Gospel Audiences* (Grand Rapids: Eerdmans, 1998), 9–48.

Beavis, M.A. *Mark's Audience. The Literary and Social Setting of Mark 4:11–12* (JSNTSup 33; Sheffield: Sheffield Academic Press, 1989).

Begg, C. 'Josephus's Portrayal of the Disappearances of Enoch, Elijah, and Moses: Some Observations', *JBL* 109 (1990), 691–3.

Benko, S. *Pagan Rome and the Early Christians* (London: B.T. Batsford, 1985).

Berlin, A. 'Point of View in Biblical Narrative', *Poetics and Interpretation of Biblical Narrative* (Sheffield: Almond Press, 1983), 71–113.

Bickermann, E.J. 'Das leere Grab', *ZNW* 23 (1924), 281–91.

'Symbolism in the Dura Synagogue. A Review Article', *HTR* 58 (1965), 127–51.

Bolt, P.G. 'The Narrative Integrity of Mark 13:24–27' (unpublished MTh thesis, Australian College of Theology, Kensington, NSW, 1991).

'The Spirit in the Synoptic Gospels: the Equipment of the Servant', in B.G. Webb (ed.), *The Spirit of the Living God, Part 1* (Explorations 5; Sydney: ANZEA, 1991), 45–75.

'The Gospel for Today's Church', in B.G.Webb (ed.), *Exploring The Missionary Church* (Explorations 7; Sydney: ANZEA, 1993), 27–59.

'What Were the Sadducees Reading? An Enquiry into the Literary Background to Mark 12:18–23', *TynB* 45:2 (1994), 369–94.

'Mark 13: An Apocalyptic Precursor to the Passion Narrative', *RTR* 54:1 (1995), 10–32.

'Jesus, Daimons and the Dead', in A.N.S. Lane (ed.), *The Unseen World. Christian Reflections on Angels, Demons, and the Heavenly Realm* (Carlisle: Paternoster, 1996), 75–102.

'Mk 16:1–8: The Empty Tomb of a Hero?', *TynB* 47:1 (1996), 27–37.

' "With a View to the Forgiveness of Sins": Jesus and Forgiveness in Mark's Gospel', *RTR* 57.2 (1998), 53–69.

'Life, Death, and the Afterlife in the Greco-Roman World', in R.N. Longenecker (ed.), *Life in the Face of Death. The Resurrection Message of the New Testament* (Grand Rapids: Eerdmans, 1998), 51–79.

'Feeling the Cross: Mark's Message of Atonement', *RTR* 60.1 (2001), 1–17.

Bonner, C. 'Traces of Thaumaturgic Technique in the Miracles', *HTR* 20 (1927), 171–81.

'Witchcraft in the Lecture Room of Libanius', *TAPA* 66 (1932), 34–44.

Boomershine, T.E. *Mark, the Storyteller: A Rhetorical-Critical Investigation of Mark's Passion and Resurrection Narrative* (Ann Arbor: UMI, 1974).

'Peter's Denial as Polemic or Confession: The Implications of Media Criticism for Biblical Hermeneutics', *Semeia* 39 (1987), 47–68.

Boomershine, T.E. and G. Bartholomew. 'The Narrative Technique of Mark 16:8', *JBL* 100:2 (1981), 213–23.

Booth, W.C. 'Distance and Point of View: An Essay in Clarification', in P. Stevick (ed.), *Theory of the Novel* (New York: Free Press, 1967), 87–107.

The Rhetoric of Fiction (Chicago: University of Chicago Press, ²1983 (1961)).

The Rhetoric of Irony (Chicago: University of Chicago Press, 1974).

The Company We Keep. An Ethics of Fiction (Berkeley: University of California Press, 1988).

Brashear, W.M. 'The Greek Magical Papyri: an Introduction and Survey; Annotated Bibliography (1928–1994)', in W. Haase (ed.), *ANRW* II.18.5 (Berlin: De Gruyter, 1995), 3380–684.

Bravo, B. 'Une Tablette Magique D'Olbia Pontique, les Morts, les Héros et les Démons', *Poikilia. Études offertes à Jean-Pierre Vernant* (Paris: EHESS, 1987), 185–218.

Brenk, F.E. 'In the Light of the Moon: Demonology in the Early Imperial Period', in W. Haase (ed.), *ANRW* II.16.3 (Berlin: De Gruyter, 1986), 2068–145.

Breytenbach, C. and P.L. Day. 'Satan', in K. van der Toorn et al. (eds), *Dictionary of Deities and Demons in the Bible* (Leiden: E.J. Brill, 1995), cols 1369–80.

Brooten, B.J. 'Is Belief the Center of Religion?', in L. Bormann, K. del Tredici & A. Standhartinger (eds), *Religious Propaganda and Missionary Competition in the New Testament World. Essays Honoring Dieter Georgi* (NovTSupp 74; Leiden: Brill, 1994), 471–9.

Brown, P. 'Sorcery, Demons and the Rise of Christianity', in M. Douglas (ed.), *Witchcraft: Confessions and Accusations* (London: Tavistock, 1970), 17–45.

Bryan, C. *A Preface to Mark. Notes on the Gospel in Its Literary and Cultural Settings* (Oxford: Oxford University Press, 1993).

Bullough, E. ' "Psychical Distance" as a Factor in Art and an Aesthetic Principle', *BritJ Psychology* 5 (1912), 87–118.

Burkert, W. *Ancient Mystery Cults* (Cambridge, Mass.: Harvard University Press, 1987).

Burn, A.R. 'Hic Breve Vivitur. A Study of the Expectation of Life in the Roman Empire', *Past & Present* 4 (1953), 2–31.

Burns, E. *Character: Acting and Being on the Pre-Modern Stage* (New York: St. Martin's Press, 1990).

Burrelli, R.J., Jr. 'A Study of Psalm 91 with Special Reference to the Theory that it was Intended as a Protection Against Demons and Magic' (unpublished PhD dissertation, University of Cambridge, 1993).

Burridge, R.A. *What Are the Gospels? A Comparison with Graeco-Roman Biography* (SNTSMS 70; Cambridge: Cambridge University Press, 1992).

Caird, G.B. 'The Transfiguration', *ExpT* 67 (1955–6), 291–4.

Camery-Hoggatt, J. *Irony in Mark's Gospel: Text and Subtext* (SNTSMS 72; Cambridge: Cambridge University Press, 1992).

Carney, T.F. *The Shape of the Past: Models and Antiquity* (Lawrence, Kans.: Coronado, 1975).

Cavallin, H.C. 'Tod und Auferstehung der Weisheitslehrer. Ein Beitrag zur Zeichnung des *frame of reference* Jesu', *SNTU* 5 (1980), 107–21.

Cave, C.H. 'The Leper: Mark 1:40–45', *NTS* 25 (1979), 245–50.

Chatman, S. *Story and Discourse: Narrative Structure in Fiction and Film* (Ithaca: Cornell University Press, 1978).

Ciraolo, L.J. 'Supernatural Assistants in the Greek Magical Papyri', in M.W. Meyer and P.A. Mirecki (eds), *Ancient Magic and Ritual Power* (Leiden: E.J. Brill, 1995), 279–95.

Clark, M.E. 'Images and Concepts of Hope in the Early Imperial Cult', in K.H. Richards (ed.), *SBL Seminar Papers 1982* (Chico: Scholars, 1982), 39–44.

Cohan, S. and L.M. Shires. *Telling Stories. A Theoretical Analysis of Narrative Fiction* (New York & London: Routledge, 1988).

Collins, A.Y. *Is Mark's Gospel a Life of Jesus? The Question of Genre* (Milwaukee, Wis.: Marquette University Press, 1990).

'The Empty Tomb and Resurrection according to Mark', in *The Beginning of the Gospel. Probings of Mark in Context* (Minneapolis: Fortress, 1992), 119–48.

'Suffering and Healing in the Gospel of Mark', in *The Beginning of the Gospel. Probings of Mark in Context* (Minneapolis: Fortress, 1992), 39–72.

'Rulers, Divine Men, and Walking on the Water (Mark 6:45–52)', in L. Bormann, K. del Tredici and A. Standhartinger (eds), *Religious Propaganda and Missionary Competition in the New Testament World. Essays Honoring Dieter Georgi* (NovTSupp 74; Leiden: Brill, 1994), 207–27.

'Apotheosis and Resurrection', in P. Borgen & S. Giversen (eds), *The New Testament and Hellenistic Judaism* (Aarhus, Denmark: Aarhus University Press, 1995), 88–100.

Cook, B.F. *Greek Inscriptions* (London: British Museum, 1987).

Cornford, F.M. *Plato's Cosmology. The Timaeus of Plato Translated with a Running Commentary* (London: Kegan Paul, Trench & Trubner, 1937).

Cotter, Wendy J. 'Cosmology and the Jesus Miracles', in W. Arnal & M. Desjardins (eds), *Whose Historical Jesus?* (Studies in Christianity & Judaism 7; Waterloo, Ont.: Wilfrid Laurier University Press, 1997), 118–31.

Miracles in Greco-Roman Antiquity. A Sourcebook (London: Routledge, 1999).

Cotton, H.M., W.E.H. Cockle & F.G.B. Millar. 'The Papyrology of the Roman Near East: A Survey', *JRS* 85 (1995), 214–35.

Cranfield, C.E.B. *The Gospel According to St Mark* (CGNTC; Cambridge: Cambridge University Press, 1979).

Crisci, E. *Scrivere Greco Fuori d'Egitto. Ricerche sui manoscritti greco-orientali di origine non egiziana del IV secolo a.C. all' VIII d.C.* (Papyrologica Florentina XXVII; Florence: Edizioni Gonnelli, 1996).

Cuddon, J.A. (ed.). *A Dictionary of Literary Terms* (Harmondsworth: Penguin, 1986).

Culler, J. *Structuralist Poetics. Structuralism, Linguistics and the Study of Literature* (London: Routledge, 1975).

Cumont, F. *Afterlife in Roman Paganism* (New Haven: Yale University Press, 1922).

Danove, P.L. *The End of Mark's Story: A Methodological Study* (BIS 3; Leiden: E.J. Brill, 1993).

Deissmann, A. *Bible Studies. Contributions Chiefly from Papyri and Inscriptions to the History of the Language, the Literature, and the Religion of Hellenistic Judaism and Primitive Christianity* (trans. A. Grieve; Edinburgh: T. & T. Clark, 1901).

New Light on the New Testament from Records of the Græco-Roman Period (trans. L.R.M. Strachan; Edinburgh: T. & T. Clark, 1908).

Light From the Ancient East. The New Testament Illustrated by Recently Discovered Texts of the Graeco-Roman World (trans. L.R.M. Strachan; London: Hodder & Stoughton, [4]1927 (German [4]1922, 1910); Peabody: Hendrickson, 1995).

Derrett, J.D.M. 'Legend and Event: The Gerasene Demoniac: An Inquest into History and Liturgical Projection', in E.A. Livingstone (ed.), *Studia Biblica II. Papers on the Gospels. Sixth International Congress on Biblical Studies. Oxford 3–7 April 1978* (JSNTSup 2; Sheffield: JSOT, 1980), 63–73.

Dewey, J. 1980: *Markan Public Debate* (SBLDS 48; Chico: Scholars, 1980).

'Point of View and the Disciples in Mark', in K.H. Richards (ed.), *SBL 1982 Seminar Papers* (Chico: Scholars, 1982), 97–106.

Douglas, M. *Purity and Danger. An Analysis of the Concepts of Pollution and Taboo* (London: Routledge & Kegan Paul, 1966, repr. 1978).

Dowden, K. *Death and the Maiden. Girls' Initiation Rites in Greek Mythology* (London & New York: Routledge, 1989).

Duling, D.C. 'The Eleazar Miracle and Solomon's Magical Wisdom in Flavius Josephus's *Antiquitates Judaicae* 8.42–49', *HTR* 78 (1985), 1–25.

Dumbrell, W.J. 'The Role of the Servant in Isaiah 40–55', *RTR* 48:3 (1989), 105–13.

Durand, J.D. 'Mortality Estimates from Roman Tombstone Inscriptions', *AmJSociology* 65 (1959), 365–73.

Dwyer, T. *The Motif of Wonder in the Gospel of Mark* (JSNTSup 128; Sheffield: SAP, 1996).

Edelstein, L. 'Rufus (4)', in N.G.L Hammond and H.H. Scullard (eds.), *Oxford Classical Dictionary* (Oxford: Clarendon, 1970), 938.

Edwards, J.R. 'Markan Sandwiches: The Significance of Interpolations in Markan Narratives', in D.E. Orton (ed.), *The Composition of Mark's Gospel. Selected*

Studies from Novum Testamentum (Leiden: E.J. Brill, 1999), 192–215. Originally published in *NovT* 21 (1989), 193–216.

Eitrem, S. *Some Notes on the Demonology of the New Testament* (Symbolae Osloenses, Sup. 20; Osloae: Universitetsforlaget, 1966).

Faraone, C.A. 'An Accusation of Magic in Classical Athens (Ar. *Wasps* 946–48)', *TAPA* 119 (1989), 149–61.

—'Aphrodite's ΚΕΣΤΟΣ and Apples for Atalanta: Aphrodisiacs in Early Greek Myth and Ritual', *Phoenix* 44 (1990), 219–43.

—'The Agonistic Context of Early Greek Binding Spells', in C.A. Faraone and D. Obbink (eds.), *Magika Hiera. Ancient Greek Magic & Religion* (Oxford & New York: Oxford University Press, 1991), 3–32.

—'Sex and Power: Male-Targetting Aphrodisiacs in the Greek Magical Tradition', *Helios* 19:1–2 (1992), 92–103.

—'Deianira's Mistake and the Demise of Heracles: Erotic Magic in Sophocles' *Trachiniae*', *Helios* 21:2 (1994), 115–35.

—'The Mystodokos and the Dark-Eyed Maidens: Multicultural Influences on a Late-Hellenistic Incantation', in M.W. Meyer and P.A. Mirecki (eds.), *Ancient Magic and Ritual Power* (Leiden: E.J. Brill, 1995), 297–333.

Farnell, L.R. *The Higher Aspects of Greek Religion* (Chicago: Ares, 1977).

Feldman, E. *Biblical and Post-Biblical Defilement and Mourning: Law as Theology* (New York: Yeshiva University Press, 1977).

Festugière, A.J. *Personal Religion among the Greeks* (University of California Press, 1954).

Finney, P.C. 'The Rabbi and the Coin Portrait (Mark 12:15b, 16): Rigorism Manqué', *JBL* 112 (1993), 629–44.

Fish, S.E. *Surprised by Sin: the Reader in Paradise Lost* (Berkeley: University of California Press, 1967, ²1971).

—*Self-Consuming Artifacts: The Experience of Seventeenth-Century Literature* (Berkeley: University of California Press, 1972).

Fisher, K.M. 'The Miracles of Mark 4:35–5:43: Their Meaning and Function in the Gospel Framework', *BTB* 11 (1981), 13–16.

Foerster, W. 'δαίμων, δαιμόνιον, κτλ', in G. Kittel (ed.), *Theological Dictionary of the New Testament* (Grand Rapids: Eerdmans, 1964), II: 1–20.

Fowler, R.M. *Loaves and Fishes: The Function of the Feeding Stories in the Gospel of Mark* (SBLDS 54; Chico: Scholars, 1981).

—'Who is "the Reader" of Mark's Gospel?', in K.H. Richards (ed.), *SBL 1983 Seminar Papers* (Chico: Scholars, 1983), 31–53.

—'Who is "the Reader" in Reader-Response Criticism?', *Semeia* 31 (1985), 5–23. A revision of previously listed item.

—*Let the Reader Understand. Reader-Response Criticism and the Gospel of Mark* (Minneapolis: Fortress, 1991).

Frankfurter, D. *Religion in Roman Egypt. Assimilation and Resistance* (Princeton: Princeton University Press, 1998).

Friedman, N. 'Point of View in Fiction', in P. Stevick (ed.), *Theory of the Novel* (New York: Free Press, 1967), 108–37. Reprinted from *PMLA* 70 (1955).

Friedrich, G. 'εὐαγγελίζομαι, εὐαγγέλιον, προευαγγελίζομαι, εὐαγγελιστής', in G. Kittel (ed.), *Theological Dictionary of the New Testament* (Grand Rapids: Eerdmans, 1964), II: 707–37.

Frier, B. 'Roman Life Expectancy: Ulpian's Evidence', *Harvard Studies in Classical Philology* 86 (1982), 213–51.

Garland, D.E. ' "I am the Lord your Healer": Mark 1:21–2:12', *RevExp* 85 (1988), 327–43.

Garland, R. *The Greek Way of Death* (London: Duckworth, 1985).

Garrett, S.R. *The Demise of the Devil: Magic and the Demonic in Luke's Writings* (Minneapolis: Fortress, 1989).

Gaston, L. 'Beelzeboul', *TZ* 18 (1962), 247–55.

Gealy, F.D. 'Legion', in G.A. Buttrick (ed.), *Interpreters Dictionary of the Bible* III (Nashville: Abingdon, 1962), 110.

Geller, M.J. & D. Levene. 'Magical Texts from the Genizah (with a New Duplicate)', *JJS* 49:2 (1998), 334–40.

Gennette, G. *Narrative Discourse: An Essay in Method* (Ithaca: Cornell University Press, 1980).

Gill, C. 'The Question of Character-Development: Plutarch and Tacitus', *CQ* 33 (1983), 469–87.

   'Ancient Psychotherapy', *J.Hist.Ideas* 46:3 (1985), 307–25.

   'Introduction', in C. Gill (ed.), *The Person and the Human Mind. Issues in Ancient and Modern Philosophy* (Oxford: Clarendon, 1990), 1–17.

   'The Human Being as an Ethical Norm', in C. Gill (ed.), *The Person and the Human Mind. Issues in Ancient and Modern Philosophy* (Oxford: Clarendon, 1990), 137–61.

   'The Character-Personality Distinction', in C. Pelling (ed.), *Characterization and Individuality in Greek Literature* (Oxford: Clarendon, 1990), 1–31.

   'Panaetius on the Virtue of Being Yourself', in A. Bulloch, E.S. Gruen, A.A. Long & A. Stewart (eds.), *Images and Ideologies* (Berkeley & London: University of California Press, 1993), 330–53.

Goldin, J. 'The Magic of Magic and Superstition', in E.S. Fiorenza (ed.), *Aspects of Religious Propaganda in Judaism and Early Christianity* (Notre Dame: University of Notre Dame Press, 1976), 115–47.

Gordon, R.L. 'Helios', in K. van der Toorn, B. Becking & P.W. van der Horst (eds.), *Dictionary of Deities and Demons in the Bible* (Leiden: E.J. Brill, 1995), cols 750–63.

Graf, F. 'Dionysian and Orphic Eschatology: New Texts and Old Questions', in T.H. Carpenter & C.A. Faraone (eds.), *Masks of Dionysus* (Ithaca: Cornell University Press, 1993), 239–58.

Griffin, J. 'Augustus and the Poets: "Caesar qui cogere posset" ', in F. Millar & E. Segal (eds.), *Caesar Augustus. Seven Aspects* (Oxford: Clarendon, 1984, repr. 1985), 189–218.

Guelich, R.A. ' "The Beginning of the Gospel" – Mark 1:1–15', *BibRes* 27 (1982), 5–15.

   'The Gospel Genre', in P. Stuhlmacher (ed.), *The Gospel and the Gospels* (Grand Rapids: Eerdmans, 1983), 174–208.

   Mark 1–8:26 (WBC 34a; Dallas: Word, 1989).

Guijarro, S. 'Healing Stories and Medical Anthropology: A Reading of Mark 10:46–52', *BTB* 30:3 (2000), 102–12.

Gundry, R.H. *Mark. A Commentary on His Apology for the Cross* (Grand Rapids: Eerdmans, 1993).

Hadas, M. *Imperial Rome* (New York: Time, 1965).

Hamilton, N.Q. 'Resurrection Tradition and the Composition of Mark', *JBL* 84 (1965), 415–21.

Harkness, A.G. 'Age at Marriage and at Death in the Roman Empire', *TAPA* 27 (1896), 35–72.

Harrison, J.E. *Prolegomena to the Study of Greek Religion* (Cambridge: Cambridge University Press, 1903).

Harvey, W.J. 'The Human Context', in P. Stevick (ed.), *Theory of the Novel* (New York: Free Press, 1967), 231–51. Reprint from *Character and the Novel* (1965).

Hasenfratz, H.-P. *Die toten Lebenden. Eine religionsphänomenologische Studie zum sozialen Tod in archaischen Gesellschaften. Zugleich ein kritischer Beitrag zur sogenannten Strafopfertheorie* (Beihefte der Zeitschrift für Religions- und Geistesgeschichte 24; Leiden: E.J. Brill, 1982).

Hawley, R. 'Female Characterization in Greek Declamation', in D. Innes, H. Hine & C. Pelling (eds.), *Ethics and Rhetoric. Classical Essays for Donald Russell on his Seventy-Fifth Birthday* (Oxford: Clarendon, 1995), 255–68.

Head, P.M. 'A Text-Critical Study of Mark 1.1 "The Beginning of the Gospel of Jesus Christ"', *NTS* 37:4 (1991), 621–9.

Heil, J.P. *The Gospel of Mark as a Model for Action. A Reader-Response Commentary* (New York: Paulist, 1992).

Hengel, M. *Judaism and Hellenism: Studies in Their Encounter in Palestine during the Early Hellenistic Period* (London: SCM, 1974).

— *The Son of God. The Origin of Christology and the History of Jewish-Hellenistic Religion* (London: SCM, 1976).

Herrmann, W. 'Baal-Zebub', in K. van der Toorn et al. (eds.), *Dictionary of Deities and Demons in the Bible* (Leiden: E.J. Brill, 1995), cols 293–6.

Holmes, B. 'In Search of God', *New Scientist* 2287 (21 April 2001), 24–8.

Hooker, M.D. *Mark* (BNTC; London: Black, 1991).

Hopfner, Th. 'Die Kindermedien in den griechisch-ägyptischen Zauberpapyri', in *Recueil d'études dédiées à la mémoire de N.P. Kondakov. archéologie. histoire de l'art. études byzantines* (Seminarium Kondakovianum; Prague: Politika, 1926), 650–74.

Hopkins, M.K. 'The Age of Roman Girls at Marriage', *Population Studies* 18 (1965), 309–27.

— 'On the Probable Age Structure of the Roman Population', *Population Studies* 20 (1966), 245–64.

Horsley, G.H.R. 'The Inscriptions of Ephesos and the N.T.', *NovT* 34 (1992), 105–68.

Huidekoper, F. *The Belief of the First Three Centuries Concerning Christ's Mission to the Underworld* (Boston: Crosby, Nichols, & Co., 1854).

Hull, J.M. *Hellenistic Magic and the Synoptic Tradition* (SBT (2) 28; London: SCM, 1974).

Hulse, E.V. 'The Nature of Biblical "Leprosy" and the Use of Alternative Medical Terms in Modern Translations of the Bible', *PEQ* 107 (1975), 87–105.

Hunter, A.M. *The Gospel according to St Mark* (Torch Bible Commentaries; London: SCM, 1949).

Huzar, E.G. 'Emperor Worship in Julio-Claudian Egypt', in W. Haase (ed.), *ANRW* II.18.5 (Berlin: De Gruyter, 1995), 3092–143.

Ilan, T. *Jewish Women in Greco-Roman Palestine* (Peabody: Hendrickson, 1996).
Iser, W. 'The Reading Process: A Phenomenological Approach', *New Literary History* 3 (1972), 272–99.
    'Interaction between Text and Reader', in S.R. Suleiman and I. Crosman (eds), *The Reader in the Text. Essays on Audience and Interpretation* (Princeton: Princeton University Press, 1980), 106–19.
Jeremias, J. 1928: *Das Evangelium nach Marcus. Versuch einer urchristlichen Erklärung für die Gegenwart* (Chemnitz & Leipzig: Max Müller, 1928).
    'ποιμήν, ἀρχιποίμην, ποιμαίνω, ποίμνη, ποίμνιον', in G.W. Bromiley (ed.), *Theological Dictionary of the New Testament* (Grand Rapids: Eerdmans, 1968, repr. 1975), VI: 485–502.
    New Testament Theology. Part 1: The Proclamation of Jesus (NTL; London: SCM, 1971).
Johnson, W.R. 'Response to E.A. Judge, "On Judging the Merits of Augustus"', in W.R. Herzog II (ed.), *On Judging the Merits of Augustus* (Colloquy 49; Berkeley: Center for Hermeneutical Studies in Hellenistic and Modern Culture, 1984), 37–9.
Jones, D.L. 'Christianity and the Roman Imperial Cult', in W. Haase (ed.), *ANRW* II.23.2 (Berlin: De Gruyter, 1980), 1023–54.
Judge, E.A. 'The Penetration of Graeco-Roman Society by Christianity', *Tyndale House Bulletin* 1:17 (1956), 5–6.
    'The Early Christians as a Scholastic Community', *JRH* 1 (1960 & 1961), 4–15, 125–37.
    The Conversion of Rome. Ancient Sources of Modern Social Tensions (Sydney: Macquarie Ancient History Association, 1980).
    'The Social Identity of the First Christians: A Question of Method in Religious History', *JRH* 11 (1980), 201–17.
    'On Judging the Merits of Augustus', in W.R. Herzog II (ed.), *On Judging the Merits of Augustus* (Colloquy 49; Berkeley: Center for Hermeneutical Studies in Hellenistic and Modern Culture, 1984), 1–25.
    Augustus and Roman History (North Ryde, NSW: Macquarie University Press, ²1987).
    'The Second Thoughts of Syme on Augustus', *Ancient History: Resources for Teachers* 27:1 (1997), 43–75.
    'Ancient Beginnings of the Modern World', in T.W. Hillard, R.A. Kearsley, C.E.V. Nixon & A.M. Nobbs (eds.), *Ancient History in a Modern University* (2 vols; Sydney & Cambridge, UK: AHDRC Macquarie University & Eerdmans, 1998), II: 468–82.
Juel, D.H. *A Master of Surprise. Mark Interpreted* (Minneapolis: Fortress, 1994).
Jung, C.G. *Modern Man in Search of a Soul* (London, 1933).
Kahl, B. 'Jairus und die verlorenen Töchter Israels. Sozioliterarische Überlegungen zum Problem der Grenzüberschreitung in Mk 5:21–43', in L. Schotroff and M.T. Wacker (eds.), *Von der Wurzel getragen. Christliche-feministische Exegese in Auseinandersetzung mit Antijudaismus* (Leiden: E.J. Brill, 1996), 61–78.
Kaiser, O. and E. Lohse. *Death and Life* (Nashville: Abingdon, 1981).
Kee, H.C. *Medicine, Miracle & Magic in New Testament Times* (SNTSMS 55; Cambridge: Cambridge University Press, 1986).
Kelber, W.H. *Mark's Story of Jesus* (Philadelphia: Fortress, 1979).

King, H. 'Bound to Bleed: Artemis and Greek Women', in A. Cameron and A. Kuhrt (eds.), *Images of Women in Antiquity* (London: Routledge, 1993), 109–27.

Kotansky, R. 'Incantations and Prayers for Salvation on Inscribed Greek Amulets', in C.A. Faraone and D. Obbink (eds.), *Magika Hiera. Ancient Greek Magic & Religion* (Oxford & New York: Oxford University Press, 1991), 107–37.

'Jesus and Heracles in Cádiz (τὰ Γάδειρα): Death, Myth, and Monsters at the "Straits of Gibraltar" (Mark 4:35–5:43)', in A.Y. Collins (ed.), *Ancient and Modern Perspectives on the Bible and Culture. Essays in Honor of Hans Dieter Betz* (Atlanta: Scholars, 1998), 160–229.

'Demonology', in C.A. Evans & S.E. Porter (eds.), *Dictionary of New Testament Background* (Downers Grove, Ill.: IVP, 2000), 269–73.

Kraeling, C.H. 'Was Jesus Accused of Necromancy?', *JBL* 59 (1940), 147–57.

Kurtz, D.C. and J. Boardman. *Greek Burial Customs* (London: Thames & Hudson, 1971).

Lane, W.L. *The Gospel according to Mark* (NICNT; Grand Rapids: Eerdmans, 1974).

Langton, E. *Good and Evil Spirits. A Study of the Jewish and Christian Doctrine, Its Origin and Development* (London: SPCK, 1942).

Lewis, T.J. 'Beelzebul', in D.N. Freedman et al. (eds.), *Anchor Bible Dictionary* I (New York: Doubleday, 1992), 638–41.

Lewy, H. 'Aristotle and the Jewish Sage According to Clearchus of Soli', *HTR* 31 (1938), 205–35.

Licht, J. *Storytelling in the Bible* (Jerusalem: Magnes, 1978).

Lightfoot, R.H. 'The Connexion of Chapter Thirteen with the Passion Narrative', in *The Gospel Message of St. Mark* (Oxford: Oxford University Press, 1950), 48–59.

Lloyd Davies, M. 'Levitical Leprosy: Uncleanness and the Psyche', *ExpT* 99 (1987), 136–9.

Lloyd, G.E.R. *Magic, Reason, and Experience. Studies in the Origin and Development of Greek Science* (Cambridge: Cambridge University Press, 1979).

Maccoby, H. 'Corpse and Leper', *JJS* 49:2 (1998), 280–5.

MacCulloch, J.A. *The Harrowing of Hell. A Comparative Study of An Early Christian Doctrine* (Edinburgh: T. & T. Clark, 1930).

Mackenzie, W. & D. Brothwell. 'Disease in the Ear Region', in D. Brothwell & A.T. Sandison (eds.), *Diseases in Antiquity. A Survey of the Diseases, Injuries and Surgery of Early Populations* (Springfield, Ill.: Charles C. Thomas, 1967), 464–73.

Maclaurin, E.C.B. 'Beelzeboul', *NovT* 20:2 (1978), 157–60.

McVann, M. 1990: 'Destroying Death: Jesus in Mark and Joseph in "The Sin Eater"', in R. Detweiler & W.G. Doty (eds.), *Biblical Text and Secular Story* (AAR Studies in Religion 60; Atlanta: Scholars, 1990), 123–35.

Malbon, E.S. 'Disciples/Crowds/Whoever: Marcan Characters and Readers', in *In the Company of Jesus. Characters in Mark's Gospel* (Louisville: Westminster John Knox, 2000), 70–99. Also published in D.E. Orton (ed.), *The Composition of Mark's Gospel. Selected Studies from Novum Testamentum* (Leiden: E.J. Brill, 1999), 144–71. Originally published in *NovT* 28 (1986), 104–30.

Narrative Space and Mythic Meaning in Mark (San Francisco: Harper & Row, 1986).

'The Jewish Leaders in the Gospel of Mark: A Literary Study of Marcan Characterization', in *In the Company of Jesus. Characters in Mark's Gospel* (Louisville: Westminster John Knox, 2000), 131–65. Originally published in *JBL* 108 (1989), 259–81.

'The Poor Widow in Mark and Her Poor Rich Readers', in *In the Company of Jesus. Characters in Mark's Gospel* (Louisville: Westminster John Knox, 2000), 166–88. Originally published in *CBQ* 53 (1991), 589–604.

Malina, B. and J.H. Neyrey. *Calling Jesus Names. The Social Value of Labels in Matthew* (Foundations and Facets; Sonoma, Calif.: Polebridge, 1988).

Marcus, J. 'A Note on Markan Optics', *NTS* 45:2 (1999), 250–6.

Martin, R.P. *Mark: Evangelist and Theologian* (Exeter: Paternoster, 1972).

Martinez, D. ' "May she neither eat nor drink": Love Magic and Vows of Abstinence', in M.W. Meyer and P.A. Mirecki (eds.), *Ancient Magic and Ritual Power* (Leiden: E.J. Brill, 1995), 335–59.

Mastermann, E.W.G. *Hygiene and Disease in Palestine in Modern and Biblical Times* (London: Palestine Exploration Fund, n.d.).

Meier, J.P. *A Marginal Jew. Rethinking the Historical Jesus. Vol. 1: The Roots of the Problem and the Person* (New York: Doubleday, 1991).

Merkelbach, R. 'Die goldenen Totenpässe: Ägyptisch, Orphisch, Bakchisch. I. Ägyptisches und Griechisches Totengericht', *ZPE* 128 (1999), 1–13.

Metzger, B.M. *A Textual Commentary on the Greek New Testament* (New York: United Bible Societies, [2]1994).

Meyer, M.W. *Who Do People Say I Am? The Interpretation of Jesus in the New Testament Gospels* (Grand Rapids: Eerdmans, 1983).

Meyer, M.W. and P.A. Mirecki (eds.). *Ancient Magic and Ritual Power* (Leiden: E.J. Brill, 1995).

Michaelis, W. 'ὁράω, κτλ', in G. Kittel (ed.), *Theological Dictionary of the New Testament* (Grand Rapids: Eerdmans, 1967) V: 315–82.

Miller, S.G. 'Excavations at Nemea, 1980', *Hesperia* 50 (1981), 45–67.

Mills, M.E. *Human Agents of Cosmic Power in Hellenistic Judaism and the Synoptic Tradition* (JSNTSup 41; Sheffield: JSOT, 1990).

Mitchell, S. *Anatolia. Land, Men, and Gods in Asia Minor. Vol. 1: The Celts in Anatolia and the Impact of Roman Rule* (Oxford: Clarendon, 1993).

Møller-Christensen, V. 'Evidence of Leprosy in Earlier Peoples', in D. Brothwell & A.T. Sandison (eds.), *Diseases in Antiquity. A Survey of the Diseases, Injuries and Surgery of Early Populations* (Springfield, Ill.: Charles C. Thomas, 1967), 295–306.

Moore, S.D. *Literary Criticism and the Gospels. The Theoretical Challenge* (New Haven & London: Yale University Press, 1989).

Moss, G.C. 'The Mentality and Personality of the Julio-Claudian Emperors', *Medical History* 7 (1963), 165–75.

'Mental Disorder in Antiquity', in D. Brothwell & A.T. Sandison (eds.), *Diseases in Antiquity. A Survey of the Diseases, Injuries and Surgery of Early Populations* (Springfield, Ill.: Charles C. Thomas, 1967), 709–22.

Murray, O. 'Kingship', in S. Hornblower & A. Spawforth (eds.), *The Oxford Classical Dictionary* (Oxford: Oxford University Press, [3]1996), 807.

Niedner, F.A., Jr. 'Gospel Dramaturgy: Dying and Rising with Christ in Mark', *CurThM* 20:6 (1993), 455–61.

Nilsson, M.P. 'Early Orphism and Kindred Religious Movements', *HTR* 28 (1935), 181–230.

Nineham, D. *Saint Mark* (Pelican NTC; Harmondsworth: Penguin, 1963, repr. 1981).

Nock, A.D. 'Note XIV: St Paul and the Magus', in F. Jackson and K. Lake (eds.), *The Beginnings of Christianity. Part 1: The Acts of the Apostles* (London: Macmillan, 1932), 164–88.

Olson, R.A. 'Between Text and Sermon: Mark 16:1–8', *Int* 47 (1993), 406–9.

Owen, G.E.L. 'Alcmaeon (2)', in N.G.L Hammond and H.H. Scullard (eds.), *Oxford Classical Dictionary* (Oxford: Clarendon, 1970), 38.

Parker, R. *Miasma. Pollution and Purification in early Greek Religion* (Oxford: Clarendon, 1983).

Patrick, A. 'Disease in Antiquity', in D. Brothwell & A.T. Sandison (eds.), *Diseases in Antiquity. A Survey of the Diseases, Injuries and Surgery of Early Populations* (Springfield, Ill.: Charles C. Thomas, 1967), 238–46.

Pease, A.S. 'Some Aspects of Invisibility', *HSCP* 53 (1942), 1–36.

Pelling, C. 'Conclusion', in C. Pelling (ed.), *Characterization and Individuality in Greek Literature* (Oxford: Clarendon, 1990), 245–62.

Pestman, P.W., M. David and B.A. van Groningen. *The New Papyrological Primer* (Leiden: E.J. Brill, 1990).

Petersen, N.R. 'The Composition of Mark 4:1–8:26', *HTR* 73 (1980), 185–217.

Petterson, A. 'Antecedents of the Christian Hope of Resurrection. Part 1: The Old Testament', *RTR* 59:1 (2000), 1–15.

'Antecedents of the Christian Hope of Resurrection. Part 2: Intertestamental Literature', *RTR* 59:2 (2000), 53–64.

Petropoulos, J.C.B. 'The Erotic Magical Papyri', in *Proceedings of the XVIII International Congress of Papyrology* (2 vols; Athens: Greek Papyrological Society, 1988), II: 215–22.

Phillips, C.R., III.: 'In Search of the Occult: An Annotated Anthology', *Helios* 15:2 (1988), 151–70.

'Seek and Go Hide: Literary Source Problems and Graeco-Roman Magic', *Helios* 21:2 (1994), 107–14.

Pike, K.L. 'Etic and Emic Standpoints for the Description of Behavior', in A.G. Smith (ed.), *Communication in Culture. Reading in the Codes of Human Interaction* (New York: Holt, Rinehart, Winston, 1966), 152–63.

Pilch, J.J. 'Biblical Leprosy and Body Symbolism', *BTB* 11 (1981), 108–13.

'Understanding Biblical Healing: Selecting the Appropriate Model', *BTB* 18 (1988), 60–6.

Pomeroy, S. *Families in Classical and Hellenistic Greece. Representations and Realities* (Oxford: Clarendon, 1997).

Porter, S.E. 'Resurrection, the Greeks and the New Testament', in S.E. Porter, M.A. Hayes & D. Tombs (eds.), *Resurrection* (JSNTSup 186; Sheffield: Sheffield Academic Press, 1999), 52–81.

Preisendanz, K. 'Akephalos', in T. Klauser, *RAC* (Stuttgart: Hiersemann, 1950), I: 211–16.

Price, S.R.F. *Rituals and Power. The Roman Imperial Cult in Asia Minor* (Cambridge: Cambridge University Press, 1984).

Rabinowitz, L.I. 'Deaf Mute', *EncJ* V (Jerusalem: Keter, 1972), 1419–20.

Ramage, E.S. 'Response to E.A. Judge, "On Judging the Merits of Augustus"',
    in W.R. Herzog II (ed.), *On Judging the Merits of Augustus* (Colloquy
    49; Berkeley: Center for Hermeneutical Studies in Hellenistic and Modern
    Culture, 1984), 47–52.

Ramsay, W.M. *The Church in the Roman Empire before AD 170* (London: Hodder
    & Stoughton, [9]1907 [1893]).

Rhoads, D. 'Social Criticism: Crossing Boundaries', in J.C. Anderson &
    S.D. Moore (eds.), *Mark & Method: New Approaches in Biblical Studies*
    (Minneapolis: Fortress, 1992), 135–61.

    'Losing Life for Others in the Face of Death. Mark's Standards of Judgment', in
    J.D. Kingsbury (ed.), *Gospel Interpretation. Narrative-Critical and Social-
    Scientific Approaches* (Harrisburg, Penn.: Trinity Press International, 1997),
    83–94. Originally published in *Int* 47:4 (1993), 358–69.

Rhoads, D. and D. Michie. *Mark as Story. An Introduction to the Narrative of a
    Gospel* (Philadelphia: Fortress, 1982).

Riley, G.J. *Resurrection Reconsidered. Thomas and John in Controversy*
    (Minneapolis: Fortress, 1995).

Rimmon-Kenan, S. *Narrative Fiction: Contemporary Poetics* (New Accents;
    London & New York: Methuen, 1983).

Robinson, J.M. 'The Problem of History in Mark (1957)', *The Problem of History
    in Mark and other Marcan Studies* (Philadelphia: Fortress, 1982), 55–133.

Rogers, L. *Fevers in the Tropics. Their Clinical and Microscopical Differentiation.
    Including the Milroy Lectures on kāla-Azār* (London: Hodder & Stoughton,
    1908).

Rohde, E. *Psyche. The Cult of Souls and Belief in Immortality among the Greeks*
    (London: Kegan Paul, Trench, Trubner, 1925).

Rohrbaugh, R. 'Introduction', in R. Rohrbaugh (ed.), *The Social Sciences and
    New Testament Interpretation* (Peabody, Mass.: Hendrickson, 1996), 1–15.

Rousseau, J.J. and R. Arav. *Jesus and His World. An Archaeological and Cultural
    Dictionary* (Minneapolis: Fortress, 1995).

Runia, D.T. *Philo of Alexandria and the Timaeus of Plato* (Leiden: E.J. Brill,
    1986).

Russell, D.A. '*Ēthos* in Oratory and Rhetoric', in C. Pelling (ed.), *Character-
    ization and Individuality in Greek Literature* (Oxford: Clarendon, 1990),
    197–212.

Russell, J.C. 'Late Ancient and Medieval Population', *TAPA* 48:3 (1958), 5–152.

Sandison, A.T. 'Diseases of the Skin', in D. Brothwell & A.T. Sandison (eds.),
    *Diseases in Antiquity. A Survey of the Diseases, Injuries and Surgery of Early
    Populations* (Springfield, Ill.: Charles C. Thomas, 1967), 449–56.

    'Diseases of the Eye', in D. Brothwell & A.T. Sandison (eds.), *Diseases in
    Antiquity. A Survey of the Diseases, Injuries and Surgery of Early Populations*
    (Springfield, Ill.: Charles C. Thomas, 1967), 457–63.

Sankey, P.J. 'Promise and Fulfilment: Reader-Response to Mark 1.1–15', *JSNT*
    58 (1995), 3–18.

Schaberg, J. 'Daniel 7, 12 and the New Testament Passion-Resurrection Predic-
    tions', *NTS* 31 (1985), 208–22.

Scherrer, S.J. 'Signs and Wonders in the Imperial Cult: A New Look at a Roman
    Religious Institution in the Light of Rev 13:13–15', *JBL* 103 (1984), 599–
    610.

Schweizer, E. 'πνεῦμα κτλ', in G. Kittel (ed.), *Theological Dictionary of the New Testament* (Grand Rapids: Eerdmans, 1968), VI: 332–455.

Scroggs, R. & K.I. Groff. 'Baptism in Mark: Dying and Rising with Christ', *JBL* 92 (1973), 531–48.

Segal, A.F. 'Heavenly Ascent in Hellenistic Judaism, Early Christianity and their Environment', in W. Haase (ed.), *ANRW* II.23.2 (Berlin: De Gruyter, 1980), 1333–94.

Shepherd, T. 'Intercalation in Mark and the Synoptic Problem', in E.H. Lovering, Jr. (ed.), *SBL Seminar Papers 1991* (Atlanta: Scholars, 1991), 687–97.

Markan Sandwich Stories. Narration, Definition, and Function (St Andrews University Dissertation Series; Berrien Springs, Mich.: St Andrews, 1993).

Shiner, W.T. *Follow Me! Disciples in Markan Rhetoric* (SBLDS 145; Atlanta: Scholars, 1995).

Singer, C. and A. Wasserstein. 'Anatomy and Physiology', in N.G.L. Hammond and H.H. Scullard (eds.), *Oxford Classical Dictionary* (Oxford: Clarendon, 1970), 58–61.

'Medicine', in N.G.L. Hammond and H.H. Scullard (eds.), *Oxford Classical Dictionary* (Oxford: Clarendon, 1970), 660–4.

Sjöberg, E. 'III. דרך in Palestinian Judaism', in G.W. Bromiley (ed.), *Theological Dictionary of the New Testament* (Grand Rapids: Eerdmans, 1968 [German: 1959]), VI: 375–89.

Smith, J.Z. 'Towards Interpreting Demonic Powers in Historic and Roman Antiquity', in W. Haase (ed.), *ANRW* II.16.1 (Berlin: De Gruyter, 1978), 425–39.

Smith, Morton. *Clement of Alexandria and the Secret Gospel of Mark* (Cambridge, Mass.: Harvard University Press, 1973).

Jesus the Magician (London: Victor Gollancz, 1978).

'O'Keefe's *Social Theory of Magic*', *JQR* 74:3 (1984), 301–13.

Smith, R. 'Wounded Lion: Mark 9:1 and Other Missing Pieces', *CurThM* 11:6 (1984), 333–49.

Smith, S.H. 'The Literary Structure of Mark 11:1–12:40', in D.E. Orton (ed.), *The Composition of Mark's Gospel. Selected Studies from Novum Testamentum* (Leiden: E.J. Brill, 1999), 171–91. Originally published in *NovT* 31 (1989), 104–24.

'The Role of Jesus' Opponents in the Markan Drama', *NTS* 35 (1989), 161–82.

'A Divine Tragedy: Some Observations on the Dramatic Structure of Mark's Gospel', in D.E. Orton (ed.), *The Composition of Mark's Gospel. Selected Studies from Novum Testamentum* (Leiden: E.J. Brill, 1999), 230–52. Originally published in *NovT* 37 (1995), 209–31.

A Lion With Wings. A Narrative-Critical Approach to Mark's Gospel (Sheffield: Sheffield Academic Press, 1996).

Smith, W.D. 'So-Called Possession in Pre-Christian Greece', *TAPA* 96 (1965), 403–26.

Spawforth, A.J.S. 'The Achaean Federal Imperial Cult I: Pseudo-Julian, Letters 198', *TynB* 46 (1995), 151–68.

Standaert, B. *L'Évangile selon Marc. Commentaire* (Paris: Éditions du Cerf, 1983). This is a version of his original thesis, *L'Évangile selon Marc, Composition et genre littéraire* (Bruges: Sint Andriesabdij, 1978), published as a commentary.

Stark, R. 1992: 'Epidemics, Networks, and the Rise of Christianity', *Semeia* 56 (1992), 159–75. Later revised to become Chapter 4 in *The Rise of Christianity*.

   The Rise of Christianity. How the Obscure, Marginal Jesus Movement Became the Dominant Religious Force in the Western World in a Few Centuries (San Francisco: HarperCollins, 1997 (Princeton: 1996)).

Steiner, G. ' "Critic"/"Reader" ', *New Literary History* 10 (1979), 423–52.

Stevick, P. (ed.). *Theory of the Novel* (New York: Free Press, 1967).

Stock, A. *The Method and Message of Mark* (Wilmington: Michael Glazier, 1989).

Stol, M. *Epilepsy in Babylonia* (Gronigen, STYX Publications, 1993).

Strubbe, J.H.M. ' "Cursed be he that moves my bones" ', in C.A. Faraone and D. Obbink (eds.), *Magika Hiera. Ancient Greek Magic & Religion* (Oxford & New York: Oxford University Press, 1991), 33–59.

Stuhlmacher, P. (ed.). *The Gospel and the Gospels* (Grand Rapids: Eerdmans, 1991).

Swete, H.B. *The Gospel According to St. Mark* (London: Macmillan, 1909).

Tabor, J.D. ' "Returning to the Divinity": Josephus's Portrayal of the Disappearances of Enoch, Elijah, and Moses', *JBL* 108 (1989), 225–38.

Tambiah, S.J. 'Form and Meaning of Magical Acts: A Point of View', in R. Horton and R. Finnegan (eds.), *Modes of Thought. Essays on Thinking in Western and non-Western Societies* (London: Faber, 1973), 199–229.

Tannehill, R.C. 'The Disciples in Mark: The Function of a Narrative Role', in W.R. Telford (ed.), *Interpretation of Mark* (IRT 7; London: SPCK, 1985), 134–57. Originally published in *JR* 57 (1977), 386–405.

   'The Gospel of Mark as Narrative Christology', *Semeia* 16 (1980), 57–95.

Taylor, V. *The Gospel According to St. Mark* (Grand Rapids: Baker, [2]1966, repr. 1981).

Temkin, O. *The Falling Sickness. A History of Epilepsy from the Greeks to the Beginnings of Modern Neurology* (Baltimore: Johns Hopkins Press, 1945, rev. 1971).

Theißen, G. *The Miracle Stories of the Early Christian Tradition* (ed. J. Riches; Studies of the New Testament and its World; Philadelphia: Fortress, 1983).

   ' "Meer" und "See" in den Evangelien: Ein Beitrag zur Lokalkoloritforschung', *SNTU* 10 (1985), 5–25.

Tolbert, M.A. 'How the Gospel of Mark Builds Character', in J.D. Kingsbury (ed.), *Gospel Interpretation. Narrative-Critical and Social-Scientific Approaches* (Harrisburg, Penn.: Trinity Press International, 1997), 71–82. Originally published in *Int* 47:4 (1993), 347–57.

Toynbee, J.M.C. *Death and Burial in the Roman World* (London: Thames & Hudson, 1971).

Trites, A. *The New Testament Concept of Witness* (SNTSMS 31; Cambridge: Cambridge University Press, 1977).

Turner, C. H. 'A Textual Commentary on Mark i', *JTS* 28 (1927), 145–58.

Twelftree, G.H. *Christ Triumphant. Exorcism Then and Now* (London & Sydney: Hodder & Stoughton, 1985).

   'Demon, Devil, Satan', in J. B. Green & S. McKnight (eds.), *Dictionary of Jesus and the Gospels* (Leicester & Downers Grove, Ill.: IVP, 1992), 163–72.

   Jesus the Exorcist. A Contribution to the Study of the Historical Jesus (WUNT 2.54; Tübingen: Mohr, 1993).

Uspensky, B. *A Poetics of Composition* (trans. V. Zavarin & S. Wittig; Berkeley: University of California Press, 1973).

Vallance, J.T. 'Medicine', in S. Hornblower & A. Spawforth (eds.), *The Oxford Classical Dictionary* (Oxford: Oxford University Press, [3] 1996), 945–9.

Vancil, J.W. 'Sheep, Shepherd', in D.N. Freedman (ed.), *Anchor Bible Dictionary* (New York: Doubleday, 1992), V: 1187–90.

van Henten, J.W. 'Typhon', in K. van der Toorn et al. (eds), *Dictionary of Deities and Demons in the Bible* (Leiden: E.J. Brill, 1995), cols. 1657–62.

van Iersel, B.M.F. *Reading Mark* (trans. W.H. Bisscheroux; Edinburgh: T. & T. Clark, 1989 (Dutch: 1986)).

— *Mark. A Reader-Response Commentary* (trans. W.H. Bisscheroux; JSNTSup 164; Sheffield, Sheffield Academic Press, 1998).

Vermeule, E. *Aspects of Death in Early Greek Art and Poetry* (Berkeley: University of California Press, 1979).

Vernière, Y. 'Le Léthé de Plutarque', *RÉA* 66 (1964), 22–32.

Versnel, H.S. ' "May he not be able to sacrifice . . .". Concerning a Curious Formula in Greek and Latin Curses', *ZPE* 58 (1985), 247–69.

— 'Beyond Cursing: The Appeal to Justice in Judicial Prayers', in C.A. Faraone and D. Obbink (eds.), *Magika Hiera. Ancient Greek Magic & Religion* (Oxford & New York: Oxford University Press, 1991), 60–106.

— 'Πεπρημένος. The Cnidian Curse Tablets and Ordeal by Fire', in R. Hägg (ed.), *Ancient Greek Cult Practices from the Epigraphical Evidence* (Stockholm: Swedish Institute Athens, 1994), 145–54.

Walsh, P.G. 'Spes Romana, Spes Christiana', *Prudentia* 6 (1974), 33–43.

Watson, G.R. and H.M.D. Parker. 'Legion', in N.G.L Hammond and H.H. Scullard (eds.), *Oxford Classical Dictionary* (Oxford: Clarendon, 1970), 591–3.

Wedderburn, A.J.M. *Baptism and Resurrection. Studies in Pauline Theology against Its Graeco-Roman Background* (Tübingen: Mohr, 1987).

Weeden, T.J. *Mark – Traditions in Conflict* (Philadelphia: Fortress, 1971).

Wegener, M.I. 'Reading Mark's Gospel Today: A Cruciforming Experience', *CurThM* 20:6 (1993), 462–70.

— *Cruciformed. The Literary Impact of Mark's Story of Jesus and His Disciples* (Lanham, Md.: University Press of America, 1995).

Weiss, K. 'πῦρ, πυρόω, πύρωσις, πύρινος, πυρρός', in G.W. Bromiley (ed.), *Theological Dictionary of the New Testament* (Grand Rapids: Eerdmans, 1968) VI: 928–59.

Wengst, K. *Pax Romana and the Peace of Jesus Christ* (London: SCM, 1987).

Wiedemann, T. *Adults and Children in the Roman Empire* (London: Routledge, 1989).

Wilder, A.N. *Early Christian Rhetoric. The Language of the Gospel* (NTL; London: SCM, 1964).

Wilken, R.L. *The Christians as the Romans Saw Them* (New Haven: Yale University Press, 1984).

Williams, C.K., II and O.H. Zerves. 'Corinth, 1986: Temple E and East of the Theater', *Hesperia* 56 (1987), 1–46.

Williams, J.F. *Other Followers of Jesus. Minor Characters as Major Figures in Mark's Gospel* (JSNTSup 102; Sheffield: JSOT, 1994).

Wilson, E. 'On the Dermopathology of Celsus', *Brit.Med.J* (1863, vol. 2), 446–9, 465–8.

Winkler, J.J. 'The Constraints of Eros', in C.A. Faraone and D. Obbink (eds.), *Magika Hiera. Ancient Greek Magic & Religion* (Oxford & New York: Oxford University Press, 1991), 214–43.

Winter, B.W. 'Acts and Roman Religion. B. The Imperial Cult', in D.W.J. Gill and C. Gempf (eds.), *The Book of Acts in Its First Century Setting. Vol. 2: The Book of Acts in Its Greco-Roman Setting* (Grand Rapids & Carlisle: Eerdmans & Paternoster, 1994), 93–103.

'The Achaean Federal Imperial Cult II: The Corinthian Church', *TynB* 46 (1995), 169–78.

Wistrand, E. *Felicitas imperatoria* (Göteborg, Sweden: Acta Universitatis Gothoburgensis, 1987).

Wright, A.G. 'The Widow's Mites: Praise or Lament? – A Matter of Context', *CBQ* 44:2 (1982), 256–65.

Young, M.O. 'Did Some Middle Platonists Deny the Immortality of the Soul?', *HTR* 68 (1975), 58–60.

Zerwick, M. *Biblical Greek Illustrated by Examples* (Rome: Scripta Pontificii Instituti Biblici, 1963).

Zias, J. 'Death and Disease in Ancient Israel', *BA* 54:3 (1991), 146–59.

Zuntz, G. *Persephone. Three Essays on Religion and Thought in Magna Graecia* (Oxford: Clarendon, 1971).

INDEX OF BIBLICAL REFERENCES

INDEX OF ANCIENT SOURCES

INDEX OF MODERN AUTHORS

Stark 27, 78, 79, 81, 273–275
Steiner 3
Stevick 23
Stock 3
Stol 231
Strubbe 78, 161, 173
Swete 74, 220, 225

Tabor 221
Tambiah 148
Tannehill 11–12, 15, 20, 22, 23, 46, 118, 131, 253, 258
Taylor 74, 89, 123, 197, 206, 220, 225
Temkin 231
Theißen 131, 132, 147, 171
Thompson 57, 68, 78, 114
Tolbert 12, 13, 19
Toynbee 181
Trites 92
Turner 90
Twelftree 35, 55, 66, 68, 191

Uspensky 18

Vallance 34, 109
Vancil 192
Van der Horst 59
Van Henten 109
Van Iersel 2–4, 9, 11, 44, 47, 131
Vermeule 88
Vernière 120
Versnel 77, 78, 84, 149
Von Harnack 274

Walsh 186
Wasserstein 105, 172, 212
Watson 149
Wedderburn 187, 188, 223
Weeden 20
Wegener 11, 12, 15, 46, 271, 278
Weiss 74, 75, 77
Wengst 40, 41, 45, 73, 134, 252, 259
White 274
Whittaker 96, 259
Wiedemann 28, 29, 81, 156–161
Wilder 21, 271
Wilken 124
Williams, C.K. 112
Williams, J.F. 6, 7, 12, 13, 15, 21, 51, 52, 74, 88–92, 102, 104, 118, 119, 131, 135, 144, 146, 154, 177, 178, 197, 201–203, 211, 224, 237–239, 241, 242
Wilson 101
Winkler 71, 162
Winter 39
Wise 35, 124
Wistrand 40, 42, 45
Wortmann 64
Wright 251

Young 183
Youtie 207

Zerves 112
Zerwich 144
Zias 79
Zilliacus 231
Zuntz 151, 185

SUBJECT INDEX

Alexander the Great   81, 140
Alexander Jannaeus   81
alignment   19, 202, 269
alternative kingdom   42, 49, 50, 266
amazement   51, 146, 177, 203, 249
amulets   33, 85
aphrodisiacs   162, 164
apotheosis   39–40, 263–264, 267, 272
  and Jesus   220–224, 259, 262, 266
Asclepius   32, 77, 128, 215
Augustus   40, 141, 199, 222, 248
  achievements of   41, 132–134
  deification of   40, 214–215, 223
  life under   41, 45, 136
  as ruler of the sea   140, 142
  as source of life   40, 167, 215
authority
  Jesus'   51, 123–129, 134, 154, 247,
    249
  and Jesus' opponents   103–104,
    246–247, 256
  and scribes   103–104
  and spirits   71, 72

Ba'al   125
banishment   95–99
barrenness   170, 171, 245–246
Bartimaeus   6, 236–243; *see also*
  Suppliant 13
Beelzebul   123–127
belief   211, 227, 274–277
  and disciple   238; *see also* disciples,
    and belief
  and Suppliant 12
binding   65, 147–149, 207
bleeding and death   170–174
blindness   209, 212, 214, 216, 238
  and the dead   214–215, 242
  and death   212–215, 242; *see also*
    death, and blindness
  and the gods   215

boys and magic   232–234; *see also*
  mediums, boys as
burial   136, 158–159, 260–261
  of Jesus *see* Jesus, burial of

Caesars   39–44, 49, 73, 132–134, 141,
  199–200, 222–224
  deification of   14, 212, 264–265,
    272; *see also* worship of rulers
  see also Augustus; Claudius; imperial
    Rome; Jesus, and Caesar; Julius
    Caesar; Nero; Tiberius; Vespasian
Celsus   77, 148, 275
character   13, 24, 277
  evaluation of   20, 90, 202, 203
  traits of   13–15, 241
characters
  major   6
  minor   6, 11, 15
charms
  and death   189, 207
  against fever   78
  Greek   37
  love   85, 87, 162–163
  separation   204
  silencing   207, 208
children
  burial of   155, 158–159, 199,
    229–233
  and death *see* death, and children
  female   159–160
chilling, of victims of curses   111, 114,
  166, 231
Christianity, rise of early   273–274
chthonic sacrifice   152, 153
cities   27, 101, 273
Claudius   40, 133, 223, 251, 265, 267
coins   248
counter-curse   70, 86, 165, 199, 214
crowds *see* Jesus, and crowds
crucifixion   253, 265–266